Frommer's™

Best Walking Trips in Scotland

My Scotland

By Felicity Martin

SCOTLAND IS A GREAT PLACE TO VISIT FOR MORE THAN JUST EXERCISE—

your mind can be as active as your feet. Wherever you walk, you'll find something to excite you—perhaps watching a herd of red deer in the hills or exploring the birthplace of Robert Burns, Scotland's national poet. More than 5,000 years of human life is visible in the landscape; the walks in this book visit stone circles erected in prehistoric times, and castles and abbeys built centuries ago.

The walks in these pages are quite varied. In the morning, you might climb a hill for a magnificent panorama of lochs and mountains, then spend the afternoon ambling along sea cliffs to an unspoiled sandy bay. A good mix of different grades of walk throughout the country means that even in the mountainous Highlands you can enjoy a gentle woodland or riverside stroll.

Scotland's beautiful scenery offers a new view around every corner—one moment a river snaking through lush farmland and the next heather moorland rising up to a rocky peak. And the abundant wildlife means you have a good chance of seeing some of the country's iconic species, such as red squirrel or osprey.

In between walks, enjoy the warm hospitality and good food—Scottish salmon, beef, and raspberries will all make your holiday one to remember. And if you have any energy left, try some of the other outdoor activities that Scotland is famed for—mountain biking and white water rafting are just a couple of the many excellent ways to enjoy the country's famous rugged beauty.

First page: top, ©iStockphoto.com; bottom, ©Allan Devlin/Scottish Viewpoint

©iStockphoto.com

©Jonathan Smith

THE FALKIRK WHEEL (left) This 19th century engineering marvel, with it's giant hook-wheel and boat-carrying baskets, ingeniously moves boats between the adjoining Forth and Clyde and Union canals. It's also the site of an extraordinary reclamation project, with the formerly industrial canals that link Edinburgh and Glasgow now home to abundant wildlife and surprising serenity.

The road to **ARTHUR'S SEAT (above)**—a 350-million year old extinct volcano in the center of Edinburgh—rises to a peak where breathtaking panoramic views extend for miles over the city and surrounding countryside. Most prominent are the nearby Scottish Parliament, Palace of Holyrood and Edinburgh Castle—all close enough to visit when you get tired of the view.

It was on the forested shores of beautiful **LOCH TROOL** (right) that Robert The Bruce and his ragtag group of 300 men fought back 1,500 English soldiers in the service of King Edward I in 1307, helping Bruce win the hearts of the Scottish people. Seven years after the Battle of Loch Trool, his forces defeated the English Army and Bruce was crowned the King of Scotland.

A man crosses a stile in front of the **KILLANTRINGAN LIGHTHOUSE** (below), near the beginning of Scotland's longest walking route, the 341km (212-mile) Southern Upland Way. On a clear day, the cliff-top walk yields breathtaking views west to Ireland, as well as of the dozens of wrecks that line the dramatic coastline.

©P. Tomkins/Scottish Viewpoint

©Keith Kirk/Scottish Viewpoint

A stone bridge spans the River Braan in the **HERMITAGE**, a woodland that inspired the tales of Beatrix Potter— the Beatrix Potter Garden is filled with bronze statues of many of her characters. The woods that inspired the famous writer are also home to the Hermitage Douglas fir, one of the tallest trees in Britain.

©Felicity Martin

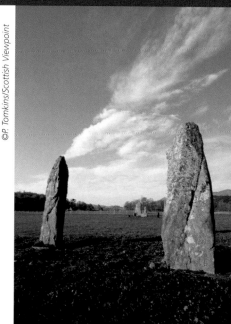

©P. Tomkins/Scottish Viewpoint

TOBERMORY (above), and its picturesque harbor, is the capital of the Isle of Mull and the setting for the hugely popular British children's television program, *Balamory*, with several houses in the town acting as the homes of the show's characters. Waterfalls and pretty lochans line the shore path on the walk into town, where the views make bringing your camera essential.

Part of the standing stones that mark **KILMARTIN GLEN (right)**, a collection of cairns and other rock monuments. Some of these mysterious stones are 5,000 years old, predating the pyramids.

A view from near the summit of **LOCHNA-GAR**, the highest mountain in the Eastern Cairngorms. The entire mountain lies within Balmoral Estate, the Scottish home of the Royal Family since 1852, which normally hosts the Royals from August to October.

School children play amidst the remains of the 18th century **FYRISH MONUMENT (right)**, a replica of India's gates of Negapatam, built by Sir Hector Munro, a former commander of the British Colonial Forces.

A sign points the way to the summit of **BEN NEVIS (below)**, the highest peak in the British Isles at 1,344m (4,408 ft). The "mountain of heaven" (in Gaelic) can be climbed in a single, lengthy day, and is considered by many Scots to be the most important hill for them to climb in their lifetime. The stunning setting has also been used as a film location for many movies, including *Braveheart*, *Highlander*, and the *Harry Potter* series.

©Mark Hicken/Scottish Viewpoint

OSPREY

Identifying features: Whistling call, chocolate eye-stripe, white underparts

Best sighting time: April to August

Habitat: Typically breeds on pine tops in old woods and plantations. Hunts over lochs and estuaries, and along soft coasts.

Where to see: Meall a' Bhucaille, Loch an Eilean, Fochabers, and Spey Bay

More than any other creature, the osprey is an icon of modern conservation success in Scotland. Persecution forced it to extinction in the early 20th century. But in the 1950s, ospreys began a comeback, breeding again in Strathspey beside the Cairngorm Mountains.

A huge effort by conservation groups helped to protect these new colonists from egg thieves and to increase the population. Now, more than 200 pairs of osprey breed at many sites on the Scottish mainland, several of which have purpose-built hides to view the birds and CCTV viewing links to their lofty nests.

Ospreys can range quite widely along sandy coasts and loch margins in search of fish. Here, they hover with slow, deep wing beats. After a plunge, an osprey always shakes its whole body as it flies off—stunning when seen against dark waters.

©iStockphoto.com

GOLDEN EAGLE

Identifying features: Long, broad wings; very large; soars along ridge tops

Best sighting time: Year-round

Habitat: Uplands, especially with a mix of hills, moors and woodland

Where to see: Upland walks in Argyll and the West Highlands and Northeast Scotland, plus the Angus Glens, Ben Lawers, and Glen Tilt in Tayside and Fife

Watched from nearby in sunshine, an adult golden eagle has gloriously honey-toned plumage. Combine that with a large hooked beak and talons, and this is a bird that demands respect.

Many would like to see a golden eagle in Scotland. But to do this takes effort, patience, and luck. Thousands of common buzzards have been inflated to eagle status by wishful thinking. It can be hard to gauge the size of a single bird soaring over a hill, but there are some good clues to a true eagle ID.

Eagles have long, rather rectangular-shaped wings that end in prominent "fingers" of primary feathers. They often glide with their wings held in a shallow "V" shape. Buzzards have shorter, more rounded wings and tend to soar with them out level to the body.

RED SQUIRREL

Identifying features: Glossy, reddish-brown upper parts, leaps between branches

Best sighting time: Year-round

Habitat: Conifer woods, both native and planted

Where to see: Ben Lomond, Callander Crags, Glen Tilt, the Knock and Hosh, the Hermitage, Kinnoull Hill, Meall a' Rhucaille, Loch an Eilean, Bennachie

©iStockphoto.com

Sometimes you hear a red squirrel before you see it. The scrape of claws on bark as it scampers up a pine trunk, the shake of branches overhead, or the "thunk" of a cone dropped from on high can all be clues that there's a little red leaper near at hand.

The red is Scotland's only native squirrel. Its ancestral home is in pine-rich forests, although it can also thrive in plantations and parks, including in cities.

In recent decades, Scottish reds have suffered from competition with North American grey squirrels. Introduced in the 19th century, greys have since spread across much of the mainland outside of the Highland Region. Where they have thrived, red squirrels have dwindled.

But there are still many places, especially in the Highlands and south of Scotland, where you can hope to see red squirrels. So keep listening for the scuffles and thuds.

GANNET

Identifying features: Long beak, white adult plumage, spectacular dives

Best sighting time: Year-round feeding around coast, April to September at colonies

Habitat: Breeds at a handful of large colonies, some on remote islands. Feeds anywhere around coast away from shallow inland parts of sea lochs.

Where to see: Cnoc nan Ghabar, Fife Coastal Path, Seaton Cliffs, Fochabers and Spey Bay, Aberdeen beaches

©iStockphoto.com

There's no mistaking a gannet. Its wingspan is the largest of any North Atlantic seabird, and the plumage of an adult is so white that you can, quite literally, see it from miles away.

Close up, a gannet has large, forward-facing eyes (an adaptation for fish-finding) and a long bill. Gannets only breed at a few colonies around the Scottish mainland and islands.

For most people, the commonest way to see gannets is from a boat or by watching from the coast when they feed inshore. Almost any part of the Scottish coast can be a hunting area for gannets, depending on weather and shoals. Look for plumes of spray flaring skywards to get a clue to where one of these big, distinctive seafarers has plunged and will soon re-emerge, flapping, from the waves.

©iStockphoto.com

RED DEER

Identifying features: Large size, stags (males) have branching antlers for much of year and bellow loudly during the "rut"

Best sighting time: Year-round; rut in October

Habitat: Widespread in hills, boglands, and woods in the Highlands and south

Where to see: All upland walks in Argyll and the West Highlands, Corrour to Rannoch, Ben Lawers, Angus Glens, Glen Tilt, Lochnagar, CairnGorm, Morrone, Bennachie

Largest of all the country's land mammals, males (stags) further emphasize their scale with branching antlers.

Since after the last Ice Age, red deer have been a source of food, tools, and ornaments. Stone Age hunter-gatherers used antler implements and feasted on venison. The hunting of red deer is still an important source of income and employment in the Scottish uplands.

For much of the year, stags stay in all-male groups. Adult stags only consort with females (hinds) at the autumn "rut." This is when stags bellow at each other and clash antlers to gain control of harems. Set against a mountain backdrop, this sight and the accompanying sound are part of the very essence of the Scottish uplands.

©Mark Hicken/Scottish Viewpoint

SCOTCH ARGUS

Identifying features: Erratic flight with few pauses, eyespots on forewings

Best sighting time: Mid-July to early September

Habitat: Tall grassland with tussocks, including lightly grazed, open areas and woodland glades

Where to see: Any walk in Argyll and the West Highlands, plus around the Cairngorms

Scotland has many fewer butterfly species than England, but these include some that live almost exclusively here. The Scotch Argus is one of these.

This brown butterfly has declined so much in England that it now breeds at only two places. But it is still widespread in much of mainland Scotland, especially in the West and the central Highlands.

Named for Argus, a mythical Greek giant with a hundred eyes, the Scotch Argus has a row of black eyespots, each centered with white, arranged in a row near the lower border of each forewing. In sunny weather, you need keen eyesight to see such detail, because the males are tireless fliers. In poorer weather they will perch on tufts of grass or twigs, on the lookout for females. Scotland's other Argus butterfly—the Northern Brown Argus—is scarcer and lives in dry grasslands, particularly in the eastern lowlands towards the coast.

RED GROUSE

Identifying features: Size of a medium domestic hen, rapid fire "go-back" call, rich brownish-red plumage

Best sighting time: Year-round

Habitat: Highest numbers on heather moors managed specifically for grouse. Scattered on heaths and bogs elsewhere.

Where to see: Ben Cruachan, The Cobbler, Corrour to Rannoch, Ben Lawers, Angus glens, Glen Tilt, Lochnagar, Bennachie

©Peter Cairns/Scottish Viewpoint

No other bird in the world makes as much use of heather as the chicken-sized red grouse. It eats the plant, nests under it, and shelters in it all year, never straying far from the heath where it hatched.

Cock grouse are most obvious in spring, when they strut on mounds, flaring their lipstick-red eye "wattles" and calling to attract hens and repel rival males. Up close, the red grouse's plumage blends many tones of brown, including the rich russet for which the species is named.

Grouse sightings often happen when one suddenly and noisily takes flight as you pass nearby. Its loud alarm call is often described as "go-back, go-back, go-back." But the only time to heed its advice is for a couple of months from August 12, when grouse shooting is at its peak on large moors managed for the harvest of this one bird.

PINE MARTEN

Identifying features: Dark brown upper coat and pale yellow underside, long tail, graceful movements

Best sighting time: Year-round; droppings most obvious in autumn

Habitat: Long-established woods, including western oakwoods and Caledonian pinewoods. Commonest in West and Central Highlands.

Where to see: Glen Nant, Creag Meagaidh, Meall a' Bhucaille, Loch an Eilean

©Niall Benvie/Alamy

Nimble as a ballet dancer, sleek of fur and bright of eye, the pine marten combines good looks with a predatory attitude. This is a creature that can turn its paw to anything from eggs, squirrels, or berries to grab a meal.

This means that some lucky householders in the West Highlands can encourage martens to make night visits to gardens by supplying jam and fruit as al fresco snacks. But you'll be much more likely to find evidence of a pine marten on a trail than to see the creature itself.

Narrow, 5.1-to-7.6cm (2-to-3-in.) droppings are the most obvious signs. In autumn, these can be so stuffed with remains of berries that they can look 100% fruity. In snow, marten paw prints look as large as a child's handprint, and back and front paws often overlap where the marten landed on each bound.

BIRCH

Identifying features: Bark smooth, mottled white and tawny, or dark gray and rutted; arrowhead leaf shape

Best sighting time: Year-round

Habitat: Old woods and plantations

Where to see: Widespread and visible on many walks, especially Creag Meagaidh, Meall a' Bhucaille, Morrone, and the Vat and Muir of Dinnet.

Several kinds of birch grow in Scotland. The most common are the silver birch, which often has a graceful droop to its branches and pale bark, and the downy birch, which has a more chaotic form and hairier branches. These species hybridize, so telling them apart is not always straightforward.

What is easy to see is that a birch is a true pioneer, able to colonize bare ground and prepare the way for other trees to follow. Each birch produces masses of tiny seeds. Scattered by the wind, these can go far, sprouting in places where they are not shaded by other trees.

That is why the youngest trees are usually at the edge of birch woods and also along the sides of paths. It is also why birches were among the first very first trees to return to Scotland after the last glaciers melted, more than 10,000 years ago.

WILDLIFE GUIDE

FLORA

BOG MOSSES

Identifying features: "Persian carpet" of rich colors where several species grow together; huge water-holding capacity

Best sighting time: Year-round

Habitat: Very wet areas, including some ditches beside forest paths and in huge, flat boglands

Where to see: Corrour to Rannoch Station, Glencoe Lochan

Look at a bog and the first thing likely to strike you is its flatness and wetness. Investigate more closely and you'll very likely be drawn in to notice ever-finer details of pattern and color. Much of this will be thanks to different kinds of *Sphagnum* bog mosses.

Cherry red, bright yellow, brown, and acid green are prominent in the bog moss palette, adding brilliance to what could otherwise be a dull-looking landscape. These plants hold an astonishing amount of water, so when dried, they can be super-absorbent. Take a handful and squeeze it, and you'll be surprised at how much liquid comes out.

In the past, this property meant that bog mosses did useful service as diaper linings, toilet aids, and wound dressings. They also, over thousands of years of build-up of bogs, are the basis for peat.

HEATHER

Identifying features: Woody stems, pale purple flowers in early autumn

Best sighting time: Year-round, but peak blooms mid-August to September

Habitat: Often on well-drained slopes in uplands. Largest expanses where moorland is burned regularly to boost heather for grouse.

Where to see: Mayar & Dreish from Glen Doll/Glen Clova, Glen Tilt Trail. Also in sunnier areas within pinewoods, and on the lower slopes of Cairn Gorm.

©iStockphoto.com

Think of Scotland and name a plant. Many people, the world over, would choose heather. Several kinds of "heath" plants grow on the moors for which Scotland is famous. But one— "ling"—is the species that packs the most purple into the late summer shows of upland color.

Ling is naturally a plant of woodland clearings and forest edges. But here people have boosted its extent to create swathes of heather moorland.

This is done by careful burning of large patches of heather every few years to encourage young growth, to give food for sheep and both food and shelter for red grouse. Look at a heather moor on a hillside and you'll see the patchwork effect created by the burning.

SCOTS PINE

Identifying features: Deeply cracked, orange-red bark, bottle-green needles

Best sighting time: Year-round

Habitat: Long-established native woods, often with birches, and in plantations

Where to see: Meall a' Bhucaille, Loch an Eilean, Bennachie, plus individual trees in woods elsewhere, such as at the Hermitage

©Dr. Kenny Taylor

In some ways, calling this tree "Scots" pine is a splendid bit of Caledonian cheek. This is the world's most widespread conifer, as familiar to many in Siberia as it is in Scotland. But there *is* something very distinctive about the Scots pine in the land for which it is named.

Set the bottle-green of pines against the tawny tones of mountains, or reflect stem, branch, and crown in the silver of a loch, and you have a classic picture. It's one repeated in many parts of the Highlands, though you can also expect to see Scots pine in plantations almost anywhere in the country.

As a long-established native tree, Scots pine is home to some distinctive wildlife. The Scottish crossbill—the only species of bird unique to Scotland—likes nothing better than a good spread of old-growth pines, and red squirrels relish its cones.

©iStock-photo.com

HAREBELL

Identifying features: Relatively large, pastel-blue flowers on thin stalks in high summer

Best sighting time: July and August

Habitat: Road verges, edges of moors, and woods

Where to see: Widespread, but some good harebell walks include Croc nan Gobhar, Craigellachie to Dufftown, The Vat and Muir of Dinnet.

When people talk about the "Bluebells of Scotland", this is the plant they mean, not the better-known spring bloomer in lowland woods. Harebells have nodding, bell-shaped, pastel-blue flowers that open in late summer.

One harebell plant can have several flowers, each carried at the end of a thread-thin stalk. So a puff of breeze can set them bouncing and swaying, as if to unheard music. Perhaps that is why harebells were once thought to have magical associations. They could tinkle a warning to hares when danger was near, it was said, and made good hats for fairies.

©Duncan Shaw/Alamy

BRACKEN AND OTHER FERNS

Identifying features: Thrives in sunny areas; other ferns in shade; large fronds

Best sighting time: April to November

Habitat: Grassy hills, lightly grazed pastures, woodland clearings, and trail edges

Where to see: Very widespread, so could occur on most walks.

Ferns thrive in Scotland's mild, moist climate. Explore the shady gully of a burn and you could find several kinds. An exception is bracken, which relishes the full sunlight of woodland clearings and treeless slopes.

At the height of summer, bracken can be a nuisance to walkers. It often grows to an adult's chest height, making for slow and sometimes wet progress where it encroaches on trails. It's another story in spring and autumn. The young shoots, formed like fiddleheads, have a simple elegance as they unfold from the ground.

Yellow, green, copper, and gold are the bracken order of the autumn days, a superb counterpoint to the purples of heather and the bronze of moorland sedges. More prosaically, bracken fronds have pest-repellant properties, which increased their usefulness when they used to be cut as bedding for both livestock and people.

ORCHIDS

Identifying features: Complex flowers, often pink, purple, or white; low growing

Best sighting time: June to August

Habitat: Moors, marshes, meadows, coastal grasslands

Where to see: Many good areas within walks, including at Ben Lawers, Loch Tay, Glen Nant, Fife Coastal Path, Seaton Cliffs

©iStockphoto.com

Part of the pleasure of walking in Scotland is the way a walk through fairly uniform heathland, coastal grassland, or inland bog can suddenly be enlivened by a mass of orchids in flower.

Commonest is the heath spotted orchid, which grows best on the acidic ground so widespread in the Scottish moors and peatlands. Where the ground is very wet, different kinds of marsh orchids, some with intensely pink or purple flowers, can be abundant.

Part of the joy of orchid appreciation is in the detailed patterns and tones on individual flowers. Look very closely, perhaps using binoculars and looking down the larger optic as a magnifier, and marvel at the calligraphy of colored freckles. These function as floral landing pad guides for pollinating insects.

SEA PINK

Identifying features: Cushion forming, with pale pink flowers on short stalks in early summer

Best sighting time: May to June for flowers, but old flower heads persist through autumn.

Habitat: Principally coastal grasslands and maritime heath; also high on some mountains

Where to see: Fife Coastal Path, Seaton Cliffs

©Dr. Kenny Taylor

There's something particularly upbeat about flowers at the coast. The headland may be gale-swept, the cliffs steep, and the seas seething, but these small blossoms can ride out the storm and the harshness of their growing place.

Sea pink, or "thrift" as it is also known, is one of this hardy group of sea-edge survivalists. Like many plants of high latitudes that need to cope with extremes of exposure, it grows in tussocks for heat conservation. Sometimes it's abundant, so an early-year walk over a carpet of sea pinks can bring spring to your step in more ways than one.

But in early summer, when the cushions sprout a covering of pale pink flowers, it would seem sacrilege to place boot on plant. By late summer, the old blossoms become tissue thin. Seen backlit against an August sunset, these translucent flower heads add another subtle note to the allure of the Scottish coast.

Frommer's®

Best Walking Trips in Scotland

1st Edition

by Felicity Martin, Colin Hutchison & Patrick Thorne

Wildlife Guide by Dr. Kenny Taylor

Here's what the critics say about Frommer's:

"Amazingly easy to use. Very portable, very complete."
—BOOKLIST

"Detailed, accurate, and easy-to-read information for all price ranges."
— GLAMOUR MAGAZINE

"Hotel information is close to encyclopedic."
—DES MOINES SUNDAY REGISTER

"Frommer's Guides have a way of giving you a real feel for a place."
—KNIGHT RIDDER NEWSPAPERS

John Wiley & Sons Canada, Ltd.

Published by:

JOHN WILEY & SONS CANADA, LTD.

6045 Freemont Blvd.
Mississauga, ON   L5R 4J3

ISBN 978-0-470-15989-7

Editor: Gene Shannon
Project Manager: Elizabeth McCurdy
Project Editor: Lindsay Humphreys
Editorial Assistant: Katie Wolsley
Project Coordinator: Lynsey Stanford
Cartographer: Lohnes & Wright
Production by Wiley Indianapolis Composition Services

Front cover photo: A rocky outcropping near Quiraing, Isle of Skye.

For reseller information, including discounts and premium sales, please call our sales department: Tel. 416-646-7992. For press review copies, author interviews, or other publicity information, please contact our publicity department: Tel. 416-646-4582; Fax: 416-236-4448.

Wiley also publishes its books in a variety of electronic formats. Some content that appears in print may not be available in electronic formats.

Manufactured in the United States

1   2   3   4   5   RRD   13   12   11   10   09

CONTENTS

TABLE OF WALKS   vi

LIST OF REGIONAL MAPS   x

1 THE BEST OF WALKING IN SCOTLAND   1

1 The Best Family Walks 1
2 The Best Walks for Seeing Wildlife . .2
3 The Best Mountain Walks. 3
4 The Best Hill Walks 4
5 The Most Scenic Walks 5
6 The Best Coastal Walks 6
7 The Walks with the
     Best Attractions. 6
8 The Best Restaurants for Dinner 7
9 The Best Places for Lunch 8
10 The Best Hotels .8
11 The Best Budget
     Accommodations. 9

2 PLANNING YOUR TRIP TO SCOTLAND   10

1 Before You Go. 10
2 When to Go. 12
     *What to Bring: The Walker's
     Checklist* 13
3 Getting There & Getting Around . .13
4 Choosing a Walk 17
     It's Easy Being Green 20
5 Walking Safety .21
6 Guided Walking Tours 23
     *Frommers.com: The Complete
     Travel Resource* .23

3 SUGGESTED ITINERARIES   25

1 Scenic Perthshire Getaway 25
2 The Historic South in 1 Week. 26
3 Deeside & Strathspey in 1 Week. . .28
4 Loch Ness & the North
     in 1 Week. 30

4 EDINBURGH & GLASGOW WALKS   33

by Colin Hutchison

Essentials 34
Yellowcraigs Beach to
North Berwick .37
Scald Law—The Pentland Hills 40
Arthur's Seat & Holyrood Park 43
Falkirk Wheel. .47
Falls of Clyde. .50

Kelvin Walkway 53
Mugdock Country Park
to Carbeth. 56
Dumgoyne Hill by Killearn 59
Queen's View & the Whangie. 63
Conic Hill 66
Sleeping & Eating 69

5 SOUTHERN SCOTLAND WALKS   72

by Colin Hutchison

Essentials 72
Dundonald Glen &
the Smugglers Trail 75
Alloway, Ayrshire. 78
Portpatrick to Killantringan
Lighthouse 81
Wood of Cree .84
Loch Trool 87

The Merrick. 90
Peebles 93
Selkirk to Abbotsford House. 96
Melrose to Harestanes 100
Coldingham—St. Abb's Head—
Eyemouth 104
Sleeping & Eating 107

6 TAYSIDE & FIFE WALKS   109

by Felicity Martin

Essentials 110
Perth & Kinnoull Hill. 112
Loch Leven Heritage Trail 115
Fife Coastal Path 118
Knock of Crieff 121
The Hermitage. 124

Ben Lawers 128
Glen Tilt. 131
Seaton Cliffs. 135
Mayar & Driesh. 138
Rannoch to Corrour. 141
Sleeping & Eating 144

7 ARGYLL & THE WEST HIGHLANDS WALKS   147

by Felicity Martin

Essentials 148
Callander Crags &
Bracklinn Falls. 150
Ben Lomond. 153
Arrochar Alps 156
Glen Nant. 159

Cruachan 162
Tobermory. 165
Kilmartin Glen. 168
Carradale 170
Kinlochleven. 173
Sleeping & Eating 177

Table of Walks

Walk	Distance
Edinburgh & Glasgow	
❶ Yellowcraigs Beach to North Berwick	9.6km (6 miles) round-trip
❷ Scald Law—The Pentland Hills	14km (8.7 miles) round-trip
❸ Arthur's Seat & Holyrood Park	5.6km (3.5 miles) round-trip
❹ Falkirk Wheel	5.6km (3.5 miles) round-trip
❺ Falls of Clyde	4.6km (2.9 miles) round-trip
❻ Kelvin Walkway	8.4km (5.2 miles) round-trip
❼ Mugdock Country Park to Carbeth	8.2km (5 miles) round-trip
❽ Dumgoyne Hill by Killearn	4.2km (2.6 miles) round-trip
❾ Queen's View & the Whangie	4.8km (3 miles) round-trip
❿ Conic Hill	4km (2.5 miles) round-trip
Southern Scotland	
❶ Dundonald Glen & the Smugglers Trail	6.2km (3.9 miles) round-trip
❷ Alloway, Ayrshire	7.2km (4.5 miles) round-trip
❸ Portpatrick to Killantringan Lighthouse	7.2km (4.5 miles) round-trip
❹ Wood of Cree	1.7km (1 mile) round-trip
❺ Loch Trool	14km (8.5 miles) round-trip
❻ The Merrick	23km (14 miles) round-trip from visitor center; 13km (8 miles) round-trip from Bruce's Stone car park.
❼ Peebles	5.3km (3.3 miles) round-trip
❽ Selkirk to Abbotsford House	11km (7 miles) one-way
❾ Melrose to Harestanes	33km (20 miles) one-way
❿ Coldingham—St. Abb's Head—Eyemouth	16km (10 miles) round-trip
Tayside & Fife	
❶ Perth & Kinnoull Hill	11km (6.9 miles) round-trip
❷ Loch Leven Heritage Trail	8km (5 miles) one-way (round-trip by bus)
❸ Fife Coastal Path	14km (8.7 miles) one-way
❹ Knock of Crieff	7.5km (4.7 miles) round-trip
❺ The Hermitage	6.8km (4.25 miles) round-trip
❻ Ben Lawers	11km (7 miles) round-trip
❼ Glen Tilt	9.7 or 14.7km (6 or 9.2 miles) round-trip
❽ Seaton Cliffs	5.6km (3.5 miles) round-trip

by Felicity Martin

Essentials 182
Loch an Eilein 183
Meall a' Bhuachaille 186
Cairn Gorm & Ben Macdui. 189
Bennachie 192
The Vat & Muir of Dinnet 194
Getting to Little Ord 195

Lochnagar 197
Morrone 201
Dufftown to Craigellachie 204
Spey Bay. 208
Creag Meagaidh 211
Sleeping & Eating 214

9 THE NORTHERN HIGHLANDS WALKS 217

by Patrick Thorne

Essentials 218
The Duke of Sutherland
Monument 221
An Teallach. 224
Dog Falls, Glen Affric 227
Fyrish Monument 230

The Start of the Great
Glen Way 233
Sandwood Bay. 237
Lael Forest 240
The Ben Nevis Tourist Path 243
Sleeping & Eating 246

APPENDIX A: FAST FACTS, TOLL-FREE NUMBERS & WEBSITES 249

1 Fast Facts: Scotland 249   **2** Toll-Free Numbers & Websites. . . 256

APPENDIX B: LANGUAGE & PLACE NAMES 261

INDEX 263

General Index. 263
Accommodations Index. 270

Restaurant Index. 271

Difficulty	Best Time to Go	Star rating	Page number
Moderate	Jun.–Sept.		37
Moderate to Strenuous	Late summer, when the hills are a sea of purple heather.	★	40
Easy	Early morning to escape the crowds; the summit is also a fantastic spot to enjoy the sunset.	★	43
Easy	Jun.–Sept.		47
Easy	Sept.–Nov.		50
Easy	Mid-summer to relax with a picnic.		53
Easy	Spring for the wildflowers and reduced crowds.		56
Strenuous	Summer evenings for spectacular sunsets over the Arrochar Alps.	★	59
Moderate	Summer evenings for spectacular sunsets over the Arrochar Alps.	★	63
Moderate	Great on any clear day, but crowded in the summer.		66
Easy to Moderate	In August the old village of Dundonald holds its fair.	★	75
Easy	Spring or autumn to avoid peak season and enjoy the colors.	★	78
Easy to Moderate	Best in the summer, but start early to have the trail to yourself.		81
Easy	In the spring, bluebells carpet the forest floor and bird-watchers may spot rare migratory visitors.		84
Easy to Moderate	Jun.–Sept.		87
Strenuous	Any clear day; in winter, be equipped for snow conditions.	★	90
Easy	Especially rewarding during the autumn colors.	★	93
Easy to Moderate	Spring and autumn to avoid the busiest period.		96
Strenuous	Colors are best in late spring and early autumn.	★	100
Moderate to Strenuous	Mid- to late summer for the wildflowers, bracing sea air, and surfing.	★	103
Moderate	April to June for spring colors.		112
Easy	At dawn to see the most wildlife.	★	115
Moderate	May to July to enjoy tempting beaches and colorful gardens.	★★★	118
Moderate	October to mid-November for autumn colors.	★	121
Easy	January and February for snowdrops and waterfalls.	★	124
Strenuous	June to August for mountain flowers.	★★	128
Moderate	October and November for autumn colors and to hear red deer rutting.		131
Easy	May to July for nesting seabirds and wildflowers.	★★	135

continues

Table of Walks

Walk	Distance
Tayside & Fife (continued)	
❾ Mayar & Driesh	14km (8.5 miles) round-trip
❿ Rannoch to Corrour	19km (12 miles) one-way (round-trip by train)
Argyll & West Highlands	
❶ Callander Crags & Bracklinn Falls	9.3km (5.8 miles) round-trip
❷ Ben Lomond	13km (8.1 miles) round-trip
❸ Arrochar Alps	14.2km (8.9 miles) round-trip
❹ Glen Nant	4km (2.5 miles) round-trip
❺ Cruachan	16km (10 miles) round-trip
❻ Tobermory	4km (2.5 miles) one-way (round-trip by bus)
❼ Kilmartin Glen	6.4km (4 miles) round-trip
❽ Carradale	12km (7.5 miles) round-trip
❾ Kinlochleven	10km (6.5 miles) round-trip
The Northeast Highlands	
❶ Loch an Eilein	5km (3.1 miles) + optional 1.6km (1 mile) round-trip
❷ Meall a' Bhuachaille	8.4km (5.25 miles) round-trip
❸ Cairn Gorm & Ben Macdui	24km (15 miles) round-trip
❹ Bennachie	8.9km (5.5 miles) round-trip
❺ The Vat & Muir of Dinnet	1.1km (0.7 miles) and 2.9km (1.8 miles) round-trip
❻ Lochnagar	20km (12.5 miles) round-trip
❼ Morrone	12km (7.5 miles) round-trip
❽ Dufftown to Craigellachie	7.2km (4.5 miles) one-way (round-trip by bus)
❾ Spey Bay	16km (10 miles) round-trip
❿ Creag Meagaidh	21km (13 miles) round-trip
The Northern Highlands	
❶ The Duke of Sutherland Monument	9.7km (6 miles) round-trip
❷ An Tellach	18km (11 miles) round-trip
❸ Dog Falls, Glen Affric	6km (3.8 miles) round-trip
❹ Fryish Monument	5.6km (3.5 miles) round-trip
❺ The Start of the Great Glen Way	6.4km (4 miles) round-trip
❻ Sandwood Bay	13km (8 miles) round-trip
❼ Lael Forest	2.9km (1.8 miles) round-trip
❽ The Ben Nevis Tourist Path	16km (10 miles) round-trip

Difficulty	Best Time to Go	Star rating	Page number
Strenuous	July to September for heather blooming.		138
Strenuous	June to August for moorland flowers.		141
Moderate	October and November for autumn colors and waterfalls.	★	150
Strenuous	September, as the crowds dwindle and autumn colors start to appear.	★★★	153
Strenuous	Make an early start to get a space in the car park.	★★	156
Easy	March and April for spring wildflowers; October for autumn colors.		159
Strenuous	May to July for long days.	★	162
Easy	May and June, to avoid summer crowds.		165
Easy	September and October, when the glen is quieter.	★★	168
Moderate	July and August for lingering on the beaches.	★	170
Moderate	April and May for spring colors and views of snowy mountains.		173
Easy	Summer evenings for quiet sunset walk.	★	183
Moderate	July and August for heather blooming.	★	186
Strenuous	May to June for the longest hours of daylight.	★★	189
Moderate	July and August for heather blooming.	★★	192
Easy	Early morning to have the Vat to yourself.	★	194
Strenuous	Arrive early to ensure a parking place.	★★★	197
Moderate	September and October for autumn birch trees.		201
Easy	April to June for fresh spring woodlands.		204
Moderate	July and August for osprey and other wildlife.		208
Strenuous	September and October for autumn colors.	★★	211
Moderate	The waterfall is most impressive in spring as the snow melts.	★	221
Strenuous	Between June and October, to enjoy the long daylight hours.	★★	224
Moderate	The route is especially stunning in the autumn with fall foliage.	★	227
Moderate	May to June, for the long, sunny spring days.		230
Moderate	Late summer to pick raspberries and blackberries.		233
Moderate	In late summer for the long days, reduced insect pests, and the warm sea temperature.	★★★	237
Easy	The woodland is full of autumn color during October and November.		240
Strenuous	June to October to make the best of daylight hours and hopefully good weather.	★	243

LIST OF REGIONAL MAPS

Scenic Perthshire Getaway........26

The Historic South in 1 Week......28

Deeside & Strathspey
in 1 Week......................29

Loch Ness & the North
in 1 Week.....................31

Edinburgh & Glasgow 35

Southern Scotland 73

Tayside & Fife 111

Argyll & the West Highlands 149

The Northeast Highlands 181

The Northern Highlands.........219

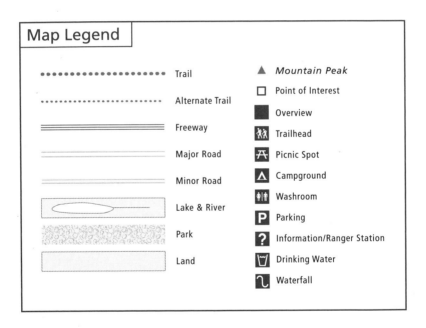

Map Legend

••••••••••••••••	Trail	▲ Mountain Peak
•••••••••••••••••	Alternate Trail	☐ Point of Interest
═══════════	Freeway	■ Overview
───────────	Major Road	🏃 Trailhead
───────────	Minor Road	🪑 Picnic Spot
⬭	Lake & River	△ Campground
	Park	🚻 Washroom
	Land	P Parking
		? Information/Ranger Station
		🥛 Drinking Water
		∿ Waterfall

AN INVITATION TO THE READER

In researching this book, we discovered many wonderful places—hotels, restaurants, shops, and more. We're sure you'll find others. Please tell us about them, so we can share the information with your fellow travelers in upcoming editions. If you were disappointed with a recommendation, we'd love to know that, too. Please write to:

Frommer's Best Walking Trips in Scotland, 1st Edition
John Wiley & Sons Canada, Ltd. • 6045 Freemont Blvd. • Mississauga, ON   L5R 4J3

AN ADDITIONAL NOTE

Please be advised that travel information is subject to change at any time—and this is especially true of prices. We therefore suggest that you write or call ahead for confirmation when making your travel plans. The authors, editors, and publisher cannot be held responsible for the experiences of readers while traveling. Your safety is important to us, however, so we encourage you to stay alert and be aware of your surroundings. Keep a close eye on cameras, purses, and wallets, all favorite targets of thieves and pickpockets.

ABOUT THE AUTHORS

Felicity Martin is an outdoors writer and photographer living in Perthshire, at the heart of Scotland. She has written walking guidebooks to Orkney and Perthshire, as well as hundreds of features about walks around Scotland for Trails, Country Walking, and many other magazines and newspapers.

Colin Hutchison is an Edinburgh-based travel and adventure sports writer whose passion for the great outdoors was nurtured by his parents from an early age. His wife Gill and baby Isla now join him on his many forays into Scotland's highlands and islands.

Patrick Thorne is a lifetime professional travel writer based in the Scottish Highlands near Inverness. He writes extensively on winter sports for publications worldwide and has written several books and features on travel in Scotland.

Other Great Guides for Your Trip:

Frommer's Scotland
Frommer's Edinburgh & Glasgow
Frommer's Edinburgh & Glasgow Day by Day

FROMMER'S STAR RATINGS, ICONS & ABBREVIATIONS

Every hotel, restaurant, and attraction listing in this guide has been ranked for quality, value, service, amenities, and special features using a **star-rating system.** In country, state, and regional guides, we also rate towns and regions to help you narrow down your choices and budget your time accordingly. Hotels and restaurants are rated on a scale of zero (recommended) to three stars (exceptional). Attractions, shopping, nightlife, towns, and regions are rated according to the following scale: zero stars (recommended), one star (highly recommended), two stars (very highly recommended), and three stars (must-see).

In addition to the star-rating system, we also use **seven feature icons** that point you to the great deals, in-the-know advice, and unique experiences that separate travelers from tourists. Throughout the book, look for:

(Finds)	Special finds—those places only insiders know about
(Fun Facts)	Fun facts—details that make travelers more informed and their trips more fun
(Kids)	Best bets for kids and advice for the whole family
(Moments)	Special moments—those experiences that memories are made of
(Overrated)	Places or experiences not worth your time or money
(Tips)	Insider tips—great ways to save time and money
(Value)	Great values—where to get the best deals

The following **abbreviations** are used for credit cards:

AE	American Express	DISC	Discover	V	Visa
DC	Diners Club	MC	MasterCard		

FROMMERS.COM

Now that you have this guidebook to help you plan a great trip, visit our website at **www.frommers.com** for additional travel information on more than 4,000 destinations. We update features regularly to give you instant access to the most current trip-planning information available. At Frommers.com, you'll find scoops on the best airfares, lodging rates, and car rental bargains. You can even book your travel online through our reliable travel booking partners. Other popular features include:

- Online updates of our most popular guidebooks
- Vacation sweepstakes and contest giveaways
- Newsletters highlighting the hottest travel trends
- Podcasts, interactive maps, and up-to-the-minute events listings
- Opinionated blog entries by Arthur Frommer himself
- Online travel message boards with featured travel discussions

The Best of Walking in Scotland

Scotland is a land of contrasts—an ancient country with a modern outlook, where well-loved traditions mingle with the latest technology. Here you can tread on some of the oldest rocks in the world and wander among standing stones and chambered cairns erected 5,000 years ago. However, that little cottage you pass may have a high-speed Internet connection and be home to a jewelry designer or an architect of eco-friendly houses.

Certainly, you'll encounter all the shortbread and tartan you expect, though kilts are normally reserved for weddings and football matches. But far more traditional, although less obviously so, is the warm welcome you'll receive from the locals. The farther you go from the big cities, the more time people have to talk—you'll find they have a genuine interest in where you come from and what you do.

Scotland's greatest asset is its clean, green landscapes, where walkers can fill their lungs with pure, fresh air. It may only be a wee (small) country, but it has a variety of walks to rival anywhere in the world. As well as the splendid mountain hikes to be found in the Highlands, there's an equal extent of Lowland terrain with gentle riverside walks and woodland strolls. The indented coastline and numerous islands mean that there are thousands of miles of shore to explore, while the many low hills offer exquisite views over the countryside. There's walking to suit all ages and tastes.

Some glorious countryside with rolling farmland, lush woods, and grassy hills can be reached within an hour's drive of Edinburgh and Glasgow. Most industry and housing is in the central belt that links the two, although there are also peaceful corners for walking. Going north from Edinburgh, you come to the Kingdom of Fife and Tayside, while Loch Lomond and the Trossachs National Park is due north of Glasgow. As you continue across the Highland Boundary Fault, the landscape abruptly changes, becoming less fertile and more rugged.

In the northeast, broad glens separate the high mountain plateau of Cairngorms National Park, and the landscape gradually softens towards the coast. In the west, rocky hills and mountains rise straight out of the Atlantic, giving views of sea lochs and sandy beaches. For the wildest, strangest looking mountain scenery, travel to the northern Highlands where steep, bare mountains punctuate a moonscape of heather moorland.

Here we highlight some of the best walks in Scotland, including several offering unusual sights and memorable experiences that you can recount to the folks back home.

1 THE BEST FAMILY WALKS

- **Yellowcraigs Beach** (near Edinburgh): With miles of golden sand, this is a fantastic location for a summer walk and picnic. It has stunning views across the Firth of Forth to the Kingdom of Fife and is only 20 miles (32km) from the hubbub of Edinburgh. The rock pools and seals are a great attraction for children, and you can see Fidra Island, which is said to have inspired *Treasure Island,* the 18th-century classic novel by Robert Louis Stevenson. See p. 38.

- **Tobermory** (Isle of Mull): This walk is a must for all kids who watched the series *Balamory* on children's television. Allow youngsters time to play in Aros Park before the coastal walk through woods and past waterfalls to the picture-postcard town. Simply getting to Mull is an adventure, with the best views of Oban and Duart Castle from the ferry. See p. 165.
- **Mugdock Park** (Glasgow): In this country park, there are heaps of attractions for children. They can let off steam in the play area at Craigend Visitor Centre; then you can entice them around the walk with promise of a ghostly 14th-century castle. Easy paths lead around lochs and through the ancient oaks of Mugdock Wood. The walk even includes a small section of the 145km (90-mile) West Highland Way long-distance trail. See p. 57.
- **Kelvin Walkway** (Glasgow): For a completely different view of the city than that gained around the shopping streets and squares, follow the path along the River Kelvin. This green route has all sorts of interesting sights, including statues, ornate bridges, an old toll house, and a gunpowder mill, although children will probably be more interested in the duck pond and play area. See p. 54.

- The start of the **Great Glen Way** (Inverness): Although hiking the whole of this 117km (73-mile) long-distance path is likely only to appeal to the fittest of teenagers, children of all ages will enjoy the first 3.2km (2 miles) along the River Ness. The route takes you over a series of footbridges linking the Ness Islands to parkland with leisure facilities and a Floral Hall, where children can meet the friendly Koi Carp in the pond and explore the cactus house. See p. 233.
- **Lael Forest** (Ullapool): This is a bit different from many woodland walks, as the Lael Forest Garden is more like a tree zoo, containing several hundred trees and shrubs ranging from common specimens to many rarities. Stroll under giant sequoia trees and look out for labels identifying the Chilean yew, Macedonian pine, Oregon maple, Serbian spruce, and many other exotic trees. See p. 240.

2 THE BEST WALKS FOR SEEING WILDLIFE

- **Seaton Cliffs** (Arbroath): This Scottish Wildlife Trust Reserve is a haven for seabirds, wildflowers, and butterflies. Waves have eroded the sandstone cliffs into fantastic formations, such as sea stacks and arches. Walk here from May to July through a riot of white, yellow, pink, and purple flowers and look down on seabird nests from the tarmac cliff-top path. See p. 135.
- **Spey Bay** (Moray Firth): Because this river estuary is constantly in flux, with shifting gravel bars and eroding banks,

it provides a wonderfully rich habitat for all sorts of wildlife, from osprey to otters. The River Spey is an important river for salmon and many other creatures, such as seals, who come to feed on them. The Moray Firth Wildlife Centre at the river mouth is home to the Whale and Dolphin Conservation Society. If you're lucky you could see some of the local population of bottlenose dolphins. See p. 207.
- **Falls of Clyde** (New Lanark): For an old industrial area close to Glasgow and

Edinburgh, there is a surprising richness of nature in this wildlife reserve. It is based on a wooded gorge where the River Clyde plunges over a dramatic waterfall. Kingfishers and dippers flit around the water, while woodpeckers and sparrowhawks live among the trees. The highlight is the nesting pair of peregrine falcons, which can be observed from a "hide" used by bird watchers. See p. 51.

- **Loch Leven Heritage Trail** (Kinross): Loch Leven, Scotland's largest Lowland loch, is designated a National Nature Reserve because of its importance for wildfowl and nesting ducks. About 20,000 pink-footed geese roost here in winter—their dawn flight is an amazing sight. In summer, broods of ducklings shelter along the shoreline, and there's a chance of seeing an osprey or white-tailed sea eagle fishing. All sorts of exotic migrants turn up here, including a spoonbill in 2008. The path runs around the loch, linking viewpoints and bird hides. See p. 115.
- **Glen Nant** (Oban): Atlantic Oakwood of this type supports more species of wildlife than any other habitat in Scotland.

Effectively, this lush west-coast woodland is Scotland's "rainforest." The Ant Trail has information about plants and animals, such as pine marten and woodpecker, and explains how the wood has survived thanks to its importance as a source of charcoal for iron smelting. See p. 159.

- **Wood of Cree** (Galloway): This ancient oakwood looks its best in spring and autumn—when bluebells carpet the ground or when the leaves become a riot of color. Here bird-watchers may spot rare migratory visitors like the redstart and pied flycatcher. Those who keep their eyes on the ground could see some of the 300 species of flowering plants, including wild garlic, primrose, and wood sorrel. See p. 84.
- **Dog Falls** (northern Highlands): Glen Affric is a very special place, where nature still holds sway. The beautiful glen has a wild feel because much of Scotland's native flora and fauna survives here. Walk among gnarled old pines and, if you're lucky, spot some of the rare wildlife such as pine martens, red squirrels, capercaillie, and crossbill. See p. 227.

3 THE BEST MOUNTAIN WALKS

- **Ben Nevis** (Fort William): As the highest mountain in the British Isles, Ben Nevis, at 1,344m (4,408 ft.), is an irresistible draw for hill walkers. It's a hard slog to the top, but the sense of achievement is incredible. If clouds don't obscure the view, you can enjoy a spectacular panorama over the west coast. See p. 243.
- **Cairn Gorm and Ben Macdui** (Cairngorms): Ben Macdui, at 1,309m (4,295 ft.), is the second highest mountain in Britain, while Cairn Gorm, at 1,245m (4,085 ft.), is the prominent summit above Aviemore that gives the whole

mountain range its name. This hike explores the most remarkable landscapes of Cairngorms National Park, where ice-gouged cliffs bite into a vast sub-arctic plateau. See p. 189.

- **Arrochar Alps** (Argyll Forest Park): These mountains are aptly named Alps, as they have an unusually rugged character for hills so far south in Scotland. They rise straight out of a sea loch in the western part of Loch Lomond and the Trossachs National Park. The Cobbler, at 881m (2,890 ft.), is the lowest but best loved of these peaks, with rock faces that played a significant role in the

THE BEST OF WALKING IN SCOTLAND

1

THE BEST HILL WALKS

development of Scottish climbing. See p. 156.

- **Ben Lomond** (Loch Lomond): Scotland's most southerly mountain also has some of the finest views, stretching on a clear day from the urban fringes of Glasgow to Ben Nevis in the north. A well-made path up Ben Lomond (974m/3,195 ft.) makes it one of the "easier" Munros (mountains over 914m/3,000 ft.) to tackle. See p. 153.
- **Lochnagar** (Deeside): Lying in the eastern part of Cairngorms National Park, Lochnagar (1,155m/3,789 ft.) is a romantic summit with great cliffs on its north side that hold snow late into the year. Balmoral, the Royal Family's summer home, lies at its foot, and Prince Charles made the most of local legends in his children's story *The Old Man of Lochnagar*. See p. 197.
- **Creag Meagaidh** (between Fort William and Aviemore): This mountain also has steep cliffs popular with climbers and a wide summit plateau where it is easy to lose your bearings. Enjoy one of the most beautiful mountain

approaches in Scotland on this hike up Creag Meagaidh (1,130m/3,707 ft.). Once on top, there are lovely views over Loch Laggan to an endless succession of mountain ridges, especially if you stay high to include two neighboring Munros. See p. 211.

- **Ben Lawers** (Tayside): Although Ben Lawers, at 1,124m (3,983 ft.), is the highest mountain in the southern Highlands, an elevated start point reduces the amount of climbing needed to reach the summit. The mountain is a National Nature Reserve because its limestone rocks support rare arctic-alpine flora and there are wonderful views over Loch Tay. See p. 128.
- **Cruachan Horseshoe** (Oban): This is one of the most challenging walks in Scotland—a circuit of a narrow, rocky ridge between Ben Cruachan (1,126m/ 3,694 ft.) and Stob Diamh (980m/3,215 ft.) where you need agility and a good tolerance for heights. On a clear summer's day there is an enchanting view over the west coast and the nearby Hebridean islands. See p. 162.

4 THE BEST HILL WALKS

- **Bennachie** (Aberdeen): Set amid rolling farmland, Bennachie is a heather-clad range of hills with rocky summits. The most prominent top, Mither Tap (518m/1,700 ft.), is ringed by an Iron Age hill fort and has views to the North Sea coast. Recent path improvements have made progress much easier across the peaty ground. See p. 192.
- **Meall a' Bhuachaille** (Aviemore): This hill is near the main Cairngorms massif and makes an excellent objective for those who feel the big mountains are a bit too challenging. Walk through ancient pine forest and past a little green loch before climbing Meall a' Bhuachaille (810m/2,657 ft.). The view

is superb, and you may spot the local herd of reindeer. See p. 186.

- **The Merrick** (Galloway Forest Park): At 843m (2,529 ft.), The Merrick is the highest hill in southern Scotland, with an exposed position that gives it mountain weather. Pick a fine day and you'll be well rewarded by the remarkable views, which stretch from the Solway to the Firth of Clyde and as far as Ireland to the west. See p. 90.
- **Scald Law** (Edinburgh): The Pentlands are the capital's local range of hills, running southwest from the edge of the city. They are full of history, including traces of Romans and Picts, and the reservoir at their heart is a haven for

wildlife. The grassy, rolling hills provide great walking, and the highest summit, Scald Law (583m/1,914 ft.), offers the widest views. See p. 41.

- **Perth and Kinnoull Hill** (Perth): You don't need to climb a mountain for brilliant views in Scotland. Just hike from the center of the "Fair City" to the cliff top on wooded Kinnoull Hill (222m/728 ft.) and gaze down on the River Tay snaking below. The view is enhanced by Kinfauns Castle nestled below. Return down Coronation Road, trod by generations of

royalty, and through colorful riverside gardens. See p. 112.

- **Dumgoyne** (Glasgow): This little hill has bags of character and shows up from miles around as a prominent bump on the end of the Campsie Hills. Its volcanic origins give it the conical shape. The steep climb to Dumgoyne's summit (427m/1,400 ft.) is well worth it for sweeping views over Loch Lomond and the Firth of Clyde. What's more, you can finish with a dram in the distillery at its foot. See p. 60.

5 THE MOST SCENIC WALKS

- **Arthur's Seat** (Edinburgh): For a three-dimensional view of Scotland's capital city, climb the volcanic hill at its heart and look out over chimneys and spires to Edinburgh Castle and Leith docks on the Firth of Forth. The walk includes a stroll along Salisbury Crags for a bird's-eye view of the Scottish Parliament building and Holyrood Palace, the Royal Family's official residence in Scotland. See p. 44.
- **Callander Crags** (Stirling): Set in the pretty Trossachs, this hike encompasses many different sights to make a truly memorable walk. It rises along a wooded cliff edge with aerial views of the resort town of Callander to a monument with views of the surrounding lochs and mountains. The return is past spectacular Bracklinn Falls where Keltie Water drops through a rocky gorge. See p. 150.
- **Conic Hill** (Loch Lomond): The Highland Boundary Fault thrust up the ridge of rock that forms Conic Hills and two islands in Loch Lomond—Inchcailoch and Inchmurrin—that are perfectly aligned with it. It is by far the best viewpoint for drinking in the beauty of Loch Lomond and its wooded isles. A great place to enjoy a summer sunset! See p. 67.

- **Knock of Crieff** (Tayside): The Knock of Crieff also lies on the fault line that divides the Highlands from the Lowlands and has wonderful views in all directions. Heathery mountains seem just a stone's throw away to the north, while woods and pastures roll away in the south to the fertile valley of Strathearn. See p. 121.
- **Peebles** (Borders region): This wonderful riverside walk is most delightful in autumn, when the warm colors of the broadleaved trees are reflected in the Tweed. On a sunny day, they contrast gloriously with the blue sky reflected in the water. Stroll past a 13th-century castle and see what wildlife you can spot—perhaps a heron fishing in the shallows or a buzzard soaring above. See p. 93.
- **Loch an Eilein** (Aviemore): The ancient Caledonian pine forest of Rothiemurchus surrounds this sparkling loch, which has been a popular beauty spot since Victorian times. Why not sit awhile on one of the benches to enjoy lovely reflections in the still waters and gaze up to the blue horizon of Cairngorm Mountains? See p. 182.

6 THE BEST COASTAL WALKS

- **Fife Coastal Path** (Fife): Follow the prettiest section of this long-distance route on a path that links the charming fishing villages of the East Neuk. This eastern corner of the Kingdom of Fife juts out into the North Sea and has sandy bays and rocky shores frequented by seals and seabirds. As well as wildlife, the area has a rich history, with landmarks such as St. Fillan's Cave and the saltpans and windmill at St. Monans. See p. 118.

- **Sandwood Bay** (northern Highlands): You don't walk to Sandwood Bay, you make a pilgrimage there. Such is its iconic status that many consider a visit almost a spiritual experience. It's not hard to see why it's so special—a great arc of pristine sand framed by sandstone cliffs and a sea stack, arched over by an enormous sky. See p. 237.

- **St. Abb's Head** (Coldingham): This famous headland is not only one of the finest on Britain's east coast, but it is also an excellent place to see nesting seabirds. The visitor center will help you tune into the flora and fauna to look out for as you follow the narrow path above dramatic coastal cliffs. Other sights include a lighthouse, secluded bays, and the surrounding patchwork of serene farmland. See p. 103.

- **Killantringan Lighthouse** (Portpatrick): Head across to the southwest tip of Galloway for another rewarding clifftop walk. This time you look out west to the distant coastline of Ireland. Starting from the picturesque fishing village of Portpatrick, this walk passes above cliffs with colonies of nesting seabirds on its way to scenically sited lighthouse See p. 81.

- **Carradale** (Kintyre peninsula): For sheer diversity of coastal views and wildlife, this walk is hard to beat. Wild goats live on Carradale Point, and you could see any size of marine mammal from a seal to a minke whale (the coast is also visited by basking sharks). The route takes in two beautiful and very different beaches—a vast stretch of golden sand and a perfect little cove with turquoise water—while the jagged mountains of the Isle of Arran are a constant presence offshore. See p. 170.

7 THE WALKS WITH THE BEST ATTRACTIONS

- **Falkirk Wheel** (between Edinburgh and Glasgow): Photographs don't do justice to this modern engineering feat—you have to walk up close and see the shiny boat lift in action to appreciate the marvel. Originally a flight of 11 locks linked the Union Canal to the Forth and Clyde Canal, but these were built over. When the canals were reopened as a Millennium project, the enormous Falkirk Wheel was created to raise boats 30m (100 ft.) from one loch to the next. This walk follows the Union Canal through a tunnel that passes under the Antonine Wall, built by the Romans 2,000 years ago. See p. 48.

- **Fyrish Monument** (Inverness): This is another man-made construction that looks most impressive when you get close and see its true size. It stands on top of a hill near Alness and looks quite quaint from a distance. The massive structure of stone towers and arches is a replica of the gates of Negapatam in India, built on the orders of the local landowner, Sir Hector Munro. See p. 230.

- **Hermitage and Braan** (Dunkeld): The walk up the River Braan to the Hermitage features a stone summerhouse that has a balcony overlooking a waterfall. Designed to amplify the sound of the crashing waters, and with mirrors to reflect the flashing light, this is just one feature of the woodland garden where the Dukes of Atholl entertained their visitors. See p. 124.

- **The Vat and Muir of Dinnet** (Deeside): Natural structures can be just as amazing as built ones, as you'll discover if you visit the unusual geological feature of the Vat. It comes as a bit of a surprise—squeeze through a crack in a gorge wall and suddenly you find yourself in an enormous circular pothole that was formed by meltwater flowing under a glacier. See p. 194.

- **Dufftown to Craigellachie** (Strathspey): You'll remember this walk for the number of distilleries it passes—or then again perhaps you won't. It starts at the famous Glenfiddich Distillery (save the whisky tasting until afterwards) and follows the River Fiddich downstream via a disused railway line to Craigellachie. See p. 204.

- **Alloway** (Ayr): Don't visit Scotland without finding out more about the national bard, Rabbie Burns, whose poems and songs—from "To a Mouse" to "Auld Lang Syne"—define what it is to be Scottish. This walk provides an ideal introduction, as it starts by the Robert Burns Heritage Museum at his birthplace and visits several sites that appear in his epic poem *Tam o' Shanter*. See p. 78.

8 THE BEST RESTAURANTS FOR DINNER

- **Stac Polly** (Edinburgh; ✆ **01315 562231**): Attentive service and suitably Scottish decor will help you enjoy the best of Scottish game and seafood at this well-established restaurant. It's named after a small but iconic mountain in the northern Highlands. See p. 71.

- **McCallum's Oyster Bar** (Troon; ✆ **01292 319339**): Dine on the best seafood for miles around while relaxing with a view out to sea. Situated on Troon harbor, this Ayrshire restaurant is packed with yachting memorabilia. See p. 108.

- **East Haugh House** (Pitlochry; ✆ **01796 472473**): The elegant restaurant in this country house hotel serves excellent local produce, such as hill-fed Perthshire lamb. Eat in the cozy bar or sample the more adventurous menu in the stylish restaurant. See p. 146.

- **Knipoch Hotel Restaurant** (Kilninver; ✆ **01852 316251**): Treat yourself to fine dining at this lochside hotel, whose daily five-course menu relies heavily on Scottish produce and is supported by an excellent wine cellar. See p. 178.

- **Craigellachie Hotel** (Craigellachie, Speyside; ✆ **01340 881204**): This classic Scottish hotel uses the finest local ingredients in its mouth-watering menu. Once you've settled into an armchair in the Quaich Bar with a dram in your hand, any aches and pains will vanish. See p. 215.

- **Crannog Seafood Restaurant** (Fort William; ✆ **01397 705589**): As the Crannog occupies the most attractive spot in town, on a pier overlooking Loch Linhe, you can enjoy wonderful west-coast views while dining. Much of the fish comes from the owners' boats or their own smokehouse. See p. 247.

9 THE BEST PLACES FOR LUNCH

- **Falko Konditormeister** (Gullane; ℂ **01620 843168**): You could end your walk at Yellowcraigs Beach in this cozy cafe that offers one of Scotland's top cake-eating experiences. Lunch on fresh breads, handmade Bavarian cakes, and excellent coffee. See p. 71.
- **Main Street Trading Company** (St. Boswells; ℂ **01835 824087**): Prepare yourself for the Melrose to Harestanes walk with a good feed on fresh organic sandwiches and home baking in this bright, friendly bookshop. The free-range chicken and hummus sandwich is recommended, as are the carrot cake and scones. See p. 108.
- **Loch Leven's Larder** (Kinross; ℂ **01592 841000**): In the past 10 years, many excellent farm shops and cafes have sprung up across Scotland. This is a prime example, with superb views over Loch Leven and a nature walk that links to a Heritage Trail. See p. 146.
- **Lade Inn** (Kilmahog; ℂ **01877 330152**): After a walk around Callander Crags and Bracklinn Falls, you'll be ready to relax in this inviting Scottish inn. Its real ales and hearty home-cooked meals are available all day in summer, at lunch and dinnertime in winter. See p. 178.
- **Ord Ban Restaurant Café** (Aviemore; ℂ **01479 810005**): Part of the Rothiemurchus Centre, this cafe is strategically situated close to all Aviemore walks. Feast on produce from the Rothiemurchus Estate deli and home baking washed down with great coffee. See p. 215.
- **Café 1** (Inverness; ℂ 01463 226200): Before stepping out along the Great Glen Way, indulge in a hearty lunch in this attractive restaurant, which combines Scottish ingredients with international dishes. See p. 247.

10 THE BEST HOTELS

- **Abode Hotel** (Glasgow; ℂ **01412 216789**): If you love style, you'll relish this chic hotel, which was formerly known as the Art House. Centrally placed, it's ideal for unwinding in unashamed luxury. See p. 70.
- **Brig o' Doon House Hotel** (Alloway; ℂ **01292 442466**): The situation of this welcoming country house hotel is hard to beat—in lovely gardens on the banks of the River Doon, within sight of the famous Brig o' Doon arched bridge that inspired Robert Burns. See p. 107.
- **Crieff Hydro Hotel** (Crieff; ℂ **01764 651670**): Kids will have a whale of a time at this stylish but family-friendly resort that has every imaginable leisure activity.
It has a scenic setting on the Knock, a hill with great walks. See p. 145.
- **Ardanaiseig Hotel** (Kilchrenan; ℂ **01866 833333**): Hidden away in mature wooded gardens on the shores of Loch Awe, this luxurious hotel offers classic Scottish hospitality. Ask for a room with a four-poster bed if you want to sleep in style. See p. 177.
- **Kildrummy Castle Hotel** (near Alford; ℂ **01975 571288**): You'll feel like a lord staying in this mansion house amid acres of landscaped gardens that contain a ruined castle. Enjoy the ambience of antiques and oak-panelled rooms, and the delicious meals—people travel miles to dine in the restaurant. See p. 215.

- **Dornoch Castle Hotel** (Dornoch; ℂ **01862 810981**): In this case you stay in the castle itself, which was once the residence of the bishops of Caithness. Test your navigation skills around the labyrinthine corridors, winding stairs, and converted cellars. See p. 246.

11 THE BEST BUDGET ACCOMMODATIONS

- **SYHA Leith Walk** (Edinburgh; ℂ **01315 242090**): Run by the Scottish Youth Hostel Association, this clean, spacious, and friendly hostel is the perfect budget solution for singles, couples, and families visiting Scotland's capital city. See p. 70.
- **SYHA Melrose** (Melrose; ℂ **01896 822521**): You may be traveling on a budget, but you'll be able to afford to stay in this Georgian mansion, since it is run as a youth hostel. The building overlooks historic Melrose Abbey and is clean and friendly with reasonable self-catering facilities. See p. 107.
- **Blair Castle Caravan Park** (Blair Atholl; ℂ **01796 481263**): The spacious grounds of Blair Castle offer one of the most picturesque places to camp or bring your campervan. Children can enjoy ranger-led activities or red-squirrel spotting, and you're right by Glen Tilt and other local walks. See p. 144.
- **Carradale Bay Caravan Park** (Carradale; ℂ **01583 431665**): This is another fun place for the kids, on the edge of a mile-long sandy beach. Bring a tent or tourer to this peaceful spot and enjoy the surrounding network of paths. See p. 177.
- **Froach Lodge** (Boat of Garten; ℂ **01479 831331**): The hostel-style accommodations in this cozy Victorian villa are geared to hill walkers and other outdoor lovers, with the Cairngorms on the doorstep. The friendly atmosphere and delicious home-cooked food will soon make you feel at home. See p. 214.
- **Ivybank Guest House** (Inverness; ℂ **01463 232796**): For great value, opt for this comfortable, centrally placed B&B. Built in 1836, it retains its original features and charm, and has a walled garden. Half the rooms have private bathrooms. See p. 246.

2

Planning Your Trip to Scotland

Scotland has an enormous amount of excellent walking, and we have picked some of the best routes amidst the most beautiful and interesting parts of the country. The countryside is so varied—from flat coastal plains, through woods and low hills, to rugged mountains—that there are walks to suit everyone. Nearly one-tenth of Scotland is covered by the national forests, which are managed for public benefit by Forestry Commission Scotland.

Many people visit Scotland specifically to climb its mountains. There are 284 Munros (mountains over 914m/3,000 ft.), and some walkers dedicate themselves to climbing them all—a sport known as "Munro-bagging." Having completed them, many set about adding the 220 Corbetts (mountains between 762m/2,500 ft. and 914m/3,000 ft.) to their tally. Although the mountains are lower than those of well-known ranges elsewhere in the world (Ben Nevis, at 1,344m/4,409 ft., is the highest), conditions on them can be as severe as in the Alps or Arctic.

Scotland is a safe, modern country to visit, and you shouldn't run into any particular problems walking here. It also has several local walking festivals during the year. Joining one can provide an excellent introduction to an area and its best walks, and give you the opportunity to follow a guide on walks that you may not have the confidence to tackle alone.

For additional help in planning your trip and for more on-the-ground resources in Scotland, please turn to the "Fast Facts, Toll-Free Numbers & Websites" appendix on p. 249.

1 BEFORE YOU GO

VISITOR INFORMATION

A good place to start your planning is on the web, where the **VisitScotland** (Scottish Tourist Board) website **www.visit scotland.com** will help you decide where to go. Half the site is dedicated to whetting your appetite with "Scotland's ultimate visitors' guide," while the other half provides a "one-stop Scottish holiday shop" for travel, accommodations, and event tickets. Individual Scottish regions are covered in more detail in separate websites, which you can link to from the main VisitScotland site.

Many other websites offer information about Scotland. The best of the bunch is easy-to-navigate Undiscovered Scotland **www.undiscoveredscotland.co.uk**, a comprehensive and reliable site that has a wealth of information about places, history, and travel.

Throughout Scotland, you'll find a network of Tourist Information Centres in the cities, towns, and villages that attract tourists. The staffs know their areas well and can help you plan your day or find a bed for the night. The centers are shown on maps with an "*i*" symbol and are well

Plan Before You Walk at Frommers.com

Want to make your walking vacation as smooth and enjoyable as possible? We've added lots of valuable information about how to plan the perfect trip on our website at www.frommers.com/go/walking. You'll find tips on how to get fit before your trip, suggestions on how best to plan your route, and useful packing tips. There are even bonus walk reviews for Scotland not found in this book!

signposted on the ground. Smaller centers in more seasonal areas are closed in the winter months.

PASSPORTS

On arrival in the United Kingdom, you must show a valid national passport or other equivalent official document that satisfactorily establishes your identity and nationality. Visitors to the U.K. who require a visa may normally stay in the U.K. up to a maximum of 6 months.

For additional information on passports and visas, please turn to the "Fast Facts, Toll-Free Numbers & Websites" appendix on p. 249.

CUSTOMS
What You Can Bring into Scotland

Look at the "Practical Information" pages in the "About Britain" section of the **Visit-Britain** website at **www.visitbritain.com** for additional guidance, appropriate to your home country, as to what you are allowed to bring into Scotland.

If you come to Scotland directly from another E.U. country, you can bring as much alcohol and tobacco as you want providing it is for your own use, and you can satisfy customs officers that you have brought it into the U.K. for personal use. "Own use" includes goods for your own consumption and gifts. If you bring in goods for resale, or for any payment, even payment in kind, they are regarded as being for a commercial purpose.

When traveling from a non-E.U. country, you can bring the following into the U.K. for your own use without paying U.K. tax or duty:

- 200 cigarettes; or 100 cigarillos; or 50 cigars; or 250 grams of tobacco
- 2 liters of still table wine
- 1 liter of spirits or strong liqueurs over 22% alcohol by volume; or 2 liters of fortified wine (such as port or sherry), sparkling wine, or other liqueurs
- 60 cubic centimeters of perfume
- 250 cubic centimeters of eau de toilette
- £145 worth of all other goods including gifts and souvenirs

What You Can Take Home from Scotland

U.S. Citizens: For specifics on what you can bring back, download the invaluable free pamphlet *Know Before You Go* online at **www.cbp.gov** (click on "Know Before You Go!"), or contact the **U.S. Customs & Border Protection (CBP),** at 1300 Pennsylvania Ave. NW, Washington, DC 20229 (© **877/287-8867**) and request the pamphlet.

Canadian Citizens: For a clear summary of Canadian rules, write for the booklet *I Declare,* issued by the Canada Border Services Agency (© **800/461-9999** in Canada, or 204/983-3500; www.cbsa-asfc.gc.ca).

Australian Citizens: A helpful brochure available from Australian consulates or Customs offices is *Know Before You Go.* For more information, call the **Australian**

Customs Service at ☎ **1300/363-263,** or log on to **www.customs.gov.au.**

New Zealand Citizens: Most questions are answered in a free pamphlet available at New Zealand consulates and Customs offices: *New Zealand Customs Guide for* *Travellers, Notice no. 4.* For more information, contact **New Zealand Customs,** The Customhouse, 17–21 Whitmore St., Box 2218, Wellington (☎ **04/473-6099** or 0800/428-786; www.customs.govt.nz).

2 WHEN TO GO

Scotland is a year-round destination for walking, with a climate that is generally mild and devoid of extremes. Lovely, sunny days can occur at any time of year, as can wet and windy ones. The only thing that can be guaranteed about the weather is that it's changeable.

Spring and autumn are ideal times for a walking holiday. These months normally have some fine spells of weather, and accommodations are cheaper than during the peak summer holiday months, except around the Easter holiday. What's more, the countryside is bright with wildflowers and fresh green leaves in spring, and with the rich autumn colors of trees, bracken, and hill grasses from late September to early November. The driest months are April, May, and June.

Around midsummer, days seem to last forever, with long, light evenings for relaxing or exploring. July and August are the main months for family holidays, and the time when accommodations rates are highest. Although this is when the warmest temperatures occur, it is rarely uncomfortably hot for walking.

Winter has a special appeal if you enjoy frosty mornings or are hoping to walk in snow. However, the days are very short, making long walks difficult, and hill walkers need to be well equipped and experienced. Hogmanay (New Year) is traditionally the major time for winter celebrations, and accommodations and dining are expensive both then and at Christmas, though good value packages are available.

Scotland is often thought of as a rainy destination, but in fact eastern Scotland has a very similar rainfall pattern to London and even more hours of sunshine during the summer because of the longer days. Western Scotland, however, is much wetter, especially where warm, wet Atlantic air meets the mountains in places such as Fort William. However, the Gulf Stream also keeps the western coastal fringe relatively mild. The coldest winter weather occurs inland, or on the east coast when storms blow in from the Arctic.

Average Temperature & Rainfall in Scotland

	Jan	Feb	Mar	Apr	May	June	July	Aug	Sep	Oct	Nov	Dec
Edinburgh Temp. (°F)	38	39	42	45	50	55	59	58	54	49	42	40
Temp. (°C)	3	4	6	7	10	13	15	14	12	9	6	4
Rainfall (in.)	2.2	1.6	1.9	1.5	2.0	2.0	2.5	2.7	2.5	2.4	2.5	2.4

	Jan	Feb	Mar	Apr	May	June	July	Aug	Sep	Oct	Nov	Dec
Fort William Temp. (°F)	40	40	42	46	52	56	59	58	54	50	43	41
Temp. (°C)	4	4	6	8	11	13	15	14	12	10	6	5
Rainfall (in.)	8.8	6.3	5.8	4.3	3.9	4.2	5.0	6.0	6.9	7.9	8.0	9.2

What to Bring: The Walker's Checklist

- Day pack
- Boots
- Socks
- Underwear
- Pants and shorts
- Long-sleeved shirt or sweater
- Outerwear: parka or windbreaker
- Waterproof jacket and pants
- Hat
- Water bottle
- Food
- First aid kit
- Map and compass
- Sunglasses
- Sun block
- Insect repellant
- Matches and fire starter
- Plastic bags

Also consider these items:

Camera, battery charger, extra memory card.

Trekking pole(s), the collapsible, telescoping variety.

A bandana has many uses. Soak one in water and tie around your neck for an instant pick-me-up in hot weather; tie around your head for a sweatband; or use as a mask tied below your eyes to protect from wind and dust.

Heart-rate monitor to wear on wrist to track target heart rate, particularly if you have any physical infirmities that would require paying particular attention to over-exertion, especially on strenuous walks at altitude or in extreme weather.

A good book for after the walk, or to enjoy during a break on the trail. A paperback is lighter to carry around.

Complete information on what to bring on your walking vacation can be found at www.frommers.com/go/walking, including tips on day packs, clothing, and equipment to pack, and recommendations for other things to bring with you.

3 GETTING THERE & GETTING AROUND

BY PLANE

If you are traveling from elsewhere in the British Isles or from Europe, you'll find a wide choice of flights from regional airports to several destinations within Scotland, offered at competitive prices by companies such as Flybe, Easyjet, Ryanair, bmi, and flyglobespan. British Airways still flies to Scotland from London airports, but Flybe have taken over most of their internal routes and also Loganair, the franchise that serves the Scottish islands.

Those needing a long-haul flight will save time and the hassle of a transfer by finding a direct flight to Scotland. However, the choice is limited, and often you'll have to arrive via one of the London airports, or perhaps another European one such as Amsterdam or Shannon.

Edinburgh airport (EDI; www.edinburgh airport.com) has flights from more than 100 destinations worldwide. The majority of these are from other British airports or from European cities, although Delta Airlines flies from New York (JFK), Continental Airlines from New York (Newark), and flyglobespan from Toronto (summer only). Edinburgh airport is on the western edge of the city, and it is a 13km (8-mile) ride by taxi or shuttle bus to the center. There are good road links in all directions, including onto the M8 for Glasgow and the west and the M90 for the north.

Glasgow airport (GLA; www.glasgow airport.com) is Scotland's principal long-haul gateway, with some 30 airlines serving more than 80 destinations worldwide. There are several flights from the US; Continental Airlines flies from New York (Newark), US Airways from Philadelphia, Virgin Atlantic Airways (summer only),

and flyglobespan from Orlando. For Canadians, the choices include Air Transat from Toronto, and flyglobespan (summer only) from Vancouver and Calgary. The airport is 32km (20 miles) west of the city center and is easily reached from the M8 motorway. The nearest rail station is Paisley Gilmour Street, 1.6km (1 mile) away by taxi or bus.

Aberdeen airport (ABZ; www.aberdeen airport.com) has several flights from U.K. and European airports, including Scandinavian ones. It is 11km (7 miles) from Aberdeen city center, off the A96 Aberdeen-to-Inverness road. Regular bus services run into the city center, and the nearest railway station at Dyce is a short taxi ride from the airport.

Inverness airport (INV; www.hial.co. uk) is the main entryway for air travel to the north of Scotland. It has flights from a variety of U.K. destinations.

Dundee airport (DND; www.hial.co. uk) is located minutes from the city center and serves the surrounding region of Tayside. It only has a few scheduled flights—from Belfast and Birmingham (both Flybe) and from London City (Air France).

For listings of the major airlines serving Scotland, please see the "Fast Facts, Toll-Free Numbers & Websites" appendix (p. 249).

BY CAR
Estimated Hours of Drive Time to Scottish Cities

	Edinburgh	Glasgow	Stirling	Dundee	Aberdeen	Inverness
London	7.5	7	7.5	8.5	10	10.5
Cardiff	7	7	7	8	9.5	10.5
Manchester	4	4	4	5	6.5	7.5
York	4	4	4.5	5.5	7	8

The two main driving routes into Scotland are up the west and east sides of England. The west route uses the M6 then the M74 through south Scotland, and is on motorway or dual carriageway (at least two lanes in either direction) all the way. You can

branch off into Dumfries and Galloway or the Scottish Borders after passing Carlisle, or follow the M74 to Glasgow. From Glasgow, good roads connect to other cities in central and northern Scotland, such as Edinburgh, Stirling, Perth, and Inverness.

(Tips) Rental Car Insurance Charges

Third-party insurance is compulsory for driving on U.K. roads and will automatically be included in the amount you pay. You are usually liable up to a specified amount, called the "excess," which can vary from £100 to £1,000 (this will be higher if the driver is under 23 or for larger vehicles, such as MPVs [SUVs]). Your credit card will be used to guarantee this sum. However, many companies allow you to pay extra to waive or reduce the excess. It's up to you whether you want to pay this amount—just remember that you must return the car in the same condition as you received it to avoid being charged.

The east route uses the A1, which follows the coast to Edinburgh, though, if you want to visit the Scottish Borders, you can branch off on to the A696 or A697, which both join the A68 to Edinburgh. From Edinburgh, the Forth Road Bridge and M90 take you to Fife and Perth, with good onward connections to Dundee, Aberdeen, and Inverness.

A good road map will help you plan your journey and find your way around. Choose one from Ordnance Survey (showing geographical details as well as roads), Collins, Phillips, the AA (Automobile Association) or HarperCollins, who publishes the official VisitScotland touring map, which includes extensive tourist information.

Holders of overseas driving licenses are permitted to drive motor vehicles for up to 12 months in the U.K.

Driving in Scotland, as elsewhere in the U.K., is always on the left-hand side of the road. At junctions, you must give way to traffic on the major road—signs and road markings usually make this clear. Roundabouts are a common feature of Scottish roads. These may vary from vast islands on motorway intersections to "mini roundabouts," which are just raised white bumps in the middle of a junction. In all cases, give way to all vehicles coming from your right, and always go clockwise (left) around the roundabout.

You will see many speed cameras on major roads—they are brightly painted,

and road signs with a camera icon give a forewarning.

Use of a hand-held mobile (cell) phone or similar device is illegal while driving.

BY FERRY

Ferry travel is popular among visitors from Ireland, Belgium, Holland, and Luxembourg. **Stena Line** (www.stenaline.co.uk; (C) **08705 707070**) sails from Belfast to Stranraer, and **P&O Irish Sea** (www.poirishsea.com; (C) **087166 449999**) sails from Larne to Cairnryan and Troon (summer only).

The Superfast ferry service between Rosyth in Fife and Zeebrugge in Belgium closed in September 2008, but Norfolkline (www.norfolkline.com) is due to resume sailings on the same route from Europe in Spring 2009. The next nearest ferry from Europe is **P&O Ferries** (www.poferries.com; (C) **08716 645645**) from Zeebrugge to Hull in northeast England.

Scotland has many islands, over 50 of which have scheduled ferry services. Most ferries carry cars, though advance booking is advisable, especially on popular routes during the holiday season. However, if you are traveling by foot or bike, you can just turn up in time to buy a ticket and board before departure. On some short services that are constantly plying back and forth, such as the Corran Ferry that crosses Loch Linhe south of Fort William, fares are collected on board.

Caledonian MacBrayne, familiarly known as "CalMac," (www.calmac.co.uk; © **08000 665000**) runs virtually all the services in the west of Scotland. They have two types of reduced-fare passes. If you're taking more than one ferry, check out the discounted Island Hopscotch tickets. If you're going to be taking a lot of ferries, you might be better off with an Island Rover, which entitles you to 8 or 15 consecutive days' unlimited ferry travel. They do not, however, guarantee a place for your car on any ferry, so you still need to book ahead.

BY TRAIN

Two main rail lines link England to Scotland, the east-coast and west-coast lines. **National Express East Coast** (www.national expresseastcoast.com) trains use the fastest and most popular route, from London King's Cross station to Edinburgh via Peterborough, York, and Newcastle, some of these continuing to Aberdeen or Inverness. **Virgin Trains** (www.virgintrains.co.uk) run up the west-coast line from London Euston to Glasgow via Crewe, Preston, and Carlisle. In addition, the overnight **Caledonian Sleeper** service (www.firstgroup.com/scot rail/caledoniansleeper) runs up the west-coast route from London Euston to various Scottish cities.

Several long-distance direct services to Scotland begin from outside London. For instance, Virgin has services from Birmingham to Edinburgh or Glasgow, and **First TransPennine Express** (www.tp express.co.uk) operates direct services to Edinburgh and Glasgow from Manchester airport via the west-coast line. You can also catch a train from Cardiff or the southwest of England with **CrossCountry** (www. crosscountrytrains.co.uk).

Rail services offer quicker journey times to Scotland than traveling by road, and often beat air travel when you take into account transfer and check-in times. You can reach Edinburgh from London in as little as 4$^1/_2$ hours and Glasgow in 5 hours.

Allow a further 2$^1/_2$ hours to continue on to Aberdeen, or 3$^1/_2$ hours to Inverness. Railway stations are generally located in the middle of cities and towns, so centrally situated hotels are only a short taxi ride away.

Train tickets can be bought at railway stations, through **National Rail Enquiries** (© **08457 484950**), online through operators' websites or via an independent retailer such as **thetrainline.com** (© **0870 010 1296**). Where railway stations are unmanned, board the train and pay when the guard comes around collecting fares.

As most Scots live in the central belt between Edinburgh and Glasgow, this is the area with the densest rail network and most frequent trains. Only a few main lines serve the rural areas, particularly in the Highlands. All Scottish cities have regular train services, and you can also reach many of the towns that are close to walks featured in this book, for instance Fort William, Aviemore, Ayr, and Arbroath.

FirstScotRail (www.firstgroup.com/scot rail) runs most of the train services within Scotland, including routes such as the West Highland Line that are rated as among the great scenic routes of the world.

BY COACH (BUS)

Long-distance buses in Britain are comfortable, modern vehicles and offer the cheapest way to travel between cities. Journey times are usually slightly longer than by train, but frequency of service can be greater on popular routes. Buses run directly to Scottish cities from many British cities and towns. The main U.K. operator is **National Express** (www.nationalexpress. com; © **08717 818181**). **Megabus** (www. megabus.com; © **09001 600900**) also offers incredibly low fares for booking early or traveling at less popular times.

The national coach operator, **Scottish Citylink** (www.citylink.co.uk; © **08705 505050**), runs services between all Scotland's major towns and cities, including many with walks featured in this book. Fares are significantly cheaper than for the equivalent train journeys, so coaches soon fill up on popular routes and at weekends and holidays. It's a good idea to book your journey as early as possible, to get the best deal on price and to reserve a seat. If you're planning lots of coach travel, you may be better off buying an Explorer Pass, which offers unlimited travel for a specified number of days; for instance, 3 days' travel out of 5 for £35. It also offers a range of discounted tickets, some specifically for children and students.

For more rural walks in and around villages, you'll need to use local bus services, which are provided by a bewildering array of companies. Routes and timetables change frequently, but are publicized at bus stops and on leaflets produced by local councils, which are available free from shops and Tourist Information Centres.

4 CHOOSING A WALK

For such a rich and diverse walking destination, there are obviously thousands of different walks you could take—so what makes these the best? While any choice is going to be subjective, we've used our years of experience to choose the best walks for all kinds of interests: the best walks for spectacular views, the best to see wildlife, the best forest walks, the best coastal routes, the best challenges, and the best to see places to explore the culture while you walk. Above all, we've strived to provide routes that show you something unique about Scotland that you won't likely find where you've come from.

ELEMENTS OF A FROMMER'S "BEST WALKING TRIP"

At the beginning of each review, there is lots of information to help you decide if a particular walk is right for you. Keeping in mind what kind of vacation experience you want, use these tools to help you plan and get the most out of your vacation.

Star Ratings & Icons

Located in the title bar at the beginning of the walk review, these ratings are the quickest way to see which hikes we believe are "the best of the best."

All routes in this book have been carefully recommended and make for an excellent walking experience; however, a few routes are so exceptional that they deserve special attention. For these, we've awarded a star (or two or three stars) for easy identification.

Likewise, some walks have special qualities that deserve recognition:

(Finds) Are lesser-known walks that don't have the crowds of some of the more popular routes—the hidden treasures.

(Kids) These choices are ones best suited for doing with young families, with easier terrain and lots to see and do to keep children engaged.

(Moments) These routes contain experiences that are so special they will leave lasting memories—something you may never have seen before, and will never forget.

Difficulty Rating

A trail's **degree of difficulty** greatly affects the time needed to complete the walk. Park agencies and guidebook writers rate the degree of challenge a trail presents to the average traveler. Of course the "average" walker varies widely, as do their skills, experience, and conditioning; assessing "degree of difficulty" is inevitably subjective.

A path's elevation gain and loss, exposure to elements, steepness, climatic conditions, and the natural obstacles a person encounters along the way (for example, a boulder field or several creek crossings would increase the difficulty rating) figure prominently in determining the route's difficulty rating.

In this book, walks are rated with an Easy-Moderate-Strenuous system. The rating in brief is:

Easy: Less than 8km (5 miles) with an elevation gain of less than 213 to 244m (700 to 800 ft.). These are easy day trails suitable for beginners and children.
Moderate: Between 8 and 16km (5–10 miles) with less than a 610m (2,000-ft.) elevation gain. You should be reasonably fit for these.
Strenuous: Walks over 16km (10 miles), and those with more than a 610m (2,000-ft.) elevation gain. These are not suitable for children or people of questionable fitness.

Distance

Distance is expressed in kilometers and miles for the complete distance to walk beginning at the trailhead. The routes in this guide range from 3 to 26km (2–16 miles) round-trip.

Estimated Time

Estimated time needed to complete the walks in this guidebook is based on the expected performance of a person in average physical and aerobic condition, traveling at a moderate pace. Age, fitness, and trail experience vary widely among people, and the estimated time may be far too long for some, far too short for others. The estimate also includes recommended amounts of time for taking breaks along the route.

Elevation Gain

Elevation gain measures the *net* gain from the trailhead to the route's highest point. Overall gain (or gross gain) on a trail with rolling terrain that climbs and loses elevation, could be substantially more. The elevation chart that appears with the trail map for each walk will show the route's topography.

Costs & Permits

There is no charge for walking anywhere in Scotland, and no permits are required.

At some popular destinations, you will have to pay for car parking—normally "pay and display" where you put coins in a machine and place the ticket it dispenses inside your windshield. This fee (usually about £2) is generally used to maintain the facilities for walkers. In a few car parks you may find a donation box for voluntary contributions to the upkeep of the car park and paths.

Pet-Friendly

Under Scottish access legislation, walkers have the right to take dog(s) with them. However, they also have the responsibility to keep their dog under control so that it doesn't cause damage and isn't a nuisance to others.

Keep your dog on a short lead around farm animals and during the bird-breeding season (Apr–July). Never let it worry or attack livestock or disturb nesting birds. Keep yourself and your dog at a safe distance, as cattle can act aggressively toward dogs, especially if they have calves. Avoid taking your dog into fruit and vegetable fields unless there is a clear path.

It is illegal not to clean up after your dog if it fouls a public place, so take a supply of "poo bags" and pick up and carefully dispose of dog waste. You'll find dog waste bins in parks and around built-up areas, but elsewhere you'll have to use an ordinary rubbish bin.

Note that most routes described in this book qualify as pet-friendly, so this information only appears in route descriptions where bringing a pet is not appropriate or requires unusual preparation.

Best Time to Go

We have suggested the best time period to take a particular walk. Scotland offers four-season hiking, but some climatic restrictions must be heeded. You can walk some of the trails in this guide all of the time, all of the trails some of the time, but not necessarily all of the trails all of the time. Deep snow in the mountains can make it physically impossible to complete long walks in daylight—apart from the safety issues of possibly getting stuck out or being caught in an avalanche. At other times, the freeze-thaw nature of Scottish weather can make the mountains very icy, so ice axe and crampons are required.

The suggested times are intended to show the best time for maximum enjoyment of the trail, but almost all of the walks are also accessible outside the suggested time period.

Website

The suggested website is the best place to go to get further information on the trail and surrounding area.

Recommended Map

We've listed our favorite trail maps, those that are reasonably easy for the traveler to obtain. These will likely provide additional detail to the map provided in this guide.

Trailhead GPS

We've listed the GPS coordinates for where the recommended trail begins. The intent is to get you to the start of your route easily, by entering the coordinates into a handheld or automotive GPS device, GPS-enabled mobile phone, or online mapping program.

Trailhead Directions

Directions to the walk's starting point are given from the nearest highway or major road to the parking area for the trailhead. For trails having two desirable trailheads, directions to both are given. A few trails can be hiked one-way with the possibility

of a public transport or a car shuttle. Suggested car shuttle points are noted.

NAVIGATION ASSISTANCE
Maps

Each trail in this guide has a map. Familiarize yourself with the map legend. To follow the map easily, first look for the north. Then find the trailhead and follow the directions given to each waypoint.

The government agency **Ordnance Survey** (www.ordnancesurvey.co.uk) produces maps covering the whole of Scotland. The most useful maps for walking are the Landranger series (1:50,000 scale) with magenta covers and the Explorer series (1:25,000 scale) with orange covers. The Explorer maps are often double sided. If you want a weatherproof map, go for the range of Explorer Active Maps, which are laminated. You can buy these OS maps directly from the online Ordnance Survey shop in the leisure section of www.ordnancesurvey.co.uk and from other map and outdoor suppliers.

Harvey (www.harveymaps.co.uk) also produces excellent maps specifically designed for walkers. They are bold and easy to read, but only cover the most popular walking areas.

Several companies produce smaller scale maps that are useful for seeing the bigger picture and for traveling around the country. An online source of such maps is www.mapsworldwide.com.

Google Maps are particularly useful for finding your way to walks. Google Maps provide highly specific driving directions from Point A to Point B—that is to say from the city to the country and from one walk to another.

Google Maps provides road maps and in some cases also shows tracks used by walks. A more specific Terrain map view displays a topographic view. In addition, the Satellite view shows terrain in a more three-dimensional way. You can create and edit Google maps on your home computer

(Tips) **It's Easy Being Green**

Here are a few simple ways you can help conserve fuel and energy when you travel:

- Each time you take a flight or drive a car, greenhouse gases release into the atmosphere. You can help neutralize this danger to the planet through "carbon offsetting"—paying someone to invest your money in programs that reduce your greenhouse gas emissions by the same amount you've added. Before buying carbon offset credits, just make sure that you're using a reputable company, one with a proven program that invests in renewable energy. Reliable carbon offset companies include **Carbonfund** (www.carbonfund.org), **Terra-Pass** (www.terrapass.org), and **Carbon Neutral** (www.carbonneutral.org).

- Whenever possible, choose nonstop flights; they generally require less fuel than indirect flights that stop and take off again. Try to fly during the day—some scientists estimate that nighttime flights are twice as harmful to the environment. And pack light—each 15 pounds of luggage on a 5,000-mile flight adds up to 50 pounds of carbon dioxide emitted.

- Where you stay during your travels can have a major environmental impact. To determine the green credentials of a property, ask about trash disposal and recycling, water conservation, and energy use; also question if sustainable materials were used in the construction of the property. The website **www.greenhotels.com** recommends green-rated member hotels around the world that fulfill the company's stringent environmental requirements. Also consult **www.environmentallyfriendlyhotels.com** for more green accommodations ratings.

- At hotels, request that your sheets and towels not be changed daily. (Many hotels already have programs like this in place.) Turn off the lights and air-conditioner (or heater) when you leave your room.

- Use public transport where possible—trains, buses, and even taxis are more energy-efficient forms of transport than driving. Even better is to walk or cycle; you'll produce zero emissions and stay fit and healthy on your travels.

- If renting a car is necessary, ask the rental agent for a hybrid, or rent the most fuel-efficient car available. You'll use less gas and save money at the tank.

- Eat at locally owned and operated restaurants that use produce grown in the area. This contributes to the local economy and cuts down on greenhouse-gas emissions by supporting restaurants where the food is not flown or trucked in across long distances.

before your trip or download them to a wireless device.

MapQuest.co.uk has excellent map-making capabilities and will enable you to get maps and directions to towns and trailheads. The company also offers a product called MapQuest Navigator 5.0 that provides GPS car navigation on your phone without the need to buy another navigation device.

Reading GPS Coordinates

In North America, GPS coordinates normally reflect a measurement of longitude and latitude given in "degrees." In Britain, coordinates are based on a grid system that covers the entire country; this grid is used on all maps published by the national mapping agency Ordinance Survey.

The national grid is divided into dozens of grids, each measuring 100km in both length and width; the particular grid relevant for the coordinate given is indicated by a unique 2-letter code. This grid is further subdivided into "eastings" and "northings," which are each measured from the southwest corner of the square. In this book, each easting and northing is represented by a five-digit number (the easting is given first) that measures the distance from the southwest corner of the square being described—for example, the trailhead for Ben Nevis (NN 12597 72978) is 12.597km east and 72.978km north of the southwest corner of the NN map grid.

For readers using a GPS device, it is important to change your map datum setting to "OSGB36" or "British Grid" to use the coordinates provided in this book.

Walks can be broken up with waypoints, or stops along the way. These waypoints can guide you back to the trailhead if you are lost, by checking the coordinates for where you are and aiming yourself towards the coordinates of the nearest waypoint.

Having a GPS reading of the trailhead and of certain trail waypoints can be both helpful and confusing. Such readings can be particularly helpful as a supplement to a map for finding obscure trailheads, unsigned junctions, or going off-trail—situations you will rarely encounter while walking any of the high-quality trails in this guide.

Where a GPS reading can be confusing to the less experienced walker and GPS user has to do with the fact that a GPS device only shows direction or gives distance "as the crow flies," or, in a straight line. But walkers are not crows! Most trails don't take a straight line from Point A to Point B, so be sure to consult the map included with the walk description along with your GPS readings.

5 WALKING SAFETY

There are many well-maintained, waymarked paths for walking, especially on land owned by government agencies—Forestry Commission Scotland and Scottish Natural Heritage—and conservation charities, such as the National Trust for Scotland. Local government authorities (councils) and local countryside trusts have also done considerable work in recent years to provide good quality walk networks. That said, there are also thousands of miles of "unimproved" paths, which may have originated as stalker's paths, farm tracks, or have simply developed from the passage of many feet following the same route up a mountain. Some of the most exciting walks

and best views are to be had in these untamed areas, so be prepared for rough walking and a lack of signposting on the more adventurous walks.

COMMON AILMENTS

FOOD & WATER Food hygiene standards in Scotland are very high, so you shouldn't encounter problems. Simply observe the normal precautions when consuming food products: that they are within their expiry date and that foods such as chicken and pork are thoroughly cooked.

Scottish tap water is of an excellent standard and tastes better than most imported bottled waters! However, you will find bottled water, including leading Scottish brands, in most shops and supermarkets. Ice cubes and drinking water supplied in bars and restaurants are safe. Occasionally you will come across taps where the water is marked not for drinking, for instance in public toilets that don't have a mains water supply.

Vegetarians will not find a great choice outside the cities. Almost all cafes and restaurants offer at least one vegetarian option, but often only one.

RESPIRATORY ILLNESSES You are probably at greatest risk of catching a cold or flu on your flight or train journey to Scotland, where you may be mixing with many people in an atmosphere of re-circulated air.

Sore throats, coughs, and other "sniffles" are the common ailments in Scotland, especially during the winter months when short days and cold, damp weather lowers people's immune systems. The classic treatment for such viruses is to rest and drink plenty of fluids. Aspirin and ibuprofen are all available over the counter, either straight or in various branded concoctions with flavorings and caffeine.

BUGS: TICKS & INSECT BITES Ticks are common wherever sheep and deer are present (in other words practically everywhere in Scotland!). They are found particularly in woodland and rough vegetation. They attach to human hosts in warm areas where they will go undisturbed—behind the ears or knees, armpits, and in the scalp.

At the conclusion of a walk in an area where ticks are present, check your fellow walkers (and have them check you!) for ticks. Brush off your clothes. In a postwalk shower, scan your body one more time. Remember that ticks can be smaller than a pinhead before they start feeding. Make sure to wash the clothes you wore while walking.

When removing a tick, your aim is to remove it cleanly without leaving its mouthparts behind or upsetting it so that it regurgitates its stomach contents (and any bacteria it is carrying) into your blood stream. Firmly grab the tick with a pair of sharp-pointed tweezers right where the head meets the skin. Slowly pull the tick straight out. Special tweezers are available that make it easier to remove them safely.

Mosquitoes used to be unheard of in Scotland, but with global warming a few are beginning to make themselves felt. However, they are unlikely to be an issue for you. Midges—tiny insects that swarm in their thousands in warm, damp, still conditions—are what prove troublesome in Scotland, though fortunately most people don't have any lasting effect from their bites, except for a bit of itchiness. However, a few do have allergic reactions and may come out in red lumps. Likewise, other bites—often from unseen, unidentified insects—may become swollen and itchy. In that case, you can ease the area by applying anti-histamine cream (available from pharmacies).

OTHER DANGERS Nature in Scotland is very harmless. The wild animals are much more scared of you than you are of them, and all the big predators, such as wolf and bear, were hunted to extinction centuries ago. The only creature that could poison you is an adder, a timid snake that has a black zigzag pattern down its back. Adders bask in sunny places, but you're unlikely to see one as they disappear as soon as they become aware that a person is about. Their bites are very rarely fatal—if you are bitten, keep calm and seek medical attention as soon as possible.

There are some poisonous plants in Scotland, but you will be quite safe if you avoid eating fruits and fungi that you can't identify. One plant that could hurt you if you brush against it or handle its sap is an introduced species that has escaped from ornamental gardens. The giant hogweed is an umbellifer with a thick, hollow stem and large flower head the shape of an upturned umbrella. As its name suggests, it grows well above head height—up to 3.7m (12ft.) tall. It is found beside rivers and around wet ground, and contact with it can cause a painful and persistent rash.

TRAILHEAD SAFETY & PARKING PRECAUTIONS

Returning to the trailhead after a joyful day on the trail to find a car window smashed and valuables missing can ruin your vacation. Thieves are known to target car parks that attract lots of tourists, as their cars may contain cameras, money, and other valuables. The greatest risk is in popular places within an hour or so of cities—crime is less prevalent in more rural areas and rare in the remoter Highlands and islands.

A few simple steps can minimize the likelihood of your car being broken into: don't leave valuables in the car (best idea); lock valuables in the trunk (second best idea); bring your wallet and keys with you rather than hiding them in your vehicle.

6 GUIDED WALKING TOURS

Wilderness Scotland (www.wilderness scotland.com; © **01316 256635**) is an award-winning adventure-travel and ecotourism company specializing in small-group walking and adventure holidays in the Highlands and islands. Accommodations vary from hotels and guesthouses to a yacht sailing between islands.

C-N-Do (www.cndoscotland.com; © **01786 445703**) is a long-established company that runs guided walking tours, independent walking holidays, and 1-day walks and courses throughout Scotland. They place an emphasis on sustainable tourism and offer accommodations options ranging from hotels, through guesthouses, to hostels.

Mountain Innovations (www.scot mountain.co.uk; © **01479 831331**) are based at Boat of Garten, near Aviemore

Frommers.com: The Complete Travel Resource

Planning a trip or just returned? Head to **Frommers.com,** voted Best Travel Site by *PC Magazine.* We think you'll find our site indispensable before, during, and after your travels—with expert advice and tips; independent reviews of hotels, restaurants, attractions, and preferred shopping and nightlife venues; vacation giveaways; and an online booking tool. We publish the complete contents of over 135 travel guides in our **Destinations** section, covering over 4,000 places worldwide. Each weekday, we publish original articles that report on **Deals and News** via our free **Frommers.com Newsletters.** What's more, **Arthur Frommer** himself blogs 5 days a week, with cutting opinions about the state of travel in the modern world. We're betting you'll find our **Events** listings an invaluable resource; it's an up-to-the-minute roster of what's happening in cities everywhere—including concerts, festivals, lectures, and more. We've also added weekly **podcasts, interactive maps,** and hundreds of new images across the site. Finally, don't forget to visit our **Message Boards,** where you can join in conversations with thousands of fellow Frommer's travelers and post your trip report once you return.

and the Cairngorms, and offer walking holidays and mountain courses. Their lodge has a relaxed and friendly atmosphere with superb home cooking, and they'll collect you from Inverness airport or Aviemore station.

Easyways (www.easyways.com; ℂ 01324 714132) is a booking agency for the West Highland Way and other long-distance trails. They tailor packages to individual customers, arranging travel, accommodations, transfer of baggage and such like.

For more information on package tours and for tips on booking your trip, see www.frommers.com/planning.

3

Suggested Itineraries

Scotland is bigger than most visitors realize—until they start traveling around. With so many varied landscapes and thousands of walks, you could spend every holiday here and not exhaust the possibilities. These itineraries provide a good starting point, and will help you make the most of a few days or a week. Families will enjoy a short break in Perthshire, while history and literary buffs will be fascinated by a tour of the South. Lovers of nature will delight in a week on Deeside and Strathspey, walking in Cairngorms National Park with a few castles and distilleries thrown in. But for the wildest landscapes and dramatic walks, head north.

1 SCENIC PERTHSHIRE GETAWAY

If you want to visit some of the prettier parts of rural Scotland, but don't have much time to spare, take a few days to relax in Perthshire Big Tree Country. You can enjoy great views on family walks around the attractive wooded valleys and hills of this area, which is only about an hour's drive north from Edinburgh and Glasgow. Distances are fairly small, so you can move on each night or base yourself in one town. Good public transport links mean you could do these walks without driving.

Day ❶: Crieff

From Edinburgh, cross the Forth Road Bridge and take the cross-country A823 road through Glen Devon in the Ochil Hills and past Gleneagles Hotel and golf courses to Crieff. If coming from Glasgow, take the motorway past Stirling and turn off the A9 at Braco, where you can visit Ardoch Roman Fort before continuing to Crieff. After lunch, enjoy views from the **Knock of Crieff** (p. 121) on a walk starting at the Famous Grouse Experience. The **Crieff Hydro Hotel** (p. 145) makes an ideal stopover.

Day ❷: Dunkeld

Drive to Dunkeld through the Sma' Glen, a rugged, steep-sided valley that gives a real taste of Highland scenery. Dunkeld is a historic little town with quaint houses and a ruined cathedral, linked by a stone bridge across the River Tay to the Victorian resort village of Birnam. Explore the **Hermitage and Braan** walk (p. 124) for waterfalls, follies and tall trees, then visit the Beatrix Potter Garden and stroll down to the ancient Birnam Oak on the banks of the Tay. More wonderful trees can be seen in the grounds of the **Hilton Dunkeld House Hotel** (p. 145).

Day ❸: Perth

Dunkeld is less than half an hour from Perth, so you can afford to do some sightseeing. Loch of the Lowes wildlife reserve just outside Dunkeld is well worth visiting, especially for nesting osprey and red squirrels. Follow quiet roads through Caputh and Stanley, where historic Stanley Mills brings to life a water-powered textile mill. Maybe lunch at **Duncan's** (p. 146) before hiking through riverside gardens and up to a cliff-top viewpoint on the **Perth and Kinnoull Hill** walk (p. 112). For great dining, stay at **Parklands Hotel** (p. 145).

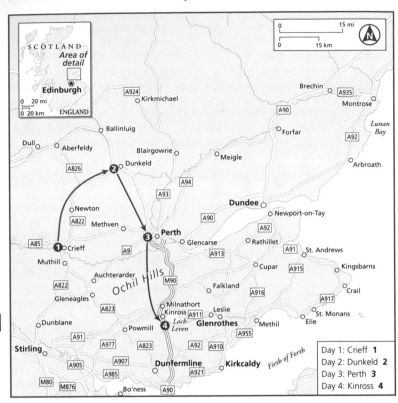

Day 1: Crieff **1**
Day 2: Dunkeld **2**
Day 3: Perth **3**
Day 4: Kinross **4**

Day ❹: Kinross

The M90 provides a fast route back to Edinburgh, but for a more scenic drive take the A912 through Glenfarg to Kinross, passing lonely Balvaird Castle. Break your journey in Kinross for a stroll on the Loch Leven Heritage Trail (p. 115) and lunch in **Loch Leven's Larder** (p. 146). If returning to Glasgow, follow the A977 and cross the Kincardine Bridge over the Firth of Forth.

2 THE HISTORIC SOUTH IN 1 WEEK

Many of the notable events in Scottish history happened in the disputed border territory between Scotland and England. As well as soldiers, the south has seen the comings and goings of monks, smugglers, and reivers (cattle thieves). It has been a fertile area for works of the imagination, stimulating the creativity of two writers who did more than any others to define Scottishness: Robert Burns and Sir Walter Scott. Follow this tour for walks that explore Scotland's history and culture.

Days ❶ & ❷: Ayr

The coastal town of Ayr has a major airport (Prestwick) and is easily reached by road from Glasgow (via the A77) or Edinburgh (via the A70). If driving up from England, you could join this circuit at Dumfries. Just south of Ayr, explore Burns' birthplace on the **Alloway** walk (p. 78), visiting several places that feature in his famous poem Tam o' Shanter. **The Secret Garden** (p. 108) makes a great lunch stop, and where better to stay than the **Brig o' Doon House Hotel** (p. 107), next to the arched bridge where Tam's gray mare Meg lost her tail to a witch?

The next day, you can do the **Dundonald Glen and Smugglers Trail** walk (p. 75) past the impressive ruins of 14th-century Dundonald Castle before lunch in Troon at **McCallum's Oyster Bar** (p. 108) or **The Old Loans Inn** (p. 108). The Ayshire coast is famous for its golf courses, including Royal Troon and Turnberry. If you've time, drive 26km (16 miles) south of Ayr to visit grand Culzean Castle and Country Park, where General Dwight Eisenhower was given an apartment as thanks for his help in World War II. On the way down the A719 you climb (or go down?) the Electric Brae, famous for its deceptive perspective.

Day ❸: Galloway

Head south, leaving the coast at Girvan for a drive through the increasingly wild Galloway hills. A snack at **Glentrool Visitor Centre** (p. 108) should fortify you for a walk in Galloway Forest Park. Choose from a circuit of **Loch Trool** (p. 87) or a climb up **The Merrick** (p. 90), the highest hill in southern Scotland. Both walks take you past Bruce's Stone, which commemorates a victory by Robert the Bruce against English forces. If you go west from Newton Stewart, you can spend the night in Stranraer at **Glenotter Guest House** (p. 107).

Day ❹: Galloway/Dumfries

Today you could start early for the **Killantringan lighthouse walk** (p. 81) along the exposed west coast, or you might prefer a short, sheltered stroll in the **Wood of Cree** (p. 84). If you need a rest day, you'll find plenty of tourist attractions as you follow the A77 east to Dumfries. Children will love Cream o' Galloway—combining ice cream parlor and farm park—near Gatehouse of Fleet, or a visit to Threave Castle on an island in the River Dee near Castle Douglas (walk 1.6km/1 mile; then ring the bell for the boatman). You can pick up the trail of Robert Burns in Dumfries, where he spent the later part of his life.

Days ❺ & ❻: Borders

A scenic drive up the A701/A708 will take you through hills and past photogenic St. Mary's Loch to the towns of the Scottish Borders. Melrose has an atmospheric ruined Abbey, where Robert the Bruce's heart is buried, and is the most attractive place to stay; depending on your budget, try **Burts Hotel** (p. 107) or the **Youth Hostel** (p. 107). Alternatively, stay at **The County Hotel** (p. 107) in Selkirk, a coaching inn frequented by Sir Walter Scott. While in the area, you must visit Scott's home, **Abbotsford House** (p. 107), preferably at lunchtime. Other good eating places in the area are **Russell's Restaurant** (p. 108) in Melrose, **Main Street Trading Company** (p. 108) in St. Boswell's, and **Sunflower** (p. 108) in Peebles.

Of course, you're really here for the walking, so don't forget to burn off some of those calories on the local routes. There's something for all tastes, an easy stroll by the idyllic River Tweed on the **Peebles** walk (p. 93), a moderate walk from **Selkirk to Abbotsford House** (p. 96), or a longer hike along the St. Cuthbert's Way from **Melrose to Harestanes** (p. 100). Near Peebles, call at the historic manor of Traquair House, where Bonnie Prince Charlie once took refuge, and try the delicious beers from their brewery.

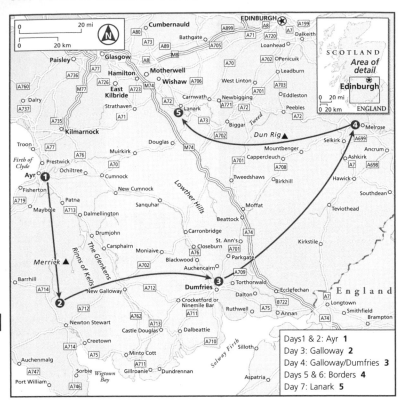

Days1 & 2: Ayr **1**
Day 3: Galloway **2**
Day 4: Galloway/Dumfries **3**
Days 5 & 6: Borders **4**
Day 7: Lanark **5**

Day ❼: Lanark
If you've time on your return journey for another walk, head back to Edinburgh or Glasgow via Lanark. Here you can catch up with Scotland's industrial history on the

Falls of Clyde walk (p. 50), which starts at the beautifully restored 18th-century cotton mill village of New Lanark and goes through a wildlife reserve beside the river.

3 DEESIDE & STRATHSPEY IN 1 WEEK

Explore the valleys of the Dee and the Spey, the two major rivers draining the Cairngorms Mountains, for some of the most evocative scenery in Scotland. This is a country of whisky distilleries and castles. Walks lead through gnarled pinewoods that are remnants of old Caledonian Forest, over heather-clad hills and up the most famous mountains of Cairngorms National Park. Reach Deeside via Aberdeen or drive from the south via Perth and Glenshee.

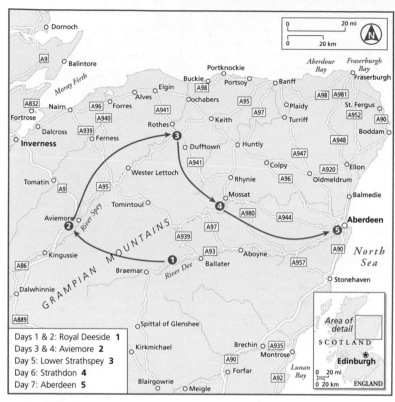

Days 1 & 2: Royal Deeside **1**
Days 3 & 4: Aviemore **2**
Day 5: Lower Strathspey **3**
Day 6: Strathdon **4**
Day 7: Aberdeen **5**

Days ❶ & ❷: Royal Deeside

Follow the salmon-rich River Dee upstream to Ballater, where virtually every
shop has a plaque proclaiming that it is a
supplier to a member of the Royal Family.
While you're in the vicinity, don't miss
Balmoral, the Royal Family's summer
home, and Braemar Castle, which has
been restored since the conflicts of the
17th and 18th centuries. For a novel first
walk, visit a strange geological feature on
the **The Vat and Muir of Dinnet** walk
(p. 194). After that easy introduction, go
for a more demanding hike up **Morrone**
(p. 201) at Braemar or a full mountain
climb up **Lochnagar** (p. 197), near Ballater, the next day.

Deeside Hotel (p. 214) is close to the
center of Ballater, or you could keep your
costs down by staying at **Rucksacks** (p. 215),
an independent hostel in Braemar. You can
enjoy meals cooked with excellent local produce, such as Aberdeen Angus beef, at The
Rowan Tree in Ballater or **The Gathering
Place** (p. 215) in Braemar.

Days ❸ & ❹: Aviemore

To reach Strathspey from Deeside, take the
A939 over the mountain pass between
Cockbridge and Tomintoul on the north
side of the Cairngorms. You'll pass the star-
shaped battlements of Corgarff Castle and
climb past the lifts of the Lecht ski slopes.

In the Aviemore area, you can fit your accommodations to your budget by staying at the **Hilton Coylumbridge** (p. 214), at **Froach Lodge** (p. 214) in Boat of Garten, or at **Glenmore Caravan and Camping Site** (p. 214).

After driving through the mountains, revive yourself with lunch at **Ord Ban Restaurant Cafe** (p. 215) before a gentle stroll around **Loch an Eilein** (p. 182). If you're feeling rich, you could dine at **The Cross** (p. 215) in Kingussie; otherwise Ord Ban is also great for an informal candlelit dinner. The next day, you should be ready to hit the hills, either heading for the summits of **Cairn Gorm and Ben Macdui** (p. 189) or taking the lower option of **Meall a Bhuachaille** (p. 186).

Day ❺: Lower Strathspey

Now follow the River Spey downstream to Craigellachie and Dufftown in the heart of malt whisky country. Once you've eaten in the **Craigellachie Hotel** (p. 215) and sampled their range of whiskies, you may feel compelled to spend the night there to drink up more of the classic Scottish ambience. Alternatively, you could sample local cuisine at the **Taste of Speyside** (p. 216) in nearby Dufftown.

For walks, you could amble from Glenfiddich Distillery along the wooded valley of the River Fiddich on the **Dufftown to Craigellachie** walk (p. 204) or step out farther on the **Spey Bay** walk (p. 207) to the Moray Firth Wildlife Centre at the mouth of the river.

Day ❻: Strathdon

Take the A941 or A96 towards Aberdeen. If you woke with a hangover from sampling too many malt whiskies, you'll find a bracing walk up **Bennachie** (p. 192) will blow away the cobwebs. You're now returning southwards, and could treat yourself to a final night in the **Kildrummy Castle Hotel** (p. 215) where you can sleep and dine in style.

Day ❼: Aberdeen

On the way back to Aberdeen, you could add to your tally of castles, visiting Castle Fraser near Inverurie or going via Banchory and stopping at Crathes Castle or Drum Castle on Deeside. Once back in the city, take a wander around the ancient University buildings and Cathedral in Old Aberdeen.

4 LOCH NESS & THE NORTH IN 1 WEEK

Loch Ness is the largest of three lochs lying along the Great Glen, the deep fault line that runs from Inverness to Fort William. Both the Great Glen Way and Caledonian Canal follow this natural dividing line between the central and northwest Highlands. You can choose to spend a week walking the length of the Great Glen Way, or you can use your time to explore the wild and often dramatic landscapes to the north. You'll need a car for the latter option—distances are great, but the roads are almost empty.

Days ❶ & ❷: Inverness

There's no better way for a walker to explore Inverness, the capital of the Highlands, than by strolling through the town from the castle, across the islands in the River Ness, to the Floral Hall on the start of the **Great Glen Way** (p. 233). Take time to relax, possibly with a leisurely lunch at nearby **Café 1** (p. 247). You'll find accommodations to suit every budget, from the **Ivybank Guest House** (p. 246) through the moderately priced **Glen Mhor Hotel** (p. 246) and **Kingsmills Hotel** (p. 247) to upmarket **Dunain Park** (p. 246).

Days 1 & 2: Inverness & Loch Ness 1
Day 3: Ullapool 2
Day 4: Far Northwest 3
Days 5 & 6: Inverness Dornoch Firth 4
Day 7: Inverness 5

On your second day, head to Glen Affric, one of the most beautiful and unspoiled glens in Scotland, for the **Dog Falls** walk (p. 227). Go or come back via Drumnadrochit on Loch Ness, so you can visit Urquhart Castle and the Loch Ness Exhibition Centre—and maybe get a glimpse of Nessie!

Day ❸: Ullapool
Today, drive towards Ullapool and the northwest coast. You'll want an early start if you're planning to do the challenging mountain climb up **An Teallach** (p. 224), but you can take it easy if you opt instead for a shorter walk around **Lael Forest** (p. 240). Ullapool is a planned fishing village with

whitewashed houses built around a grid system and a small award-winning museum and visitor center.

Day ❹: Far Northwest
Now you really head into the wilds, as you drive north through some of the most remarkable scenery in Scotland. Bare, steep-sided mountains rise like islands out of a sea of empty moorland punctuated by myriad lochs. Cross the bridge at Kylesku and continue up the coast to Kinlochbervie and beyond for a walk to **Sandwood Bay** (p. 237), one of the most atmospheric spots in Britain. You're now just short of Cape Wrath, the northwest tip of mainland Britain, and could continue on along the north

coast to John o' Groats. However, with only a week to spare, you probably want to be heading back.

Days ❺ & ❻: Inverness Dornoch Firth

Drive down the largely single-lane A838 past Loch Shin and Lairg to Dornoch Firth, an estuary on the east coast. If you want to finish your holiday in style, splash out on a couple of nights at **Dornoch Castle Hotel** (p. 246). From here you can easily tackle the **Duke of Sutherland Monument** walk (p. 221) at Golspie and the **Fyrish Monument** walk (p. 230) near Alness. Both have superb views and monuments poignantly connected to the social history of the area. While in Golspie, you could lunch or dine at the **Golf Links Hotel** (p. 248).

Day ❼: Inverness

On your drive back to Inverness, you can take the windier A836, which climbs uphill, giving a great view back to the Dornoch Firth, or you could take the A9 through Tain. An interesting route, if you're in no rush, is to go to Nigg and take the small ferry across the Cromarty Firth to Cromarty. Look for seals as you drive down the shore of the Firth.

Edinburgh & Glasgow Walks

by Colin Hutchison

If arriving from outside of the United Kingdom, it's likely your visit to Scotland will begin in Edinburgh or Glasgow.

On the east coast, nestled under the rolling Pentland Hills and looking north to the sweep of the Firth of Forth, Edinburgh is Scotland's capital city. Hordes of annual visitors and students lend the city a cosmopolitan ambience to go with its well-known historic and aesthetic beauty. Consequently, "Auld Reekie" is packed with buzzing cafes; cozy, atmospheric eateries; and fascinating attractions, including the National Museum of Scotland and Dynamic Earth. Moreover, as hinted by the slopes of the Pentlands 11km (7 miles) south, the fine beaches just 24km (15 miles) east, and the dramatic Salisbury Crags lying almost within earshot of Parliament's debating chamber, you don't need to roam far from the bright lights to access wild and varied walking terrain and world-class views.

Only 77km (48 miles) directly west and less than an hour's journey time by car or train, the once heavily industrialized city of Glasgow sits astride the River Clyde, on which 17th-century merchant ships sailed for the Americas to develop lucrative trade links and fortune. Today, the grand buildings on Virginia Street reflect the affluence once enjoyed by sugar and tobacco merchants whose ships braved the Atlantic.

Despite its industrial heritage, visitors who arrive clinging to the stereotypical vision of Glaswegians being a tough, hard-drinking lot are set for disappointment. For though, like the back streets of Edinburgh, Glasgow continues to have its problems, for the past 2 decades the city has undergone quite a renaissance.

Reflecting its growing reputation as the style capital of Scotland, well-heeled, ever more confident Glaswegians are spoiled with a wealth of boutique shopping outlets and trendy west-end cafes. No visitor should leave Glasgow without exploring the Botanic Gardens and the fascinating interactive interior of Scotland's busiest no-charge tourist attraction—the Kelvingrove Museum and Art Gallery.

Moreover, like in the east, there are parks and river walkways galore to enjoy in this proud city that's preparing to host the 2014 Commonwealth Games.

Yet for walkers, the real attractions lie just beyond the city limits. Readily accessed by train or car, the wild natural beauty of Loch Lomond and the southern boundary of the Highlands are just 30 minutes north. Like Queen Victoria, you may choose to walk at Queen's View looking north to the Arrochar Alps, tackle the steep, rewarding slopes of the volcanic remnants of Dumgoyne, or marvel at the autumn colors of the oak woodland and rushing waters of the Falls of Clyde.

Wherever you choose to roam, in and around these two great cities, you'll be truly spoiled for choice.

ESSENTIALS

GETTING THERE

By Air

If you fly into Glasgow airport (www.glasgowairport.com), it will cost you around £18 to £20 for a taxi into the city center 13km (8 miles) to the east. The taxi rank is directly outside the terminal building. Alternatively, the Service 500 bus service operated by Arriva departs every 7 minutes from the airport (£4.20 single) for the 30-minute journey into Glasgow. The bus stops at Buchanan Street Bus Station, just a 5-minute walk from Queen Street (railway) station (www.firstgroup.com/scotrail) for trains north, west, and east. From Buchanan Street it's a 10-minute walk to Central Station for trains to the southwest of Scotland and England.

If you fly into Edinburgh (www.edinburghairport.com), expect to pay between £16 and £20 for the 25-minute cab fare 9.7km (6 miles) east into the city center. Arguably the best (and certainly cheapest) option is to catch the regular (every 10 min. during peak time) Airlink 100 express bus service from stand 19 outside the airport terminus. This costs just £3 (single) and takes around 25 minutes to reach its terminus at Waverley Bridge. This is directly opposite the entrance to Waverley Station where you can catch a host of train services including to Glasgow (£9.20 single), Aberdeen, Inverness, North Berwick, and London (www.firstgroup.com/scotrail).

By Car

The M8 motorway is the main highway linking Glasgow and Edinburgh. To access either city centre by car, simply follow the M8 then all signs for the respective city centre.

If driving north to Glasgow from England, you will travel up the M74 motorway then join the M8 outside Glasgow. To reach Edinburgh from the south, either follow the A1 coastal road or the A68 that cuts through the Borders from the north of England. There's plenty of city centre parking in Glasgow and Edinburgh, though note that the latter becomes very congested in summer.

By Train

The main railway line linking Glasgow (Queen Street Station) and Edinburgh (Waverley Station) is operated by **First ScotRail** (www.firstgroup.com/scotrail). Expect to pay £9.80 single / £16 return for the 50-minute journey.

To travel further north by train (www.firstgroup.com/scotrail) from Glasgow, catch the train from Queen Street Station. In Edinburgh, Waverley also serves all routes north—including Inverness and Aberdeen.

Trains from London (www.nationalexpresseastcoast.com) arrive first in Edinburgh (Waverley) then Glasgow (Central Station). The journey time is around 4.5 hours. Fares vary greatly. Expect to pay from £42 to £100 for a single journey.

For comprehensive details on your travel options to Scotland by rail, contact **National Rail Enquiries** (© **08457 484950**; www.nationalrail.co.uk).

By Bus (Coach)

National Express (www.nationalexpress.com) operates a regular London to Glasgow/Edinburgh coach service (around 8 hours). Fares vary and are cheaper than the train, with prices from around £25 one-way (© **08717 818181**). From Glasgow (Buchanan Street Bus

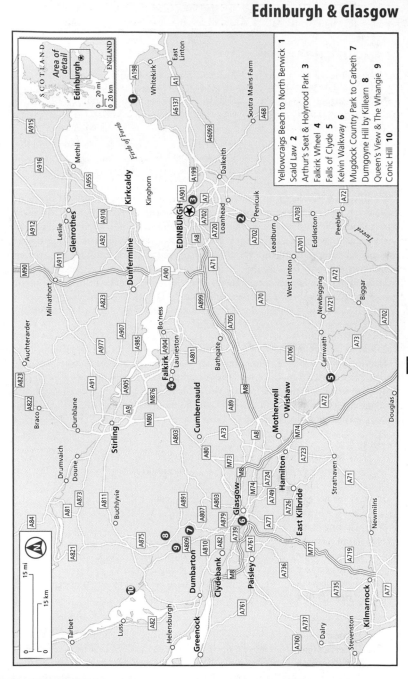

1 Yellowcraigs Beach to North Berwick **1**
Scald Law **2**
Arthur's Seat & Holyrood Park **3**
Falkirk Wheel **4**
Falls of Clyde **5**
Kelvin Walkway **6**
Mugdock Country Park to Carbeth **7**
Dumgoyne Hill by Killearn **8**
Queen's View & The Whangie **9**
Conic Hill **10**

Station) and Edinburgh (Edinburgh Bus Station), **Scottish Citylink** (𝄐 **08705 505050**; www.citylink.co.uk) runs daily services to all the major towns and cities, including Aberdeen and Inverness.

VISITOR INFORMATION

In Glasgow, the main **VisitScotland Tourist Information Centre** is at 11 George Square (𝄐 **01412 044721**) directly opposite Queen Street Railway Station. The busy though helpful staff will be able to help with accommodations inquiries, travel links, and advice on tourist attractions both near and far. The office is open daily year-round, though hours vary.

In Edinburgh, the tourist office is in the east end at 3 Princes St. (𝄐 **08452 255121**) just 10m (33 ft.) from the grand interior of the Balmoral Hotel and beside steps leading down to Waverley Station. Like elsewhere, the open hours vary.

ORIENTATION

In Glasgow, George Square is the very center of the city. From its north side you can catch trains to the north and west of the city and to the Highlands. Behind (to the north) of the train station is **Buchanan Street Bus Station** on Killermont Street. Directly outside the side entrance of Queen Street is the sign for the Clockwork Orange (www.spt. co.uk).

In Edinburgh, use Princes Street and the sight of Edinburgh castle to get your bearings. With your back to the castle and standing on Princes Street at the junction with Lothian Road, you are looking north. To your right and a mile down Princes Street is Waverley Station (just past Scott's Monument).

GETTING AROUND

Lothian Buses (www.lothianbuses.com) is your most convenient way of traveling across the city. It costs £1.10 for a single journey, and with buses running from 6am to midnight (plus limited night bus service), you'll rarely have to wait long for a bus.

While you can walk to Arthurs Seat under your own steam, the likes of the Pentland Hills are best accessed by car or using Lothian Buses from Lothian Road at the west end of Princes Street.

The likes of Yellowcraigs is most accessible by car, though there are occasional buses that leave from Edinburgh Bus Station.

The Glasgow Underground (www.spt.co.uk; single £1.10; Mon–Sat 6:30am–11pm, Sun 10am–6:30pm) is ideal for quickly reaching the south side or west end of the city, including to reach the Kelvin Way and star attractions like the Kelvingrove Museum and Art Gallery (www.glasgowmuseums.com).

However, to reach walks like the Falls of Clyde in the southeast, you'll need to catch the Lanark train from Glasgow Central. For walks to the north of Glasgow, including Dumgoyne and Conic Hill, you'll need to catch the bus from Buchanan Street Bus Station or drive. If you are prepared to hike, it's possible to reach the Falkirk Wheel using the Glasgow–Edinburgh train and getting off at Falkirk High.

Hiring a car is the best way to maximize the flexibility of your itinerary. Car rentals start from around £35 per day or £140 per week. You'll need an international drivers license, credit card, and often need to be over 21 years old. Both Glasgow and Edinburgh airport have car hire offices, and these are also found in the city centers. Try **Arnold Clark** (𝄐 **08445 765425**), **Avis** (𝄐 **08706 086338;** www.avis.co.uk), and **Kira Rentals** (𝄐 **08702 856191;** www.kirarentals.co.uk).

YELLOWCRAIGS BEACH TO
NORTH BERWICK (Kids)

Difficulty rating: Moderate

Distance: 9.6km (6 miles) round-trip

Estimated time: 2.5 hours

Elevation gain: Minimal

Costs/permits: None

Best time to go: June to September

Recommended map: O/S Explorer Map no: 351 Dunbar

Trailhead GPS: NT 51605 85574

Trailhead directions: Sixteen kilometers (10 miles) east of Edinburgh, turn off the A1 at Bankton Junction, following the signs for the North Berwick Coastal Trail. About 3.2km (2 miles) east of Gullane, turn left for Dirleton. Midway through this village, turn left at the sign for Yellowcraigs Beach and follow the road to the car park (£2).

By public transport, take the X5/124 bus from Edinburgh for North Berwick until you reach Fidra Stores in Dirleton; then walk to the trailhead (Bus times: Mon–Sat every 40 min. and Sun every hour.)

Just 32km (20 miles) east of the hubbub of Edinburgh lies the calming, golden sweep of Yellowcraigs Beach. Perfect for a family hike and picnic, enjoy stunning views of the Firth of Forth and north to the Kingdom of Fife. Beyond the rock pools and seals, spot Fidra Island, said to have inspired *Treasure Island,* the 18th-century classic novel by Robert Louis Stevenson. Later, off North Berwick, you'll spy the fortress-like cliffs of Bass Rock, home to one of the world's largest gannet colonies.

For visitors with children, the fun of this walk begins even before you leave the car park, for there are the double temptations of the Treasure Island Adventure Playground amidst the trees and ice cream from Toni's van.

Yet it's at the beach itself, found 182m (597 ft.) farther along a wide sandy trail, that you are truly rewarded for your decision to venture beyond the streets of Edinburgh. For as you emerge through a gap in the marram grass–strewn dunes, the sweep of the Forth mesmerizes the eye, while directly offshore lies the gnarled black rock of Fidra Island, complete with its striking 18th-century lighthouse.

❶ Yellowcraigs Beach After reaching the beach, turn right to walk 4.8km (3 miles) eastwards along the huge expanse of soft sands to the pretty fishing village of North Berwick, where Stevenson enjoyed many a childhood holiday.

The sea views are fantastic, and the beach is a kids' dream for building sand castles, so don't forget a bucket and spade! Useful, too, is a pair of binoculars. This area is teeming with fauna and flora, from seals lounging on the rocks to seabirds swooping for a tasty fish supper. Inland, you may spot skylarks and bumblebees and pretty wildflowers including wild thyme, harebell, and birdsfoot trefoil.

❷ View of Bass Rock Gazing out to sea towards the distant outline of the Kingdom of Fife, reflect that in 1561, Mary Queen of Scots may have cast her eyes on Yellowcraigs while sailing from France to the Port of Leith in Edinburgh. Innumerable wrecks lie below these waters.

EDINBURGH & GLASGOW WALKS

4

YELLOWCRAIGS BEACH TO NORTH BERWICK

(Fun Facts) **The Treasures of Fidra**

Robert Louis Stevenson (born 1850) occasionally stayed in the nearby fishing village of North Berwick as a boy. In his book *Catriona* he described the islands of the Firth of Forth. Close to shore, Fidra is believed to have been his inspiration for the classic children's novel *Treasure Island*. The lighthouse on Fidra was built in 1885 and in 1970 was the first in Scotland to be fully automated. The ancient remains of a dwelling connected with the (now ruined) 12th-century Cistercian nunnery in North Berwick can still be seen on Fidra.

As you round the first headland, the full glory of Yellowcraigs Beach meets the eye, its wide sands galloping straight ahead for over 1.6km (1 mile). Moreover, a mile offshore you will spy the unmistakable gray ramparts of the cliffs and dome-shaped hulk of Bass Rock, a nesting site for thousands of seabirds. In the 1600s, it's also where dozens of souls perished as political and religious prisoners.

❸ **Craigleith Island** As you walk farther down the beach, your eye will also be drawn to low-lying islands to the west of Bass Rock, including Craigleith. Deserted, it's a popular destination for sea kayakers. You can enjoy a 1-hour circumnavigation of this island and out to Bass Rock with the likes of **Seabird Seafari** boat trips (✆ 01620 890202; £20) that depart from the pier at North Berwick.

❹ **Wooden bridge** After over 1.6km (1 mile) of walking east, you will cross a small stream via a wooden bridge behind the beach. You are now halfway to North Berwick and your reward of dining by the sea.

The terrain now changes, with the beach narrowing and the foreshore much rockier. Here, grayish blue rock pools offer opportunities for kids to search for crabs. There's also the option to progress along a narrow, marram grass–lined path above the beach, but be wary of stray golf balls from the adjacent fairway.

Pressing on, you'll soon round another headland, beyond which the pier at North Berwick is clearly visible. You may also start to spot empty lobster pots left on the beach by local fishermen, an indication that despite the presence of heavy industry far to the west, these waters are rich in marine life.

❺ **North Berwick Pier** Finally, after nearly an hour and a half (or all day if you've ambled), you'll climb up a few natural stone steps and round the headland to walk the final 457m (1,500 ft.) of beach that ends at the tiny North Berwick pier overlooked by the RNLI Lifeboat Station.

There are now several attractions in this picturesque, popular seaside town to enjoy, most notably a visit to the acclaimed **Scottish Seabird Center** (✆ 01620 890202; www.seabird.org) by the pier. Here, young and old alike can find out about the wealth of birdlife around these shores and relax with breakfast or lunch in the fabulous child-friendly cafe, with its sun-deck looking out to Bass Rock.

By the pier you'll also spot the impressive Celtic cross and remains of St. Andrew's Old Kirk. In the Middle Ages, pilgrims came here from all over Scotland before braving the Forth to journey on to St. Andrew's in Fife.

By the ruins of the kirk, there's also a poignant memorial to the members of

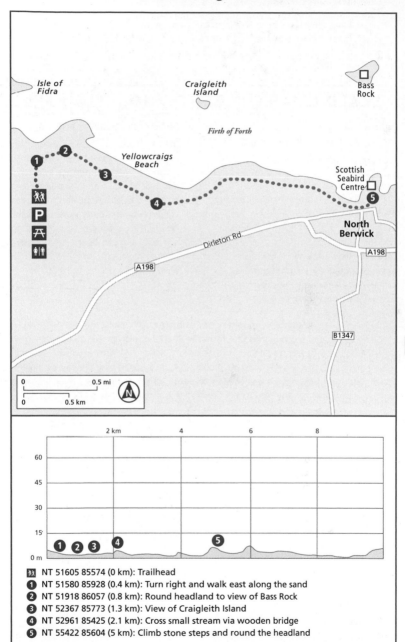

NT 51605 85574 (0 km): Trailhead

1. NT 51580 85928 (0.4 km): Turn right and walk east along the sand
2. NT 51918 86057 (0.8 km): Round headland to view of Bass Rock
3. NT 52367 85773 (1.3 km): View of Craigleith Island
4. NT 52961 85425 (2.1 km): Cross small stream via wooden bridge
5. NT 55422 85604 (5 km): Climb stone steps and round the headland

RAF Coastal Command who lost their lives during World War II flying dangerous anti-submarine reconnaissance and bombing missions.

Retracing your steps back to the car park at Yellowcraigs is no less rewarding a walk, for now you can enjoy the westward-looking views down the Firth of Forth. Look carefully and 37km (23 miles) beyond the southern shoreline of the Forth, you'll spot the distinctive hump of Arthur's Seat that overlooks Edinburgh.

SCALD LAW—THE PENTLAND HILLS ★

Difficulty rating: Moderate/strenuous

Distance: 14km (8.7 miles) round-trip

Estimated time: 3 to 3.5 hours

Elevation gain: 397m (1,302 ft.)

Costs/permits: None

Best time to go: Late summer, when the surrounding hills are a sea of purple heather

Website: www.pentlandhills.org

Recommended map: Pick-up "Discover the Pentland Hills Regional Park" from rangers' center at the trailhead.

Trailhead GPS: NO 23271 63058

Trailhead directions: From Edinburgh city center, follow signs for the A702 heading south. Cross over the city bypass and stay on the A702. Continue for 6.4km (4 miles) to Flotterstone Inn, passing the entrance to the ancient Castlelaw Hill Fort. At the sign for Flotterstone, turn right and park by the ranger post. Lothian Bus nos. 4, 10, 11, 15, and 16 all enable access to the area by public transport.

Rising steeply on the southern periphery of Edinburgh's city limits, the elongated string of rolling brown and green humps that form the Pentland Hills are just 20 minutes' drive from the heart of the city. You'll find ancient history, 90km (56 miles) of waymarked trail, fishing on deep lochs, and innumerable picnic spots. Moreover, from the highest peak of the range, Scald Law, there's the chance to savor truly breathtaking views, including north across Edinburgh and the Firth of Forth to the ancient Kingdom of Fife beyond.

Park 18m (59 ft.) past the cozy Flotterstone Inn, beside the ranger center. The rangers can provide free maps of the area. Strike out west for 0.5km (⅓ mile) along a peaceful, tree-lined, single-track road, past a BBQ and picnic site. You'll quickly feel a world away from the cacophony of city life.

This first part of your route is part of the 4.3km (2.7-mile) Heron Trail that explores the picturesque area around Glencorse Reservoir and offers an easy outing with young children.

❶ **Sign for Scald Law** After 5 minutes of walking, the canopy of trees recedes to reveal the rolling brown, purple, and green

southerly range of the Pentlands. Just before the road turns sharply uphill, towards Glencorse Reservoir, look for the waymarked sign for Scald Law. Go through the metal gate, heading south along a rough, dirt footpath between rough pastures.

Though the area is popular with walkers and cyclists, the majority don't stray far from the road that cuts through the glen as far as the trout-rich Loganlea Reservoir, following the line of the Logan Burn. So, you could have the trail to yourself!

❷ **Wooden Bridge** The path forks after less than 30m (98 ft.) of walking between the fields, with the right path

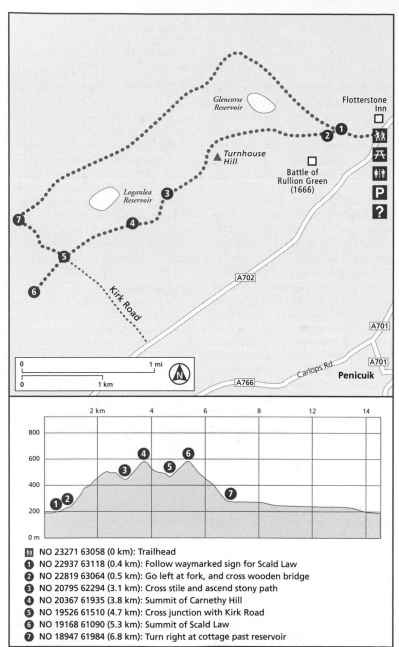

🏃 NO 23271 63058 (0 km): Trailhead
❶ NO 22937 63118 (0.4 km): Follow waymarked sign for Scald Law
❷ NO 22819 63064 (0.5 km): Go left at fork, and cross wooden bridge
❸ NO 20795 62294 (3.1 km): Cross stile and ascend stony path
❹ NO 20367 61935 (3.8 km): Summit of Carnethy Hill
❺ NO 19526 61510 (4.7 km): Cross junction with Kirk Road
❻ NO 19168 61090 (5.3 km): Summit of Scald Law
❼ NO 18947 61984 (6.8 km): Turn right at cottage past reservoir

(Tips) **Stalking**

August is the start of the stalking (deer hunting) season in Scotland. It's important to stick to the marked paths during this time of the year. The high ground
around Castlelaw Hill to the southeast of the Pentlands forms part of a military
firing range. Avoid this area when red flags are flying.

leading to Glencorse Reservoir. Stay left, admiring the range of hills to the southwest over which you'll soon climb. The clearly marked sign-post for Scald Law tells you to cross the adjacent wooden bridge.

The path now steadily climbs the broad shoulder of Turnhouse Hill via a narrow, muddy path carved into the hillside by years of erosion. As you climb above the sheep fields, note that to your left is where the Battle of Rullion Green took place in November 1666, pitching Covenanters against Royalists in bloody fighting. Nearby, archaeologists have also found the remains of an ancient hill fort.

More obvious as you gain height above the narrow finger of Glencorse Reservoir, where fishermen cast for rainbow trout, is the swathe of eye-catching purple heather that covers the hills in late August.

Within 30 minutes of leaving the car park you will have ascended over 75m (246 ft.) to be midway up Turnhouse Hill. Around here there's a narrow copse of trees that runs across the hillside. This is a good place to stop for a quick bite and to admire the views. With very young kids, it may also be a handy turning-back point.

After about 1.6km (1 mile) you will spot the village of Penicuik to the south of the Pentlands. As you ascend, the going can occasionally be quite steep in places, though never technically difficult, and very soon you'll be walking over the rounded summit of Turnhouse. From Turnhouse Hill, look north over Edinburgh. You'll easily spot Edinburgh Castle

and working east observe the dramatic rise of Salisbury Crags and the pointed summit of Arthur's Seat. Look farther north to the Port of Leith overlooking the vast expanse of the Firth of Forth.

After Turnhouse, the path drops away to become occasionally rockier. After a further small climb, the terrain again drops sharply away for several hundred feet before climbing again. As a student, I recall mountain-biking this section and head-planting into the peaty soil.

❸ **Stile Crossing** After crossing a stile and continuing to ascend a rough stony path, observe the contrast in the terrain. To the east, there's the patchwork of yellow and green fields of the farmlands of East Lothian and south over Border country. To the northwest you can just spot the rise of the first mountains of the central Highlands.

❹ **Carnethy Hill** Pressing ever westwards, after ascending over Whitecraig Heads, you'll reach a huge jumble of rocks that marks the summit of Carnethy Hill. Some almost form a natural sheltered cairn—useful to huddle within if it's windy. Below, directly to the north you can easily see the small road that runs through the middle of the Pentlands past the reservoirs of Loganlee and Glencorse.

❺ **Kirk Road Junction** From Carnethy Hill you can see the triangulation point atop Scald Law about 0.8km (¹/₂ mile) ahead. Pressing on, it's not long before you descend to a junction where your path crosses directly over another called Kirk Road. This runs south to north over the lower slopes of Scald Law and is a useful escape route should the weather suddenly deteriorate.

⑥ Summit of Scald Law   After crossing over Kirk Road path, it's a 10-minute steady ascent to the summit. The view from the top definitely makes your trek to this point worthwhile.

The views are spectacular, so have the camera ready. Look north beyond Edinburgh and the distant Forth Rail Bridge towards the Ochil Hills, while on a clear day you can see the peak of Ben Lomond, Scotland's most southerly Munro far to the northwest. Eastwards, you can't miss the distinctive peak above the seaside town of North Berwick and the cliffs of Bass Rock just 1.6km (1 mile) offshore.

From the summit, it takes less than 30 minutes to descend northwards to reach the westernmost edge of Loganlea Reservoir down in the glen. Retrace your steps to the junction with Kirk Road path. Here, turn left and follow the stony-then-grassy trail down by a fence and through fields of sheep until you reach the tarmac road running past a cottage and the reservoir.

⑦ Loganlea Reservoir   On reaching the road by the cottage and reservoir, turn right and start down the road for the 4km (2¹/₂-mile), easy walk back to Flotterstone car park. En route, savor the uninterrupted view along the peaks to the south you have just hiked. Before making the 6.4km (4-mile) journey back to the city center, consider celebrating your discovery of the Pentland Hills with a well-earned bite to eat or drink in the atmospheric Flotterstone Inn.

ARTHUR'S SEAT & HOLYROOD PARK ★ Kids

Difficulty rating: Easy

Distance: 5.6km (3.5 miles) round-trip

Estimated time: 2 hours

Elevation gain: 206m (676 ft.)

Costs/permits: Parking (£1 per hour)

Best time to go: Early morning is the best time to escape the crowds. The summit is also a fantastic spot to enjoy sunset.

Website: www.historic-scotland.gov.uk

Recommended map: The Holyrood Lodge Information Centre (0131 652 8150; 0900-1500) beside the Scottish

Parliament has a ranger service and offers the free map "Welcome to Holyrood Park." See also www.historic-scotland.gov.uk.

Trailhead GPS: NO 26945 73732

Trailhead directions: Follow signs for the Palace of Holyrood and Scottish Parliament, parking in the car park just south of the Parliament. Alternatively, walk down the Royal Mile to the Palace of Holyrood. Turn right past the Parliament into Holyrood Park. The car park (start point) is on your left.

Many of the world's great cities boast spectacular skylines for visitors to enjoy. Not Scotland's capital city. It simply invites visitors, including intrepid young walkers and their parents, to climb Arthur's Seat. A 350-million-year-old extinct volcano, its summit guarantees breathtaking panoramas over the city and north to the Firth of Forth and Kingdom of Fife. All within a mile of another historical vantage point—Edinburgh Castle.

Holyrood Park

Six-thousand years ago, man eked out an existence farming on this wild protected terrain that's designated a Site of Special Scientific Interest (SSSI) and encircled by the city. Today, its crags and grass are devoid of the woodland that 12th-century Scottish kings explored for royal game hunting. Instead, this rugged, spectacular expanse of steep, volcanic hills is crisscrossed by rough paths, with a 5.6km-long (3½-mile) road running around its perimeter. On Sundays the majority of the road is closed to traffic. Due to its proximity to the city center, the area is popular with walkers at all times of the year.

At the north entrance to Holyrood Park, and with your back to the Palace of Holyrood, the Royal Family's home in Edinburgh, lift your gaze to admire the sheer cliffs and steep, naturally terraced slopes of Salisbury Crags. A kilometer south, the conical summit of Arthur's Seat is also clearly visible.

From the car park, turn left and head east along the road until you spot the 14th-century ruin of St. Anthony's Chapel on a bluff above the swan- and duck-filled waters of St. Margaret's Loch.

On approaching the loch, where excited kids watch the ducks, you'll see a sign reading SWANS – SLOW ON THE ROAD. Go round tiny St. Margaret's Loch in a clockwise direction before steeply climbing south towards the ruin up a narrow, rocky path.

❶ **St. Anthony's Chapel** On reaching the bluff atop which the chapel stands, 120m (394 ft.) above sea level, you are rewarded with views of the Palace of Holyrood, where you can spot the wonderful partially ruined archways of Holyrood Abbey. Founded in the 12th century, several Scottish monarchs, including King James III, married here until it fell into disrepair.

To the right of the palace is a flat expanse of grass, in public use since the 1800s and a perfect place for young children to play or a family to picnic.

Then there's St. Anthony's Chapel. Only a few walls—which were once 12m (40 ft.) high—remain standing, the origins of which are obscure. In 1426 the Pope gave money for its repair. Today, it's a Scheduled Ancient Monument.

From the chapel, several rough paths cut southwest above a broad cleft that naturally divides Salisbury Crags from Arthur's Seat. Whatever path you choose, continue to ascend until your route joins the gravel "tourist" path running steadily upwards from Holyrood towards the summit.

Fifty meters (164 ft.) below Arthur Seat's rocky summit and 0.7km (½ mile) above the chapel, the path meets a wide, flattish grassy area. Stop here to feast on the views over northern Edinburgh, past the ancient Port of Leith where Mary Queen of Scots landed in 1561, and out over the spectacular expanse of the Firth of Forth.

On this ascent I like to study the distinctive changes in architecture across the city, which includes the ancient walls of the castle; fine, Georgian, terraced houses; and the distinctive, 17th-century street lines of the "New Town."

From this vantage point, follow the stone path with the hand-guard rail for 50m (164 ft.) of further easy ascent to the rocky summit of Arthur's Seat. Keep

NO 26945 73732 (0 km): Trailhead
1 NO 27573 73696 (1.1 km): St. Anthony's chapel
2 NO 27515 72942 (2.1 km): Summit of Arthur's Seat
3 NO 27578 73090 (2.8 km): Turn left where path splits
4 NO 27271 72820 (3.4 km): Turn right and ascend narrow rocky path
5 NO 26873 73430 (4.3 km): Enjoy views of Scottish Parliament as path descends

children close, and be wary of the precipitous drop over the summit's westernmost crags.

❷ Arthur's Seat To this point you've walked and climbed over 1.6km (1 mile), so with camera and binoculars at hand take a moment to savor the 360-degree panorama.

Start by looking west to the once impregnable fortifications of Edinburgh Castle. Let your gaze track northwest, glimpsing the metallic frame of the Forth Rail Bridge, one of the engineering wonders of the world, spanning the Forth to the Kingdom of Fife. Farther northwest you'll spot the rise of the Ochil Hills, whilst far to the west-northwest you may glimpse the summit of Ben Lomond, Scotland's most southerly Munro.

Now, gazing across the islands within the Firth of Forth, look directly east 32km (20 miles) to the distinctive domed peak above North Berwick. Just beyond, 1.6km (1 mile) out at sea sit the grayish cliffs of Bass Rock—home to one of the world's largest colonies of gannets.

To the south, the Pentland Hills, including on their easternmost flank the white streak of the artificial ski slope of the Midlothian Snowsport Center, provide a spectacular backdrop to the city.

❸ Descent to Salisbury Crags From the summit, avoid the temptation to descend via the steep paths to the southwest. Despite path improvements, this remains a treacherous route for the unwary, especially when wet.

Instead, retrace your steps back down the summit path with the handrail and continue down the main gravel path you ascended earlier. After 100m (328 ft.), turn left where the path splits and skirt

southwest around the hulking crags of Arthur's Seat. Remain on this narrow path that winds past thick thorn bushes, observing the wild grassy expanse above the cliffs of Salisbury Crags to your right.

❹ Along Salisbury Crags After 15 minutes descending off the summit, on a small bluff your trail meets a broad, low-level path that has cut through the park between the steep slopes of Arthur's Seat and Salisbury Crags. Here, turn right and immediately ascend the narrow, rocky path that winds along the spectacular cliff top, gouged out long ago by glacier activity. If accompanied by young children, think twice about taking this route. Instead, continue south over the bluff and follow the lower path that runs for a mile below the cliffs back to the start point.

For those who choose to go right and along the cliff top, watch your footing. Though the cliffs are popular with local climbers who (illegally) scale the rock faces, there are no barriers to prevent an unwelcome 40m (131-ft.) fall.

From your elevated position, the city still looks almost toy-like below as you hike northwest.

❺ Scottish Parliament After continuing along the cliff top for 15 minutes, the path steadily veers north and descends towards the your start point. Now you have a bird's-eye view of the new Scottish Parliament. The seat of the Scottish government, this unique complex, intricately constructed in wood, glass, and concrete, was opened in 2004 at a cost of over £400 million. The Parliament is built on the site of an old brewery.

From this vantage point, continue wandering along the cliffs as the path steeply descends towards the road and the car park.

Difficulty rating: Easy

Distance: 5.6km (3.5 miles) round-trip

Estimated time: 2 hours

Elevation gain: 54m (177 ft.)

Costs/permits: None

Best time to go: June to September

Website: www.thefalkirkwheel.co.uk, www.scottishcanals.co.uk

Recommended map: British Waterways map (£ 4.95): Forth and Clyde and Union Canals.

Trailhead GPS: NS 86873 80011

Trailhead directions: This walk starts at the historic Union Inn by lock 16 in Camelon. From Glasgow follow the M80/A80 signs for Falkirk and then the brown-and-white tourist signs for the Falkirk Wheel. Instead of parking by the Wheel, continue east along the A803 (Glasgow Rd.) and Main Street in Falkirk to a large roundabout. Turn right onto B816 Glenfuir Road. After 0.8km (½ mile) along here, on the right is lock 16 by the canal. There is parking on nearby streets.

The Falkirk Wheel is a marvel of engineering that ensures hikers, cyclists, and anyone seeking a fun boat ride can explore all or only a small section of the fascinating Forth and Clyde and Union canal networks. Linking Edinburgh in the east with Glasgow in the west, the Forth and Clyde and Union canals are a humbling example of what can be achieved by inspired 17th-century engineering and the hard work of thousands of shovel-wielding workers. Your hike around the area of the Falkirk Wheel will possibly be one of the easiest in this book. Perfect for a family day out or a brisk walk, the route combines the novelty of visiting the Wheel with rich wildlife and scenic waterways that were once central to the development of Scotland's rich industrial heritage.

The interpretive boards outside the attractive Georgian-styled Union Inn in Camelon tell you this is lock 16 of the Forth and Clyde Canal and where—until paved over by a road—11 locks once ran down from the Union Canal to connect with the Forth and Clyde. It's worthwhile popping into this atmospheric inn for a pint of beer or a great value pub meal.

From outside the inn, cross the road bridge over the Forth and Clyde Canal. Now turn left to follow the well-maintained path along the northern side of the canal bank towards the distant Falkirk Wheel.

As you amble west along almost a mile of serene waterway, there's a good chance you'll spot swans, cygnets, and moor hens feeding by the canal bank. To your right is the town of Falkirk, an ancient meeting place for drovers bringing their cattle from the Highlands and where, in 1298, Scottish freedom fighter William Wallace fought the English forces of King Edward I.

❶ **Falkirk Wheel Visitor Centre** After crossing a small bridge, you can't miss the enormous and impressive engineering feat that is the Falkirk Wheel, on which you can take a memorable boat trip (see sidebar). As you walk along the canal bank from Camelon, the huge gleaming metal structure dwarfs the surrounding canal basin and attractive grassy banks by which the visitor center has been built.

It's worthwhile popping into the visitor center, where a free interactive exhibition offers a myriad of facts and a working model about the construction of the wheel and the canal network. There's also a children's play area nearby and an excellent child-friendly cafe that offers uninterrupted views across to the wheel.

EDINBURGH & GLASGOW WALKS

4

FALKIRK WHEEL

Falkirk Wheel Boat Trip

This is great fun for young and old walkers alike. Amazingly, laborers in the 17th century had only rudimentary picks, shovels, and volatile gunpowder to dig out these miles of waterway. Two-hundred years later, the construction of the Falkirk Wheel marked yet another milestone in engineering. Its ingenious hook-wheel (35m/115 ft. in diameter) and two 27m-long (89-ft.) watertight boat-carrying baskets, hydraulically lift the passenger-carrying barges 35m (115 ft.) from the lower Forth and Clyde Canal to the Union Canal.

For those looking to experience the marvel firsthand, boat trips begin in the basin outside the **Falkirk Wheel Visitor Centre** (*C* **08700 500208;** £8 adults; open year-round 10am–4:30pm). After sailing into the bottom gondola of the wheel, you are whisked over 30m (98 ft.) up to the Union Canal.

For the rest of the tour, you pass along the aqueduct, through the 180m (591-ft.) Roughcastle Tunnel and even under the ancient remains (A.D. 142) of the Antonine Wall before returning back down into the basin by the visitor center.

② **Rough Castle Tunnel** From the visitor center, turn right out the door and follow the signs for the Union Canal and Antonine Wall. As you walk up the fairly steep path, it's fascinating to watch the giant wheel turn and sweep the boats up to the viaduct high above your head.

Continuing south, your canal experience takes an unexpected turn as you enter Rough Castle Tunnel, Britain's first canal tunnel to be built in over 100 years.

This 145m-long (476-ft.) tunnel has been designed to carry the Union Canal towards the Falkirk Wheel without disturbing a section of the 60km-long (37-mile) Antonine Wall that cuts directly overhead as it runs west to east.

Emerging from the tunnel, continue south along what is now the Union Canal. At the old lock-keeper's house you'll briefly veer right to pass between white gates before continuing east along the canal bank. On your right, you'll presently spot the periphery of Tamfourhill Wood. While you can't see it, between you and the wood archaeologists have found remains of an old Roman camp. The remains of another have also been found just to the northwest of the Falkirk Wheel.

For the next 30 minutes you'll amble along the Union Canal. Like me, you may be struck by the serenity of these canal banks that were once a key part of Scotland's transportation network. Ironically, the main Glasgow-to-Edinburgh railway line that partially led to the demise of the canals runs just to the south of where you are walking.

③ **Old Canal Link** There is the option to continue east, all the way to distant Edinburgh if you so desire. However, assuming you want to return to the Union Inn and your car, the white gates with a signpost to the Forth and Clyde Canal just past a road bridge mark the spot where you wave goodbye to the Union Canal.

As you turn left down the path, this is the original route of the Union Canal, as a series of 11 locks enabled barges and ships to descend over 30m (98 ft.) to the Port Downie Basin of the Forth and Clyde Canal where the Union Inn and lock 16 still stand.

As you descend the path and go through a white gate, you can still see signs of the old canal. Now, you'll pass under the Glasgow-to-Edinburgh railway bridge, beyond which a sign points you up onto

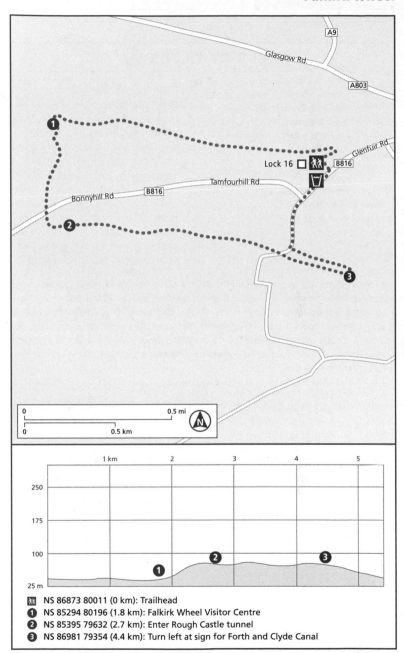

NS 86873 80011 (0 km): Trailhead
1 NS 85294 80196 (1.8 km): Falkirk Wheel Visitor Centre
2 NS 85395 79632 (2.7 km): Enter Rough Castle tunnel
3 NS 86981 79354 (4.4 km): Turn left at sign for Forth and Clyde Canal

the main (Glenfuir) road. Walk down this road for around 0.4km (¹/₄ mile) until you reach a set of traffic lights. Here, turn off to your left down a small path through grass that leads directly to the canal bank and the entrance to the Union Inn.

FALLS OF CLYDE Kids

Difficulty rating: Easy

Distance: 4.6km (2.9 miles) round-trip

Estimated time: 2 hours

Elevation gain: 60m (197 ft.)

Costs/permits: None

Best time to go: September to November

Website: www.swt.org.uk, www.newlanark.org

Recommended map: Pick up the information leaflet at the Falls of Clyde Visitor Centre

Trailhead GPS: NS 88099 42346

Trailhead directions: Traveling east from Glasgow (or west from Edinburgh) along the M8, take the road signposted for New Lanark and follow all signs south on the A73 for Lanark. New Lanark is approximately 1.6km (1 mile) southwest of Lanark and clearly signposted. Park in the designated area and make your way to the trailhead by the entrance to the Falls of Clyde Visitor Centre and Wildlife Reserve. There are also frequent trains to Lanark from Glasgow city center.

The Falls of Clyde, the centerpiece of the Falls of Clyde Wildlife Reserve, is a wonderful sight as its waters tumble westwards towards Glasgow and out into the Forth of Clyde. Even on the wettest day this gentle walk lifts the spirits with its abundance of wildlife, including the woodpecker and rare peregrine falcon and the tranquillity of the deciduous woodland. It's also rare to have the chance to combine your walk with a visit to a UNESCO World Heritage Site, the beautifully restored 18th-century cotton mill village of New Lanark, near the trailhead.

Start by walking through the archway and up the step by the New Lanark Nature Reserve Centre.

As you walk south, the river is on your right. Almost immediately you'll spot the Mill Weir, with an old, tall chimney stack rising above the water's edge.

You may have been walking for less than 5 minutes, but consider taking a rest! The reason is it gives you the chance to admire both the woodland view across the river and the intricately carved benches that line your well-maintained path.

❶ Carved Bench One bench has a beautiful carving of a butterfly, another of fish. Farther along, it's apparent that artists have devoted considerable time and energy to carving images of birds, butterflies, fish, flowers, and trees onto the seats.

As you go, keep your eyes peeled for kingfishers and dippers that occasionally make an appearance over the fast-moving water. In the distance, the wind carries the unmistakable sound of rough, tumbling water.

The path now winds between trees and shrubbery, including magnificent stands of oak, ash, and birch.

❷ House with Tree Nursery Your route follows a sturdy boardwalk and then a tarred path beside which there's a house with a small tree nursery. The path passes around the side of the Bonnington Linn Power Station, opened in 1927. Behind the station, huge green pipes fall over 45m

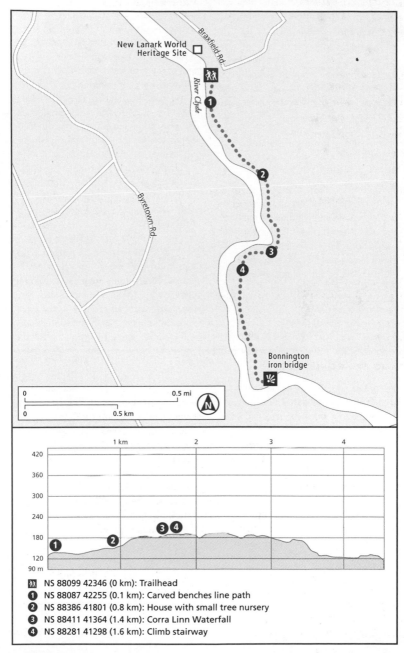

🏃 NS 88099 42346 (0 km): Trailhead
❶ NS 88087 42255 (0.1 km): Carved benches line path
❷ NS 88386 41801 (0.8 km): House with small tree nursery
❸ NS 88411 41364 (1.4 km): Corra Linn Waterfall
❹ NS 88281 41298 (1.6 km): Climb stairway

(148 ft.) down the wooded hillside into the building. Follow the path behind the power station and up the flight of steps.

❸ Corra Linn Waterfall   As you walk, the sound of a powerful rush of water greets your ears. Arriving at a clearing, your gaze will quickly turn to your left, to the water tumbling over 27m (89 ft.) into the spectacular gorge. This is the dramatic Corra Linn Waterfall.

It's a beautiful location but you've still plenty of fascinating sights to see, so press on.

❹ Stairway   Indeed, as you climb another series of steps, keep a sharp eye out for signs of badgers and woodpeckers in the trees. As you wind through the trees with the river far below, it's not long until you discover the Operation Peregrine Bird Hide. Directly across the river you'll spot the high, rocky cliffs plunging down into the gorge that forms part of the hunting territory of the peregrine.

There are only around 1,500 pairs of peregrine falcons in Scotland. Fortunately, since 1997, one pair has chosen to nest under the cliffs near this viewpoint. Enthusiasts, supported by rangers, use this hide to monitor their breeding and hunting habits and to safeguard their nesting sites.

From the hide, continue to walk south along the woodland trail, noting that at night bats are among the nocturnal guests. As you walk, three further viewpoints offer opportunities for photographs of the rapids, gorge, and the waterfalls.

Finally, the path bears left to the old Bonnington iron bridge (built 1926), from which you can enjoy excellent views of Bonnington Weir and up and down the Falls of Clyde.

From here, it's time to retrace your steps back to the visitor center, where children will enjoy the many interactive exhibits (including a "honey bee hotel," where they can watch 15,000 bees create their intricate honeycomb) and a tour of the award-winning mills of New Lanark.

Mills of New Lanark

Born in 1771, Robert Owen was the son-in-law of David Dale (1739–1806), an entrepreneurial Scot who founded giant sandstone mills at New Lanark, close to the Falls of Clyde. Utilizing child labor, life in the mills of 18th-century Scotland was notoriously hard. However, when Owen started to manage the mills in 1800, the visionary steadily began to introduce enlightened working practices that by 1825 had established his reputation as a social pioneer. Out went child labor and in came the first nursery school in the world, free health care and decent homes for workers, improved wages, and an education system.

Today, the award-winning **New Lanark Visitor Centre** (𝄐 **01555 661345;** www.newlanark.org; daily 11am–5pm; £6.95) is one of Scotland's top visitor attractions. In the care of an independent charity, over 400,000 people a year come to this historic village that 200 years ago was at the center of revolutionary social change. You can also stay within the village by booking into the **New Lanark Mill Hotel and Waterhouses** (𝄐 **01555 667200;** www.newlanarkhotel. co.uk).

Difficulty rating: Easy

Distance: 8.4km (5.2 miles) round-trip

Estimated time: 2 to 2.5 hours

Elevation gain: Minimal

Costs/permits: None

Best time to go: Mid-summer to relax with a picnic while savoring the views over the River Kelvin

Website: www.glasgow.gov.uk

Recommended map: O/S Explorer Glasgow Active map: 342

Trailhead GPS: NS 56687 66280

Trailhead directions: This walk assumes you are staying in the west end or city center of Glasgow. The best way of reaching the trailhead is to hop aboard the Glasgow Underground (www.spt.co.uk)—affectionately known as the "clockwork orange" because the train is bright orange and the Inner Circle runs in a clockwise direction.

From Buchanan Street Subway Station ("U" sign on street) take the Outer Circle six stops (£1.10) west to Kelvinhall station. Emerging from the station, turn left and walk 0.3km (¼ mile) east up Dumbarton Road until you see a sign by the Kelvin Hall Sports Arena that reads KELVIN WALKWAY. This is the trailhead.

If your itinerary affords little time to be in Scotland's largest city, this short easy hike along the attractive, leafy Kelvin Walkway offers a fascinating insight into Glasgow's abundance of cultural treasures, and an opportunity to enjoy the diversity of flora beyond the urban streets. While this account refers only to a 4.8km (3-mile) stretch of the majestic Kelvin, you can explore all 14km (9 miles) of the route that finishes in the genteel northern suburb of Milngavie, where the 145km-long (90-mile) West Highland Way trail to Fort William begins. Alternatively, you can use this short walk to access the serene banks of the Forth and Clyde Canal and hike 23km (14 miles) farther west to Bowling or almost 90km (56 miles) east to Scotland's capital of Edinburgh.

On your left, the River Kelvin tumbles south towards the River Clyde, while directly ahead you can't miss the majestic 18th-century architecture of the Kelvingrove Museum and Art Gallery—Scotland's most popular free visitor attraction. Across the road you'll also see the red sandstone building of the Kelvin Hall Sports Arena.

Follow the paved path that runs under a canopy of deciduous woodland on the right-hand side of the Kelvin. Across the water on a hill to your left you'll easily spot the impressive ancient facade and tower of the University of Glasgow.

After only a few minutes of walking, the path emerges behind the stunning, red sandstone facade of the Kelvingrove Museum and Art Gallery, which reopened its doors in 2007 following a £28-million refurbishment. Packed with interactive displays of priceless exhibits from ancient times to the present day, it's highly recommended to pay even a short visit to the museum. Admission is free.

With the museum on your right, the path veers to the left past a bowling green to meet the attractive tree-lined avenue of the Kelvin Way by an ornate sandstone bridge.

❶ **Kelvin Way Bridge** Spanning the Kelvin, this 19th-century bridge is easily recognizable with its four groups of bronze statues.

EDINBURGH & GLASGOW WALKS

4

KELVIN WALKWAY

Across the road is Kelvingrove Park, the attractive tree- and flower-rich Victorian gardens established in 1852. It's overlooked by the sweep of the mansion houses of Park Circus on a hill to the east.

Cross the road and head into the park, following the blue sign marked FORTH AND CLYDE CANAL. Turn first left along a tree-lined path with a children's play area and a lovely pond inhabited by ducks on your right.

If in doubt of the route, stick to the path that winds north, following the River Kelvin upstream.

② Highland Light Infantry Statue
After 5 minutes, you'll come to an impressive statue of a helmeted colonial-era soldier looking west towards the University. It's dated 1906 and commemorates the fallen in overseas battles of the Highland Light Infantry.

③ Under Gibson Street Beyond this statue, ignore the attractive bridge on your immediate left and continue directly ahead along the river. As the broad path climbs past an avenue of oak trees, there's a small path to your left about 6m (20 ft.) before the main path rises to meet Gibson Street.

Take this unlikely narrow path, and you'll emerge into open parkland with the river on your immediate left. Continue

following the path, passing a pub. It's here there's an option to go up the steps onto Great Western Road for a quick exit to the Kelvinbridge subway or to enjoy one of the west end's many cafes.

To stay on the route, follow the path as it goes through the graceful arch of the red sandstone Kelvin Bridge. Admire the ornate wrought-iron work of this arched span and note the lion rampant metal shields placed on either side of the bridge above the river.

As you press north, you'll note the river is intermittently rapids or tranquil water. In places small finches and robins flit amongst the trees, while in the evening you may spot the occasional fox.

Certainly, as you walk along the banks you'll be struck by the serenity of this leaf-strewn walkway that's surrounded by wild shrubbery and steeply wooded hillsides yet within shouting distance of the city streets.

④ North Woodside Flint Mill The path then crosses the river via a small arched footbridge. Here lie the stone remains of the former site of the North Woodside Flint Mill. Built in 1765, it was used to grind barley and later gunpowder during the Napoleonic Wars before being developed into a flint mill. It was even bombed during World War II.

ⓕun Facts Kelvin Who?

You could argue modern society owes a debt of gratitude to William Thomson Lord Kelvin. Born in 1824, by the time the gifted scientist, inventor, and engineer died in 1907 he had published 661 scientific papers and created over 70 patents. As the pioneer of thermodynamics, we have Kelvin to thank for the likes of refrigeration and electric light, whilst ship captains were grateful for his development of a compass for iron ships. You could also argue he was a founding father of modern communications thanks to his work on the telegram cabling system from Europe to America. In recognition of his phenomenal contribution to humankind's scientific understanding, much of the area around the University of Glasgow where Kelvin studied and lectured is named after the learned professor.

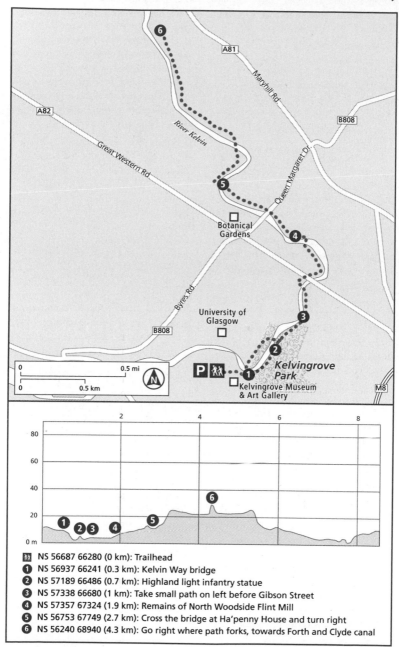

🚶 NS 56687 66280 (0 km): Trailhead
❶ NS 56937 66241 (0.3 km): Kelvin Way bridge
❷ NS 57189 66486 (0.7 km): Highland light infantry statue
❸ NS 57338 66680 (1 km): Take small path on left before Gibson Street
❹ NS 57357 67324 (1.9 km): Remains of North Woodside Flint Mill
❺ NS 56753 67749 (2.7 km): Cross the bridge at Ha'penny House and turn right
❻ NS 56240 68940 (4.3 km): Go right where path forks, towards Forth and Clyde canal

Just 91m (300 ft.) farther north, the arched footbridge to your left leads into the acclaimed and landscaped Botanic Gardens.

⑤ Ha'penny House A little farther north, the broad path splits. Keep left to walk by the river. After almost 3.2km (2 miles), you'll find a small red-brick building sitting by a bridge. This is the Ha'penny House, where for over 100 years the toll to cross the river was one half-penny—hence the name.

Cross the bridge over the river and turn right to walk through the Botanics Arboretum on the opposite bank. The terrain ahead is picturesque open parkland interspersed with a myriad of deciduous tree species. Very soon you'll pass through the arch of yet another massive red sandstone bridge spanning the river. This one is adorned with huge Corinthian pillars. It

would seem Glasgow's 19th-century architects spared no expense!

Continuing along the path, you'll again cross over the river and follow the tree-lined paved path for a further 0.8km (1/2 mile). After ascending almost 30m (100 ft.) above the riverbank, you'll pass by the walls of a tower block before meeting a road. Cross this road and continue through the parkland on the opposite side for a further 10 minutes.

⑥ Forth and Clyde Canal On reaching a major fork in the path, going left means walking the further 8km (5 miles) to Milngavie. Instead, turn right and a minute's stroll up the path you'll find the 18th-century engineering marvel of the Forth and Clyde Canal.

From here retrace your steps to the front entrance of the Kelvingrove Art Gallery, from where you'll recognize the trailhead just 45m (148 ft.) to your right.

MUGDOCK COUNTRY PARK TO CARBETH (Kids)

Difficulty rating: Easy

Distance: 8.2km (5 miles) round-trip

Estimated time: 2.5 to 3 hours

Elevation gain: 70m (230 ft.)

Costs/permits: None

Best time to go: Spring lets you enjoy the wildflowers while avoiding the peak summer crowds.

Website: www.mugdock-country-park.org.uk

Recommended map: "Mugdock Country Park," available from the rangers' office at the Craigend Visitor Centre.

Trailhead GPS: NS 54432 77795

Trailhead directions: From Glasgow city center, follow the signs for Aberfoyle and go north on the A81. After passing through the commuter villages of Bearsden and Milngavie, the A81 passes Milngavie reservoir on your left, and shortly afterwards you'll see a sign on your left for Mugdock. Take this road, passing a stable, and park at the Craigend Visitor Centre.

This easy walk is packed with natural and man-made attractions. After prying the kids away from the play area at Craigend Visitor Centre, there's a ghostly 14th-century castle, lochs, and the ancient oaks in Mugdock Wood to explore before strolling along a small section of the 145km (90-mile) West Highland Way trail. Along the way there's oodles of places to stop for a picnic, or wait until you return to the Craigend Visitor Centre for a well-earned bite to eat in the Stables Tea Room.

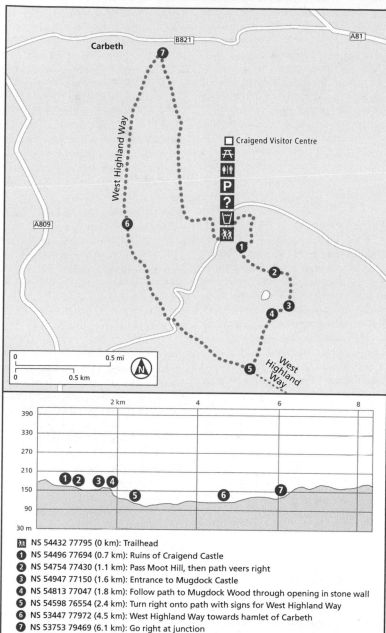

🏃 NS 54432 77795 (0 km): Trailhead
❶ NS 54496 77694 (0.7 km): Ruins of Craigend Castle
❷ NS 54754 77430 (1.1 km): Pass Moot Hill, then path veers right
❸ NS 54947 77150 (1.6 km): Entrance to Mugdock Castle
❹ NS 54813 77047 (1.8 km): Follow path to Mugdock Wood through opening in stone wall
❺ NS 54598 76554 (2.4 km): Turn right onto path with signs for West Highland Way
❻ NS 53447 77972 (4.5 km): West Highland Way towards hamlet of Carbeth
❼ NS 53753 79469 (6.1 km): Go right at junction

Your hike through the woods and open moors of the 260-hectare (642-acre) Mugdock Country Park starts at the arched entrance of Craigend Stables, where amenities include toilets, a ranger center, tea room, and an arts and craft gallery.

Originally built around 1816 as a stable and coach house to support nearby Craigend Castle, from 1949 until 1955 this area formed part of Craigend Zoo.

There are no animals in sight as you leave the center and bear left to follow a broad path signposted for Mugdock Castle, believed to date back at least to 1372.

Flanked by deciduous woodland, you'll pass a small loch on your left where wildfowl feed and then turn left to follow a path that skirts past the ruins of Craigend Castle.

❶ Craigend Castle It's hard to believe the forlorn, blackened walls that meet your gaze were once part of a grand edifice built in 1816 in a Regency Gothic style. In its heyday, the castle also featured landscaped gardens and a sumptuous interior befitting a succession of monied residents that included Sir Andrew Buchanan, a 19th-century British ambassador to Vienna, and James Outram, the former proprietor of the *Glasgow Herald* newspaper.

Press on towards Mugdock Castle, remaining on the main path when there's the option of following another smaller path to your left.

❷ Moot Hill A little farther along your tree-lined trail you'll spot a raised wooded area of ground known as Moot Hill.

Once an island in Mugdock Loch, until the 18th century this was where court meetings were held to settle local disputes and where convicted prisoners were taken to await their sentence. Nearby, Gallow Hill marks the spot where the last public execution took place in 1817.

The path now veers right, again signposted to Mugdock Castle and passing over a series of boardwalks that keeps you from sinking up to your knees in bog. In summer

you may spot the likes of the small pearl-bordered fritillary around here.

❸ Mugdock Castle After 0.8km (½ mile) of walking, you'll finally arrive at the entrance to the fortress-like Mugdock Castle. Standing on a rocky promontory and looking out over Mugdock Loch, when first built in the 13th century as a stronghold for Clan Graham, its walls would have been impregnable. However, in the reign of Charles I, it was ransacked twice.

From Mugdock Castle you leave the main path, to bear right and then immediately left onto a narrower path signposted for Mugdock Wood and the West Highland Way.

❹ Path to Mugdock Wood After walking across a brief stretch of rough grassland, you'll come to a curved stone wall with a small opening on the right that leads down a rocky, muddy path under a thick canopy of trees. Here, you'll also spot a series of etched wooden shapes embedded into the ground that name the different types of trees in the wood.

For the next 0.8km (½ mile), you will descend through this thick, ancient woodland of oak trees, initially walking along boardwalks over the marshy ground. At the first major junction of paths, take the right-hand fork signposted for the Kyber Pass. Descend down this trail for a further 152m (500 ft.) before you come a wide path signposted for the West Highland Way.

❺ West Highland Way Having turned right onto the West Highland Way, you are now walking a trail that runs 145km (90 miles) from Milngavie to the town of Fort William, in the shadow of Britain's highest peak, Ben Nevis.

You're just walking another 3.2km (2 miles) to the wooden huts of Carbeth. The going is easy here, as you follow the stony path until you pass through an iron gate to meet a road. Turn left and walk down the road for around 30m (98 ft.). Before a stone bridge and meeting the Allander

Water, you'll turn right through the wooden gate with a sign for the West Highland Way.

The path now uses a series of wooden boardwalks to cross a stretch of bog. Immediately ahead, the views open up towards the central Highlands, the broad sweep of the valley through which you now walk peppered with forest plantations and rolling green fields of farmland. To your right, you'll see the dramatic rise of the Campsie Fells, the deep horizontal scars in its brown crags a reminder that this landscape was gouged and scraped during the last Ice Age.

❻ Craigallian Loch and Carbeth As you walk along the western banks of Craigallian Loch, you'll note the distinctive hump of Dumgoyne dead ahead, a rewarding and steep hill-walk described below.

Your gentle path soon meets the series of green-and-brown painted wooden huts for which the hamlet of Carbeth is famous. Though many have been replaced, the original huts were built in the 1930s to provide affordable holiday accommodations for people in Glasgow who wished to escape into the fresh air of the countryside.

❼ Iron Gate and Public Footpath Just past the final hut on your left, the path goes through an iron gate and onto a public footpath. Passing uprooted, rotting trees left to attract insects and wildlife, ascend this muddy path until you meet a junction. Take the right-hand path through mixed woodland, following the deer fence on your left.

When you come across a gate, go through it and turn left, walking up the road for 91m (300 ft.).

Ignore the first gap on your right that is signposted for horses. Instead, continue up the road to a second gap in the wall. Turn right here. Follow the path all the way down until you cross a small bridge. Here, turn left where you meet another path, and follow this wider, main path all the way back to Craigend Visitor Centre.

DUMGOYNE HILL BY KILLEARN ★ (Find)

Difficulty rating: Strenuous

Distance: 4.2km (2.6 miles) round-trip

Estimated time: 1.5 to 2 hours

Elevation gain: 391m (1,283 ft.)

Costs/permits: None

Best time to go: Midsummer evening to enjoy the spectacular sunsets over the Arrochar Alps above Loch Lomond

Website: www.glengoyne.com

Recommended map: O/S Landranger No.57, Stirling and The Trossachs, 1:50,000

Trailhead GPS: NS 52692 82756

Trailhead directions: From Glasgow city center, follow the signs for Aberfoyle and go north on the A81. After passing through the well-heeled commuter "villages" of Bearsden and Milngavie, the A81 winds over the moors to Strathblane. 4.8km (3 miles) farther north is Glengoyne Distillery and the trailhead.

You can also catch the no.10 bus from Buchanan Street Bus Station in Glasgow to Dumgoyne.

If you fancy what the Scots would describe as a "wee" (small) challenge, then you'll find a clamber up the heather-strewn hillside of Dumgoyne hard to beat. The remnants of an ancient volcanic eruption, Dumgoyne (391m/1,283 ft.) protrudes like a fat thumb from the westernmost flank of the Campsie Hills. Though a short walk, the views from the summit are breathtaking, while its steep path will test the lungs of even the fittest walker. Kids may not appreciate the climb, but many an adult hiker has enjoyed this hill before descending to savor a dram within the walls of one of Scotland's most southerly malt whisky distilleries.

Scotland boasts scores of wonderful walking routes. However, few offer start and finish points from a malt whisky distillery.

Parking off the road, 18m (60 ft.) north of the entrance to the whitewashed walls of Glengoyne Distillery, take care as you cross the road (eastwards) to immediately head up a rough track found adjacent to a 40 mph road sign.

Note there are few waymark signs on this route, though you will be hard pushed to miss the dome-shaped hulk of Dumgoyne! Though it's a short hike, take water with you, wear walking boots, and carry waterproof clothing regardless of the weather when you start up the trail.

From the A81 and after passing two cottages, your route climbs steadily between a plantation of conifers and open farmland. Within 5 minutes, and staying on the main track lined with ferns, wild raspberry bushes, and a rash of purple thistles (the emblem of Scotland), you'll cross a quaint, old stone bridge with a river 14m (45 ft.) below.

Pressing uphill, ignore the first farm gate immediately ahead and continue to follow the now stony farm track for a further 274m (900 ft.) as it winds steeply past a thick canopy of oak and beech trees.

❶ Farm Gate The track veers south towards a farm gate and open moorland beyond. Don't be put off by the stark sign pinned to a tree that reads PRIVATE ROAD. KEEP DOGS ON LEAD. In Scotland, land access legislation gives you the right to roam as long as you do so responsibly and don't interfere with livestock or damage crops. So relax—but make sure you close the gate!

Though the track now disappears completely, the steeply rising bulk of Dumgoyne Hill directly east offers a heavy hint of the direction you must go.

From the farm gate, walk directly uphill to the narrow footpath. Cross this, jumping the shallow ditch on its far side, and start walking over the open, rough grazing land. For orientation, as you walk head for the far right-hand corner of the large field. You'll also see an old oak tree in the midst of the field and begin to see the scar of the main path gouged into the lower, boggy hillside of Dumgoyne.

❷ Wooden Stile After 25 minutes of walking uphill, the field ends abruptly at a fence and old crumbling stone wall with a wooden stile. After crossing this and a small stream, immediately join the muddy path that strikes directly up the west-facing slope of Dumgoyne. Looking up the path with its few deviations, you can see why the tree-less hill merits the description of a short, sharp ascent!

As you start the ascent surrounded by indifferent sheep, be sure to occasionally turn around to admire the views west over the glen of Strathblane with its patchwork of green, rolling pasture and forest plantations. Directly below you'll spot the farm directly opposite the distillery, while on gaining further altitude the southernmost islands of Loch Lomond will also come into view 24km (15 miles) to the northwest.

Dumgoyne isn't a walk for people who are unsteady on their feet. At times the terrain is surprisingly steep. Fortunately, over the years, bootprints have made large indents in the grassy slope, and this aids your climb as you pass sprouts of purple heather and yellow-petaled wildflowers.

❸ Viewpoint High above the distillery and after almost 1 hour of continual ascent, the steep track suddenly veers south to skirt along the west side of Dumgoyne. As the path veers south, don't

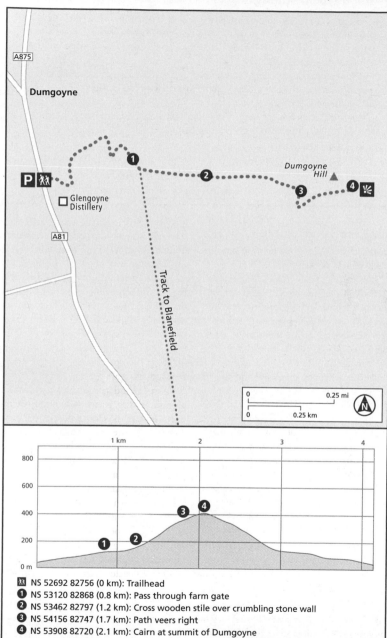

NS 52692 82756 (0 km): Trailhead
❶ NS 53120 82868 (0.8 km): Pass through farm gate
❷ NS 53462 82797 (1.2 km): Cross wooden stile over crumbling stone wall
❸ NS 54156 82747 (1.7 km): Path veers right
❹ NS 53908 82720 (2.1 km): Cairn at summit of Dumgoyne

Glengoyne Distillery

Founded in 1833, Glengoyne Distillery is one of few single malt whisky distilleries to be found in the south of Scotland and close to Glasgow. Nestled amidst trees in the shadow of Dumgoyne, the character-filled distillery is a collection of traditional, whitewashed buildings.

Before an Act of Parliament was passed in the 1820s that reduced the levy on spirit production, the hills around Glengoyne (glen of the geese) reportedly supported many an illicit still.

However, when the Act came into force, it became easier to legally produce whisky. So, granted a license, Glengoyne began the distillation process that continues to this day.

You can visit the distillery (see review at end of this chapter) and enjoy a malt whisky tasting of what, in Gaelic, Scots refer to as *uisge beatha*—"the water of life."

be tempted to continue scrambling directly east up the alternative, narrow, dangerously eroded track.

So, veering southwards along a goat track, you may momentarily feel exposed as the ground falls sharply away to the west over crags. Yet your efforts are now truly rewarded, as on rounding a small bluff the whole of Glasgow comes into view to the south. With binoculars, on a clear day you may even spot the Isle of Arran in the Firth of Clyde to the southwest. Don't be surprised if you also see twinkling lights in the sky, for Dumgoyne isn't far from the final turn aircraft make before landing at Glasgow airport almost 32km (20 miles) to the south.

All the while the path continues to wind uphill, revealing the long west-facing ridge and wild moors of the Campsie Fells, of which Dumgoyne forms the westernmost edge. Though it may feel you are deviating away from the summit, don't be tempted to take a shortcut either on ascent or descent, for the ground falls away sharply onto hidden crags on Dumgoyne's southeast face.

④ Dumgoyne Summit Just when you start to believe you've strayed too far south, the track again veers east for a final, gentle

18m (60-ft.) ascent to the pancake summit of Dumgoyne, complete with cairn.

Unless it's blowing a gale or bucketing with rain, this is definitely the best place to reward yourself with a well-earned flask of tea and the food you've hopefully remembered to pack. But first there are photos to take and fabulous views to savor.

 Standing at 390m (1,282 ft.), take time to drink in the panorama. Gazing northwest, enjoy the sweep of the southern section of Loch Lomond, the U.K.'s largest expanse of fresh water. Over a dozen islands dot the loch, while above its western shoreline the striking Munro peaks of the Arrochar Alps create a wonderful backdrop—especially at sunset. Now look directly west into the valley of Strathblane, trying to spot the route of the West Highland Way, at 145km (90 miles) one of Scotland's many long-distance hiking trails. To the immediate north, there's the picturesque village of Killearn and the wildlife-rich forests and mountains of the Trossachs beyond. Behind you, in late summer and fading light, the rolling, barren moors adopt the appearance of a huge brown-and-orange sponge, while far to the south, beyond historic and densely forested Mugdock Park, lie the many attractions of Glasgow.

Whatever the conditions when you finally pry your eyes away from the view, take extreme care on the descent. Make no mistake, though only a small hill in comparison to Scotland's countless grander crags and mountains, the terrain on the upper reaches of Dumgoyne is no less forgiving should you slip. So, take your time to retrace your steps and ensure you are in fine fettle for toasting your climb at the Dumgoyne Distillery.

QUEEN'S VIEW & THE WHANGIE ★

Difficulty rating: Moderate

Distance: 4.8km (3 miles) round-trip

Estimated time: 1.5 hours

Elevation gain: 176m (577 ft)

Costs/permits: None

Best time to go: A clear summer evening to enjoy a stunning sunset over Loch Lomond and the Arrochar Alps

Recommended map: O/S Landranger map no.64: Glasgow

Trailhead GPS: NS 51069 80825

Trailhead directions: From Glasgow city center, follow the A739 and all subsequent signs north for Bearsden and Drymen. On entering Bearsden, at a large roundabout take the left fork for the A809 and drive through Bearsden Cross. Continue 1.6km (1 mile) farther north, and take the right fork to stay on the A809. On your right is the artificial ski slope of Bearsden Ski Club. Continue on the A809 for 6.4km (4 miles), passing the Carbeth Inn before ascending over moorland for 1.6km (1 mile) and locating Queen's View car park on your left.

Queen's View isn't a difficult or long walk. Yet as its name implies, the views are fit for a Queen. Indeed, in the 1800s Queen Victoria is reported to have walked here during one of her many jaunts into the Scottish Highlands. Undoubtedly, it's the views north to Loch Lomond, the jagged Munros of the Arrochar Alps, and the peak of Ben Lomond that make this such a worthwhile walk. This hike is also ideal for visitors with only limited time to explore the country. Less than 30 minutes' drive from Glasgow Airport, from the hilltop you can feast on some of Scotland's most famous landmarks—and still make your flight.

You can't miss the green knoll of Queen's View that rises gently from the car park and curves westwards out of sight behind a small plantation of conifers.

From the car park, cross over the wall at the obvious stone-stepped stile. Then use the old railway sleepers set into the ground to cross the short stretch of bog. If you try to take a shortcut here, be prepared to sink up to your knees in mud!

Beyond the bog, the well-worn path climbs steadily westwards up a broad, grassy slope interspersed with the occasional large boulder.

The first 183m (600 ft.) of ascent is fabulous for walkers accompanied by small children because after an easy climb you are quickly rewarded with heart-warming views of the surrounding countryside.

The A809 running north to the former droving village of Drymen quickly assumes toylike proportions as you ascend rapidly towards a TV tower. Turn to look east, taking care not to step on one of many cow-pats, and across the valley of Strathblane you'll see the distinctive, extinct volcanic hump of Dumgoyne Hill rise up above the malt whisky distillery of Glengoyne at the edge of the Campie Fells.

❶ Wooden Stile Unless it's mended by the time you do this walk, the huge hole in the fence by the stile means there's no need to use the 2.1m-high (7-ft.) stile that meets the path.

Ignore the path to your left and proceed to your right (westwards) along the increasingly muddy path that follows the natural contours of the heather-strewn hillside. Steadily, a vast expanse of boggy moorland opens up below to your right.

As your walking boots splash along the muddy, rocky trail, see if you can spot the carefully cut rectangle of grass on a small hillock about a quarter-mile to the right and close to the A809. It's the unlikely runway for the local model aircraft club. Throughout the year, all manner of remotely controlled aircraft entertain onlookers with their controlled acrobatic displays.

A bit farther along the red clay path that runs along a natural escarpment leading to The Whangie, the path winds through a series of huge boulders that once crashed down from the 9m-high (30-ft.) rocky slope on your left. Pick your way through what can seem like walking though a giant's game of marbles.

❷ Views of Loch Lomond As you climb, you reach an altitude where Loch Lomond, its myriad of islands, and the peaks of the Arrochar Alps above its western shore all suddenly come into sight. Midway up the loch's eastern shoreline, you can also spot the peak of Ben Lomond, Scotland's most southerly Munro, while farther east the peak of Ben Ledi is among the many craggy hills that jut above the dense areas of forestry in the Trossachs.

As you press ever westwards, the path continues to gently ascend, offering uninterrupted views over Loch Lomond, Scotland's largest expanse of fresh water and the centerpiece of the Loch Lomond and Trossachs National Park. Established in 2002, the park is 1,865 sq. km (720 sq. miles) and includes 20 Munros (peaks over 914m/3000 ft.) in its boundary.

Approximately 40 minutes after leaving the car park, the path veers to the left and climbs sharply past a gnarled rowan tree to reach a wide expanse of peaty moorland. The route remains obvious, with the white triangulation point on the summit clearly visible beyond a shallow rise immediately west.

❸ Queen's View Summit After squelching through the oily, peaty bog, you'll reach the summit. Now you can enjoy a 360-degree panorama. Make sure you have your camera ready.

 Loch Lomond lies to the north, while to the southwest the Firth of Clyde is now visible. Look carefully and on a clear day you'll spot the Isle of Arran with its distinctive jagged peaks. Directly south is the sweep of Glasgow, with the River Clyde splitting the city in two. Let your eyes track eastwards. Across the valley from where you stand, admire the long, prominent ridge of the Campsie Fells, its south-facing crags sculpted long ago by glacial activity. Immediately to your southeast, amidst the carpet of deciduous forest that is Mugdock Country Park, you can also roughly track the route of the West Highland Way (90-mile) long-distance hiking trail as it winds its way through the broad glen, past Dumgoyne and north to the village of Drymen before meeting the southeastern shoreline of Loch Lomond.

When you're ready to come down, you'll note there's a choice of several paths. Walk directly north, heading just slightly to the left of Loch Lomond on the horizon. Initially a broad grassy path, your route soon falls away into the cleft of the hillside, with the track narrowing to follow the contours of a second lower hill.

Loch Lomond now briefly disappears from view, but there's a water reservoir about 0.8km (1/2 mile) to your left. Stay on the path as it rounds the hillside in a clockwise direction.

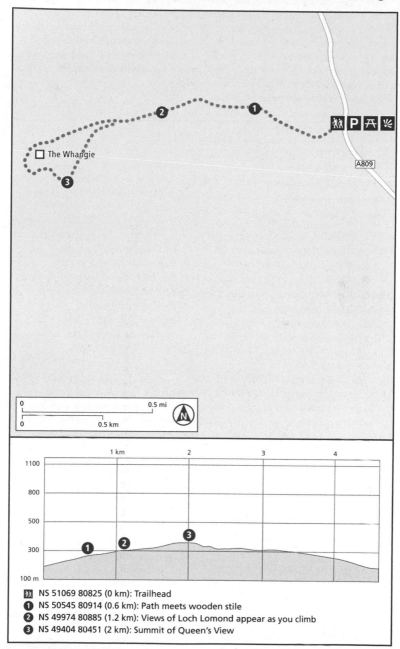

NS 51069 80825 (0 km): Trailhead
1 NS 50545 80914 (0.6 km): Path meets wooden stile
2 NS 49974 80885 (1.2 km): Views of Loch Lomond appear as you climb
3 NS 49404 80451 (2 km): Summit of Queen's View

It's not long before you arrive at the mighty rocks of The Whangie. A climber's haven, 18m (60-ft.) walls of grayish stone rise almost vertically as part of an impressive escarpment. On the day I visited, the area was deserted save for a dozen black bullocks grazing nearby on the succulent grass. If you shout, the walls of The Whangie produce an eerie but fabulous echo.

From here, the path loops back around towards the car park. Don't deviate from the main path, and within 40 minutes to an hour of walking you will once again pass the large wooden stile and descend to the car park, no doubt agreeing that this small hill does indeed offer views fit for Her Majesty.

CONIC HILL

Difficulty rating: Moderate

Distance: 4km (2.5 miles) round-trip

Estimated time: 2 hours

Elevation gain: 309m (1,014ft.)

Costs/permits: None

Best time to go: A great hike on any clear day, but the height of summer is very busy with walkers

Website: www.lochlomond-trossachs.org

Recommended map: O/S Explorer Map no: 347 Loch Lomond; there are also interpretive signs at the trailhead.

Trailhead GPS: NS 42131 91038

Trailhead directions: From Glasgow city center, follow the A739 and all signs north for Bearsden and Drymen. On entering Bearsden, at a large roundabout take the left fork for the A809 and continue north through Bearsden Cross, following the A809 for another 18km (11 miles). Take the B858 into Drymen; then turn left by the village square onto the B837 for Balmaha, which is 4.8km (3 miles) along the road past Milton of Buchanan. Park in the large car park opposite the Oak Tree Inn.

Conic Hill is small in stature when compared to its famous cousin, mighty Ben Lomond, 24km (15 miles) to the north. Yet a walk up this rounded hill offers spectacular views right across the southern islands of Loch Lomond and to the mighty, jagged peaks of the Arrochar Alps beyond. Moreover, few mountains in Scotland can boast that they sit astride the geophysical boundary of the Highlands and the Lowlands. It's here that the Highland Boundary Fault cuts right across the hillside on a line that runs from the Isle of Arran in the west to the fishing port of Stonehaven in the east. There are also fine choices that await after descending Conic Hill, including a boat trip to the nearby historic isle of Inchcailloch or a delicious meal and well-earned pint in the atmospheric Oak Tree Inn within the ancient village of Balmaha.

The village of Balmaha is located within the Loch Lomond and The Trossachs National Park, designated Scotland's first national park in 2002. Starting from the rear of the car park, the forested and bald slopes of Conic Hill rise directly north of where you stand.

Initially, you follow the marker posts for the West Highland Way, the oldest long-distance route in Scotland, and stretching an energy-sapping 145km (90 miles) from the outskirts of Glasgow to the town of Fort William in the west

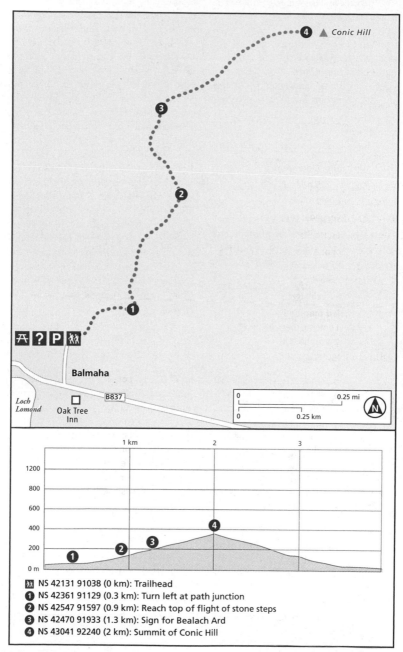

🏕 NS 42131 91038 (0 km): Trailhead
❶ NS 42361 91129 (0.3 km): Turn left at path junction
❷ NS 42547 91597 (0.9 km): Reach top of flight of stone steps
❸ NS 42470 91933 (1.3 km): Sign for Bealach Ard
❹ NS 43041 92240 (2 km): Summit of Conic Hill

Highlands. The broad path is easy to follow and relatively flat as you walk beside Balmaha Plantation.

❶ Path Junction At a junction of the paths, turn left to begin a steep ascent through stands of old Scots Pine and larch. The path can be muddy and slippery in places. Despite the relative brevity of this walk, you'll quickly appreciate why it's imperative to dress for the hills with sturdy hiking boots.

At the top of the steep, irregular steps, you'll pass through a wooden gate. Look to your right to admire the hump of Dumgoyne Hill at the end of the Campsie Fells.

❷ Top of Stone Stairs Continue climbing the stone steps for a few minutes longer until you reach open countryside. Now turn around and enjoy your first taste of the spectacular views over Inchcailloch and the other isles that dot the bonnie banks of Loch Lomond.

Westwards, in the near distance you'll spot the dome of Duncryne Hill. Looking north, you can also see the upper, wild slopes of Ben Lomond, while to the northwest Ben Vorlich is among the craggy Munro peaks that form a wonderful backdrop to the loch. Indeed, one of the most rewarding times to hike up Conic Hill is to enjoy the pinkish-red glow of a summer sunset over Loch Lomond.

❸ Bealach Ard Signpost As you press on, the terrain becomes steeper, narrower, and muddier, until at the top of a flight of rocky steps you come to a signpost by a stream. This is the Bealach Ard (Gaelic for "high pass"). As you continue to ascend to the top of the pass, keep your eyes peeled for the photogenic Highland cattle grazing nonchalantly amidst the bracken. Hopefully, you haven't forgotten your camera or your binoculars, for almost with every footstep there's something to admire amidst the breathtaking scenery.

Though your legs may protest, the advantage of continuing to ascend is clear. For at close to 305m (1,000 ft.) of elevation, you can see for almost 64km (40 miles) southwest and east. The jagged peaks on the Isle of Arran paint the horizon far to the southwest, while across the moorland and mixed woodland to the east you can make out the pillar of Wallace Monument by Stirling Castle.

❹ The Summit From where the path splits and you bear left, it won't take you long to reach the rounded summit less than 61m (200 ft.) above. The stony, narrow path isn't the easiest at this point, so keep in mind that you will also descend this path—if you find the route slippery on the ascent, allow plenty of time for the return journey.

Ⓕun Facts   Loch Lomond and The Trossachs National Park

Designated a national park in 2002, Scotland's first national park (the other is the Cairngorms) incorporates a staggering 1,865 sq. km (720 sq. miles) of lochs, rivers, forests, and woodland packed with nature and opportunities for outdoor pursuits. Within its boundaries, the majority of which lie less than 90 minutes' drive from 70% of Scotland's population, you'll find over 20 Munros (peaks over 914m/3,000 ft.), including Ben Lomond, Scotland's most southerly Munro. The West Highland Way (www.west-highland-way.co.uk) also runs through the park.

However, your labors will be rewarded as you reach the summit of Conic Hill and savor the panorama. Looking northeast, you can look right across the forested slopes of the Trossachs towards Ben Ledi and distant Stirling, whilst southwards there's the distinctive hump of Dumgoyne protruding from the northwestern edge of the Campsie Fells.

However, your eyes will likely be drawn westwards across the southern sweep of Loch Lomond to the fabulous peaks of the Arrochar Alps that rise sharply from the western shores of the loch. In the loch and close to Balmaha, you can easily spot the steeply sloping and forested terrain of Inchcailloch, an ancient burial ground for Clan MacGregor. Nearby is the flatter isle of Clairinch, and in the distance Inchmurrin, at over 1.6km-long (1 mile), is the largest of over 20 islands scattered across Britain's largest area of fresh water.

Having enjoyed the views from Conic Hill, retrace your steps back down to the car park at Balmaha. Here, consider popping over to Inchcailloch by boat or sample the fine food served daily in the Oak Tree Inn in the village.

SLEEPING & EATING

ACCOMMODATIONS

★ (Finds) **Abode Hotel** With a stylish interior that oozes chic, this isn't the place to tramp in with muddy hiking boots. This central hotel is the place to unwind in unashamed luxury and enjoy fine dining in its acclaimed restaurant.

129 Bath St., Glasgow G2 2SY. (C) **01412 216789.** www.abodehotels.co.uk. 59 units. Doubles from £90; suites from £130. AE, MC, V. **Close to:** River Kelvin.

(Value) **Black Bull Hotel** This welcoming, family-run hotel with views towards Dumgoyne and Loch Lomond blends the charm of its heritage as a 19th-century coaching inn with the comfort and style of a Scottish country house hotel.

2 The Square, Killearn, G63 9NG. (C) **01360 550215.** www.blackbullhotel.com. 15 units. Doubles from £100; suites from £140. MC, V. **Close to:** Dumgoyne, Queen's View, and Conic Hill.

★ (Finds) **Macdonald Holyrood Hotel** Few luxury modern hotels can boast being 2 minutes' walk from the Palace of Holyrood, the Scottish Parliament, and the spectacular crags of Arthur's Seat. Moreover, this stylish hotel with a reasonably priced restaurant often has special deals.

81 Holyrood Rd., Edinburgh. EH8 8AU (C) **01315 504500.** www.macdonald-hotels.co.uk. 156 units. Doubles from £85; suites from £125. AE, MC, V. **Close to:** Arthur's Seat.

★ **Malmaison** Yup, you'll need to take your muddy hiking boots off here too. This classy, centrally located boutique hotel doesn't skimp on luxury with its individually styled rooms and a wonderful, dreamy ambience.

278 West George St., Glasgow G2 4LL. (C) **01415 721000.** www.malmaison-glasgow.com. 72 units. Doubles from £160; suites £210. AE, MC, V. **Close to:** Kelvin Walkway.

(Value) **SYHA Leith Walk** Brand new and located in the heart of the capital, this clean, spacious, and friendly hostel is the perfect budget solution for exploring Auld Reekie.

9 Haddington Place, Edinburgh EH7 4AL. (C) **01315 242090.** www.syha.org.uk. 298 beds. £10–£26 per bed. MC, V. **Close to:** Arthur's Seat.

(Value) **SYHA Park Circus** Located in a grand terrace and handy for both the west end and city center, this clean and safe hostel is close to pubs and restaurants and ideal for budget-conscious families and others.

8 Park Terrace, Glasgow G3 6BY. (C) 01413 323004. www.syha.org.uk. 159 beds. £10–£21 per bed, all en suite. MC, V. **Close to:** Dumgoyne, Conic Hill, Falls of Clyde, River Kelvin.

RESTAURANTS

★★ (Finds) **Falko Konditormeister** GERMAN This cozy cafe is possibly Scotland's top cake-eating experience. For light, mouthwatering, and authentic hand-made Bavarian cakes, fresh breads, and excellent coffee, this is heaven.

1 Stanley Rd., Gullane. (C) 01620 843168. www.falko.co.uk. Main courses £3–£6. MC only. Open Sun 1100-1730; Wed, Thur and Fri 0800-1730; Sat 0900-1730. Reservations recommended. **Close to:** Yellowcraigs Beach.

(Kids) **Papilio** ITALIAN If you want flavorful, simple, and authentic Italian dishes and wines that won't break the bank, this buzzing, friendly, and laid-back family-friendly restaurant won't disappoint. Terrific mid-week lunch deals.

158 Bruntsfield Place, Edinburgh. (C) 01312 293325. www.papiliorestaurant.com. Reservations recommended. Main courses £7–£14. All major credit cards. Daily lunch and dinner. **Close to:** Pentland Hills.

Schottische FRENCH Above the convivial atmosphere and real ale-swilling pub of Babbity Bowster's in the Merchant City, this cozy escape offers classic, rustic French fare with a twist of Scots. Fancy scallops with black pudding?

16–18 Blackfriars St., Glasgow. (C) 01415 525055. Reservations recommended. Main courses £8–£15. MC, V. Tues–Sun, dinner only, from 1700-2200. **Close to:** Falls of Clyde and River Kelvin.

Scottish Seabird Centre CAFE Tuck into a tasty full Scottish breakfast, Sunday brunch, or traditional homemade rock scone in this bright, family-friendly cafe with the stunning cliffs of Bass Rock as your backdrop.

The Harbour, North Berwick. (C) 01620 890202. www.seabird.org. Main courses £3–£7. MC, V. Open 1000-1700 daily. Reservations recommended on weekends. **Close to:** Yellowcraigs or St. Abb's Head.

★ **Stac Polly** SCOTTISH For the best of Scottish game and seafood with attentive service and a touch of tartan, this Edinburgh institution consistently hits the mark. No fried Mars bars here!

29-33 Dublin St., Edinburgh. (C) 01315 562231. www.stacpolly.co.uk. Main courses £17–£20. MC, V. Open for lunch Mon–Fri, 1200–1400; dinner Mon–Sun, 1800–2130. Reservations recommended. **Close to:** Arthur's Seat.

★★ (Finds) **Urban Angel** CAFE This hidden gem is a central cafe-cum-restaurant where the relaxed air is infused with the homemade aromas of a wide range of wholesome, organically sourced stews, soups, cakes, and sandwiches.

121 Hanover St., Edinburgh. (C) 01312 256215. www.urban-angel.co.uk. Main courses £6–£12. V only. Open Mon–Thur, 1000–2200; Fri–Sat, 1000–2300; Sun, 1000-1700. Reservations recommended. **Close to:** Arthur's Seat.

(Value) **Wagamama** JAPANESE Just minutes' walk from Glasgow's Queen Street station, this is the place to enjoy informal dining on fabulously fresh oriental seafood, vegetarian, and meat dishes. You'd never know it's part of a global chain.

97-103 West George St., Glasgow. © **01412 291468.** www.wagamama.com. Main courses £9–£14. MC, V. Open Mon–Sat, 1200–2300; Sun 1230–2200. Reservations recommended. **Close to:** Kelvin Walkway.

(Finds) **Wee Curry Shop** INDIAN   Glaswegians have a healthy appetite for a curry, and this tiny, friendly restaurant above the renowned Jinty McGinty's Irish pub is hard to beat for a spicy treat.

23 Ashton Lane, Glasgow. © **01413 575280.** Reservations recommended. Main courses £9–£12. V. Open Mon–Thur, 1200–1400 and 1730–2230; Fri–Sat, 1200–2300; Sun, 1700–2230. **Close to:** Kelvin Walkway.

Southern Scotland Walks

by Colin Hutchison

Head south from Glasgow and Edinburgh, cities at either end of the broad valley of the central belt, which holds 70% of Scotland's population, and you'll discover a landscape shaped by mixed woodland and coniferous forest, rich agricultural land, salmon-rich rivers, wild moors, and rolling hills.

You'll not find the high, jagged peaks of the Highlands in this picturesque country. Yet the scenery is no less pleasing to the eye. For east and west there are dramatic, high sea-cliffs to hike; charming villages to discover; and hundreds of miles of scenic, wildlife-rich trails to wander—and all with a story to tell.

These lands are rich in history. There are ancient, ghostly castles and the site of bloody battles, including Robert the Bruce's 13th-century ambush of English soldiers by the shores of Loch Trool.

Northeast of Galloway you can even follow the footsteps of Roman legionnaires who almost 2000 years ago patrolled hill forts and the ancient byway of Dere Road. Little wonder these lands have inspired the writings of two of Scotland's most iconic literary figures—Sir Walter Scott and Robert Burns, whose beloved countryside and homes form the basis of fascinating walks in these pages.

For the serious hiker, there's the challenge of The Merrick, southern Scotland's highest hill to climb. Moreover, walks in these pages reveal the history and wildlife to be enjoyed while visiting sections of long-distance trails including the 341km-long (212-mile) Southern Upland Way, the Borders Abbeys Way, and St. Cuthbert's Way.

So, whatever you seek, follow your compass into southern Scotland and let your adventures begin.

ESSENTIALS

GETTING THERE
By Air

If flying directly to southern Scotland, you'll arrive at Prestwick International Airport (www.gpia.co.uk), the closest departure point for all the southwest trails referred to in these pages. Because Prestwick is the only airport in Scotland with a railway station (www.firstgroup.com/scotrail), it only takes 50 minutes to reach Glasgow, and half that time to take the train south to the coastal town of Ayr and "Burns country."

If arriving at Glasgow airport (www.glasgowairport.com), it's around £18 to £20 to take a taxi the 13km (8 miles) east to the city center. Alternatively, the Service 500 bus service operated by Arriva departs every 7 minutes from the airport (£4.20 single) for the 30-minute journey. The bus stops at Buchanan Street Bus Station, handy for buses to Ayrshire and the far southwest. Alternatively, it's a 10-minute walk to Central Station for trains to Ayr and Stranraer.

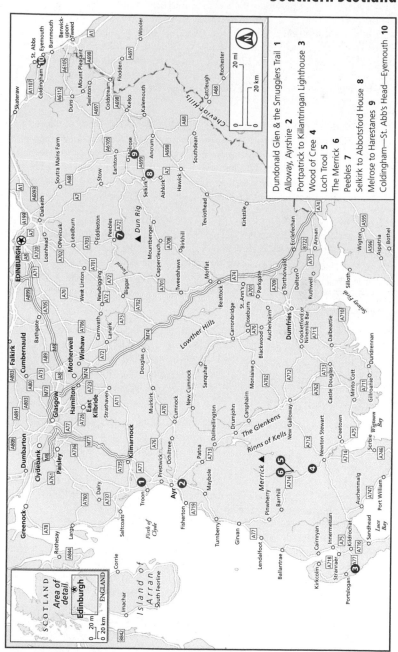

Dundonald Glen & the Smugglers Trail **1**
Alloway, Ayrshire **2**
Portpatrick to Killantringan Lighthouse **3**
Wood of Cree **4**
Loch Trool **5**
The Merrick **6**
Peebles **7**
Selkirk to Abbotsford House **8**
Melrose to Harestanes **9**
Coldingham—St. Abb's Head—Eyemouth **10**

If flying into Edinburgh (www.edinburghairport.com), expect to pay between £16 and £20 for the 25-minute cab fare 9.7km (6 miles east) into the city center. Arguably the best (and certainly cheapest) option is to catch the regular Airlink 100 express bus service from stand 19 outside the airport terminus (every 10 min. during peak time). This costs just £3 (single) and takes around 25 minutes to reach its terminus at Waverley Bridge. This is directly opposite the entrance to Waverley Station, where you can catch the east-coast line south down the coast to the likes of Dunbar and Berwick, then catch local buses to explore the likes of Eyemouth and St. Abb's.

By Car
There are several key routes to explore in southern Scotland. On the east coast, your trailhead is likely to be just off the A1 from Edinburgh, while farther inland both the A7 and the A68 will help you quickly explore Border country. From Glasgow, the west-coast routes are best reached via the A77 that stretches all the way to Stranraer. If you are driving up from England, the western areas of southern Scotland are best reached off the M74, while the A1 serves the east coast.

By Train
As noted above, Prestwick Airport is served by a railway station—handy if heading south for Stranraer. Unfortunately, there's no train line through the Borders, so you'll need to take a bus or drive. On the east coast, several trains from Edinburgh stop at North Berwick and Berwick-upon-Tweed, from where you can take a taxi or bus into Border country. Visit www.firstgroup.com/scotrail for timetable information.

VISITOR INFORMATION
In the Borders, the **VisitScotland Tourist Information Centres** in Hawick, Jedburgh, Kelso, Melrose, and Peebles are open all year (© **08706 080404;** www.visitscottish borders.com). Also visit www.ayrshire-arran.com and www.visitdumfriesandgalloway. co.uk. The main tourist information centres in Glasgow (11 George Sq.) and Edinburgh (3 Princes St.) will also be able to help with accommodations and transport inquiries.

ORIENTATION
The largest town in the south of Scotland is Ayr, a west coastal settlement almost 80km by road (50 miles) south of Glasgow, with roots stretching back to at least the 12th century. Travel another 48km (30 miles) and you'll reach Stranraer, the port from which ferries sail to distant Ireland.

Inland stretch the spectacular hill country, pasture lands, rivers, and former mill towns of the Borders and Dumfries and Galloway, while on the east coast, sleepy fishing villages like St. Abb's hug a rugged coastline beloved by surfers.

GETTING AROUND
From Glasgow and Edinburgh it's possible to catch a train down the west and east coasts respectively. Unfortunately, the Borders region hasn't been directly served by trains for almost 50 years. However, with careful planning (www.travelinescotland.com) and patience, the majority of the walks in this chapter can be accessed by public transport with the occasional use of a taxi to return to your start point.

Undoubtedly, unless you're planning to hike considerable mileage along the long-distance trails, it will prove more practical and less time consuming to simply hire a car. Currently, rentals start from around £35 per day or £140 per week. You'll need an international drivers license, credit card, and often need to be over 21 years old. There are plenty of car hire outlets in Glasgow, Edinburgh, and Prestwick. Try **Arnold Clark** (*©* 08445 765425) or **Avis** (*©* 08706 086338; www.avis.co.uk).

DUNDONALD GLEN &
THE SMUGGLERS TRAIL ★

Difficulty rating: Easy to moderate

Distance: 6.2km (3.9 miles) round-trip

Estimated time: 2 hours

Elevation gain: 70m (230 ft.)

Costs/permits: None

Best time to go: The wood is a riot of color in autumn, and in August the old village of Dundonald holds its fair.

Website: www.dundonaldmusicfest.org.uk

Recommended map: You can download three online maps of the Smuggler's Trail from the countryside pages of

South Ayrshire Council at (www. south-ayrshire.gov.uk).

Trailhead GPS: NS 34773 32860

Directions: Traveling south from Glasgow on the A77, after 40km (25 miles) turn right at the roundabout onto the A78 (northbound). After 1.6km (1 mile) along this road, take the left slip-road, sign-posted B746 for Loans. Drive through the village and after 0.4km (¼ mile) turn right at the sign for Smugglers Trail and park at the side of the road.

Ayrshire is renowned as the birthplace of "Rabbie" Burns, Scotland's national bard. Less well-known is the key role the quiet Dundonald Glen, a densely wooded area 4.8km (3 miles) east of the seaside town of Troon played in the illegal but highly lucrative 18th-century smuggling trade. At that time, dozens of people and up to 500 horses could be deployed from the likes of Dundonald village to spirit contraband whisky, tobacco, or coffee from Troon through Dundonald Glen to evade the Excisemen. Moreover, this peaceful woodland walk offers views over the Ayrshire coast and the chance to visit the impressive ruins of a castle built for King Robert II in 1371.

Over the bridge spanning the A78 and beyond a cluster of farm buildings, park in the shadow of Collennan Quarry, which supplied much of the gray stone for the grand houses in nearby Troon.

From the barred and overgrown entrance point to the quarry, turn right to walk northeast up the rough road for 152m (500 ft.), where you'll find an interpretive board that outlines the history of the Smugglers Trail.

The route ahead now becomes a narrow, steeply ascending stone track that initially skirts the southern boundary of a reservoir before plunging through Aught

(hanging) Wood and into Dundonald Forest beyond.

① Benches and Sea Views As you skirt the side of the reservoir enjoyed by fishermen, there are several benches that provide the perfect spot for a quick sandwich while you savor the sea views across the Firth of Clyde. It was from these waters that 18th-century ships slipped ashore from the likes of Ireland and the Isle of Man to land their illicit contraband.

As you walk along the main path, which is quite steep in places, it's obvious this was no easy route for the smugglers to haul their load north towards Glasgow.

> ## (Fun Facts) Smuggling
>
> Whether building or sailing with naval, merchant, or passenger ships, for centuries many a family from the west of Scotland has had links with the high seas. Yet if 17th- and 18th-century Glasgow merchants made their fortune from sailing to the Americas to trade in tobacco, it's less well-known how many people benefited from Dundonald Glen's reputation as one of the most lucrative smuggling routes in the country.
>
> Smuggling was highly organized; reports suggest one illicit haul of 18th-century tobacco, brandy, wine, and coffee seized by Excisemen in Dundonald was in today's currency worth over £120,000.

On either side of you, the ground is thickly carpeted with undergrowth. Today, the forest floor sprouts nettles, ferns, wildflowers, and wild berries, while countless stands of ash and larch trees provide a rich canopy to hide the singing birdlife. The area is also home to the rare Coleopetra beetle. If you are very lucky, you may spot one of the many roe deer that roam the forest.

❷ Small Cliff After almost a mile of winding through the silent forest, a small cliff, over which several trees are destined to fall, will come into view on your right. Standing in the midst of this dense woodland, it's a strange feeling to know that somewhere to your right lie ancient dwellings. For near this smuggling route archaeologists have also found the remains of an Iron Age dun (fortified dwelling).

❸ Path Junction Beyond the cliff, the path sharply descends to meet another path. Turn left and look for arable farmland through the trees. However, remain in the forest, continuing to wind past the gnarled branches of elm and ash in an area that, as ancient woodland, was designated a (protected) Site of Special Scientific Interest (SSSI) in 1975.

Press on down the path, descending to a wire fence beyond which a vast expanse of rough grazing land runs up to the boundary of the village of Dundonald,

whose inhabitants long ago played a role in spiriting away the contraband.

The path now runs parallel with the village, running northwest following the fence. It isn't long before you spot the next attraction of this walk—the gray fortress walls of Dundonald Castle.

❹ Wooden Bridge to Dundonald Castle To reach the castle and village, you must continue walking west along the path until you meet a small wooden bridge that crosses a stream. Cross over the bridge and follow the stony path for 5 minutes in an easterly direction. Houses will appear on your left, and after ascending a small hill the path ends outside the **Dundonald Castle Visitor Centre** (open daily Apr to end of Oct, 10am–5pm; £2.50).

The castle entrance itself is a further minute's walk up the hillside, beyond the bright and airy visitor center with its small interpretive display and cafe looking out towards the castle tower. It's definitely worth making the effort to tour inside this ancient fortress where King Robert II died in 1390 and which was used by the Stuart dynasty for a further 150 years. The timber floors may have rotted long ago, but a steel staircase allows you to explore the upper floors, including where the king would have enjoyed his private quarters. There's also the chilling oubliette, or pit, where prisoners would have been left to rot.

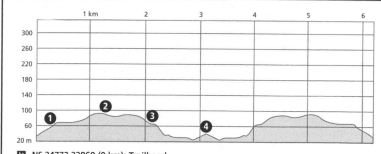

- NS 34773 32860 (0 km): Trailhead
- **1** NS 35050 32992 (0.4 km): Benches with views across Firth of Clyde
- **2** NS 35657 33650 (1.3 km): Pass small cliff on your right
- **3** NS 36176 34037 (2.1 km): Turn left at path junction
- **4** NS 36423 34617 (3.1 km): Cross small wooden bridge

On emerging from Dundonald Castle, pop back into the visitor center for a coffee or sandwich before retracing your steps back through the spooky woods of Dundonald to your starting point. Thereafter, before heading back to Glasgow or Edinburgh, there's the option of pondering the rich seam of history you've just discovered over a meal, whisky, or real ale at the welcoming **Old Loans Inn** (see review in chapter 5) in Loans.

ALLOWAY, AYRSHIRE ★

Difficulty rating: Easy

Distance: 7.2km (4.5 miles) round-trip

Estimated time: 2 to 2.5 hours

Elevation gain: 25m (82 ft.)

Costs/permits: None

Best time to go: Spring or autumn to avoid the peak tourist season and enjoy the colors in the trees and fields along the route.

Website: www.burnsheritagepark.com

Recommended map: O/S Explorer Map no.326: Ayr and Troon

Also: "Historic Alloway: A Guide for Visitors" with maps, £2 from the Robert Burns Heritage Museum.

Trailhead GPS: NS 33233 18118

Trailhead directions: Sixty-one kilometers (38 miles) southwest of Glasgow, follow the A77 south past Ayr towards Stranraer. Continue 4.8km (3 miles) south of Ayr, and then turn right at the brown sign marked ALLOWAY. Follow this road for 3.2km (2 miles) into the village, parking outside the visitor center for the Robert Burns Heritage Museum.

This walk is a must for devotees of Robbie Burns, Scotland's national bard and a literary hero. It was his hand that penned *Tam o' Shanter* and whose name is popularly associated with the verses of Auld Lang Syne that Scots sing at ceilidh's and traditional celebrations. The route of this walk takes in the thatched-roof cottage where Robbie Burns was born, the ghostly Auld Kirk (built 1516) where in 1784 Burns buried his father William Burnes, and the arched (bridge) of "Brig o' Doon" over which the hapless Tam o' Shanter fled upon his horse while pursued by witches.

Yet, this gentle walk also offers spectacular sea views towards Ireland and Kintyre, often overlooked by tourists, and the chance to savor the rolling countryside that long ago inspired Scotland's most celebrated bard.

After parking and paying a quick visit to the Robert Burns Heritage Museum, cross the road and descend the path that leads through a well-lit, 274m-long (900-ft.) underpass. This is the route of the old Maidens and Dunure Light Railway, part of the long-defunct Glasgow and South Western Railway that opened in 1906 and steamed passengers to the Ayrshire coast. The line didn't pay and finally closed in 1968.

On emerging from the tunnel, you'll see a sign beside an old stone well that reads in the Old Scots words of Burns, "Whare Mungo's mither hang'd herself"—where St. Mungo's mother hanged herself. Nine meters (30 ft.) farther and as you contemplate whether this tragic deed really occurred, your spirits will be lifted by the magnificent views to the left over the River Doon.

For 366m (1,200 ft.) upstream, beyond the first arched stone bridge, you'll spy the graceful gray-stone walls of the Brig o' Doon (Bridge of Doon) that inspired the words of Burns.

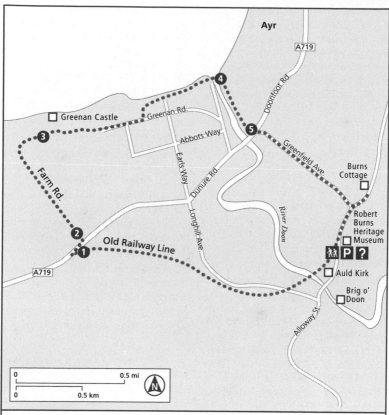

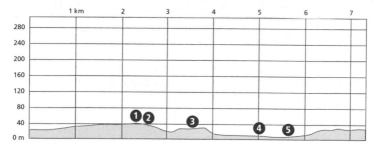

🚶 NS 33233 18118 (0 km): Trailhead
1 NS 31309 18234 (2.3 km): Cross the A719 at junction
2 NS 31346 18370 (2.5 km): Walk along farm road past High Greenan House
3 NS 31050 19076 (3.5 km): Greenan Castle
4 NS 32418 19501 (5 km): Cross small metal footbridge and turn right immediately
5 NS 32672 19077 (5.6 km): Secret Garden tearoom

❶ Junction with A719 After ambling along the paved route of the old railway line for over 1.6km (1 mile), listening to the farm birds whistling and chirping in the trees, you'll come to where the path meets the A719 road.

Crossing directly over, you'll easily spot the sign pointing northwest down a small, muddy path between rough grazing farmland. I love walking through here in late summer when there's a profusion of deliciously plump wild blackberries and raspberries to pick.

After 183m (600 ft.), you'll come to a junction with the town of Ayr and the coast clearly visible 3.2km (2 miles) to the north. Turn left down the farm road running between the fields, savoring fine views over rolling fields similar to those Scotland's 17th-century bard once ploughed.

❷ Farm Road The way ahead now runs directly west for over 0.8km (½ mile). On your right is arable farmland, with the church spires of Ayr in the distance. On your left, by the sprawling mansion of High Greenan House, horses graze on open pasture. As you walk, look southwest for the unmistakable green hump of the "Heads of Ayr" towering above the waters of the Firth of Clyde.

❸ Greenan Castle On reaching a cluster of farm cottages, the road abruptly veers right. As you turn, look left through the trees to watch the sea lapping onto soft Ayrshire sands. Behind the shoreline, birds caw in the surrounding farm fields.

Less than a minute's walk farther north along the rough road, you'll suddenly spy the ruined gray-stone walls of once-proud Greenan Castle towering above the coastline. Though this impressive, ruined stone tower house was built in 1603 for Kennedy of Baltersan, archaeologists believe it was Roger de Scalebroc who in the 12th century first built a wooden fortress on this windswept site.

Continuing north between farmland and past thriving rowan trees, the road now gently descends to meet a small housing estate forming the southernmost boundary of Ayr. With the beach 91m (300 ft.) to your left and houses on your right, continue along Greenan Road for 183m (600 ft.) before veering left. Continue walking north through a car park and past banks of wildflowers and bushes laden with rosehips in early autumn.

❹ Metal Footbridge A small metal footbridge marks the spot where the salmon-rich River Doon meets the sea. Here, I found a man scanning the water for signs of salmon. Cross the bridge and turn immediately right along a tarmac footpath, enjoying the reflection of the deciduous trees on the opposite bank reflecting over the water.

❺ The Secret Garden Walking east, a couple of minutes upriver from where the Doon tumbles over a weir, you'll pass a Spar supermarket and again meet the A719 that you crossed earlier.

If you're hungry, before crossing the busy A719, avoid crowds by your start/end point and pop into the cozy Secret Garden tearoom immediately on your right for a good-value coffee, delicious cake, or sandwich (£4–£6).

From here, your route back to the start point follows the road. Cross the A719 and for 0.8km (½ mile) walk directly southeast, with housing on your right and a golf course and park on your left.

At the top of this road, turn left onto the B7024 and you'll find the thatched cottage and birthplace (in 1759) of Robbie Burns just 137m (450 ft.) farther along the road. At the time of writing, your £5 "Discovery Pass" ticket to the Burns Heritage Museum includes entry to the cottage that claims to contain the world's largest collection of Burns artifacts and manuscripts.

Alternatively, at the top of the road, turn right and walk south for 0.8km ($^1/_2$ mile) along the B7024 until spotting your start point to the left through the trees.

However, if you've time, instead of turning left into the car park continue walking along the B7024 for less than a minute to visit the Auld Kirk (old church). Dating back to 1516, this is the resting place of William Burnes (d. 1784), Robbie Burns' father and also the setting in Burns' writing where *Tam o' Shanter* encountered a Satanic ritual amidst the ruins of the kirk. It's certainly a spooky place!

PORTPATRICK TO KILLANTRINGAN LIGHTHOUSE (Finds)

Difficulty rating: Easy to moderate

Distance: 7.2km (4.5 miles) round-trip

Estimated time: 2 to 2.5 hours

Elevation gain: 41m (135 ft.)

Costs/permits: None

Best time to go: Enjoy this walk in summer sunshine, but start early to have the trail to yourself.

Website: www.southernuplandway.com, www.southernuplandway.gov.uk

Recommended map: O/S Stranraer and The Rhins, no. 309, 1:25,000.

Trailhead GPS: NW 99740 54231

Trailhead directions: From Glasgow, follow the A77 2 hours south to Stranraer then travel 11km (7 miles) farther on the A77 to the village of Portpatrick. Park by the harbor.

By bus, take the Citylink from Buchanan Street Bus Station in Glasgow to Stranraer (2.5 hours; £16), then the local service to Portpatrick. FirstScotRail (www.firstgroup.com/scotrail), the national rail operator, also runs to Stranraer.

Tucked into the extreme southwest corner of Scotland, the Portpatrick to Killantringan Lighthouse cliff-top walk offers a rewarding hike for families and leisurely hikers. On a fine day, there are spectacular sea views west to Ireland and north to the extinct volcanic isle of Ailsa Craig. Moreover, it's the most westerly start point of Scotland's longest hiking route—the 341km (212-mile) Southern Upland Way. On a route that attracts 30,000 walkers a year, don't expect to be alone as you enjoy fine Portpatrick food and accommodations before your walk, then observe the seabirds and keep a sharp eye out for one of dozens of wrecks that have foundered on this dramatic coastline.

It's easy to find the start of this walk. On the quayside and by the HM Coastguard building and public toilets, just look for the small kids' play-park, beside which a flight of concrete steps ascends the side of the rock face.

The views from the top of this headland offer a taste of the wonderful scenery ahead. Directly below, the picturesque fishing port of Portpatrick is huddled below, and 0.8km ($^1/_2$ mile) farther south

the ruins of an ancient castle sit above the waves. Far to the west, the coastline of Ireland also greets the eye.

The wildlife is also immediately evident. From your vantage point over 30m (100 ft.) above the sea, watch as the surf constantly booms against the sea-cliffs far below, while on every nook in the gray cliff walls, herring gulls, fulmars, black guillemots, and even gannets on migratory patrols from Ailsa

Craig nest and squawk. This is no place to forget your camera or binoculars.

① Wooden Steps Walking northwest along the cliff top on a narrow, muddy path, you'll soon walk round the side of a British Telecom building and ascend a short flight of wooden steps. Turn left here onto a brief stretch of tarmac road and keep an eye out for whizzing stray golf balls from the Dunsky Golf Club on your right. Keep the boundary fence of the fairway on your right and continue north as the road once again forms a muddy path above the cliffs.

After 15 minutes of easy walking, the path suddenly corkscrews down towards one of many remote coves indented into this coastline. Take care not to slip on the wet rocks as you sharply descend and cross a secluded pebbly beach. On your right is a tiny wooden hut grandly entitled the Coastal Interpretative Centre. Shaped like a Victorian folly, externally it's visually impressive— sadly, it's also closed. On the far side, the path again climbs steeply, cutting into the cliff face 18m (60 ft.) above the water. This section will test the nerves of anyone afraid of heights and is potentially one of the trickiest sections for walkers with children.

② Second Beach After 1.6km (1 mile), the exposed cliff path broadens out to become a grassy path that traverses rolling, grassy moorland supporting wild raspberries and colorful wildflowers, including bird-foot-trefoil.

The path narrows again as it descends onto a second pebbly beach, though the route ahead isn't immediately obvious since a sheer cliff face appears to block your passage north.

The secret is to follow the walls of the cliff's face right down the beach until you're almost in the sea. On your right, a Southern Upland Way marker post suddenly becomes visible behind a giant boulder, and beyond you'll see a steep climb up two successive natural stone staircases set into the cliffs. There's a guard-rail to aid your ascent, but watch your footing.

③ Wooden Stile Near the top of the natural stone staircase is a wooden stile. From here to the lighthouse, the terrain is much easier, as it crosses wild, undulating grassland strewn with wildflowers overlooking the sea.

Briefly, as you walk north, the sea view is obscured and you'll become conscious that the sound of crashing waves is mixed with that of sheep braying on nearby pasture.

④ Grassy Hill With Lighthouse View After around 2.5km (1¹/₂ miles) and on ascending a small grassy hill, the impressive white tower of Killantringan Lighthouse comes into view. Perched over 30m (100 ft.) above a rocky promontory, from dusk its distinctive bulbous glass dome sweeps light westwards towards distant Ireland. Way to the northwest, I could just spot the faint outline of the cliffs of Mull of Kintyre, and 24km (15 miles) directly north I saw the sheer cliffs of the volcanic isle of Ailsa Craig in the Firth of Clyde.

With the lighthouse now almost always in sight, the grassy path continues across rough pasture before abruptly descending into the cleft of a hill. You'll now pass through several wooden gates and descend to almost sea level to find that the lighthouse is almost within touching distance. Now, there's just a small grassy knoll to ascend.

⑤ Shipwreck and Killantringan Lighthouse If it's dry and windless, the exposed, bald knoll serves as a fabulous spot for a picnic. For after 3.7km (2¹/₃ miles) and 1.5 hours of easy walking, this marks the northernmost extent of your coastal walk before directly retracing your steps back to Portpatrick. Scanning the horizon, you can watch ships ply the 48km (30-mile) stretch of sea between Scotland and Ireland and imagine how it must have felt for missionaries, almost 1,500 years ago, to undertake the hazardous passage eastwards in tiny wooden craft.

If you plan to walk more of the Southern Upland Way or return to Portpatrick via the B738 road (not recommended),

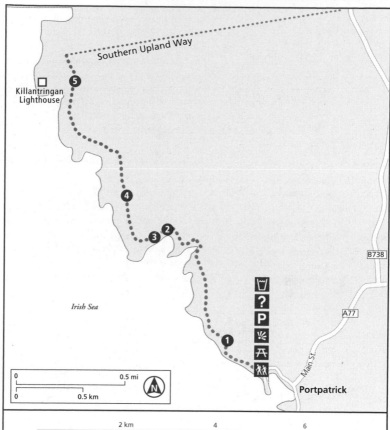

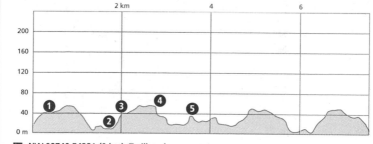

NW 99740 54231 (0 km): Trailhead
1 NW 99474 54450 (0.5 km): Climb short flight of wooden steps and turn left
2 NW 99009 55304 (1.8 km): Path descends to pebbly peach
3 NW 98906 55242 (2 km): Wooden stile at top of stone staircase
4 NW 98702 55554 (2.4 km): First view of Killantringan Lighthouse
5 NW 98246 56610 (3.8 km): Ascend grassy knoll close to lighthouse

Fun Facts Shipwrecks

Though spectacular, the waters off Portpatrick's coastline are littered with over 70 wrecks that have come to grief on the jagged rocks in the last 150 years while bound for Ireland, Liverpool, or even Australia. In 1850, the iron paddle steamer *Orion* foundered and sank less than a mile from the safety of Portpatrick harbor. Over 60 of its 200 passengers drowned.

More recently, in February of 1982 the Cypriot-registered coaster *Craiganlet* lost power and drifted ashore to hit the gnarled black rocks in Portamaggie bay. Fortunately, the 11-man crew was rescued with the aid of the RNLI lifeboat at Portpatrick and a helicopter. Today, seabirds have colonized the shards of steel that poke above the waves.

you'll need to continue 183m (600 ft.) past the knoll to meet the tarmac road running to the (private) lighthouse by the southern edge of Killantringan Bay. Turn right onto the tarmac road and walk for 2.4km (1$^1/_2$ miles) to the B738 and turn right again to walk the 4.8km (3 miles) back to Portpatrick via Dunsky Gardens.

On your return to Portpatrick, take the time to pop into the **RNLI lifeboat station** by the harbor (free entry; daily 2–4 pm, Easter–Oct), where there's a logbook and photographs of daring rescues undertaken by the volunteer crew over the years.

WOOD OF CREE (Kids)

Difficulty rating: Easy

Distance: 1.7km (1 mile) round-trip

Estimated time: 1 hour

Elevation gain: 40m (131 ft.)

Costs/permits: None

Best time to go: In the spring, bluebells carpet the forest floor and bird-watchers may spot rare migratory visitors like the pied flycatcher.

Website: www.rspb.org.uk

Recommended map: O/S Map no.319: Galloway Forest Park South, 1: 25,000

Also: "RSPB Wood of Cree Nature Reserve Trail Guide" leaflet, which can be picked up at the information board located in the Wood of Cree car park.

Trailhead GPS: NX 38109 70841

Trailhead directions: Traveling southeast from the Ayrshire coast on the A714, pass through the village of Glentrool. At 3.2km (2 miles) south of the hamlet of Bargrennan and 13km (8 miles) north of Newton Stewart, turn off left at the signpost for Wood of Cree. After crossing the river, take the first right turn and drive 4,8km (3 miles) down the single-track road to the Wood of Cree car park.

As a very short forest walk, Wood of Cree is ideal for walkers with young children in tow. Nature-lovers will discover this designated National Nature Reserve (NNR) is teeming with fauna and flora, including mighty stands of oak, birch, and ash, and over 300 species of flowering plants. This is also where to spot butterflies in the summer and the rare migratory pied flycatcher, or simply revel in the peacefulness of this ancient woodland.

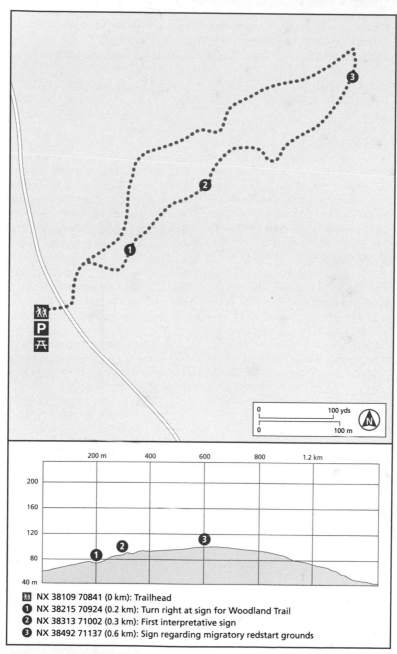

🚶 NX 38109 70841 (0 km): Trailhead
1 NX 38215 70924 (0.2 km): Turn right at sign for Woodland Trail
2 NX 38313 71002 (0.3 km): First interpretative sign
3 NX 38492 71137 (0.6 km): Sign regarding migratory redstart grounds

(Fun Facts)   **Spooked Woodcutters**

In days gone by, superstitious woodcutters used to dislike felling rowan because it was believed the tree species kept witches at bay!

From the car park, cross the single-track road and ascend the obvious rough track through the trees.

About 46m (150 ft.) up the stony path, go through the wooden farm gate and follow the sharp bend to your right. Now take the right fork in the path and continue walking east, winding through the dense forest canopy. Stop to listen to the bird calls from high in the trees and the gurgling waters of the burn (stream) to your right.

❶ **Woodland Trail**   Presently, you'll come to a simple sign marked WOODLAND TRAIL. Proceed to your right, following the clear path as it meanders through the woodland. In late May, the heavy scent of bluebells accompanies your bootprints, while wild garlic and yellow primroses also thrive amid the thick stands of trees that have inhabited this area since the last Ice Age.

Walking deeper into the forest, you'll notice the path veers slightly south towards a series of deep rock pools and an attractive, tumbling, small waterfall.

❷ **First Interpretive Sign**   After less than 0.8km (½ mile) of walking, you'll come to the first of a series of interpretive signs erected by the path, each offering an insight to the local fauna and flora.

While today the forest is a sanctuary for nature with little signs of human interference, experts believe in centuries past it was very different. There's evidence that the trees have been intensely cultivated

since at least the mid-1600s. Indeed, in the 1800s, the oak wood was felled for use as charcoal in the area's once-thriving lead-smelting industry.

The burn has its own natural story to tell. Scarce mosses thrive on the wet rocks lining its banks, while the clever stone fly larvae have evolved a specially flattened body in order to live under the boulders of the fast-flowing stream.

❸ **Migratory Redstart Grounds**   The path continues to climb into the deciduous forest, finally abandoning its parallel run with the burn to turn northwards. After a total of around 30 minutes of gentle walking, you will come to another interpretive sign that reveals this particular area of the forest is where several pairs of the migratory redstart species are known to fly in from Africa every May to nest in the trees. You can identify the male by its red breast and gray plumage.

If you visit between mid-April and late July, you may even be fortunate enough to spot the pied flycatcher nesting in the woods before also making its long return journey to the sunnier climes of Africa.

Before turning back, there's a further interesting interpretive feature by the path. On a board, seven different types of wood to be found in the forest have been hung on hooks to allow the walker to understand how soil and light conditions in the forest have enabled each tree species to develop.

Difficulty rating: Easy to moderate

Distance: 14km (8.5 miles) round-trip

Estimated time: 3 hours

Elevation gain: 60m (197 ft.)

Costs/permits: None

Best time to go: June to September

Website: www.southernuplandway.com

Recommended map: O/S Map no319 — Galloway Forest Park South

Trailhead GPS: NX 37187 78532

Trailhead directions: Heading southeast from Ayrshire on the A714, turn left off the main road at Bargrennan, following the signs for Glentrool village. After passing the Glentrool Holiday Park and House o' Hill pub, turn right at the sign for the Glentrool Forestry Commission for Scotland visitor center. Drive a further 0.8km (½ mile), cross the stone bridge, and park adjacent to the center in the large car park.

In 1307, the forested shores of picturesque Loch Trool were witness to one of Robert (later king) Bruce's earliest victories over the invading English army of Edward I. Yet it's not just history that draws walkers to this beautiful, rugged area of the vast Galloway Forest Park. For the southern shoreline of the brooding loch forms part of the Southern Upland Way, at 341km (212 miles) the longest walking route in the country. If you are feeling fit, the walk described here can form the latter 14km (9 miles) of an epic 29km (18-mile) full-day hike that includes an ascent of The Merrick, the highest hill in Southern Scotland. The route is outlined below.

Assuming you choose to walk from the visitor center, head east along the tarmac road past the visitor center car park, following the sign for Bruce's Stone car park.

Almost immediately, you've the opportunity to appreciate the views down the glen as the mixture of native deciduous trees and conifer plantations gives way to the heather-clad hills and crags east and south. Look for wild blackberries and raspberries growing by the roadside.

At 2.4km (1½ miles) down the road you'll pass the turn off to the Loch Trool car park on your right. This is another potential start point, but for ease of navigation, hike in a clockwise direction.

Continue walking east. Along the way you'll also spot a profusion of wild fungi sprouting amongst yellow-, orange-, and blue-colored wildflowers. After Loch Trool comes into view, the road ascends to pass Glen Trool Lodge before finally ending at Bruce's Stone car park.

❶ Bruce's Stone Car Park Bruce's Stone car park is where to gain a wonderful panorama over Loch Trool, east to the crags of Craiglee and south to the equally impressive craggy hilltops of Mulldonoch and Bennanbrack.

As suggested by its name, 10 minutes down a path accessed to the right from the car park is also where to find the famous granite Bruce's Stone, where it's said Robert (later king) the Bruce rested in 1307 after using guerrilla tactics to defeat English soldiers under the command of King Edward I. It's well worth the detour for the photo opportunity of the fantastic views down to Loch Trool.

At the easternmost point of car park, the road becomes a broad gravel track. Now on your left is a sign highlighting the start of the ascent of The Merrick. It's a

Fighting for Scotland

Twice in the forest I hear rustling in nearby trees. Is it the wind, a grazing deer, or a ghost from the distant past? It could easily be the latter. A historic, bloody ambush took place on this very path almost 1,000 years ago.

On 31 March 1307, a relatively minor guerrilla battle took place on the southern shore of Loch Trool, when 300 men led by Robert (later King) the Bruce defeated 1,500 pursuing English soldiers. The battle—or ambush—was a turning point in Scottish history, for it's said victory helped Bruce win the hearts and minds of the Scottish people.

In 1314, 7 years after the Battle of Loch Trool, Robert the Bruce crushed King Edward I's English army at Bannockburn near Stirling to give Scotland independence, and he was crowned King of Scotland.

Walking on, you too may find your mind imagining the bloody scene that resulted from the brutal sword and axe fighting that raged along this steep hillside and saw many an English horseman consigned to a watery grave in Loch Trool.

long, strenuous climb, and a 13km (8-mile) return trip. Assuming you only seek a rewarding hike around Loch Trool, ignore the sign and stay on the main path.

Initially, the road dips towards the lochside then levels out to cut through a swathe of deciduous trees. As a wilderness area designated a Site of Special Scientific Interest (SSSI), the area may reveal ravens in early spring and the black-and-white plumage of a pied flycatcher, or in early summer the eye-catching redstart.

After passing through a series of gates and a cattle grid, your next route indicator is a stout wooden bridge over a burn.

❷ **Forest Walk Sign** Beyond the bridge by 0.8km (½ mile), a broad, grassy footpath veers off the rough road to the right. A large, scrawled sign pinned to a tree stating FOREST WALK instructs you to turn right in order to reach the south side of the loch.

The path now snakes through the trees for around 183m (600 ft.) with the rushing burn on your right. Look out for the series of bird boxes positioned high up on the tree trunks. After just a minute's amble

along this path, you come to another wooden bridge.

❸ **Wooden Bridge** Here, deep in Galloway Forest Park, you finally have an opportunity to explore several miles of the Southern Upland Way.

On crossing the bridge, ignore the path on your left and walk to the right along an obvious stony path. A lovely old dry-stane (stone) wall is on your right and towering conifers are on your left.

Veering west, the path begins to undulate with the contours of the steeply wooded hillside. Tree roots cross the path, below which the heather falls away to the lochside 30m (100 ft.) below. Across the water, it's just possible to spot the faint track winding toward the distant Merrick.

❹ **Trail Intersection with Road** After almost 4.8km (3 miles) of walking, the track suddenly climbs and turns inland, obscuring the black waters of Loch Trool from view. It then abruptly falls into the woods, crossing a stream as it veers northwest for 91m (300 ft.). Here, the path meets a rough road.

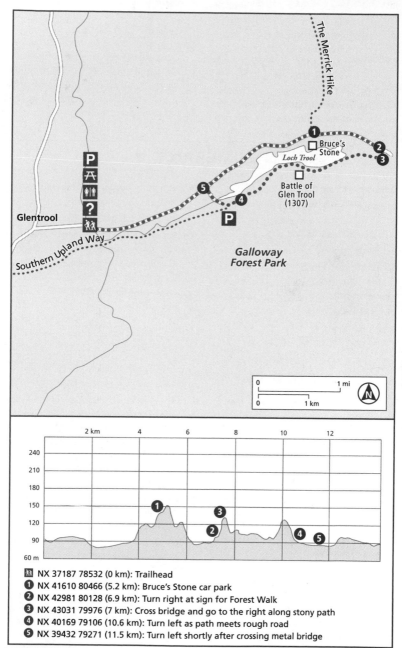

5

LOCH TROOL

🚶 NX 37187 78532 (0 km): Trailhead
❶ NX 41610 80466 (5.2 km): Bruce's Stone car park
❷ NX 42981 80128 (6.9 km): Turn right at sign for Forest Walk
❸ NX 43031 79976 (7 km): Cross bridge and go to the right along stony path
❹ NX 40169 79106 (10.6 km): Turn left as path meets rough road
❺ NX 39432 79271 (11.5 km): Turn left shortly after crossing metal bridge

Turn left onto this rough road. After a minute's walk, it suddenly divides again. Take the right fork, wandering along an old tarmac road that curves around a vast open clearing of high grass, nettles, and wildflowers. Another few minutes of walking and you'll turn right again to cross an old, metal bridge.

❺ Glen Trool Road Junction Just past the metal bridge, you come to a junction.

Turn right here and follow the tree-lined tarmac road for 0.8km ($^1/_2$ mile) as it first crosses a wooden bridge and then passes through the Glen Trool car park to the junction with the Glen Trool Road you walked earlier in the day. Turn left to walk 3.2km (2 miles) west to the visitor center at the trailhead, reflecting on your walk amidst natural surroundings that long ago helped shape Scottish history.

THE MERRICK ★

Difficulty rating: Strenuous

Distance: 23km (14 miles) round-trip from visitor center; 13km (8 miles) round-trip from Bruce's Stone car park.

Estimated time: 5 to 6 hours from the visitor center; 4 hours if starting at Bruce's Stone car park.

Elevation gain: 764m (2507 ft.)

Costs/permits: None

Best time to go: Any clear day; in winter, be equipped for snow conditions.

Website: www.forestry.gov.uk/scotland; www.southernuplandway.com

Recommended map: O/S Map no.318— Galloway Forest Park North

Trailhead GPS: NX 37187 78532

Trailhead directions: Heading southeast from Ayrshire on the A714, turn left off the main road at Bargrennan, following the signs for Glentrool village. After passing the Glentrool Holiday Park and House o' Hill pub, turn right at the sign for the Glentrool Forestry Commission for Scotland visitor center. Drive a further 0.8km ($^1/_2$ mile), cross the stone bridge, and park adjacent to the center in the large car park.

One hundred thirty kilometers (81 miles) south of Glasgow and in the midst of the Galloway Forest Park, the grass- and heather-clad hump of The Merrick rises high above the surrounding landscape. If you seek a challenging hike, The Merrick (770m/2,529 ft.), the highest mountain in southern Scotland, fits the bill. On a clear day, from its summit you can scan right across Galloway and the Borders, even as far as Ireland and Mull of Kintyre to the west and the distant Munro peak of Ben Lomond, 48km (30 miles) north of Glasgow. Moreover, if you are feeling very fit, The Merrick can form part of an epic 29km (18-mile) full-day hike. For after descending from the hill there's the option to include a circuit of historic Loch Trool where, in 1307, Robert (later king) the Bruce ambushed English soldiers under King Edward I. Refer to the Loch Trool walk above.

From the visitor center, head east along the tarmac road past the visitor center car park, following the sign for Bruce's Stone car park.

There is the option to walk paths through the dense coniferous plantations on your left, but it's all too easy to become disorientated. So remain on the road for this first section. Certainly, you've the chance to appreciate the views east down the glen, a mixture of native deciduous trees and conifer plantations giving way to heather-clad hills and crags. In late summer, wild blackberries, raspberries, nettles,

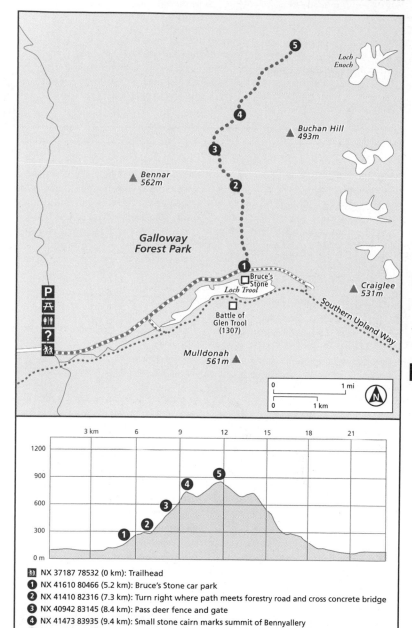

SOUTHERN SCOTLAND WALKS

5

THE MERRICK

NX 37187 78532 (0 km): Trailhead

❶ NX 41610 80466 (5.2 km): Bruce's Stone car park

❷ NX 41410 82316 (7.3 km): Turn right where path meets forestry road and cross concrete bridge

❸ NX 40942 83145 (8.4 km): Pass deer fence and gate

❹ NX 41473 83935 (9.4 km): Small stone cairn marks summit of Bennyallery

❺ NX 42762 85545 (11.6 km): Summit of the Merrick

Time Saver

The visitor center by Stroan Bridge has an excellent cafe (℡ **01671 840302;** open daily, 9am to 5pm, Easter–October) that sells maps and has picnic tables with lovely views over the river. It's worthwhile to enjoy a breakfast roll, scone, or mug of tea here before setting off, for there's no facility farther east. There are also toilets by the car park. However, if pressed for time, drive your car to Loch Trool car park or the full 3 miles east up Glen Trool to park at the road end near Bruce's Stone.

SOUTHERN SCOTLAND WALKS

5

THE MERRICK

thistles, and all manner of fungi can be spotted growing by the roadside.

Down the road 2.4km (1¹/₂ miles), you'll pass the turn off to Loch Trool car park on your right. This is another potential start point but, for ease of navigation, hike in a clockwise direction.

Continue walking east. Beyond Glen Trool Lodge and mid-way along the southern banks of Loch Trool you'll meet Bruce's Stone car park (no charge) at the road end.

❶ **Bruce's Stone Car Park** Bruce's Stone car park is where to gain a wonderful panorama over Loch Trool, east to the crags of Craiglee and south to the equally impressive craggy hilltops of Mulldonoch and Bennanbrack.

From the car park, a small path winds down to the right to Bruce's Stone, a granite stone where there's fabulous views over the loch. The simple stone marks the spot where it's said Robert (later king) the Bruce rested in 1307 after using guerrilla tactics to defeat English soldiers under the command of King Edward I. The actual Battle of Glen Trool took place amidst the trees on the opposite shore. This is also a good spot for an impromptu bite to eat before ascending The Merrick.

At the easternmost point of Bruce's Stone car park, the road becomes a broad gravel track. On your left is a sign that marks the start of the ascent of The Merrick.

Arguably, the first 20 minutes offer a taste of the varied terrain that lies ahead. Initially, the narrow path ascends gently through the heather, following the Buchan Burn. The path soon becomes progressively steeper, ascending towards the east-facing, forested slopes of Bennan.

As you ascend, high above the Buchan waterfall to your right, you gain a good view of the landscape to the north. The crags of the Braes of Mulgarvie become clearly visible, hanging from the southern slopes of Benyellary, over which you'll eventually pass to reach The Merrick.

Pressing north, you'll briefly walk through a coniferous forest, the path carpeted with pines and the landscape cloaked in silence. The route then passes through a torn and gray landscape of felled trees before directly passing an old, abandoned and windowless bothy (cottage) called Culsharg. Long ago, the occupant enjoyed a beautiful southern view across the rolling, forested hills. This is another good place for a quick bite to eat before being exposed to the elements high above the tree-line.

❷ **Forestry Road** Ten minutes' steep ascent from the bothy, the path meets a forestry road. Turn right and over the concrete bridge, 4.6m (15 ft.) beyond which a sign now points left to a path that ascends directly through a gap in the coniferous plantation. If you're very lucky you'll spot deer in the adjacent forest. But on emerging above the tree-line onto the mud and gravel path, it's more likely your thoughts will be filled with the realization that your destination lies way beyond the rounded, distant hump of Benyellary. Keep going!

❸ Gate and Moorland Continue to ascend over high, boggy moor to a solitary deer fence and gate. Beyond this the path veers north east towards the cairn on Benyellary, though the summit of The Merrick remains hidden. As you ascend the grassy west-facing slope of Benyellary, take the time to admire the view south. From this altitude a series of deep blue lochans looks like puddles formed by the footsteps of a giant.

Look west to see the gray volcanic dome of Ailsa Craig poke over the horizon. Lying several miles off the Ayrshire coast in the Firth of Clyde, it's renowned as a nesting site for gannets and all manner of seabirds. Moreover, the blue granite quarried from the isle is prized by curlers around the world and provided the stones used by Scotland's curlers to win Olympic gold at the 2002 Winter Olympics.

❹ Summit of Benyellary Finally, after over 2 hours of hiking, you'll reach the flattish, grassy summit of Benyellary, where a huge jumble of small stones marks the summit cairn.

If the weather is turning for the worse, this is where to turn back, because the

remainder of the walk is very exposed. From the summit, you can clearly see The Merrick, sitting above the long, curving spine of a ridge called the Scars of Benyellary.

It's still over 0.8km ($^1/_2$ mile) to the summit, and on the day I made the ascent I was glad to have packed a cozy fleece and windproof jacket. From Benyellary, follow the obvious path downhill, keeping the dry-stane wall on your left. Soon you are on the aforementioned Scar of Benyellary, offering a superb view east towards the impressive crags of Buchan Hilland right across the Forest of Galloway. As you walk this ridge, keep to the left, hugging the boundary wall. The eastern slope falls away sharply to the forest far below.

❺ Summit of The Merrick From the ridge, the path becomes far less defined, and though the wall heads northwest, the summit cairn lies more north-northeast.

The ascent can be a slog, but the panorama from the top makes your labor worthwhile. To the east, the lochans sit like puddles in the depression of craggy brown hills, while to the north, the farming and forestry lands of Galloway Forest Park create a patchwork of yellows, greens, and browns. To the west, Ailsa Craig is just visible, and much farther west you may be able to spot the faint outline of Ireland.

PEEBLES ★

Difficulty rating: Easy

Distance: 5.3km (3.3 miles) round-trip

Estimated time: 1.5 hours

Elevation gain: Minimal

Costs/permits: Parking £1 for 5 hours

Best time to go: Peebles is especially rewarding during the kaleidoscope of autumn colors.

Website: www.peebles.info

Recommended map: Ask at the tourist office in Peebles for a map of its local riverside walks.

Trailhead GPS: NT 24897 40382

Trailhead directions: Follow the A703 out of Edinburgh and south for 40km (25 miles), passing through Penicuik and rolling farmland with the Pentland Hills initially on your right. At the roundabout in Peebles, turn right, drive along the main street and immediately take the first left to park by the river.

A small, bustling market town with attractive 18th-century architecture and commanding views over the salmon-rich Tweed, King David (1080–1153) obviously understood Peebles' appeal when he proclaimed it a royal burgh. Archaeological finds of Iron Age dwellings in nearby Glentress Forest also suggest these fertile lands in the Tweed valley have been settled for millennia. Add the fact that this glorious riverside walk includes a 13th-century castle and wonderful opportunities for capturing nature and autumnal reflections by the Tweed and you'll understand why Peebles is a popular location to explore.

Park and walk southwest across the car park to the river bank. Here, beyond a small metal footbridge, a stone path runs along the northern shore of the River Tweed and past many quacking ducks. Strike west, walking upstream away from the town and the distinctive red sandstone 18th-century arched road bridge just visible from your starting point.

Initially, the path is suitable for wheelchairs, as it tracks towards a metal footbridge 0.4km ¹/₄ mile) upstream. Within 5 minutes you'll be strolling through open parkland. On the day I visited, wisps of mist hung over the dense coniferous and deciduous oak woodland that rise steeply from the riverbanks.

Continuing west, ignore the metal footbridge and follow the narrow path at the western edge of the park that begins to wind above the Tweed.

As you walk, enjoy the sight of birds feeding in the river's clear waters. The tall, slender herons stand like sentries, their long beaks poised to skewer a juicy fish.

❶ Neidpath Castle After almost a mile of walking, you pass through a small wooden gate to find yourself walking by the river surrounded by wild grassland. Look up to your right and you can't miss the star attraction on this hike—the 13th-century Neidpath Castle.

Above overgrown terraces, its sheer gray and black peppered walls tower over 46m (150 ft.) above the river. Privately owned, it's remarkably intact, with only some of its upper tower sections having crumbled away.

After marveling at the castle, continue southwest along the picturesque river bank. The path now narrows again, twisting and turning through the silent trees. Two hundred meters (656 ft.) beyond the

---

ⓕFun Facts   Neidpath

Locals will tell you that the original castle was built around 1260, possibly by a Sir Simon Fraser, who supported freedom fighter William Wallace (later to be betrayed and martyred in London) against the English. What's certain is that by 1370 it had been rebuilt by the Hays of Yester, fashioning the L-shape structure to be seen today.

Many famous visitors are known to have walked inside the walls of this imposing structure, including Mary Queen of Scots (1563); her son James VI (1587); and 300 years later, Sir Walter Scott, one of Scotland's most famous literary figures.

Though severely damaged, the castle walls also survived a prolonged siege by Cromwellian forces in the 1600s. It's said the Maid of Neidpath is the ghost who can occasionally be seen within this ancient castle.

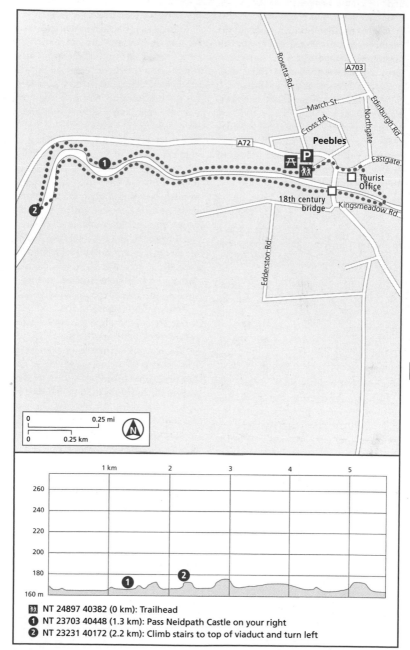

🚶 NT 24897 40382 (0 km): Trailhead
❶ NT 23703 40448 (1.3 km): Pass Neidpath Castle on your right
❷ NT 23231 40172 (2.2 km): Climb stairs to top of viaduct and turn left

castle, the river sweeps around a corner and the landscape again rewards you for your decision to walk this route.

In the distance upriver, through the overhanging trees, six graceful arches of a beautifully engineered viaduct come into view, a reminder that steam trains once puffed through this part of the Borders.

Sadly, financial realities forced the railway to close in 1962, though there are murmurings that the Borders will someday again be serviced by a railway line. However, this particular viaduct seems destined to continue as an ornate and unusual means for walkers to cross the Tweed.

❷ Stairway to Viaduct On reaching the bridge, you'll easily spot the flight of steps that leads to the top of the viaduct. At the top, turn left to enjoy the views east and west as you walk 18m (60 ft.) above the river.

On reaching the southern bank, ignore the path to your right and head immediately left, following the trail as it threads through stands of mixed woodland.

Walking east back towards Peebles, within 20 minutes you have the perfect unobstructed view of Neidpath Castle to photograph it in all its glory.

Continue hiking east. For a few minutes, as the path becomes increasingly rocky and narrow, you may wonder if you are on the right route. However, just as you begin to question your navigational skills, you'll suddenly emerge from the woods onto the type of stone path that also formed the start of your walk.

Once again, (unless you want a shortcut back to your car on the northern riverbank) ignore the metallic Tweed footbridge and continue east along the southern shoreline, admiring the views of Peebles now coming into view. For a few minutes, your riverbank walk now goes a short distance through a park.

A short flight of stone steps then leads up onto the roadway of a beautiful stone bridge that crosses the Tweed adjacent to the former town courthouse. Here too you can choose to curtail your walk, turning left to cross the bridge and locate the car park just round the corner from the old courthouse.

However, to enjoy a lovely perspective of the town's 18th-century architecture from the riverbank, walk across the road and descend the steep steps to once again stroll by the Tweed.

Follow this path for 152m (500 ft.) before crossing to the north bank via the ornate metal cantilever bridge.

Now cut directly north for a few minutes, walking up the old mews passageways to emerge onto Main Street. Turn left and walk to the end of the street to find your car and starting point. Alternatively, celebrate the end of your rewarding walk with a visit to **Sunflower** (© **01721 722420**), arguably the best restaurant in town.

SELKIRK TO ABBOTSFORD HOUSE

Difficulty rating: Easy to moderate

Distance: 11km (7 miles) one-way

Estimated time: 2.5 hours

Elevation gain: 150m (492 ft.)

Costs/permits: None

Best time to go: Spring and autumn to enjoy the landscape in full color and avoid the busiest period at Abbotsford House.

Website: www.scottsabbotsford.co.uk / www.bordersabbeysway.fsnet.co.uk

Recommended map: O/S Explorer Map no.338: Galashiels, Selkirk and Melrose (1:25,000)

Trailhead GPS: NT 47012 28477

Trailhead directions: Driving east on the Edinburgh city bypass, take the turnoff for the A7 and follow all road signs for

Selkirk, 64km (40 miles) south. In the town square, turn right and immediately take the first left to park for free. By bus, catch the no.X95 (3 times daily, 1hr. 35 min.) from Edinburgh Bus Station to Selkirk via Galashiels. Note that you will need to take a taxi at the end of the walk to return to the start point.

The Borders Abbeys Way winds through 105km (65 miles) of countryside rich in history and attractive, rolling Borders scenery. Yet the picturesque walk could arguably be renamed Sir Walter Scott's Way. From 1799 he ruled as sheriff in Selkirk, while he ended his days at his fascinating baronial home of Abbotsford House, close to his beloved Eildon Hills. It was also in Selkirk in 1298 that William Wallace was proclaimed the "Guardian of Scotland" following his victory over the English at the Battle of Stirling Bridge.

Whether you drive or take the bus, your start point is the grand monument to Sir Walter Scott in the tiny square. But before heading east up Kirk Wynd, pop into the bakery for a taste of the famous Selkirk bannock, best described as a cross between a scone and an oatcake. Then pop into the old courthouse where Sir Walter Scott meted out justice as the sheriff from 1799. From the statue, walk directly up Kirk Wynd and past the "Auld Kirkyard." It was near here that in 1113 a Tironensian abbey was founded before being moved to nearby Kelso in 1138.

Continue up the road that becomes South Port then The Loan. After 0.8km (½ mile), you'll reach the A7 with a petrol station on your left. Go directly across to briefly follow the A699. At 4.8km (3 miles) east beyond Selkirk Hill, you'll see the large television tower close to which you'll soon walk.

Now follow a low wall with horses in the field to your left. After 183m (600 ft.) there's a path on your left marked "Borders Abbeys Way."

❶ **Wooden Sign** At the wooden sign, marked BORDERS ABBEYS WAY, that appears 1.6km (1 mile) after leaving Selkirk, turn left down the narrow path that cuts through farmland and initially runs just below the fairways of Selkirk Golf Club. Almost immediately you are rewarded by fine views of Selkirk and the long, undulating profile of the hills to the north, once carpeted by the ancient Ettrick Forest.

You'll begin to spot different varieties of deciduous trees and wildflower along the path, the latter including harebell. Occasional hoof marks on the grassy path are also a reminder of Selkirk's annual Common Riding Event, dating back to the Battle of Flodden in 1513.

It won't be long before you spy a picnic bench from which to enjoy the superb views west and north. You may also already spot buzzards, ravens, and bullfinches. Just beyond a modern rain shelter, the path divides. Take the route that goes up a flight of wooden steps.

The grassy path then meets a tarmac road by Buxton House. Turn right, continuing through a gate beyond which the road becomes a muddy farm track overlooked by holly trees and wild fruit bushes.

❷ **Trail Diversion** Three kilometers (2¾ miles) after leaving Selkirk, a sign off the farm track instructs you to take the diversion to the left and skirt the boundary of a field of sheep. Ten minutes later, after passing a wooden bench that offers wonderful views west to Selkirk, you'll go through two obvious farm gates to emerge onto a tarmac road. As indicated by the sign, walk east up the road past farmland.

At a farm called Woodlands, 4.8km (3 miles) into your walk, the Borders Abbeys Way abruptly points left off the road and down a muddy path. This section is littered

(Fun Facts)   Ancient Crafts

Dry-stane walls crisscross Border country and indeed much of mainland Scotland. Built by landowners to mark boundaries, these impressive structures are hand-crafted. No cement is used to seal each of the scores of large and small rough stones in place. Only the craftsman's eye and skillful hand ensure the wall is solidly built.

with feathers discarded by the dozens of geese, ducks, and hens bred by the farmer, and it's easily the noisiest part of the entire walk!

❸ Farm Road and Gate   One hundred meters (328 ft.) down this track, the path crosses a farm road and passes through a wooden gate. The path then climbs steadily east through the rough moorland of the Whitlaw Kips. An impressive, meter-high (3.2-ft.), dry-stane wall accompanies your progress on the right.

You are now walking a drove route used in centuries past by hardy clansmen to drive their cattle to the markets in England. Scott is among the writers who have drawn inspiration from the tales of the Border reivers (outlaws) who stole cattle along such routes. This region still has a rugby team called the Border Reivers.

After 6.4km (4 miles), you pass a long avenue of wild berry trees with the rolling moorland to the right suddenly breaking to reveal the striking humps of the Eildon Hills above the market town of Melrose to the southeast. Atop Eildon Hill North, beloved by Sir Walter Scott, archaeologists have discovered a Roman signal station.

❹ Faldonside Loch   After your brisk hike over the moor, a sign points right towards Faldonside Loch. Take this turn and after 6m (20 ft.) turn left before the loch to wind through a copse of deciduous trees. Keep left and the path soon comes to a small car park. Go through here and follow the tarmac road for 0.8km (1/2 mile). At the

bottom of the hill, turn right at the junction onto another stretch of farm road.

❺ Heathery Rig Plantation Junction   After you turn right at the junction called Heathery Rig Plantation and pass countless sheep, another farm road will quickly appear on your left. Take this and hike north for almost 1.6km (1 mile), noting a lovely building on your left called Abbotsmoss House.

❻ Road Junction at Shillinglaw Plantation   Turn left at the next road junction by another plantation of conifers to make your final push towards Abbotsford House. En route you'll pass a large farm with barns before descending to the B6360 where a car park for Abbotsford House sits on your immediate left.

The Borders Abbeys Way now directly crosses the B6360 and dives through the trees to the right of a high stone wall.

Instead of following the road, go to the left of that high wall to enter the grounds of the baronial former home of Sir Walter Scott.

Turreted and overlooking a beautiful walled garden, it's packed with fascinating antiquities collected by Scott, including armor from the Napoleonic Wars and the gun of 17th-century Scottish clan hero, Rob Roy. Almost 200 years after Scott's death, Abbotsford House, where the library ceiling is painted as a copy of Rosslyn Chapel (think *The Da Vinci Code*) remains almost a shrine to the works and memory of one of Scotland's greatest masters of letters.

SOUTHERN SCOTLAND WALKS

5

SELKIRK TO ABBOTSFORD HOUSE

NT 47012 28477 (0 km): Trailhead
1 NT 47796 7916 (1.2 km): Turn left at sign for Borders Abbey Way
2 NT 48851 29330 (3.2 km): Follow diversion to the left and skirt sheep field
3 NT 50934 32474 (8.2 km): Path crosses farm road and passes through wooden gate
4 NT 51085 32999 (8.9 km): Turn right at sign for Faldonside Loch
5 NT 51638 33591 (10 km): Turn right at Heathery Rig Plantation junction
6 NT 51430 33884 (10.4 km): Turn left at junction adjacent to Shillinglaw Plantation

Even if you don't wish to pay (£7 adult) to explore the house and gardens (☎ **01896 752043**; www.scottsabbotsford.co.uk), it's recommended to pop into the Quill Tea Room for tasty homemade soup and a sandwich before calling a taxi (try **Star Taxis**; ☎ **01896 756789**; £8.50 one-way) back to Selkirk and your start point.

MELROSE TO HARESTANES ★

Difficulty rating: Strenuous

Distance: 33km (20 miles), one-way

Estimated time: 7 to 8.5 hours, one-way

Elevation gain: 249m (817 ft.)

Costs/permits: None

Best time to go: The landscape's vibrant colors are best in late spring and early autumn.

Website: www.st-cuthberts-way.co.uk

Recommended map: "St. Cuthbert's Way Trail Map," by Harvey Maps (£7).

Trailhead GPS: NT 54787 34109

Trailhead directions: This walk starts an hour's drive south of Edinburgh down the A7, in the proud and picturesque Border town of Melrose. Leave the A7 at Galashiels for the A6091 and enter Melrose along the B6374. On entering the town and passing the rugby ground, park opposite the ruin of Melrose Abbey by the visitor center.

In Scottish sport, the Borders region is renowned for their quality of rugby, producing many of the nation's top players. Yet on this long walk, which follows a picturesque section of the 100km-long (62-mile) St. Cuthbert's Way, you can see how Borders country is also rich in ancient history, spectacular views, world-class salmon fishing, and tasty food stops. Note that this is a one-way hike that requires returning to your start point by taxi.

With your rucksack prepared for a full day's hike, your day begins on Abbey Street outside the impressive 14th-century ruins of Melrose Abbey, believed to be where the heart of King Robert the Bruce, who defeated the English army at Bannockburn in 1314, is buried. It's a fitting reminder that your walk will be retracing the route taken by the 6th-century apostle St. Cuthbert, whose body was for a period interred here.

Facing the entrance to the abbey, turn right and walk up Abbey Street, crossing through Market Square. Continue until you pass under a bridge carrying the A6091.

Now keep a sharp eye out for the small green ST. CUTHBERT'S WAY sign that appears a minute or two beyond the town boundary, pointing left onto a rough farm road. Take this and immediately cross the stile on your right to follow the muddy path for 61m (200 ft.) alongside farmland. On crossing another stile, turn left and follow the path to the end. Over the next stile, turn right to spot the distinctive cross-shaped waymarker of the St. Cuthbert's Way. As you'll see, the path runs directly up into the Eildon Hills.

❶ **Bench "To Old Friends"** The words "To Old Friends" inscribed on a bench by the path is a reminder that many have enjoyed the spectacular view over Melrose.

The climb here is unrelenting, but press on, passing through a series of wooden gates, through the thick, red mud.

❷ **Right Turn at Post** The path veers right at a wooden post to traverse under the flattish summit of Eildon Hill North,

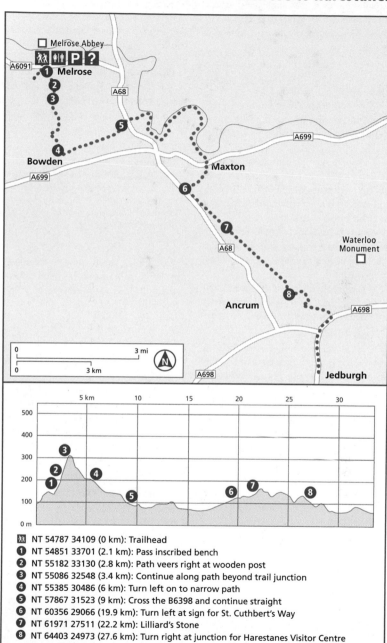

🧍 NT 54787 34109 (0 km): Trailhead
❶ NT 54851 33701 (2.1 km): Pass inscribed bench
❷ NT 55182 33130 (2.8 km): Path veers right at wooden post
❸ NT 55086 32548 (3.4 km): Continue along path beyond trail junction
❹ NT 55385 30486 (6 km): Turn left on to narrow path
❺ NT 57867 31523 (9 km): Cross the B6398 and continue straight
❻ NT 60356 29066 (19.9 km): Turn left at sign for St. Cuthbert's Way
❼ NT 61971 27511 (22.2 km): Lilliard's Stone
❽ NT 64403 24973 (27.6 km): Turn right at junction for Harestanes Visitor Centre

SOUTHERN SCOTLAND WALKS

5

MELROSE TO HARESTANES

where, almost 2,000 years ago, a Roman signal station on the summit was garrisoned by hardy centurions.

❸ Trail Junction After nearly 3.2km (2 miles) of ascent, you'll finally pass between the two summits, with the option at a small junction to climb to the remains of the signal station.

With over 26km (16 miles) to go, I recommend pressing on, savoring the views south over rolling farmland towards the border.

The route now plunges through Broad Wood, initially following a farm track. Shortly after taking a right fork in the road, you veer left down a muddy path lined by a high hedgerow that skirts a farmer's field. For the next 0.8km ($^1/_2$ mile), the route includes several wooden stile gates before emerging onto a clearing above the village of Bowden.

Where the path meets the road, turn right and 30m (100 ft.) later turn left at the signpost for Bowden Kirk.

❹ Left Turn at Sign At the first bend on this tarmac road, a sign directs you left along a narrow path running beside a barley field. You now hike east past wildflowers and huge oaks.

You eventually emerge from the secluded path at a road by Whitelee Farm Cottages. Turn left and walk the next 1.6km (1 mile) into Newtown St. Boswell's. En route you pass under a viaduct that until the 1960s carried the Borders railway line.

❺ Road Crossing The route now meets the B6398 running through Newtown St. Boswells. Cross the road. Now walk straight ahead, following the road until at a corner you come to a red stone house called "Rowena." Turn left here and wind down past the cattle market until you come to a sign under a road bridge carrying the A68. Here, turn right onto a narrow path.

It's along this stretch of forest above the River Tweed that I met a couple finding rich pickings of purple slough berries for preparing their festive gin.

Press on south above the Tweed as birdsong and occasional St. Cuthbert waymarker posts accompany you through the forest. Eventually you emerge on Hamilton Road into St. Boswell's.

Turn left onto the main street and walk south through the village past the post office, a hunting shop called Borders Gunroom, and a supermarket.

If you're hungry, it's worthwhile tucking into hearty fresh sandwiches and coffee at the **Main Street Trading Company** located halfway through the village.

Continuing south through the village, turn left into Braehead Road and descend towards the river again. After turning right where indicated below the golf club, you'll wander the southern banks of the idyllic Tweed for several miles, possibly watching fishermen cast for salmon, before climbing through forest to emerge at the peaceful Maxton Kirk.

Walk past the church, a site of worship for 1,000 years, until you meet the A699 at a pink painted house. Turn right. Down this road 61m (200 ft.), turn left and follow the road for almost 1.6km (1 mile) while spotting the Eildon Hills you hiked over several hours earlier.

❻ Dere Street Path Just before your road meets the busy A68 Edinburgh/Jedburgh road, a St. Cuthbert's Way sign points left down a tree-lined path. Passing through an avenue of gnarled trees flanked by farmland, this path is actually a 1,500-year-old Roman highway called "Dere Street."

❼ Lilliard's Stone As if to reinforce the fact you are taking steps back in history, several miles south the grassy, undulating path lined by varieties of fungi and bright wildflowers passes Lilliard's Stone. The Stone marks the grave of a Maxton girl who in 1544 bravely fought the English invaders sent by King Henry VIII. As part of the inscription by her grave relates in verse, "Upon the English loons, she laid monie thumps an' when her legs were cuttit' off she fought upon her stumps." Her final resting place is in an idyllic spot overlooking the Borders country for which she fought and died so long ago.

The route continues pressing south along Dere Street, crossing the bleak expanse of Ancrum Moor, where in 1545 the Scots defeated an English raiding force. On your left is the 46m-high (150-ft.) Waterloo Monument, built in 1817 to commemorate the Battle of Waterloo.

Eventually, your tired legs will scale a 2.1m-high (7-ft.) stile at the end of a field. Beyond this you'll cross a road to follow a wide path through deciduous forest. You'll then cross a high wooden bridge spanning a stream and shortly thereafter cross over the B6400.

❽ Harestanes Junction As you continue to follow the ST. CUTHBERT'S WAY, DERE STREET signs, it won't be too long before your path meets a junction with the option to turn right for **Harestanes Visitor Centre,** just 15 minutes' walk to the west. It is recommended that you take this route, completing your walk at the lovely cafe in Harestanes (📞 **01573 224808;** open Apr–Oct daily, 10am–5pm) and calling a taxi to return to your start point in Melrose.

Alternatively, continue south along Dere Street for another 4.8km (3 miles) to Jedburgh. Initially, you'll head southeast along the river bank, cross a bridge, and wind through a forest before veering south.

At a road bridge, climb the steps and ignore the Dere Street sign, turning right to walk for a few minutes up the A698. Turn left at the first road junction and left again at the end to walk the final mile into the historic village of Jedburgh. Here you can eat before catching a taxi (£20 one-way) back to Melrose.

COLDINGHAM—ST. ABB'S HEAD—EYEMOUTH ★

Difficulty rating: Moderate/challenging

Distance: 16km (10 miles) round-trip

Estimated time: 4 to 7 hours

Elevation gain: 57m (187 ft.)

Costs/permits: None

Best time to go: Mid- to late summer for the wildflowers, bracing sea air, and surfing.

Website: www.marine-reserve.co.uk

Recommended map: O/S Landranger map, Duns, Dunbar and Eyemouth, 1:50,000

Trailhead GPS: NT 91527 66504

Trailhead directions: Sixty-eight kilometers (42 miles) east of Edinburgh, turn off the A1 onto the A1107 for the 13km (8-mile) drive to Coldingham. In the village, follow signs for St. Abb's Head, but turn right down the road at the caravan park. Park 1.6km (1 mile) down this road, by the St. Vedas Hotel. Via public transit, buses N235 and 260 run four times daily among St. Abb's, Coldingham, and Eyemouth. The bus also runs to the train station in Berwick to return to Edinburgh.

This is a spectacular coastal walk, sections of which include hiking along the edge of very exposed sea cliffs. Aside from the fabulous views across the North Sea, the route includes historic lands managed by the National Trust for Scotland. The coastal waters around St. Abb's Head also form Scotland's only Marine Conservation Park. Don't overlook the visitor center and cafe on the outskirts of quaint St. Abb's village; and aside from bird-watching, you can also pop into the St. Vedas Hotel above Coldingham beach to rent a surfboard.

Park by the St. Vedas Hotel that overlooks the nearby golden sands and colorful beach huts. You may spot surfers in the waves. Assuming you opt first for St. Abb's Head, walk along the side of the hotel and follow the tarmac road uphill for 137m (450 ft.) until the road ends at a series of apartments. Here, follow the yellow way-markers skirting the eastern edge of the property, to a gate positioned high above Coldingham beach.

❶ Creel Path and St. Abb's Through the gate, follow the narrow track by a dry-stane wall until you reach a sign marked CREEL PATH. Turning right, you'll spot the raised hump of St. Abb's Head in the distance to the west. Walk 274m (900 ft.) north into sleepy St. Abb's, with its attractive stone-built cottages perched above the sea.

Entering the village, turn left at the first road junction and walk to the very end where the old red sandstone schoolhouse sits at the junction of the main road. Turn left, walking up the B6438 past the striking red-roofed church.

❷ St. Abb's Head Cliff Walk Another 183m (600 ft.) up the road, another sign points right. Walk along this tree-lined path until you reach another gate.

A sign says COASTAL PATH—ST. ABB'S NATIONAL NATURE RESERVE. This is the start of some really exposed and dramatic cliff walking.

Going through the gate, you have no option but to turn left. Fifty-two meters (170 ft.) below, the sea is crashing against ancient, gnarled volcanic rocks sculpted by millennia of erosion.

As you strike northwest, look down and south towards toylike St. Abb's and its stone harbor built in 1832. Scan the cliffs for the signs of over 60,000 seabirds, including kittiwakes, razorbills, fulmars, shags, and guillemots that inhabit this National Nature Reserve.

Beneath these waves lies a myriad of sea life, including rare colorful sponges, eels, and sea-fish. This diversity of fauna and flora in the waters below the cliffs was designated Scotland's first (and still only) Voluntary Marine Reserve (VMR) in 1984. Today, it's a magnet for divers.

After braving the initial 0.8km ($^{1}/_{2}$ mile) of cliff-walking, the obvious route is less exposed as you wind up and down high, grassy slopes away from the cliff edge. In the near distance, sheep cling to the steep slope of Kirk Hill.

On its summit, archaeologists have found the remains of St. Aebbe's monastery and hence the name of St. Abb's.

❸ St. Abb's Lighthouse Before walking a final exposed section of path close to the lighthouse, there's time to admire the swathe of countryside to the west.

As a sign indicates, the grassland around Kirk Hill is the habitat of the rare northern brown argus butterfly, just one of many rare species to be found within the reserve. With a white spot on its wings, it can be spotted from late June to the end of July, feeding on the nectar of wild thyme.

After over 3.2km (2 miles), the path skirts around the southern flank of the whitewashed walls of St. Abb's Lighthouse. Built in 1862, it's perched an eye-watering 85m (280 ft.) above the sea.

Just west of the lighthouse, the coastal path then meets a tarmac road. Follow this for 366m (1,200 ft.) until you come to a hairpin bend overlooking Myre Loch.

❹ Myre Loch to the Visitor Center At the hairpin, leave the road and head southeast along a narrow path that cuts through rough pasture above the small, finger-shaped Myre Loch. Keep an eye out for swans as you hug the hillside and eventually descend to meet the southern extremity of the loch. At a T-junction, turn right, pass through a gate, and follow the rough

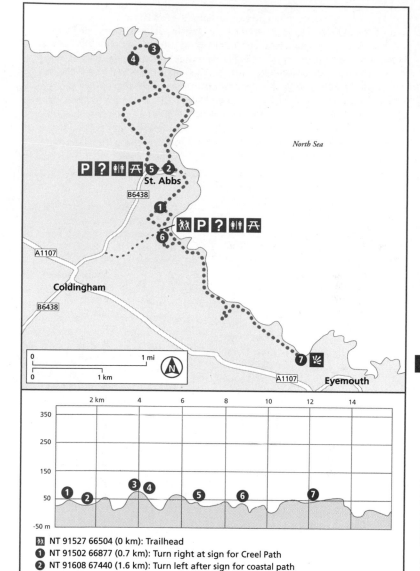

NT 91527 66504 (0 km): Trailhead
1 NT 91502 66877 (0.7 km): Turn right at sign for Creel Path
2 NT 91608 67440 (1.6 km): Turn left after sign for coastal path
3 NT 91391 69171 (3.9 km): St. Abb's Lighthouse
4 NT 91105 69030 (4.4 km): Join narrow path at hairpin bend above Myre Loch
5 NT 91369 67429 (6.7 km): Visitor Center
6 NT 91582 66301 (8.7 km): Turn left onto path marked Coastal Path
7 NT 93540 64698 (12.2 km): First views of Eyemouth

> **(Tips)** **Splitting the Route and Avoiding the Cliffs**
>
> You can easily split this hike into two sections, the first 8.9km (5.5 miles) heading north for a circuit of St. Abb's Head before retracing your steps past the St. Vedas Hotel for a similar return distance hike along the cliffs to Eyemouth. The cliff walk above St. Abb's Head isn't recommended for walkers with young children, in high winds, or if you are susceptible to vertigo. Wear good boots and stick to the path.
>
> If you'd prefer to avoid the high cliffs on St. Abb's Head, after the first waypoint (Creel Path) follow the B6438 out of St. Abb's for 0.8km ($^1/_2$) to the St. Abb's Visitor Centre by a farm on your left. Here, there's an interpretive center describing the area's fauna and flora, including marine life; a wonderful cafe; artists' workshops; and toilets. From here you can hike to the lighthouse by taking the inland route that also forms the latter section of the route described below.

road for 0.8km ($^1/_2$ mile) through farmland and hedgerows laden with wild fruits.

Soon you'll again meet the tarmac road. Turn left and follow it for 1.6km (1 mile) until you descend to a series of farm buildings. It's along this section I spotted two roe deer bolting for cover amidst a copse of trees.

❺ Visitor Center to St. Vedas Hotel After 7.2km (4.5 miles), you'll spot a small car park and the low-roofed cottages that house the visitor center, toilets, craft shops, and excellent Old Smiddy cafe. The cafe serves delicious, good-value sandwiches, soups, and cakes.

After gleaning information about the area's history, fauna, and flora within the visitor center, turn left and head down the B6438 into St. Abb's village. Passing the red-roofed church, retrace your steps back to the St. Vedas Hotel.

❻ Coldingham Bay to Eyemouth You've still 3 hours of walking ahead if you plan to hike the southern cliffs towards Eyemouth.

With your back to the St. Vedas Hotel, walk up the rough track for 122m (400 ft.), passing the youth hostel before turning left onto a small path at a wooden sign marked COASTAL PATH.

After winding along a path lined with wildflowers, including knapweed, birds-foot-trefoil and rockrose, you'll enjoy sweeping views over the dolphin-inhabited waters of Coldingham Bay.

The trail is again obvious as it winds up, down and along the edge of the reddish cliffs. After only 1.6km (1 mile) you'll be forced to jump across a wide stream by the beach before ascending a series of steep wooden steps.

A delight of this walk is the opportunity it gives to appreciate the sharp contrast between the dramatic coastal cliffs that tower over secluded bays and the surrounding patchwork of serene farmland that has been cultivated for centuries. When I startled a pheasant, I was also reminded of the area's wonderful birdlife that includes wrens, stonechats, and thrush.

❼ Eyemouth and Turning for Home After more than 11km (7 miles) of skirting barley fields and climbing over occasional stiles, the path veers close to the cliff edge to reveal the outskirts of Eyemouth directly southeast.

You can't miss the caravan site sprawled across a high promontory. However, it's a further 0.8km ($^1/_2$-mile) walk into the center of the village and its harbor area full of banks and bars.

After exploring, return north to the start point and the St. Vedas Hotel.

SLEEPING & EATING

ACCOMMODATIONS

(Finds) Brig o' Doon House Hotel   Beautifully situated above the River Doon, this welcoming country house hotel combines traditional Scottish hospitality with uninterrupted views of the famous Brig o' Doon arched bridge that inspired the verse of Robert Burns.

High Maybole Rd., Alloway, Ayrshire KA7 4PQ. ℂ **01292 442466.** www.costley.biz. 5 units. Doubles from £120. MC, V. Reservations recommended. **Close to:** Alloway.

Burts Hotel   Who knows if ghosts abound in this delightful small hotel by the market square that dates back to 1722 and is now a listed building (officially protected due to its age)? In the summer, the window boxes are in full bloom and the restaurant serves good-value Scottish fare.

Burts Hotel, Melrose, TD6 9PN. ℂ **01896 822285.** www.burtshotel.co.uk. 20 units. Doubles from £130. MC, V. Reservations recommended. **Close to:** Melrose to Harestanes walk, Selkirk to Abbotsford.

(Value) The County Hotel   Situated close to the historic town square, this friendly, simple, former coaching inn once housed Sir Walter Scott himself. The decor is tasteful and warm, and there's the option of dining on tasty homemade fare in the Souter Lounge.

3-5 High St., Selkirk. TD7 4BZ ℂ **01750 721233.** www.countyhotelselkirk.co.uk. 6 units, all en suite. Doubles from £80 with breakfast. Children under 5 stay free; 6–15 year-olds half price. MC, V. **Close to:** Selkirk to Abbotsford House.

Glenotter Guest House   Sylvia and Graham Holden run a very welcoming, simple guesthouse that definitely goes the extra mile to ensure you enjoy your stay. Delicious traditional breakfast, clean and spacious rooms, and great shower!

Leswalt Rd., Stranraer, DG9 0EP. ℂ **01776 703199.** www.glenotter.co.uk. 3 units. Doubles from £56. Children under 4 stay free. Cash only. **Close to:** Killantringan.

★ **(Value) Scottish Youth Hostel Association (SYHA)**   This Georgian mansion is a budget option with a difference, as from here you overlook historic Melrose Abbey. A superb location, clean and friendly with reasonable self-catering facilities.

Priorwood, Melrose, Roxburghshire, TD6 9EF. ℂ **01896 822521.** www.syha.org.uk. 75 beds. From £14. **Close to:** Melrose to Harestanes.

(Finds) Whitie's Guest House   Right on the main street, this friendly guesthouse and Victorian villa blends old-world character with modern comfort, great views, and every amenity just a few footsteps from your door. You'll love the buffet breakfast.

69 High St., Peebles, EH45 8AN. ℂ **01721 721605.** www.whities.co.uk. 3units, all en suite. Doubles from £75. No credit cards. **Close to:** Peebles.

RESTAURANTS

★ **(Finds) Abbotsford House** CAFE   Within the atmospheric former baronial home of Sir Walter Scott, one of Scotland's literary greats, feast on delicious, great value homemade soup and huge open sandwiches before paying to tour the house and gardens.

Abbotsford House by Melrose. ℂ **01896 752043.** www.scottsabbotsford.co.uk. Soup £3; mains £4.50. Castle/gardens £7. Mar–Oct daily. **Close to:** Selkirk to Abbotsford House.

★ ⓀⒾⒹ**ds Glentrool Visitor Centre** CAFE Aside from the lovely woodland setting, there's good home-baking, and surely you can't resist the haggis toasties!

Glentrool, 16km (10 miles) north of Newton Stewart. ℂ **01671 840302.** www.forestry.gov.uk. Main courses from £3.65. Daily, daytime, Mar–Oct.

★ ⓀⒾⒹ**ds Main Street Trading Company** CAFE This bright, friendly bookshop serves freshly made organic and homemade sandwiches and baked goods, including carrot cake and scones. Try the free-range chicken and hummus sandwich.

Main St., St. Boswells. ℂ **01835 824087.** www.mainstreetbooks.co.uk. Main courses from £3.50. Daytime Tues–Sun. **Close to:** Melrose to Harestanes.

★★ Ⓕ**inds McCallum's Oyster Bar** SCOTTISH This Ayrshire seafood on the harbor is packed with yachting memorabilia. In this rustic setting you'll feast on the best seafood for miles, and the views out to sea.

Harbour Rd., Troon. ℂ **01292 319339.** Reservations recommended. Main courses from £14. AE, V. Closed Mon. **Close to:** Dundonald Glen and Alloway.

Ⓥ**alue The Old Loans Inn** BISTRO/BAR This archetypal country pub serves up a good range of bar meals, real ales, and whiskies in a friendly atmosphere. The Sunday roast is great value for lunch.

Main St., Loan. ℂ **01292 315976.** Main courses from £8. Daily. MC, V. Reservations recommended. **Close to:** Dundonald Glen.

Russell's Restaurant SCOTTISH Overlooking the square, this prim eatery also serves delicious lunches, including a hearty Border Roast as its specialty. Nip in for afternoon tea, but leave your muddy boots at the door!

28 Market Sq., Melrose. ℂ **01896 822335.** Mains from £8.50. AE, V. Tues–Sun. **Close to:** Melrose.

Ⓥ**alue The Secret Garden** CAFE This simple cafe sits in the heart of Burns country and offers no-nonsense, hearty sandwiches and good light bites that won't break the bank.

94 Doonfoot Rd., Alloway. ℂ **01292 442465.** Lunch mains from £4. V only. Open 0900–1700 Mon–Sat. **Close to:** Alloway.

★★ Ⓥ**alue Sunflower** SCOTTISH From chicken-and-fig salad to succulent Scottish beef and dreamy desserts, this airy, cozy restaurant always tickles your tastebuds and doesn't empty your wallet.

4 Bridgegate, Peebles. ℂ **01721 722420.** www.thesunflower.net. Reservations recommended. Main courses £7–£14. V only. Open for coffee Mon–Sat, 1000–1130; lunch Mon–Sat, 1200–1500; dinner Thur–Sat only, 1800–2100. **Close to:** Peebles.

The Waterfront Bistro and Bar BISTRO Pleasant harbor-front bar bistro with al fresco dining. Varied menu includes lobster (£30) and gargantuan seafood platter (£50). Good-value Sunday specials and open sandwiches.

7 North Crescent, Portpatrick. ℂ **01776 810800.** www.waterfronthotel.co.uk. Main courses from £7. Open 7 days; coffee all day, starting at 0800; lunch 1200–1500; dinner 1800–2100. Daily lunch and dinner. MC, V. **Close to:** Killantringan lighthouse.

SOUTHERN SCOTLAND WALKS

5

SLEEPING & EATING

6

Tayside & Fife Walks

by Felicity Martin

A great diversity of scenery makes this part of Scotland an ideal base if you want to enjoy coastal and mountain scenery and everything in between. It is also highly accessible from the major cities, so it is easy to explore on day trips.

The old county of Perthshire, which makes up the largest part of this region, covers the whole of the catchment of the River Tay, Scotland's mightiest river. Many tributaries and lochs feed the Tay, which is famed for its salmon- and trout-fishing. The "Fair City" of Perth has a beautiful location on the river, just where it becomes tidal, and is adjoined by Scone, the ancient seat of kings. Perth is the capital of Perth and Kinross, the administrative area that includes smaller Kinross-shire to the south.

Perthshire is also dubbed "Big Tree Country" because of its rich heritage of trees and woods, which include specimens such as the Birnam Oak and Fortingall Yew, Europe's oldest tree. Its scenery ranges from rich farmland through verdant woods and rolling hills to soaring mountains. The Lowland straths and Highland glens contain many well-heeled towns and villages that have good facilities for visitors, including networks of paths that provide great walking.

The Kingdom of Fife—as it has long been known—lies on the north side of the Firth of Forth, just a bridge-hop from Edinburgh. Fifers are a proud and independent people—perhaps because they almost live on an island, surrounded by the sea on three sides. Another great estuary, the Firth of Tay, bounds Fife on the

north side. Its beaches and fishing villages face the North Sea, and historically there were strong trade links to the Low Countries. St. Andrews, the home of golf, is Fife's most famous and historic town.

Road and rail bridges span the Firth of Tay to Dundee, Scotland's fourth largest city after Edinburgh, Glasgow, and Aberdeen. Dundee's riches were founded on its port, with "jam, jute, and journalism" as the main industries. It still produces newspapers, magazines, and comics—including *The Dandy* and *The Beano*—but information technology businesses have replaced the heavy industries. You can glimpse the past by visiting the HMS *Discovery,* Captain Scott's expeditionary ship, and the Verdant Works, a restored jute mill.

The agricultural county of Angus encircles Dundee to the north. It stretches across the fertile vale of Strathmore, which specializes in growing soft fruit and potatoes, to the southeast part of the Cairngorms National Park. During the 1970s and '80s, Angus, Dundee, and Perthshire were combined administratively into the Tayside region. This joint organization still exists for the police, fire, and health services.

As this region extends over both Highlands and Lowlands, you can choose to walk in mountain scenery in the north or gentler landscapes in the south. Perthshire probably has more walks for its size than any other part of Scotland; I've been exploring it for over 20 years and still haven't tried all the routes. It has a bit of everything, except dramatic coastal scenery—for that you'll have to visit Fife or Angus. The region has two long-distance walks: the Fife Coastal Path and the Cateran Trail, which starts in Blairgowrie and is the only circular route in Scotland.

ESSENTIALS

GETTING THERE
By Air
Edinburgh airport (www.edinburghairport.com) has flights arriving from the widest choice of airlines, with connections to Tayside and Fife available by hired car or public transportation. In addition, **Dundee airport** (www.hial.co.uk/dundee-airport.html) welcomes flights from London, Belfast, and Birmingham.

By Car
If driving from the south to Perth, take the M80/A9 from Glasgow or the Forth Road Bridge/M90 from Edinburgh. The A9 continues north through Highland Perthshire. To reach St. Andrews, Dundee, and Angus, branch off the M90 at Kinross and head east on the A91.

By Bus
Scottish Citylink (② 08705 505050; www.citylink.co.uk), the national coach operator, has bus service to the major towns in the region. Edinburgh to Perth takes 1 hour and 15 minutes, and a standard single costs £9.40; Edinburgh to Dundee takes 1 hour and 45 minutes for £13.

By Ferry
The Superfast ferry service between Rosyth in Fife and Zeebrugge in Belgium closed in September 2008, but **Norfolkline** (www.norfolkline.com) is due to resume sailings on the same route to Europe in 2009.

By Train
Rail services from Edinburgh go north to Perth and beyond on the Highland line, to Dundee and beyond on the Express East line, and to mid-Fife on the Fife Circle line. **First Scotrail** (② 08457 484950; www.firstgroup.com/scotrail) runs these trains. Edinburgh to Perth takes 1 hour and 20 minutes, and an anytime single costs £12; Edinburgh to Dundee takes 1 hour and 15 minutes for £18.

VISITOR INFORMATION
VisitScotland (② 0845 2255121; www.visitscotland.com), the Scottish tourist board, provides information on the area and a booking service. It has many Tourist Information Centres throughout the region; they include Perth (② **01738 450600**) at Lower City Mills, West Mill Street, and Crail (② **01333 450869**) at 62-64 Marketgate and Arbroath (② **01241 872609**) at Harbour Visitor Centre, Fish Market Quay. For in-depth information, see VisitScotland's websites www.perthshire.co.uk, www.visitfife.com, and www.angusanddundee.co.uk.

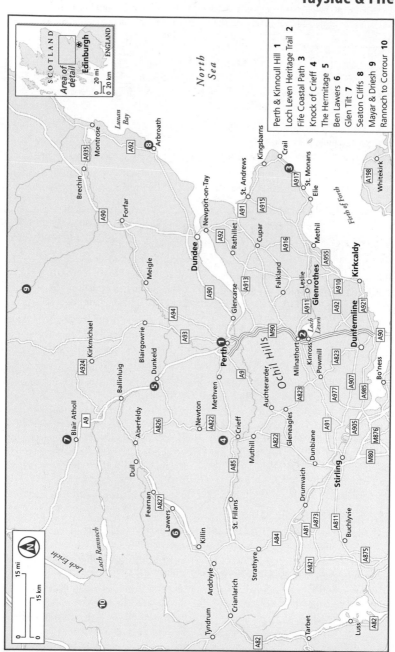

Perth & Kinnoull Hill **1**
Loch Leven Heritage Trail **2**
Fife Coastal Path **3**
Knock of Crieff **4**
The Hermitage **5**
Ben Lawers **6**
Glen Tilt **7**
Seaton Cliffs **8**
Mayar & Driesh **9**
Rannoch to Corrour **10**

North Sea

SCOTLAND

Area of
detail
Edinburgh
ENGLAND
0   20 mi
0   20 km

Perth is at the heart of this region and has good transport links in all directions. It is an hour's drive from Edinburgh via the M90 and not much more from Glasgow via the M80/A9. Most of Perthshire lies to the north, where you'll find Dunkeld, Pitlochry, and Aberfeldy, or to the west, where Crieff is the main town.

Fife bulges out into the North Sea between Edinburgh and Perth and has a network of trunk and minor roads. St. Andrews is on the east coast, just north of the East Neuk of Fife fishing villages, and not far from the Tay Road Bridge. Angus and Dundee lie east of Perthshire and north of Fife, and are easily reached via the A85 dual carriageway from Perth or the Tay Road Bridge from Fife.

GETTING AROUND

Traveline Scotland (℅ **08712 002233;** www.travelinescotland.com), the national travel service, can help you plan your journey using public transport. The service has details for both small bus companies that provide local services and major transport operators.

PERTH & KINNOULL HILL

Difficulty rating: Moderate

Distance: 11km (6.9 miles) round-trip

Estimated time: 4 hours

Elevation gain: 215m (705 ft.)

Costs/permits: Car parking £2.10 for up to 6 hours

Best time to go: April to June for spring colors

Website: www.kinnoull.org.uk

Recommended map: OS Explorer 369 (OS Landranger 58)

Trailhead GPS: NO 11973 23052

Trailhead directions: Start from the South Inch car park at the intersection of Edinburgh Road (the A912) and Marshall Place on the south edge of Perth city center, not far from rail and bus stations.

See firsthand why Perth has the nickname "The Fair City", as you stroll through its riverside gardens and climb to a tower that was built to look like a romantic ruin perched on the cliffs of Kinnoull Hill. You cross Scotland's largest river and later look down on it snaking towards the Firth of Tay. In medieval times, Scottish monarchs crossed the Firth by boat then rode along Coronation Road to the religious capital at Scone; this walk includes part of that royal route.

Go out of the car park entrance and cross the road by a mini roundabout to a viewpoint overlooking the River Tay. The domed Ferguson Gallery is on the other side of the road; it started life as Perth's waterworks and now houses paintings by the Scottish colorist J. D. Ferguson.

❶ Railway Bridge Turn upriver and walk under a railway; then immediately go up steps to a walkway on the rail bridge over the river. Information boards describe the history of the railway and of golf in Perth. The bridge curves over (and provides the access to) Moncreiffe Island, which is the home of the King James VI Golf Club. At the far end, walk beside a high wall then turn left up shallow steps to the Dundee Road. With care, cross the busy road and go up the lane on the right, signed BRANKLYN GARDEN.

❷ Branklyn Garden Turn left at the entrance to Branklyn, now following signs

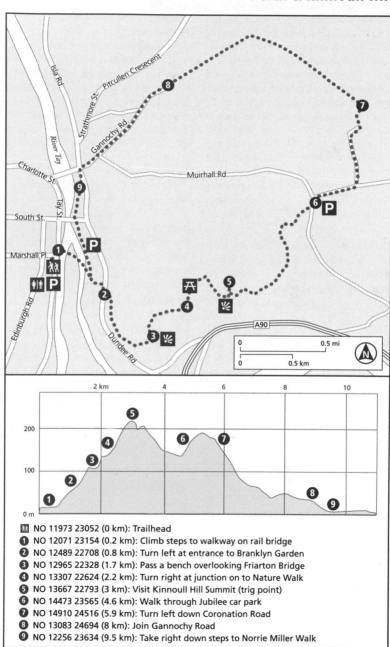

🚶 NO 11973 23052 (0 km): Trailhead
❶ NO 12071 23154 (0.2 km): Climb steps to walkway on rail bridge
❷ NO 12489 22708 (0.8 km): Turn left at entrance to Branklyn Garden
❸ NO 12965 22328 (1.7 km): Pass a bench overlooking Friarton Bridge
❹ NO 13307 22624 (2.2 km): Turn right at junction on to Nature Walk
❺ NO 13667 22793 (3 km): Visit Kinnoull Hill Summit (trig point)
❻ NO 14473 23565 (4.6 km): Walk through Jubilee car park
❼ NO 14910 24516 (5.9 km): Turn left down Coronation Road
❽ NO 13083 24694 (8 km): Join Gannochy Road
❾ NO 12256 23634 (9.5 km): Take right down steps to Norrie Miller Walk

for Kinnoull Hill. (Branklyn is one of Scotland's smallest but most famous gardens, developed by John and Dorothy Renton using many seeds collected by Scottish plant hunters active in the early 20th century—well worth a visit.) At a crossroads, turn right along Fairmount Terrace. Beyond the houses there, take the left fork up a trail, and then follow a grassy path climbing beside a hedge. Soon you can see back to the town—Perth Prison is the large building across the Tay. Enter Kinnoull Hill Woodland Park and continue ahead on the hard-surfaced path. As the path climbs, it bends left to run above the rising cliffs of Kinnoull Hill. You'll need to keep children and animals away from the edge for the next 3.2km (2 miles).

❸ Seat with a View   The path levels off by a bench overlooking Friarton Bridge, where the M90 motorway crosses the River Tay. Turn left when you come to a dip and cross a grassy area to a bench. Go right uphill to a T-junction and turn right along a wider path. The path rises through an open area to a row of beech trees, then continues downhill. Dip down across a small valley with a thicket at the bottom.

❹ Nature Walk Route   Go up steps to a junction and turn right, now on the route of the red-marked Nature Walk. The path bends left and climbs to a junction beside a picnic table, where you turn right towards the summit. Follow the surfaced path right at a crossroads and rise up to an open grassy area with a stone table.

The benches around this sunny, south-facing spot make it a good place to rest after the climb. Or you could have a picnic on the stone table, which is positioned with a bird's-eye view of the River Tay. Looking along the cliffs (which are home to ravens and peregrine falcons) you see Kinnoull Tower, which was built as a landscape feature, to resemble—from a distance—a castle of the Rhine Valley in Germany.

❺ Kinnoull Hill Summit   Turn left and walk a short distance up to the trig point marker for a view northwards to the Highlands.

A viewpoint indicator identifies the mountains ranged around the horizon, including—beyond the Drumderg wind farm—many Cairngorms peaks. Nearer at hand, look down on Perth and Scone, and follow the course of the Tay as it flows through the rolling Perthshire countryside. An information plaque highlights major events in Perth's history and the places associated with them.

Return to the stone table and continue on the cliff-top path, going downhill to a junction. Keep right up to Kinnoull Tower, another good viewpoint. Continue above the cliffs and eventually turn away from them to a T-junction. Go right and follow a track downhill through woodland and around a field, ignoring all left turns.

❻ Jubilee Car Park   Go around a gate and cross a minor road to the Jubilee car park, beside the entrance to the Jim Aitken Arboretum. This is Perth's newest horticultural attraction, opened in September 2008. And it contains some tall redwoods and other exotic trees. Walk through the car park and go right on a stony track. Climb up to gateway then turn left onto a path that follows the edge of a forested hill. Come to a post and turn left. A dirt path through tall Scots pinewood leads downhill, then goes right.

❼ Coronation Road   Beyond a metal gate, turn left down a path called the Coronation Road.

You are now walking in the footsteps of the kings and queens of Scotland. This was the way they traveled between Falkland Castle, a hunting lodge in Fife, and Scone, which was the traditional place of coronation until the Stone of Destiny was stolen from there by the English king, Edward I.

The narrow path runs steeply downhill between fields, widening as it reaches lower ground. At the bottom, meet a road on the outskirts of Scone and turn left along the Milkboys Path, which runs across fields back to Perth.

8 Gannochy   Cross a footbridge over a ditch and climb gently up to Gannochy, a district of Perth containing model cottages built for the deserving poor by local philanthropist A. K. Bell. Walk straight ahead along Gannochy Road for 1km (²/₃ mile), passing Murray Royal Hospital. At a T-junction, turn right down Lochie Brae to a set of traffic lights. When the pedestrian light shows, cross over diagonally to

Cupcakes cafe and walk along the pavement in front of it.

9 Riverside Parks   Pass a set of flats (apartments) and go right down steps into Norrie Miller Walk, the first of the riverside parks. Keep right and go through a gap in a wall to a pavilion. Continue past a sundial and a pond, always keeping on the path closest to the river. Go through an arch under Queen's Bridge and pass Rodney Gardens and then Bellwood Park. Go right at the far end to return over the railway bridge.

LOCH LEVEN HERITAGE TRAIL ★

Difficulty rating: Easy

Distance: 8km (5 miles) one-way (return by bus)

Estimated time: 2 hours

Elevation gain: 30m (100 ft.)

Costs/permits: Bus fare (£1.80 single)

Best time to go: At dawn to see the most wildlife

Website: www.discoverlochleven.com

Recommended map: Loch Leven Heritage Trail leaflet, available from local shops and Kinross Tourist Information Centre

Trailhead GPS: NO 12180 01716

Trailhead directions: Leave the M90 at the junction for Kinross, and in the town center turn right at a T-junction with a mini roundabout. Then take the third left, signed KINROSS PIER, and continue to the car park at the end of the road. Bus and coach services stop in Kinross.

Opened in 2008, the Loch Leven Heritage Trail links heritage sites around Scotland's largest Lowland loch, which is a National Nature Reserve because of its importance for wintering wildfowl and nesting ducks. Artworks and interpretation reveal much of the loch's history, from the imprisonment of Mary Queen of Scots on Castle Island to the birth of the sport of curling. Children will be intrigued by the images and verse, and will love the Kirkgate play park.

The full Trail runs 14km (8.7 miles) from Kinross Pier to RSPB's Vane Farm Reserve, though this walk only covers the first part. It is a linear route, completed by a short bus ride back to Kinross. The path is flat and smooth—suitable for bikes, pushchairs (strollers), and wheelchairs as well as people on foot—though the Nature Walk link at the end is on grass.

1 Kinross Pier   Historic Scotland boatmen ferry visitors from the small

stone jetty at Kinross Pier to ruined Lochleven Castle on Castle Island, while Kinross Fisheries boats are kept in the little harbor. An adjacent building houses the Boathouse Bistro and a Scottish Natural Heritage office.

Go through the stone-walled gateway feature marking the start of the Loch Leven Heritage Trail and follow the raised boardwalk through a reed bed.

(Finds)   Sail Away

You get a whole different perspective on Loch Leven by taking the boat trip out to Castle Island and enjoying the view that the swans, ducks, and geese have. The ruined castle is fun to explore—discover a 14th-century tower house and climb to the top of the castle walls. It's open late March to the end of October, daily 9:30am to 5:30pm (4:30pm in Oct). Admission is as follows: adult £4.70, child £2.35, concession £3.70. Make time to visit before or after your walk—the trip starts from Kinross Pier, and the ticket includes the boat trip.

2 Kirkgate Park After crossing a stream, you arrive at the grassy expanse of Kirkgate Park and turn right on the path along the shore.

The Park has some exciting and imaginative play equipment, including climbing frames and a zip wire. You may need to look twice at some of the contraptions, though children don't take long to figure them out.

At the end of the Park, pass a watchtower and ancient graveyard. Walk outside it to a viewpoint overlooking the loch. Geese roost in the field here, so keep dogs under close control. As you continue, look out for the ornamental Fish Gate, through which you glimpse Kinross House.

3 Bird Hide Soon a wood comes between you and the loch. Part way along it, detour right to the Boathouse bird hide (for watching the wildlife unobserved) built on stilts in a reed bed.

From here, watch Loch Leven's waters reflecting the ever-changing skies. Bring binoculars so that you can survey the varied birdlife—a chart on the wall helps with identification. Volcanic hills ring the loch: West Lomond is the conical hill on the left, next to the long escarpment of Bishop Hill, while Benarty Hill lies to the right.

Return to the main path and continue through wetlands and woods. Look out for Mary's Ponds, two shady pools with wooden viewing platforms.

4 Mary's Gate The path winds through willow scrub to a stone wall at the north end of Kinross golf course, where you'll find the old stone pillars of Mary's Gate, named after Mary Queen of Scots. Continue to the right on a path that bends around a field corner to the North Queich, a wide stream flowing into the loch. Cross the curving wooden bridge and keep straight ahead.

5 Burleigh Sands Pass some benches looking out over the water and then come to Burleigh Sands, an arc of beach at the north end of the loch.

This is a popular place for picnics and for dog walkers to let their dogs have a swim (they are discouraged from doing so in more sensitive parts of the loch). Some birds that live here year-round are used to the disturbance—you'll often see mallard ducks and the resident greylag geese.

Under a large Scots pine, the path bends left towards Burleigh Sands car park. Turn right to continue under tall pines fringing the shore. Farther on, the path crosses a bridge over a small pool. Loch Leven's native strain of brown trout used to be bred here and shipped to fisheries around the world. At the next footbridge, a small pedestrian gate gives access to the now vegetated fishponds.

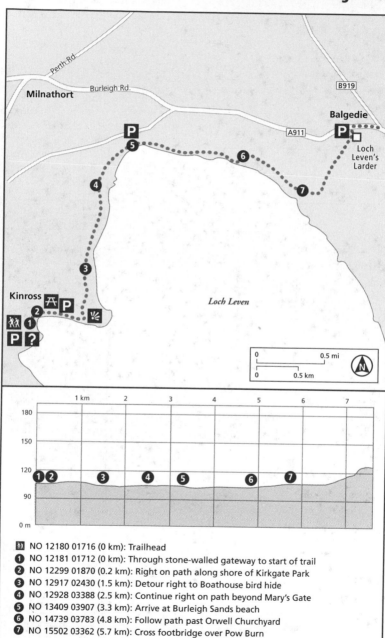

Milnathort

Perth Rd.

Burleigh Rd.

B919

Balgedie

A911

Loch Leven's Larder

Kinross

Loch Leven

0   0.5 mi
0   0.5 km

1 km   2   3   4   5   6   7

180

150

120

90

0 m

🥾 NO 12180 01716 (0 km): Trailhead
① NO 12181 01712 (0 km): Through stone-walled gateway to start of trail
② NO 12299 01870 (0.2 km): Right on path along shore of Kirkgate Park
③ NO 12917 02430 (1.5 km): Detour right to Boathouse bird hide
④ NO 12928 03388 (2.5 km): Continue right on path beyond Mary's Gate
⑤ NO 13409 03907 (3.3 km): Arrive at Burleigh Sands beach
⑥ NO 14739 03783 (4.8 km): Follow path past Orwell Churchyard
⑦ NO 15502 03362 (5.7 km): Cross footbridge over Pow Burn

⑥ Orwell Churchyard The path runs near the shore and then bends left towards a walled area with yew trees—historic Orwell churchyard, containing old gravestones and a ruined church. Before it, the path bends again to skirt a wetland area used by birds ranging from shelduck to snipe.

⑦ Pow Burn At a footbridge, cross the Pow Burn and continue to a woodland strip. Here, leave the surfaced trail and turn left up Channel Farm's Nature Walk. The way runs gently uphill through fields and past flowers planted for bumblebees and other wildlife. After 0.8km (¹/₂ mile), you

arrive at **Loch Leven's Larder** (☎ **01592 841000;** www.lochlevenslarder.com), a farm shop and cafe with superb views back over the loch. Children will want to say hello to the goats, chickens, pigs, and Highland cow.

You can enter the restaurant through the patio or walk around the outside of the building to the car park. To return to Kinross, walk up to the road at the entrance to Loch Leven's Larder to catch the bus—stick out your arm to request the driver to stop here (the official stop is to the right at Wester Balgedie). There are roughly two buses per hour, with no service on Sundays.

FIFE COASTAL PATH ★★★

Difficulty rating: Moderate

Distance: 14km (8.7 miles) one-way

Estimated time: 4.5 hours

Elevation gain: 20m (65 ft.)

Costs/permits: None

Pet friendly: Yes, but beware of livestock

Best time to go: May to July to enjoy tempting beaches and colorful gardens

Website: www.fifecoastalpath.co.uk

Recommended map: Fife Coastal Path map available from local Tourist Information Centres

Trailhead GPS: NO 52557 01958

Trailhead directions: Take the A917 along the southeast Fife coast. Park in the center of Crail and catch the number 95 bus to St. Monans from the stop opposite the Post Office, or arrive by bus from St. Andrews or Leven.

The prettiest part of Fife is the East Neuk (Corner), where lush farmland rolls down to a rocky coast strung with old fishing villages. Whitewashed houses with traditional crow-stepped gables and red pantile roofs line the harbors, and gardens are a riot of colorful flowers. This linear walk between St. Monans and Crail follows part of the Fife Coastal Path, which runs 130km (81 miles) from the Forth Bridges to the Tay Bridge.

I chose to take the bus journey first, so that I was walking back to my car. However, if you are not sure whether you'll want to do the whole walk, you could start in St. Monans and get the bus back from Pittenweem or Anstruther. The buses are generally hourly. From the Elm Row bus stop at St. Monans, walk down a passageway, then right along Gourlay Crescent and left down Station Road, passing the Mayview Hotel.

① St. Monans Harbor At the bottom, you come to St. Monans harbor with a view of houses curving round to the Auld Kirk, the closest church to the sea in Scotland. Return up the road and turn right along Rose Street, at signs for the Windmill. Past houses, the coastal path runs across grass from a small car park overlooking the sea. St. Monans Windmill is perched above you, and the indentations below are the remains of old saltpans,

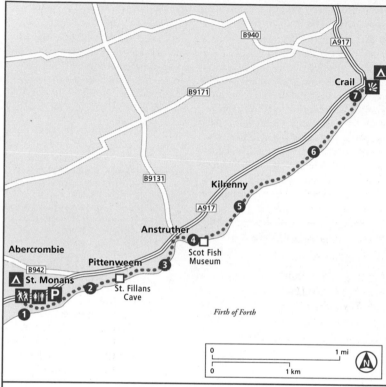

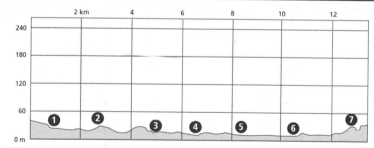

🏃 NO 52557 01958 (0 km): Trailhead

❶ NO 52611 01631 (0.8 km): St. Monans Harbor

❷ NO 54254 02262 (2.5 km): Left by old swimming pool before Pittenweem

❸ NO 56172 02920 (5.1 km): Join lane below turreted tower

❹ NO 56819 03502 (6.5 km): Anstruther Harbor

❺ NO 58045 04386 (8.2 km): Ends at caravan park, around gate to continue

❻ NO 59972 05807 (10.7 km): Arrive at Caiplie Caves past stone stile

❼ NO 61005 07276 (12.7 km): Follow path to Crail Harbor

where workers boiled seawater raised by the windmill. The path sticks close to the shore, with fine views to the lighthouse-topped Isle of May and Bass Rock.

❷ **Pittenweem** Shortly before Pittenweem, fork left above the ruins of an old swimming pool among the rocks. Go right behind a shelter on a path skirting a play area. The path curves around a bay to a promenade, where you walk past fishermen's cottages that are painted in pastel colors and decked with hanging baskets of flowers. Pass the fish market and harbor—the center of the East Neuk fishing industry—then turn left up a passageway to St. Fillan's Cave, which has an ornamental metal gate at its entrance.

"Pittenweem" is Pictish for "place of the cave" and is named after the grotto where Saint Fillan was believed to pray by a mysterious light emanating from his left arm. To visit the Cave (admission £1, including descriptive leaflet), collect the key from the Cocoa Tree Shop or Little Gallery on High Street above the Cave, at the top of the passageway that goes steeply up from the harbour. Pittenweem is famed as an artists' village and abounds in galleries and cafes.

When you've had your fill of hermits and hot chocolate, return to the harbor and continue along the shore road. At a bend, go straight ahead onto a path that runs between houses and the sea. On the edge of a cultivated field, it drops to the shore and skirts the edge of Anstruther Golf Course.

❸ **Stone Tower** Below a turreted tower, which is a war memorial, join a lane around a sandy beach lined by shrub roses. Pass the golf clubhouse and go over a crossroads into Anstruther Wester and left at a T-junction to join High Street. At a bend beyond the historic Dreel Tavern, you have a choice of routes depending on the tide. Either go right to a quay and cross stepping stones over the Dreel Burn, or follow the road left then go right after

the Smugglers' Inn and right again down a passageway.

❹ **Anstruther Harbor** Both routes bring you to Anstruther Harbor, where the promenade is lined with ice cream parlors and fish-and-chip shops, including the award-winning Anstruther Fish Bar and Restaurant. Look out for the Reaper, a traditional herring drifter belonging to the Scottish Fisheries Museum, which is opposite the car park.

The **Scottish Fisheries Museum** (www.scotfishmuseum.org) has a nationally important collection of boats, equipment, and photographs associated with the fishing industry. Its Tammie Norie tearoom—named after the Scots name for a puffin—welcomes walkers and sells homemade soups, rolls, and cakes at very reasonable prices. Museum entry is adult £5, concessions £4, accompanied children free; it's open weekdays 10am to 5:30pm (4:30pm Oct–Mar) and Sundays 11am to 5pm (noon–4:30pm Oct–Mar).

A second harbor, just beyond, has a sandy beach. Keep on along James Street and over a staggered crossroads to continue on a quiet road to the dainty little harbor at Cellardyke. Continue past a play area on the edge of town.

❺ **Kilrenny Mill** The road ends at Kilrenny Mill caravan park, where you go around a metal gate and continue along the wildest bit of coast. Cross a stream and walk beside a field of free-range pigs, then pass another grazed by cattle. Go through two kissing gates at picturesque Caiplie Farm. After a stone wall with steps built into it, stepping stones lead across a salt marsh. The path continues along the tide line.

❻ **Caiplie Caves** Beyond another stream and stone stile, come to a sandstone outcrop. This is weathered into pillars, arches, and caves, known locally as Caiplie

Caves (shown as Hermit's Well on the OS map). Cattle graze this part of the shore, so take care if you have a dog. After another stone stile, you pass the ruins of an old salmon-fishing bothy (small hut) and salt works. It is rougher going beyond, as you cross a stony path then climb steep steps.

❼ Crail Beyond the next bay, the path bends around a headland, giving a view of photogenic Crail harbor. A kissing gate leads onto a road, where you soon branch right onto a grassy path between houses. Join the main road; then, beyond the cottages, go right down cobbled steps for a pretty approach to Crail harbor. Leave the harbor by Shoregate, and either follow it back to High Street or go right up steps onto Castle Walk for a panorama over the Firth of Forth. Turn left beyond the high wall then weave left and right past a pottery to reach High Street.

KNOCK OF CRIEFF ★ (Kids)

Difficulty rating: Moderate

Distance: 7.5km (4.7 miles) round-trip

Estimated time: 3 hours

Elevation gain: 216m (710 ft.)

Costs/permits: None

Best time to go: October to mid-November for autumn colors

Website: www.crieffandstrathearn.co.uk

Recommended map: Crieff walks leaflet available from Crieff or Perth Tourist Information Centres

Trailhead GPS: NN 85662 23431

Trailhead directions: Head west out of Crieff on the A85 towards Comrie; after crossing a bridge, go right at a sign for the Famous Grouse Experience; then in 0.8km (½ mile) turn into the distillery car park.

Crieff is an attractive resort town, situated on the Highland edge at the foot of the Knock, a hill with panoramic views over mountain, wood, and farmland. This circuit of the Knock links the town's two most famous institutions—the Famous Grouse Experience at Glenturret Distillery and the Crieff Hydro Hotel. It's a great family walk, with plenty to see along the way.

This walk combines the Hosh walk, marked by red disks, with part of the Knock walk, marked by blue disks. From the distillery car park, follow signs for Woodland Walks and cross a footbridge over the Turret Burn. Keep right of a play and picnic area on a woodland path that bends up to a path junction. Turn right to walk downstream above the fast-running stream on a path with wooden railings that guard the steep slope below.

❶ Lovers' Walk The woodland becomes more open and you continue down Lovers' Walk, crossing two small side streams, to a footpath sign where you turn left on the path to Culcrieff. This path soon bends left and then zigzags up to a higher level, where it runs right to a paved lane. Turn left and walk towards the Crieff Hydro self-catering lodges at Culcrieff, the site of an old estate farm.

❷ Culcrieff Just before the lodges, go right on a marked path and, at a junction above them, keep straight ahead on a track through trees. The view opens up over a field to the right; then you bend into more trees and come to a T-junction. Go right and soon after you have left the wood come to Jesus Well, dated 1874.

❸ Viewpoint The second seat you pass, about 150m (492 ft.) beyond the well, has a superb view westwards.

As you look up Strathearn towards Comrie, the scenery becomes more rugged, with mountains rising up to the conical peak of Ben Vorlich. To the right, another Munro—Ben Chonzie—stands at the head of Glen Turret, beyond a delightful mix of pasture and wood. To the south, a gentler landscape rolls away to rounded Torlum Hill.

The path winds around the hillside, going back into trees and then drawing level with another field where there is a view southwards over Crieff. Come to a paved lane and keep straight on.

❹ Crieff Hydro Hotel The lane runs through a high wall to the Crieff Hydro Hotel (where refreshments are available in the Winter Garden cafe). Just before the wall, turn left through a kissing gate and walk up the side of a pony field. Beyond another gate, keep ahead on a paved drive past more lodges and come up to a junction.

For a shorter walk, you can climb the Knock from the Lower Knock parking area, which is just on the right, above Crieff Hydro's stables. If you start from here, keep left when you return past the Upper Knock car park.

Otherwise, go straight across the junction to an artistic walks information board and follow the path beside it uphill.

❺ Knock Viewpoint Walk up through broadleaved woodland, passing a grassy area with benches, to the summit of the Knock, where there is a viewpoint indicator on a plinth.

Take time to enjoy the view, possibly from one of the benches arranged around the open summit area. The high mass of Ben Chonzie and the rocky slopes of Blue Craigs look very close—they mark the Highland Boundary Fault, where there is a sudden transition from lush Lowlands to heather-covered Highlands.

Continue straight over the summit, across a heathery dip and up to a deer fence. Go over stile and continue ahead through a recently felled area with another stile on the far side. Keep ahead up a steep, stony path into dense conifers.

❻ Upper Knock Summit The gradient soon eases and the path runs over spruce needles and tree roots to a small cairn, marking the Upper Knock summit. Although higher, this top is enclosed by

Witch's Curse

In 1563, the Scottish Witchcraft Act made witchcraft an offence punishable by death and, until the death penalty for witchcraft was abolished in 1735, waves of persecutions spread through the country like a fever. Kate McNieven was one of the victims of this scourge, burned at the stake for being a witch. The site—crags at the eastern end of the Knock—came to be known as Kate McNieven's Craig.

Legend has it that the laird of Inchbrakie, who employed Kate as a nursemaid, tried to save her at the last minute. Just as the fire was being lit, she bit a blue bead from her necklace and spat it at him, saying that as long as it was kept at Inchbrakie the lands would pass from father to son. For many generations the bead, set in a gold ring, was kept in a casket in the house. After it was inadvertently taken away in a box of papers, no more sons were born to inherit the estate and it was sold.

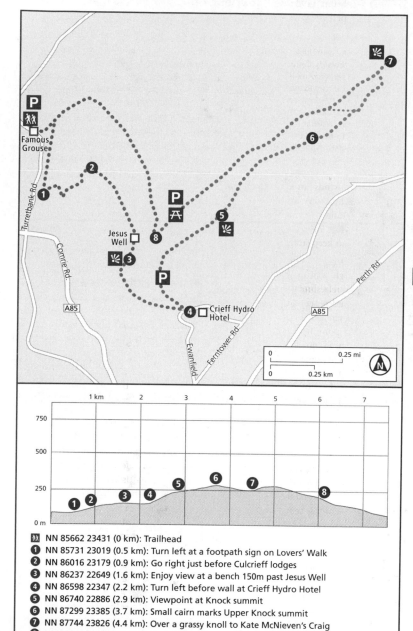

NN 85662 23431 (0 km): Trailhead
1. NN 85731 23019 (0.5 km): Turn left at a footpath sign on Lovers' Walk
2. NN 86016 23179 (0.9 km): Go right just before Culcrieff lodges
3. NN 86237 22649 (1.6 km): Enjoy view at a bench 150m past Jesus Well
4. NN 86598 22347 (2.2 km): Turn left before wall at Crieff Hydro Hotel
5. NN 86740 22886 (2.9 km): Viewpoint at Knock summit
6. NN 87299 23385 (3.7 km): Small cairn marks Upper Knock summit
7. NN 87744 23826 (4.4 km): Over a grassy knoll to Kate McNieven's Craig
8. NN 86354 22726 (6.1 km): Turn right at footpath sign to Hosh

The Famous Grouse Experience

Glenturret Distillery, the oldest in Scotland, was established in 1775. It produces Glenturret single-malt whisky, some of which goes into the Famous Grouse blend. The distillery is open daily (9am–6pm) and has a visitor center, shop, restaurant, and bar. The Famous Grouse Experience tours include a high-tech wraparound audio visual show, as well as the more traditional guided walk around the production process and a whisky tasting (first tour 9:30am, last tour 4:30pm; £4.95 per person).

Look out for two animal statues—a giant red grouse and a life-size bronze of Towser, the distillery cat who lived from April 1963 to March 1987. In nearly 24 years, she caught 28,899 mice and was acknowledged by the Guinness Book of Records to be the World Mousing Champion. The statue is on the slope up to the restaurant, which does weekday special lunch deals; for instance soup, cake, and a drink for £4.99. Get more information from ℂ **01764 656565** or www.the famousgrouse.com.

Norway spruce and has no view. Keep straight on through dark trees and then bend left as the woodland becomes less dense. Join a forest path and turn right along it, soon gaining a wide view eastwards over a felled area. At a bend, go left on a path between two deer fences to a corner, then straight ahead through a high wooden gate.

⑦ Kate McNieven's Craig   Go over a grassy knoll and continue about 50m (164 ft.) to the right to Kate McNieven's Craig, where there is a spectacular view over Monzie Castle of the whole of the northern skyline. Return through the wooden gate and turn right, on a path between deer fences. Rise uphill, beside larch trees, and return to the forest track. Go right

and walk gently downhill for 1km ($^2/_3$ mile) to the Upper Knock car park.

⑧ Hosh Path   Beyond the car park, turn a sharp right at a path sign to the Hosh and go downhill on a paved lane past various Crieff Hydro activities. Culcrieff Wood has a disc golf course and beyond is a ropes adventure course. Just after Culcrieff Golf Centre, leave the paved road and walk ahead through the Activity Centre car park. Keep straight past the building on a stony trail that goes downhill. Lower down, the path curves under large beech trees to a bend, where you go left on a trail. This returns to the path junction above Glenturret Distillery, where you go right and descend to the footbridge over Turret Burn.

THE HERMITAGE ★★★ Ⓚⁱᵈˢ

Difficulty rating: Easy	**Costs/permits:** £2 car parking
Distance: 6.8km (4.25 miles) round-trip	**Best time to go:** January and February for snowdrops and waterfalls
Estimated time: 3 hours	
Elevation gain: 137m (449 ft.)	**Website:** www.nts.org.uk/multimedia

Recommended map: Dunkeld & Birnam walks leaflet available from Dunkeld or Perth Tourist Information Centres

Trailhead GPS: NO 01282 42124

Trailhead directions: From Perth, drive north 24km (15 miles) on the A9 and turn left 1.6km (1 mile) north of Dunkeld and Birnam at a sign for The Hermitage. If you catch a train to Dunkeld & Birnam Station or a bus to Birnam from Perth, you can follow an attractive riverside path to the Hermitage (see sidebar).

This walk illustrates why Perthshire calls itself Big Tree Country—the home of many of the finest woods and trees in Scotland, thanks to a history of tree-planting landowners combined with favorable soils and climate. The Second Duke of Atholl planted the Hermitage as a woodland garden 250 years ago, and it is now the site of one of the tallest trees in Britain. The natural history of this area inspired Beatrix Potter, who spent family holidays here, to start writing her children's stories.

This circuit—the Braan Walk—goes through the Hermitage then up the River Braan, a boulder-strewn river that crashes over noisy falls. The Hermitage is a good place to see the endangered red squirrel, one of Scotland's iconic species. Also look out for two species of small bird that bob for insects from rocks in the river—white-breasted dippers and yellow-breasted gray wagtails. The walk has green waymarkers and starts from the lower car park where there are information boards about the Hermitage and Perthshire Big Tree Country.

Go through a narrow archway and walk upstream beside the River Braan, through woods that are good for spring wildflowers. The path merges with a track, then almost immediately forks left. Stroll under a grove of tall Douglas fir to a bench overlooking the Black Linn pool. On the far side is the Hermitage Douglas fir, one of the tallest trees in Britain. Continue up rough steps and keep right past the Hermitage Bridge to a stone building.

❶ **Ossian's Hall**   Push open the door to enter Ossian's Hall, a summerhouse built in 1758 as a memorial to Ossian, a 3rd-century blind bard.

 It is quite dark in the circular lobby, but slide open the next door to enter a room overlooking a dramatic waterfall on the River Braan. For the best view, go through the glass doors onto the balcony. You can't help but be impressed by the power of nature in this awesome spot. In autumn, especially when the river flow is high, you may see salmon trying to leap the falls.

Continue upriver and, after crossing a stone slab over a ditch, keep left to pass a bench at a bend in the river. The trees here are Scots pines with blaeberries (also known as bilberries or blueberries) underneath. In summer, I pause to feast on the juicy black berries.

❷ **Hermit's Cave**   Soon the path goes uphill between boulders and levels off beside a post. On your right is the well-camouflaged Hermit's Cave. After trying the rather austere stone bed, take the path to the left (right leads back to the car park). Walk through a grove of tall Sitka spruce and then past an area of natural regeneration thick with young trees. Go straight over a crossroads of paths and walk uphill to a T-junction.

Birnam to the Hermitage on Foot

A traffic-free 2.7km (1.7-mile) path leads from Birnam past interesting sights to the Hermitage. The Birnam Institute, a community arts and conference center, houses the Beatrix Potter exhibition and has an adjacent garden with many bronze statues of her characters. The author spent her childhood holidays around Birnam and based many of her stories and illustrations on the people and animals she met here.

Get off the bus at the Beatrix Potter Garden or go downhill under the A9 from the railway station to this point. Cross the road and follow a sign for the Birnam Oak, going down a lane to the River Tay. Turn left on the riverside path and, in about 100m (328 ft.), pass the ancient tree, supposedly the only remnant of Birnam Wood, which Shakespeare immortalized in his play *Macbeth*.

After passing under Thomas Telford's bridge, which links Birnam and Dunkeld, you can see across the river to partially ruined Dunkeld Cathedral, which dates from 1325 and was the center of the Celtic Church. Beyond the confluence of the Tay and Braan, go right at a T-junction, under the A9 and over a footbridge across the Braan. Keep straight ahead, past Tay Forest District headquarters, and then turn right through pretty Inver. Beyond the houses, a path runs beside the A9 for 100m (328 ft.) before turning into the Hermitage.

③ Craigvinean Cottage Turn left onto a broader path and immediately pass a stone cottage on the edge of Craigvinean Forest. Cross a wooden bridge and enter a meadow of grass, bracken, and wildflowers. Enormous flat-topped boulders lie on either side of the path.

The left-hand boulder is my favorite spot for a picnic. From here you look over the wooded valley of the Braan to the return route.

At the end of the meadow, turn left onto a minor road and walk downhill.

④ Rumbling Bridge Deciduous trees—willow, birch, aspen, and alder—line the road and obscure views of the river. But as you approach Rumbling Bridge, you'll hear thundering water. Here the boiling River Braan crashes down a waterfall into a deep, dark chasm.

Walk 100m (328 ft.) beyond the bridge and then turn left by a post into a grove of trees. Follow a rough earth path, which is soon joined by another from the car park above. It meanders through trees to the A822, which should be crossed with care.

⑤ Tomgarrow Go straight ahead up a hard track through grassland with scattered trees. Wildflowers abound, and there may be cattle or sheep. After 600m (1,969 ft.), turn left and walk towards Tomgarrow, which was once a busy hamlet. Pass to the right of the one remaining house and continue on a grassy path. You can see up the Tay valley all the way to Beinn a' Ghlo, a mountain by Blair Atholl. Cross a boardwalk over a wet dip and come to a gate in a stone wall.

⑥ Ladybank Forest Continue straight ahead through a birch wood until the path skirts around a cottage. In another 200m (656 ft.), go through a gateway into Ladybank Forest. Now the trees are conifers, although the immediate area has many

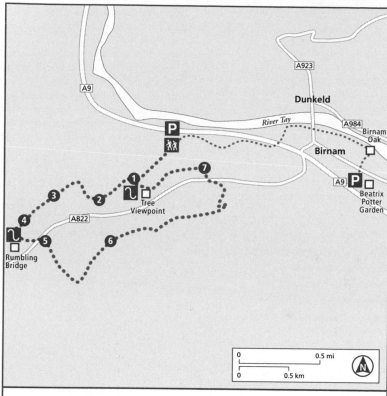

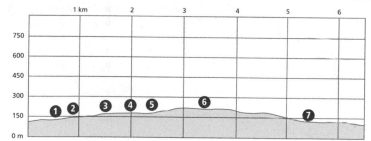

🏃 NO 01282 42124 (0 km): Trailhead
❶ NO 00874 41706 (0.5 km): Enter Ossian's Hall
❷ NO 00569 41598 (0.9 km): Hermit's Cave on your right from post
❸ NO 00067 41614 (1.5 km): Turn left and pass stone cottage
❹ NN 99700 41275 (2 km): Walk road to Rumbling Bridge over River Braan
❺ NN 99998 41189 (2.4 km): Go ahead up a track after crossing the road
❻ NO 00568 41132 (3.4 km): Gateway to birch wood at Ladybank Forest
❼ NO 01586 41897 (5.4 km): Leave Inver car park on path to the Hermitage

felled trees. In 100m (328 ft.), come to a trail and turn left along it. Keep left at the next junction to walk downhill between fir trees to a wide junction, where you turn sharp left.

If you walked to the Hermitage from Birnam, you can take a shortcut back by turning right here and following the brown Inver Walk signs. They lead through the forest to a footbridge over Inchewan Burn then downstream to the village.

Walk downhill to the main forest entrance and cross the A822 to a path that leads down through trees to another, quieter road. You can now see Inver car park; go right then left down steps to it.

❼ Hermitage Bridge Leave the car park by a path beside the information board and walk downhill through trees. Keep left at a fork and pass a memorial bench with a wooden sculpture. The path contours above the Braan to an information post with a view to the Hermitage Douglas fir. Continue under the tree and over Hermitage Bridge. For a different way back, go up to Ossian's Hall and turn right onto the all-abilities trail.

BEN LAWERS ★★

Difficulty rating: Difficult

Distance: 11km (7 miles) round-trip

Estimated time: 5 hours

Elevation gain: 780m (2,560 ft.)

Costs/permits: £2 voluntary donation

Best time to go: June to August for mountain flowers

Website: www.nts.org.uk

Recommended map: Harvey Superwalker Ben Lawers

Trailhead GPS: NN 60867 37897

Trailhead directions: From Perth go north on the A9 to Ballinluig, take the A827 through Aberfeldy and Kenmore, and then drive 19km (12 miles) along the north side of Loch Tay. Turn right at a sign for Ben Lawers on a single-track road up to the visitor center car park.

Perthshire's highest mountain rises steeply above Loch Tay and has superb views over lovely Glen Lyon to a vast array of mountain peaks. Ben Lawers' limestone-rich rocks and harsh climate make it the best place in Britain for Arctic-alpine flora, including many rare species. It is a National Nature Reserve and has a visitor center with exhibitions about the wildlife present and human influences on the landscape.

The visitor center is open from late March to the end of September, from 10am to 5pm, and is run by the National Trust for Scotland, who own Ben Lawers and neighboring mountains. It is on a single-track road, which is often closed by snow during the winter and is high enough (nearly 457m/1,500 ft.) to significantly reduce the climb up the mountain. The route approaches Ben Lawers over the top of a lower Munro, Beinn Ghlas, and returns around the north side of that mountain.

❶ Nature Trail Leave the car park by a boardwalk that leads across a marshy area towards the Nature Trail around the Burn of Edramucky. Go through a gate into a fenced area where the vegetation flourishes with protection from grazing deer and sheep. Keep to the main path, signed BEN LAWERS, rather than adding more boot wear to the grassy Nature Trail. Halfway up, the path swings over the burn and continues uphill on the far side. It exits the enclosure at the top right-hand corner, by another gate.

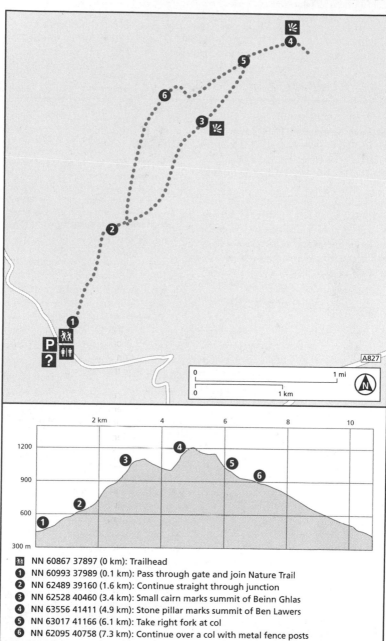

A827

0   1 mi

0   1 km

- NN 60867 37897 (0 km): Trailhead
- **1** NN 60993 37989 (0.1 km): Pass through gate and join Nature Trail
- **2** NN 62489 39160 (1.6 km): Continue straight through junction
- **3** NN 62528 40460 (3.4 km): Small cairn marks summit of Beinn Ghlas
- **4** NN 63556 41411 (4.9 km): Stone pillar marks summit of Ben Lawers
- **5** NN 63017 41166 (6.1 km): Take right fork at col
- **6** NN 62095 40758 (7.3 km): Continue over a col with metal fence posts

(Fun Facts) **Top Rank**

Ben Lawers was believed to belong to the select group of Scottish mountains that exceed the 1,219m (4,000-ft.) mark, until more accurate surveying revealed that it was 5.1m (17 ft.) too low. In 1878, a group of local men, frustrated by their mountain's loss of status, built a 6.1m-high (20-ft.) cairn on top. This didn't survive the erosive power of wind, rain, and ice for long.

2 **Path Junction** Walk 150m (492 ft.) beyond the gate to a path junction by a large boulder and keep straight on uphill. The good path with some natural rock steps zigzags steeply uphill. When you pause for a breather, admire the view westwards over Loch Tay and see the visitor center looking tiny below. The gradient eases for a while as it reaches a ridge and bends left along it. You can now see over the ridge to the east end of Loch Tay. More steep slopes lead to a flattening where a final ascent of rock slabs takes you to the summit.

3 **Beinn Ghlas** Only a small cairn marks the top of Beinn Ghlas (1,103m/ 3,619 ft.), but it is a distinct peak with a precipitous drop on the north side where ravens often play in the air currents. There is a fine view of grassy Meall Corranaich to the northwest and of higher, craggy Ben Lawers straight ahead.

Follow the path down a steep-sided ridge to the col before Ben Lawers. The wind often gusts very strongly through the gap between the two hills. Cross the col, where there is a tiny lochan on the right, and continue on the steep rocky path up Ben Lawers.

4 **Ben Lawers** After a steep haul over eroded rock steps and loose stones, you reach the summit, which has a round stone pillar and a concrete trig point marker at 1,214m (3,983 ft.).

A stunning view stretches ahead of the Munros—An Stuc, Meall Garbh, and Meall Greigh—encircling a corrie containing beautiful Lochan nan Cat. Ben More and Stob Binnein are prominent in the southwest and, on a clear day, Ben Nevis peers above other mountains in the northwest.

Choose the side of the mountain sheltered from the wind and find a rock to sit on for a panoramic picnic. It is worth walking a little way down the gently sloping southeast ridge to get a fuller view of Loch Tay and to see the summit from a different perspective, before returning down the path to the col.

5 **Fork at the Col** As soon as you reach the col, fork right on a narrow path that trends gently downhill below the steep north face of Beinn Ghlas. Below, the long, wide valley of Allt a' Chobhair runs away to Glen Lyon. Step over one of the headwaters, and then bend around the north ridge of the mountain.

6 **Ruined Fence** Cross a line of old metal fence posts at the marshy col between Beinn Ghlas and Meall Corranaich. Keep straight ahead on the path, which now angles down the left side of the Burn of Edramucky at a steady gradient that is kind on the knees. At the path junction you passed on the way out, turn right to return through the fenced enclosure.

(Fun Facts) Historic Landscape Project

Look closely at a detailed map of Ben Lawers and you'll see many shielings dotted around, especially on the southern slopes of the mountain. They reflect the now-abandoned practice of transhumance and are the summer shelters where people used to stay while watching over their cattle grazing on the lush mountain grass. You pass several at the top and the bottom of the Nature Trail enclosure, though remains of the low stone walls are grassed over, making them difficult to see.

Because Ben Lawers National Nature Reserve has many traces of past human activity, it was chosen for a major archaeological project, lasting from 2002 to 2007. This explored the shielings and lower agricultural lands through a series of surveys and excavations.

Radiocarbon dating of material from the shielings gave dates from the late 16th century to about 1840, indicating that for at least 200 years people were moving up to these pastures each summer. Also, ancient field patterns showed that crops used to be grown much higher than they are today, reflecting a greater number of people living on the land and possibly a warmer climate.

GLEN TILT

Difficulty rating: Moderate

Distance: 9.7 or 14.7km (6 or 9.2 miles) round-trip

Estimated time: 3 or 5 hours

Elevation gain: 125m (410 ft.)

Costs/permits: £1 suggested donation for upkeep of car park and paths

Best time to go: October and November for autumn colors and to hear red deer rutting

Website: www.athollestatesrangerservice. co.uk

Recommended map: Walks booklet downloadable from Atholl Ranger website or available at the Information Centre in Blair Atholl

Trailhead GPS: NN 87446 66267

Trailhead directions: Turn off the A9 (53km/33 miles north of Perth) into Blair Atholl and take the Old Blair Road at the south end of the village. After going left over a bridge, take the first left into the Glen Tilt car park (signed). If arriving by train or bus, take the path up the right side of Blair Castle gateway and fork right after the campsite to reach the car park.

This is one of the loveliest Highland glens, running from woods and farmland around Blair Castle into the heather-covered mountains of the southern Cairngorms. Wildlife thrives here, though some species are more elusive than others—you're likely to see red squirrels, roe deer, and buzzards, but need a lot of luck to spot otter, pine marten, or a golden eagle.

The Glen Tilt Trail goes up the west side of the River Tilt and returns down the east side. It is waymarked by yellow arrows on posts, with a choice of longer or shorter routes when you reach Gilbert's Bridge. On a few summer days, the track through

Eating Locally

Need to fuel up before your walk or feeling peckish afterwards? If so, visit the Blair Atholl Watermill tearoom, where bread and cakes are baked using flour ground in the traditional fashion on-site. Rami Cohen, who is both miller and baker, does guided tours of the mill (adults £1.50; children 75p; family £5), which is over the railway crossing from the village center. It's open April–October from 10am to 5:30pm.

Glen Tilt also supports plenty of sheep, which graze freely on lush grass that is enriched by underlying limestone. Eight farms on Atholl Estates have obtained organic certification and now jointly market their beef and lamb under a common brand—Atholl Glens. It's delicious and one of my favorite purchases at Perth Farmers' Market (held on the first Sat of every month).

the rifle range is closed for long-range shooting (these dates are listed on the information board in the car park and on the website). On those days the Glen Banvie Trail makes an attractive alternative.

❶ Arched Bridge From the information board, follow yellow arrows towards the River Tilt. Walk upstream and over an arched bridge, which spans the road below. The path continues beside the river and then joins the main hard path up the glen. In 40m (131 ft.), another section of riverside trail takes you past the Falls of Fender before rejoining the track. Walk past a pasture field, where buzzards often circle. After returning into trees, look out for the next arrow, directing you diagonally left up a grassy track. This runs pleasantly through an open birch wood, then crosses over a stream and bends uphill through a lovely stand of tall larch trees.

❷ Rifle Range Meet a dirt track and turn right along it, soon entering the Jubilee rifle range.

On reaching the rifle range, a marvelous view of the glen opens up, revealing almost all the walk ahead. The bowl on the heathery hill in the middle is Braigh Clais Daimh (Sloping Grassy Hollow of the Stag); both glen and longer route bend right along the foot of the hill. A couple of

benches beside the parking area are a great place to stop and survey the scene.

Cross a bridge and go through a gate to follow the track downhill through the range. Keep right where the rifle-range track forks, then right again at another fork where the left option runs uphill to a row of targets. At the bottom, cross a concrete bridge over a stream and soon come to a post where the routes divide.

❸ Gilbert's Bridge The shorter route goes right and crosses Gilbert's Bridge over the River Tilt. It then turns right on the trail back down the glen, but leaves this after 180m (591 ft.) to climb left through a woodland strip to a stile, where it rejoins the longer route (at point 7).

The longer route goes through a diamond-shaped gate in a deer fence and follows a path uphill. Soon it levels off to run along the bottom of a pine plantation before dipping down to a gate. Continue on a grassy track through gnarled old birches, passing the scattered ruins of ancient stone cottages.

❹ Allt Mhairc The path crosses a stone bridge over the Allt Mhairc, at a point where the stream squeezes down a narrow fall. Not far beyond, go left at a viewpoint sign up to a row of ruined cottages on a level promontory. Turn right along the low

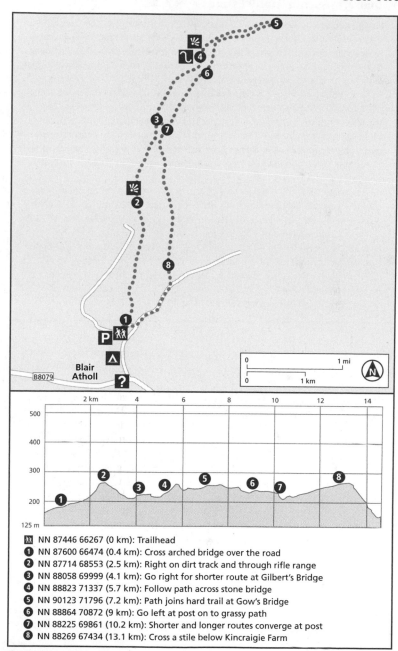

NN 87446 66267 (0 km): Trailhead
1. NN 87600 66474 (0.4 km): Cross arched bridge over the road
2. NN 87714 68553 (2.5 km): Right on dirt track and through rifle range
3. NN 88058 69999 (4.1 km): Go right for shorter route at Gilbert's Bridge
4. NN 88823 71337 (5.7 km): Follow path across stone bridge
5. NN 90123 71796 (7.2 km): Path joins hard trail at Gow's Bridge
6. NN 88864 70872 (9 km): Go left at post on to grassy path
7. NN 88225 69861 (10.2 km): Shorter and longer routes converge at post
8. NN 88269 67434 (13.1 km): Cross a stile below Kincraigie Farm

Blair Castle and Atholl Estates

Dating back to the 1200s, Blair Castle is the historic home of the Earls and Dukes of Atholl. Both castle and grounds are open to the public; attractions include walled Hercules' Garden and Diana's Grove, a pinetum (arboretum) where many record-breaking trees can be seen. Pony trekking stables and a spacious camping and caravan site are located within the grounds.

Surrounding Atholl Estates encompass some 58,000 hectares (143,321 acres) of farm, forest, and heather-clad hills. From mid-August to late October, stag-stalking brings the estate income and helps to control red deer numbers, but that happens well above this route. The woods are managed to conserve endangered species such as capercaillie—a large forest grouse—and red squirrel. Red squirrels are common in the larch and pine trees around Glen Tilt car park, and on the short Red Squirrel Trail.

The estate has its own ranger service and an information center where you can buy walk and bicycle route booklets. The rangers run a program of guided walks and children's nature activities, and a new addition in the summer of 2008 was a webcam trained on a golden eagle nest.

Blair Castle (✆ **01796 481207;** www.blair-castle.co.uk) is open daily April through October (or Easter if earlier) from 9:30am to 4:30pm; Tuesday and Saturday from November to March from 9:30am to 12:30pm. House and grounds admission is adult £7.90, senior £6.90, child £4.90, and family £21; grounds admission only is adult £2.70, senior £2.70, child £1.40, and family £6.

---

ruins before dropping back down onto the narrow grassy path.

This sunny spot above a bend in the river has a view up and down the glen. In olden days, it would have been a great place to live, with good grazing for livestock and plentiful running water nearby. Each cottage had two rooms and a byre (cowshed) for the animals.

The path runs along the top of a steep slope of birch, hazel, rowan, and alder trees. After crossing a stream, clamber above the remains of a small landslide; then continue on riverside grassland where bog plants grow in wet flushes.

5 Gow's Bridge The path joins a hard trail at Gow's Bridge, where there is a view of the Beinn a' Ghlo mountains. Turn right,

over the River Tilt, and return down the far side past Marble Lodge. More of the river is now visible, including, opposite the stream you recently crossed, the "Queen's Ford," used by Mary Queen of Scots when on a hunting trip. Beside a wooden shed, turn left onto a grassy track. It cuts the corner and then rejoins the hard track.

6 Grassy Pathway Beyond a bend, a post again points left onto a grassy path. Follow it up and through a gate (with a strand of electric fence you have to unhook—be careful to grip the plastic handle and to avoid touching the wire, which would give you a small shock); then walk along a flat section above Auchgobhal farm.

Go through another gate and across a stream, passing below a birch forest.

7 Routes Rejoin At a post the shorter route joins the longer one and they continue along the upper edge of fenced woodland. Beyond Croftmore Burn, walk through fields above the cottage of Croftmore. Then a gate leads back into woodland and you soon go left at a fork. After leaving the wood, go through a gate to open farmland. Below, you can see white Blair Castle where Glen Tilt meets broad Strath Garry. If it's clear, Schiehallion will show over the hills beyond the castle, with lumpy Farragon Hill further left.

❽ Glen Fender Walk through a field to a stile below Kincraigie farm; then follow a hard track to the minor road through Glen Fender. Turn right, downhill, and walk through the pretty hamlet of Fenderbridge. Keep right beyond the bridge then go right over Old Bridge of Tilt to return under the arched bridge you crossed at the start.

SEATON CLIFFS ★★

Difficulty rating: Easy

Distance: 5.6km (3.5 miles) round-trip

Estimated time: 1.5 hours

Elevation gain: 49m (160 ft.)

Costs/permits: None

Best time to go: May to July for nesting seabirds and wildflowers

Website: www.swt.org.uk

Recommended map: Seaton Cliffs leaflet available from Arbroath Tourist Information Centre and SWT website

Trailhead GPS: NO 65836 41130

Trailhead directions: Take the A92 from Dundee to Arbroath (24km/15 miles), and in the town turn right after the harbor roundabout at a junction signed VICTORIA PARK AND CLIFFS. Follow the road all the way to the park, entered through white pillars, and drive to the car park at the far end.

The popular Scottish Wildlife Trust Reserve at Seaton Cliffs on the outskirts of Arbroath is a haven for seabirds, wildflowers, and butterflies. A paved path runs along the top of the sandstone cliffs, which the sea has eroded into weird and wonderful formations, such as the Deil's Heid and the Blowhole. Frequent seats provide plenty of resting places.

The walk starts from the end of the long promenade that curves east from Arbroath, at a car park with a toilet block and information board about the SWT Reserve. By the start of the path, a trickle of water flows out of a rock face—this is St. Ninian's Well, which was believed to have curative powers, though it is no longer fit for drinking.

❶ Whiting Ness The path slopes up the first bluff, known as Whiting Ness. From the top, you can look back over the large town of Arbroath, the main seaport of Angus.

A large notice with instructions on how to call the Coastguard is a pertinent reminder that the cliffs are dangerous—keep children and pets under close control and stay away from the edge. To enable people to give a precise location for a rescue, there are yellow-topped posts with numbers beside the path.

❷ Needle E'e After 0.8km (¹/₂ mile), you draw level with the Needle E'e (Eye), a natural arch, through which you see the sea churning below. Mermaid's Kirk (Church), a chasm that goes down to sea level, is to the left. Not far beyond, a sign marks the start of the SWT Reserve.

(Fun Facts) **Power of the Sea**

All the formations you see are different stages of the sea's inexorable work of wearing down the rock into grains of sand, which is what this Old Red Sandstone originally was when laid down some 400 million years ago. First the sea erodes a cave, which may penetrate deep into the cliffs, until the roof collapses, creating an inlet. The headlands between these coves are slowly worn down to leave sea stacks. One day the waves will undercut the Deil's Heid and the sea will reclaim it.

You will see the most seabirds during the breeding season, May to July, when they use ledges on the cliffs to nest. Puffin, guillemot, razorbill, shag, fulmar, and eider duck are found in the reserve. Herring gulls hang around all year, and, if you're lucky, you may see a peregrine falcon.

The grass on either side of the path is rich in wildflowers, including thrift, red clover, knapweed, and sea campion. The next sheer-sided inlet is called Seamen's Grave—don't get too close, you don't want to join them!

❸ The Blowhole When you draw level with post AS10, you can see the Blowhole on the right side of the inlet below—in stormy weather the sea drives right up through this spout. The path then bends left to run around Dickmont's Den, a creek where the sea has penetrated deep inland along a weakness in the rock. Ignore a path across the fields and continue round the Den to another rocky bay. Beside post AS16, a headland with a seat has a view to a bulbous sea stack.

❹ Deil's Heid Walk on past the sea stack, admiring the profile of the Deil's Heid (Scots for Devil's Head).

At the Deil's Heid, you round a corner and pass another path junction. Now there is a pebbly beach (Cove Haven) below, and

set behind it is the earth mound of Maiden's Castle, an Iron Age fort. Its slopes are pock-marked with rabbit burrows.

❺ Castle Gate A narrow spine of rock encloses the far end of Cove Haven. This is called Castle Gate or the Three Sisters, because it is eroded into three grass-topped stacks. Beyond lies the wide sweep of Carlingheugh Bay, where a golden strip of sand curves above a wave-cut rock platform that stretches far out to sea. A narrow path angles diagonally down the grassy slope to the beach, providing the only safe access to the shore. Continue on the paved path that now runs inland beside a sheer-walled valley. Suddenly you enter a different ecosystem, with trees, ferns, and woodland birds.

❻ Seaton Den Cross a wooden bridge over a chasm in the side of the valley and come to the end of the path beside another sign marking the top end of the SWT Reserve. If you want a closer look at Seaton Den, continue 50m (164 ft.) onwards down an earth path to the small stream flowing down the valley. Turn around here (the path continues along the cliffs all the way to Auchmithie 2.9km/1.8 miles away), and return along the paved path. You will see the cliffs from a different angle on your way back.

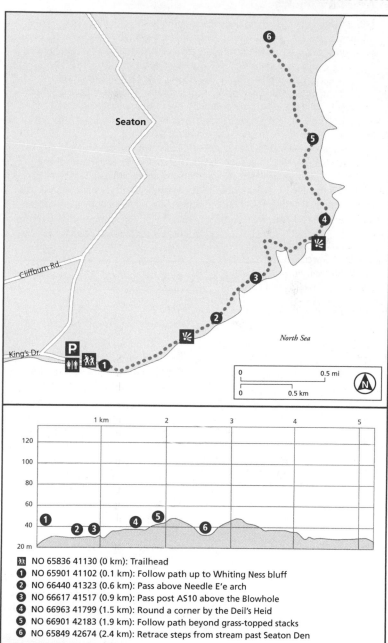

North Sea

🏃 NO 65836 41130 (0 km): Trailhead
❶ NO 65901 41102 (0.1 km): Follow path up to Whiting Ness bluff
❷ NO 66440 41323 (0.6 km): Pass above Needle E'e arch
❸ NO 66617 41517 (0.9 km): Pass post AS10 above the Blowhole
❹ NO 66963 41799 (1.5 km): Round a corner by the Deil's Heid
❺ NO 66901 42183 (1.9 km): Follow path beyond grass-topped stacks
❻ NO 65849 42674 (2.4 km): Retrace steps from stream past Seaton Den

Arbroath Smokie

Arbroath has an active fishing fleet and is home to a traditional delicacy—the Arbroath Smokie. As you pass the harbor on the way to the start, you will see some small shops selling them. It is very much a cottage industry, with the same families specializing in smoking fish for generations.

Only haddock are used to produce authentic Arbroath Smokies. Using a method that originated at nearby Auchmithie in the 1800s, the fish are gutted, dry salted, and then tied in pairs and hung over sticks for smoking over a hardwood fire. The resulting fish, with their orange-brown wrinkled skin, may not look very attractive, but they are packed full of flavor.

Like Champagne and Parma Ham, Europe has awarded the Arbroath Smokie Protected Geographical Indication status. That means the name can only be applied to haddock smoked in the traditional manner within an 8km (5-mile) radius of Arbroath. The Spink's website at www.arbroathsmokies.net includes the Fraser Collection gallery of old photographs, showing fisherwomen producing Smokies 100 years ago.

MAYAR & DRIESH

Difficulty rating: Strenuous

Distance: 14km (8.5 miles) round-trip

Estimated time: 6 hours

Elevation gain: 701m (2,300 ft.)

Costs/permits: £1.50 for car parking

Best time to go: July to September for heather blooming

Website: www.angusanddundee.co.uk

Recommended map: OS Explorer 388 (OS Landranger 44)

Trailhead GPS: NO 28390 76065

Trailhead directions: From Kirriemuir, follow signs for Glen Clova and drive all the way up the glen to the Glendoll car park.

The drive to the foot of these two Munros takes you up Glen Clova, one of the prettiest of the Angus Glens—long, U-shaped valleys in the southeast of Cairngorms National Park. The head of the glen bends round into Glen Doll, a forested valley hemmed in by cliffs and steep heather slopes. From there you climb through spectacular scenery to the barren landscape of a vast, rolling mountain plateau.

For many people, the Glendoll car park is a destination in itself; dramatic hillsides provide a backdrop to picnic tables on the grassy banks of the River South Esk.

A number of walks are waymarked through the forest, and this longer route starts by following the Corrie Fee walk, which has green-ringed posts.

1 Glendoll Turn right out of the car park and walk by the Angus Ranger Service headquarters. Keep straight ahead past the white farm buildings of Acharn and walk up Glen Doll beside the White Water. When Jock's Road branches off on the right, remain on the main track, which dips down to cross the fast-flowing river.

TAYSIDE & FIFE WALKS

6

MAYAR & DRIESH

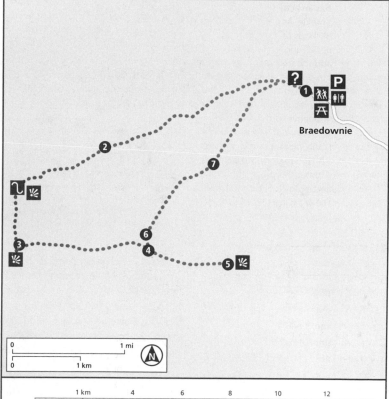

Braedownie

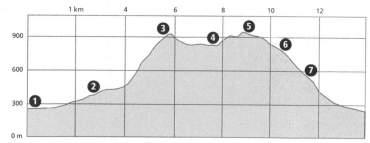

0   1 mi
0   1 km

🏃	NO 28390 76065 (0 km): Trailhead
❶	NO 28391 76060 (0 km): Walk past the Angus Ranger Service headquarters
❷	NO 25376 75253 (3.4 km): Pass through gate and enjoy view of Corrie Fee
❸	NO 24081 73732 (5.8 km): Small cairn marks the summit of Mayar
❹	NO 26021 73786 (7.8 km): Veer right down to a col
❺	NO 27116 73573 (9 km): Low shelter cairn at trig point at summit of Driesh
❻	NO 25961 73987 (10.3 km): Follow path to the right and rejoin Kilbo Path
❼	NO 26890 74987 (11.7 km): Use stepping stones to cross Burn of Kilbo

Continue alongside the rapids, ignoring side turns, to a major junction and fork left on a track climbing uphill. When the track ends, keep straight ahead on a well-made path through boulder-strewn pine forest.

❷ **Corrie Fee** At the top of the forest, you go through a gate and suddenly have a dramatic view of Corrie Fee. The wild, remote corrie is ringed by cliffs and has a waterfall cascading down the back wall. A good path weaves around and over heathery knolls of moraine as it crosses the corrie to the foot of the waterfall. It becomes rougher as it zigzags steeply uphill on the left of the falls, giving a great view back over the corrie. At the lip of the corrie the gradient suddenly eases as you gain the grassy plateau.

❸ **Mayar** In poor visibility, careful navigation is needed, but normally you can see a worn trail leading up to the summit of Mayar (928m/3,045 ft.), a stony height on the plateau marked by a small cairn.

Look north over the great rolling mountain plateau, the White Mounth, which stretches up to Lochnagar and is bitten into by cliff-girt glens. Higher peaks of the central Cairngorms can be seen farther off to the northwest, while your second summit, Driesh, lies due east and is merely a larger bump in the vast plateau. Lovely Glen Prosen lies below you, and the Backwater Reservoir gleams in the distance.

From Mayar, head northeast and then east, following a broad ridge down to a low swelling in the plateau where you meet the Kilbo Path. Walk east along it, with a fence on your right.

❹ **Col** At a rocky top where the Kilbo Path bends left to descend the Shank of Drumfollow, veer slightly right to drop down to a col separating the two mountains. Climb straight up the far side. A worn path skirts the left side of a broad hillock and then rises up towards the wide, stony summit of Driesh, passing a 1m-high (3.3 ft.) cairn.

❺ **Driesh Cairn** A low shelter cairn surrounds the trig point marker on Driesh (947m/3,107 ft.).

Driesh isn't the prettiest viewpoint—you have to walk to the edge of the flattish top to get a view into the glens—but it does have shelter, a rare commodity on the bare, windswept White Mounth. This is a good place to stop for a quick sandwich before descending.

Retrace your steps down to the col; then climb back up towards the Kilbo Path, which angles at a steady gradient down the side of the ridge ahead.

❻ **Kilbo Path** You don't need to climb all the way back up, as a small, rough path to the right contours across to the Kilbo Path. The narrow but well-worn Kilbo Path descends the side of a deep valley before bending right to the forest, which you enter through a gate.

❼ **Burn of Kilbo** The path runs through trees along the edge of the forest and then bends away from the open and comes to the Burn of Kilbo. Stride over the massive stepping stones and continue downhill. On the way down, you cross one forest path, then cut over a U-bend in another before continuing through the trees. Turn right on a level path near the river; then go left over a bridge to rejoin the outward track. Head right to return past Acharn to the car park.

Jock's Road

Three ancient pathways climb over the hills from Glendoll: the Capel Mounth to Ballater, the Kilbo Path to Glen Prosen, and Jock's Road over Tolmount to Braemar. For centuries, they have provided a link for foot and horseback travelers between Angus and Deeside. The one that the first 1.6km (1 mile) of this walk follows—Jock's Road—has played a significant role in upholding access rights.

Duncan Macpherson, who owned Glen Doll in the late 1800s, attempted to close the route to Braemar, an action that was contested by the Scottish Rights of Way and Recreation Society. The Society proved that it had long been the practice of drovers to take sheep from Braemar over the Tolmount to the market at Cullow, near Kirriemuir, and that it was therefore an established right of way.

The case went to the House of Lords on appeal, and in 1887 they ruled in favor of the Society, leaving Duncan Macpherson with substantial costs to pay—a result that deterred other landowners from trying to close similar routes. The Society is now called the Scottish Rights of Way and Access Society, Scotways for short (www.scotways.com), and it takes an interest in all types of access. You will see their footpath signs throughout Scotland, many marking traditional hill tracks, such as Jock's Road.

RANNOCH TO CORROUR

Difficulty rating: Strenuous

Distance: 19km (12 miles) one-way (return by train)

Estimated time: 6 hours

Elevation gain: 250m (820 ft.)

Costs/permits: None, except rail fare

Best time to go: June to August for moorland flowers

Website: www.perthshire.co.uk/index.asp?pg=356

Recommended map: OS Explorer 385 (OS Landranger 41 and 42)

Trailhead GPS: NN 42272 57794

Trailhead directions: Leave the A9 at Calvine and take the B8467 to Kinloch Rannoch, then the B846 for 29 slow kilometers (18 miles) to Rannoch Station car park at the end of the road. Alternatively, arrive via a West Highland Line train or catch the bus from Kinloch Rannoch.

Cross the great wilderness of Rannoch Moor, following the "Road to the Isles," an ancient route that drovers, soldiers, merchants, and missionaries used to travel to Skye and the Western Isles. The Moor is Britain's largest area of blanket peat bog—a huge, high amphitheatre, ringed by mountains, that soaks up rainfall and feeds rivers flowing in all directions. There is no shelter from the elements along the route, and the destination—lonely Corrour Station—is not on any public road, so you must return by train.

This desolate landscape and the rough, muddy trail are not for the faint-hearted, but they do provide a great sense of remoteness from civilization—somewhere you can truly be alone. Don't tackle the route in bad weather; there are many tales of people becoming lost, including engineers who surveyed the route of the railway in 1889 and had to be rescued from a blizzard by shepherds.

❶ **Rannoch Station** Walk back along the road, immediately passing the Moor of Rannoch Hotel. Continue gently downhill for 2km (1¼ miles) across the open moor to Loch Eigheach, where you cross a bridge over the River Eigheach.

❷ **Start of Trail** About 400m (1,312 ft.) beyond the bridge, turn sharply left onto a track, marked by a public footpath sign (facing the other way). Pass a padlocked gate and follow the hard track across flat moorland before rising around the shoulder of Meall na Mucarach. The track levels off by a quarry, where you can pause to drink in the view—over Rannoch Station to Loch Laidon and the distant Glencoe Mountains.

Just north of Rannoch Station, you can see a viaduct that was built to span a very wet area of moorland where the sponge-like peat is 6.1m (20 ft.) deep. Elsewhere across the moor the construction team was able to float the railway line on a raft of brushwood. Beyond the viaduct, the line goes through a cutting that tended to fill with snowdrifts, so it was roofed over to create a snow tunnel.

As you round a bend, the track stretches ahead up the U-shaped valley of the Allt Eigheach. Descend gently and cross a side stream, the Allt Gormag, at a ford (go slightly downstream to get over dry-shod).

❸ **Allt Eigheach** Continue 300m (984 ft.) beyond the ford, and then turn left across a footbridge over the Allt Eigheach. Follow a grassy track upstream, rejoining the hard track once it has forded the river. Now a long, steady, 4.8km (3-mile) climb begins. Initially, the track rises parallel to the river; then, at an arrow, it bends left to climb the flanks of Sron

Leachd a' Chaorainn. The young plantation of Scots pines on the left contains the last trees you will see until Loch Ossian.

❹ **Trail Junction** At a trail junction, keep straight ahead on a grassy path, ignoring the eroded track climbing to the right. The scene becomes wilder and emptier as you rise, gaining a view of little Lochan a' Chladheimh below and the Blackwater Reservoir snaking away between the mountains. After the gradient levels off, you can see a distant white building in the middle of nowhere—Corrour Station House. You have to bypass a gully where the track has been washed away. Beyond, several smaller gullies have to be negotiated.

❺ **Old Corrour Lodge** The path dips gently into the wide bowl containing the roofless gray ruin of Old Corrour Lodge. Just before it, you have to cross the Allt a' Choire Odhair Mhoir—the "stream of the dappled corrie."

From a distance, the remaining walls appear to be formed by breezeblocks, but closer inspection reveals massive granite slabs. After life as a shooting lodge, the building served as an isolation hospital—it is hard to imagine anywhere more isolated. This is a good spot for a picnic, as grassy lawns remain and there are rectangular stones to sit on.

Beyond the ruins, the track climbs gently for another 20m (66 ft.) and rounds the shoulder of Carn Dearg. From the high point of 550m (1,804 ft.), the track begins a gradual descent towards Loch Ossian.

❻ **Peter's Rock** Beside a wooden post, turn left, heading more steeply downhill. Peter's Rock, the boulder on the junction,

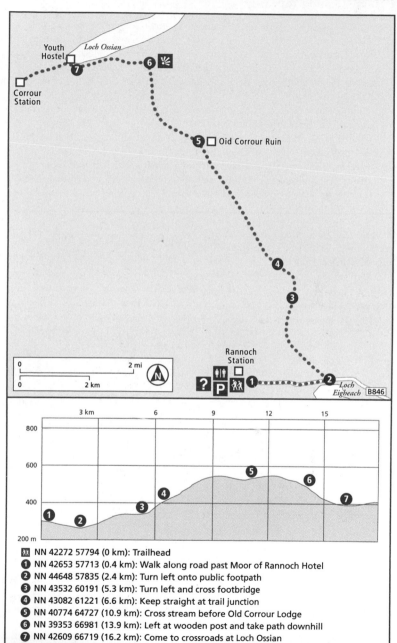

NN 42272 57794 (0 km): Trailhead
1 NN 42653 57713 (0.4 km): Walk along road past Moor of Rannoch Hotel
2 NN 44648 57835 (2.4 km): Turn left onto public footpath
3 NN 43532 60191 (5.3 km): Turn left and cross footbridge
4 NN 43082 61221 (6.6 km): Keep straight at trail junction
5 NN 40774 64727 (10.9 km): Cross stream before Old Corrour Lodge
6 NN 39353 66981 (13.9 km): Left at wooden post and take path downhill
7 NN 42609 66719 (16.2 km): Come to crossroads at Loch Ossian

6

> **(Tips) Timing Your Day**
>
> Rannoch Station has a cozy tearoom and an exhibition about the Moor and the building of the West Highland Line across it. Unless you make a very early start, you will need to return on the 6:25pm train, by which time Rannoch Station's facilities are closed, so it's worth visiting before you set off. Dinner is usually available for non-residents at the Moor of Rannoch Hotel if pre-booked ((C) **01882 633238**).
>
> Corrour Station House is a restaurant and B&B, open most days until 9pm, though closing days can vary, so it is worth checking in advance ((C) **01397 732236**).
>
> Neither station is manned by railway staff, so you must buy your ticket on the train; the standard single is £2.50 (if the conductor asks for your fare!) and the ride takes 12 minutes. Alternatively, you could take the train first and do the route in reverse. However, the views are better heading north, and you can enjoy the romance of stepping out across the wilderness in the direction of the Isles.

has a plaque (on the side facing the loch) bearing a poignant inscription to Peter J. Trowell, who died at age 30 at Loch Ossian.

> You can easily see why this spot was chosen for a memorial to someone who loved walking in the hills. Mountains rise on all sides of Loch Ossian. Westward, the Mamores and Grey Corries lie on either side of Glen Nevis, while the horizon beyond the Blackwater Reservoir is rimmed by the heights of Glencoe.

Descend diagonally towards the loch, passing a line of metal fence posts as you draw level with the top of a forestry plantation. The wet, eroded track skirts the north side of Meall na Lice and heads towards the wooded islands at the head of the loch.

7 Loch Ossian As you near Loch Ossian, the track swings over a knoll and then drops across a boggy area (go further left to avoid this) to a crossroads of tracks. The route goes left, but it is worth first walking straight across to Loch Ossian Youth Hostel, one of the most remote hostels in Britain. The small wooden building on the shore is probably the first place you'll meet anyone on the moor. Take the main track away from the hostel, rising westwards away from the loch. Turn left when you meet a wider track and follow this for 1.6km (1 mile) to Corrour Station.

SLEEPING & EATING

ACCOMMODATIONS

★ (Kids) **Blair Castle Caravan Park** This site for touring caravans, motorhomes, and tents has a lovely, spacious parkland setting where children can roam free and parents can find peace walking the dog in the woods. The modern facilities are spic and span, and village shops, bars, and restaurants are a few minutes' walk away.

Blair Atholl PH18 5SR. (C) **01796 481263**. www.blaircastlecaravanpark.co.uk. 280 units. £14–£16 touring pitch for 2. MC, V. Closed Dec–Feb. **Close to:** Glen Tilt, The Hermitage.

Craigtay Hotel   A mile from the center of Dundee, this friendly, family-run hotel is handy for both Angus and Fife. It was constructed around an 18th-century farm building, but has been much enlarged and modernized. The functional guest rooms are individually shaped and decorated. Gavin's Bistro serves moderately priced dinners nightly.

101 Broughty Ferry Rd., Dundee DD4 6JE. ℂ **01382 451142.** www.craigtay.co.uk. 18 units. £35–£50. Rates include breakfast. AE, MC, V. Free parking. **Close to:** Seaton Cliffs, Fife Coastal Path.

★★ (Kids) **Crieff Hydro Hotel**   This family-run resort spreads over 364 hectares (900 acres) of woods and meadows above Crieff. Starting life as a grand spa hotel 140 years ago, it has been fully modernized. It has self-catering lodges in secluded little villages and a staggering selection of sporting activities, including play centers for children and teenagers.

Crieff PH7 3LG. ℂ **01764 651670.** www.crieffhydro.com. 263 units. £99–£195 hotel including breakfast, £14–£60 in self-catering. AE, MC, V. **Close to:** Perth and Kinnoull Hill, Knock of Crieff, The Hermitage.

★★ **Hilton Dunkeld House Hotel**   Set in peaceful grounds on the banks of the River Tay, this hotel has the atmosphere of a grand country house and excellent leisure facilities. Guests can luxuriate in the health club, walk in the woods, fish from the riverbank, or participate in other outdoor activities.

Dunkeld PH8 0HX. ℂ **01350 727771.** www.hilton.co.uk/dunkeld. 96 units. £54–£135 double; £135–£150 suite. Rates include Scottish breakfast. AE, DC, MC, V. **Close to:** The Hermitage, Perth and Kinnoull Hill, Knock of Crieff, Glen Tilt.

★ **Parklands Hotel**   On opening as a hotel in 1991, this classic Georgian townhouse immediately became Perth's most fashionable lodging. The spacious and beautifully decorated guest rooms, filled with wood paneling and cornices, overlook the South Inch Park. It is conveniently close to the rail station and is acclaimed for its dining.

2 St. Leonard's Bank, Perth PH2 8EB. ℂ **01738 622451.** www.theparklandshotel.com. 14 units. £50–£60. Rates include breakfast. AE, DC, MC, V. **Close to:** Perth and Kinnoull Hill, Loch Leven Heritage Trail, Knock of Crieff, The Hermitage.

Sauchope Links Holiday Park   The Fife Coastal Path runs though this holiday park, which is primarily dedicated to static caravans, but has some touring spaces for motorhomes, caravans, and tents. The tranquil retreat is situated on the seashore, within walking distance of the charming town of Crail, and has an attractive area for tents.

Crail, Fife. KY10 3XJ. ℂ **01333 450460.** www.largoleisure.co.uk. 20 units. £14–£25 touring pitch for 2 (tents can be no bigger than 3.7×1.8m/12×6 ft.). MC, V. Closed Nov–Mar. **Close to:** Fife Coastal Path, Loch Leven Heritage Trail.

RESTAURANTS

Balaka   BANGLADESHI/INTERNATIONAL   Behind a facade of gray stone, this Indian restaurant has a garden planted with vegetables, flowers, and herbs, which are used by the kitchen staff. The hospitable Rouf family offers dishes such as Mas Bangla, Scottish salmon marinated in lime juice and flavored with turmeric, green chilli, and spices.

3 Alexandra Place, St. Andrews, Fife. ℂ **01334 474825.** www.balaka.com. Reservations recommended. Main courses £8.50–£15. AE, MC, V. Mon–Sat noon–3pm and 5pm–1am; Sun 5pm–1am. **Close to:** Fife Coastal Path, Seaton Cliffs.

Ben Lawers Hotel   SCOTTISH   A reputation for "good food and plenty of it," makes a meal at this 300-year-old hotel just what you need after climbing a mountain. Try "A Wee Taster" of Stornoway black pudding and Simon Howie haggis with whisky cream sauce for a delicious starter, followed by the Scottish platter.

Lawers, Loch Tay, Perthshire. ✆ **01567 820436.** www.benlawershotel.co.uk. Main courses £9–£13. MC, V. Daily 11am–9pm. Reservations recommended at peak times. Closed mid-Nov to Jan. **Close to:** Ben Lawers.

★ **Duncan's** INTERNATIONAL   Head chef and owner James Duncan sources fresh food from the best local suppliers and cooks it in imaginative combinations, such as slow-roasted Puddledub pork shoulder with baked fennel and cider sauce, or the roast loin of Fletchers of Auchtermuchty venison with red wine–poached pear, fondant potato, and kale.

33 George St., Perth. ✆ **01738 622016.** www.duncansinperth.com. Reservations recommended. Main courses: lunch £7.95, early supper £8.50, dinner £15 (3-course dinner £23). AE, MC, V. Mon–Sat noon–2:30pm and 5:30–9pm. **Close to:** Perth and Kinnoull Hill.

★★ **East Haugh House** MODERN BRITISH   Meals in the cozy bar may include mixed grills, steaks, and haggis, while the elegant restaurant has a more adventurous menu, featuring such dishes as terrine of local pigeon with orange salad and mange tout, and roast best end of Perthshire lamb on a minted mash.

Old Perth Rd., East Haugh, Pitlochry, Perthshire. ✆ **01796 472473.** www.easthaugh.co.uk. Reservations recommended. Set-price dinner menu £45; bar platters £4.50–£19. MC, V. Restaurant daily 7–9pm; bar daily noon–2:30pm and 6–9pm. **Close to:** Glen Tilt, The Hermitage.

Loch Leven's Larder BRITISH   This family-run farm shop and cafe has proven so popular that they have had to expand. A favorite of walkers on the Loch Leven Heritage Trail, the cafe serves wholesome meals made with fresh, seasonal ingredients sourced as locally as possible, including their own beef, eggs, and vegetables.

Channel Farm, Milnathort, Kinross. ✆ **01592 841000.** www.lochlevenslarder.com. Reservations recommended in summer. Main courses £4–£9. MC, V. Daily 9:30am–6pm (to 5pm Oct–May). **Close to:** Loch Leven Heritage Trail.

The Mayview Hotel SEAFOOD   This St. Monans hotel has a relaxing, modern interior. It specializes in seafood, but also offers chicken dishes and steaks. The same menu is available for lunch and dinner, with dishes such as monkfish tail stuffed with Pittenweem prawns.

40 Station Rd., St. Monans, Fife. ✆ **01333 730564.** www.mayviewhotel.co.uk. Main courses £11–£15. MC, V. Thurs–Tues 12:30–2:30pm and 6–8:30pm; closed Wed. Reservations recommended at peak times. **Close to:** Fife Coastal Path.

Argyll & the
West Highlands Walks

by Felicity Martin

Lying north of Glasgow, west of Stirling, and south of Fort William, this is the most watery part of Scotland, with more miles of coast than you can imagine from a quick glance at a large-scale map. It is a landscape of long, winding lochs, wooded peninsulas, green islands, and mountains that rise straight out of the sea. These are Scotland's Atlantic shores, where the Gulf Stream ensures a mild, damp climate—don't be surprised to see palm trees growing in gardens.

Loch Lomond and the Trossachs National Park covers the eastern part of the region and is only half an hour from Glasgow or Stirling. The National Park includes Loch Lomond, which is Britain's largest body of inland water, and the pretty wooded glens and lochs of the Trossachs, as well as Argyll Forest Park on the Cowal peninsula in the west and soaring mountains in the north.

Oban, the largest town, lies on the west coast. It is a popular holiday resort and a busy ferry port. The stone buildings encircle a sheltered bay, from which the eye-catching black, white, and red Caledonian MacBrayne ferries sail to the southern Hebrides. Many other smaller towns and villages, such as Callander, Inveraray, Lochgilphead, and Carradale, also rely on the tourist trade, offering peace and quiet in picturesque surroundings.

The walking here ranges from gentle strolls along the shore to scenic hill walks and challenging mountain climbs. If you enjoy guided walks, come for Mull Wildlife Week in May or Cowal Walking and Arts Festival in October, or look out for the regular ranger-led events in the National Park. Forestry Commission Scotland, which manages vast tracts of public forest across the region, encourages recreation by providing many car parks with waymarked walking and cycling trails. Leaflets describing these routes are available at visitor centers. Two long-distance routes run through the area: the well-trodden West Highland Way, which runs up the east shore of Loch Lomond and goes north through the mountains to Fort William, and the newer, much less frequented Kintyre Way, which runs the length of that peninsula.

You'll find plenty of English accents in Argyll, especially in places like the Isle of Mull, where people have escaped to live the dream of a rural life with beautiful views to wake up to every day. It's a laid-back, welcoming area, where you too will soon leave your everyday cares behind.

The pace of life is slow, and so is travel. There are no straight lines here, and the topography means that roads weave around lochs and mountains. Don't try to squeeze in too many places on your visit. Allow time to sit on the shore watching a family of eider duck bob on the waves, or to explore a fairytale wood where hoary old oaks drip with lichens, mosses, and ferns, and bluebells carpet the ground.

ESSENTIALS

GETTING THERE

By Air

If you're flying into Scotland, chose Glasgow airport (www.glasgowairport.com), from where you can hire a car and head straight across the Erskine Bridge and up the A82 trunk road to Loch Lomond. At Tarbet, on the west shore of the loch, either continue north and then turn left at Tyndrum onto the A85 for Oban, or take the A83 west to Lochgilphead and down the Kintyre peninsula. The A816 meanders up the west coast between Lochgilphead and Oban. If driving from the south, you can also come via Stirling, taking the A811 to Loch Lomond or the A84 to Callander.

By Bus

Scottish Citylink (℗ 08705 505050; www.citylink.co.uk), the national coach operator, has service to the major towns in the region; Glasgow to Oban takes about 3 hours, and a standard single costs £15.

By Train

First Scotrail (℗ 08457 484950; www.firstgroup.com/scotrail) runs trains on the West Highland line to Oban; Glasgow to Oban takes about 3 hours, and a single fare costs £18.

VISITOR INFORMATION

VisitScotland (℗ 08452 255121; www.visitscotland.com), the Scottish tourist board, provides information on the area and a booking service. It has 24 Tourist Information Centres throughout the region; they include the National Park Gateway Centre at Loch Lomond Shores in Balloch (℗ 08707 200631) and one in Oban (℗ 01631 563122) at Argyll Square. For in-depth information, see VisitScotland's website for this region, www.visit scottishheartlands.com, and the National Park website, www.lochlomond-trossachs.org.

ORIENTATION

The best way to get a handle on the geography of the area is by its lochs. The region starts at the Firth of Clyde, where sea lochs bound the Cowal peninsula: Loch Long on the east and Loch Fyne on the west. Lochgilphead lies on the far shore of Loch Fyne, and from here a long tongue of land extends southwards to Knapdale and the Kintyre peninsula, which encloses the west side of the Firth of Clyde. Heading north from Lochgilphead takes you through Kilmartin Glen to Oban.

The Firth of Lorn separates Oban from the Isle of Mull, and two sea lochs extend from it—Loch Etive running inland into the mountains, with its tidal falls racing under the Connel Bridge, and Loch Linhe running north to Fort William. Freshwater lochs abound, including two of Scotland's largest—Loch Lomond in the east of the region and Loch Awe in the west. The Trossachs lie to the northeast of Loch Lomond, nearer Stirling, and here practically every glen contains a sparkling loch, including Loch Katrine, home of the steamship *Sir Walter Scott*.

GETTING AROUND

Traveline Scotland (℗ 08712 002233; www.travelinescotland.com), the national travel service, can help you plan your journey using public transport. The service has details of both small bus companies that provide local services and major transport operators.

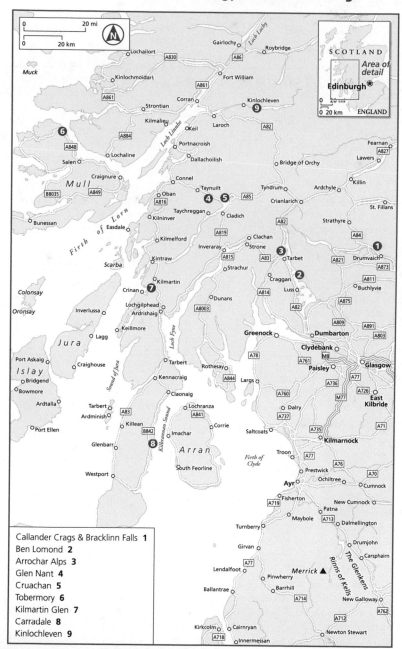

Callander Crags & Bracklinn Falls **1**
Ben Lomond **2**
Arrochar Alps **3**
Glen Nant **4**
Cruachan **5**
Tobermory **6**
Kilmartin Glen **7**
Carradale **8**
Kinlochleven **9**

Caledonian MacBrayne (☎ **08705 650000;** www.calmac.co.uk), locally known as CalMac, runs ferry services to the islands.

In the summer, the **Trossachs Trundler** (☎ **01786 442707**) provides a service for walkers and other explorers, with day rover tickets (£8) that allow you to hop on and off where you like.

CALLANDER CRAGS & BRACKLINN FALLS ★

Difficulty rating: Moderate

Distance: 9.3km (5.8 miles) round-trip

Estimated time: 4 hours

Elevation gain: 261m (855 ft.)

Costs/permits: None

Best time to go: October and November for autumn colors and waterfalls

Website: www.incallander.co.uk

Recommended map: OS Landranger 57 (or OS Explorer maps 365, 366 & 368)

Trailhead GPS: NN 63364 08168

Trailhead directions: Take the A84 from Stirling into Callander. On the main street, take the turn (opposite the Roman Camp Hotel) signposted BRACKLINN FALLS AND LOWER WOOD. Go over a bridge, round a double bend, and turn left into a forest car park at a sign for Callander Crags. Buses run from Stirling to Callander.

Callander is the main resort town in the pretty Trossachs, an area of wooded hills at the heart of Loch Lomond and the Trossachs National Park. This walk encompasses the local beauty spots, starting with a vigorous climb up Callander Crags, a line of cliffs topped by a cairn that commemorates Queen Victoria's Diamond Jubilee in 1897, followed by a stroll to Bracklinn Falls, where a river tumbles over enormous blocks of stone.

If staying in Callander or arriving by bus, walk up the Bracklinn Falls road from the High Street to the Lower Wood car park.

❶ **Lower Wood** The first part of the route follows the waymarked Callander Crags walk. From the car park, go around a barrier and along a trail. Ignore a path to the right, which comes down from the crags. Beyond a mobile phone tower, enjoy a view up to the tree-lined cliffs. The track soon ends, and the path continues down to the left. At a junction by a footbridge and bench, go right down steps and continue below the crags.

❷ **Road Intersection** The path takes a sharp right bend at the bottom of the crags, where a road runs up to the wood

from the west end of Callander High Street. This is where the work really begins, as you start a steep and sustained climb under spreading beech trees. Cliffs drop away just to the right of the path, so keep dogs and children under close rein. Trees screen the vista until you come to a clearing and get a bird's-eye view over Callander. Where the path dips down to a footbridge, the waymarked walk turns right downhill. Instead, keep straight on across the bridge and up a short rocky scramble to a kissing gate.

❸ **Jubilee Cairn** As the rocky ground levels off, the view opens up all around and you come to a tall cairn with a stone plaque on the side.

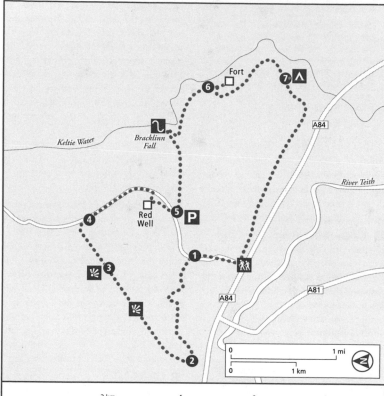

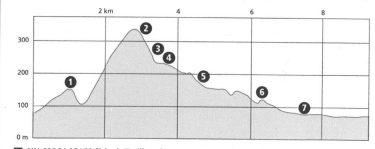

🚶 NN 63364 08168 (0 km): Trailhead
❶ NN 63366 08164 (0.4 km): Follow the waymarked Callander Crags walk
❷ NN 62362 08180 (1.6 km): Take sharp right at path at bottom of the crags
❸ NN 63204 08980 (2.8 km): Tall cairn with stone plaque
❹ NN 63656 09153 (3.3 km): Turn right at narrow lane
❺ NN 63721 08316 (4.6 km): Continue downhill to Bracklinn Falls car park
❻ NN 64880 08021 (6.2 km): Turn down past path to fort remains
❼ NN 65008 07346 (7.4 km): Pass camp and cross ridge of Auchenlaich cairn

Malcolm Ferguson picked a grand spot to honor Queen Victoria. Lovely Loch Venachar nestles between the Menteith Hills and Ben Ledi, the high grassy hill due west. To the southeast, Stirling lies on the flat plain of the River Forth with the Wallace Monument and Stirling Castle visible on rock outcrops. Ahead, you can see a much more recent addition to the view—the Braes of Doon wind farm.

Continue on the path beyond the cairn, which goes downhill, crossing several sloping rock slabs where you may need to use your hands to steady yourself. Eventually the path bends away from the fence it has been running beside and into birch trees.

4 Keltie Glen Road The path is rougher through the wood, but it soon takes you down to a narrow lane. Turn right and follow it downhill through rough grassland that is full of wildflowers, including several species of orchid. A bench on a bend overlooks Callander, but there is another place to stop just beyond.

Soon after the bend, go right at a sign for Red Well. A short path leads up to a curved stone feature, out of which flows a rust-red stream of water. In the 17th century, iron-rich Chalybeate springs such as this became very popular for their health-giving properties. Enjoy a great view from the bench in this peaceful spot.

5 Bracklinn Falls Keep going downhill until you see the Bracklinn Falls car park on your left. Go through it, down steps, and turn left along a level path. Keep straight on through woods and open land until steps lead down to Bracklinn Falls. Again take care near the edge.

Amazingly, the river has broken through a hard layer of rock, eroding the strata into great rectangular blocks. The river cascades down a series of falls between these tumbled rocks. A bridge dating from Victorian times spanned the gorge until 2006, when a summer storm brought a flood that washed it away (as well as six other nearby bridges). When you see how high above the river the path ends, you'll be amazed by how great the torrent must have been.

Return up the steps and, just before two benches, go left on a grassy path. This takes you downhill between trees to the end of a wide, gravel track.

6 Pictish Fort If you continue on the path, it leads uphill to the remains of an Iron Age fort built by the native Picts, a Celtic people encountered by the Romans when they first invaded the country 2,000 years ago. However, in summer there is little to see, as the mound is thick with bracken. Turn down the track and stay on it all the way through forest and out into farmland, where you are likely to see sheep and cattle grazing. After a right bend, look right for a view back to Callander Crags.

7 Auchenlaich Pass a gate that leads into Keltie Bridge Caravan Park; then cross the stony ridge of Auchenlaich cairn, at 351m (1,150 ft.) the longest Megalithic burial cairn in Britain. The track goes around the right side of Auchenlaich farm and bends left to a junction of fenced paths. Turn right and walk through woods, then houses, back into Callander.

The path follows the course of a disused railway line and is also part of a cycle route. Where the path ends, continue on Livingstone Avenue and follow the bicycle signs to the bridge you crossed earlier. Here turn left for Main Street or go over the bridge and up the road to the Lower Wood car park.

BEN LOMOND ★★★

Difficulty rating: Strenuous

Distance: 13km (8.1 miles) round-trip

Estimated time: 6.5 hours

Elevation gain: 937m (3,075 ft.)

Costs/permits: None

Best time to go: September, as the crowds dwindle and autumn colors start to appear

Recommended map: Harvey Superwalker Ben Lomond & Loch Katrine

Website: www.nts.org.uk/Property/11

Trailhead GPS: NS 35917 98679

Trailhead directions: From Glasgow, drive north on the A82 to Balloch at the south end of Loch Lomond and turn right onto the A811. After 13km (8 miles), turn left through Drymen onto the east Loch Lomond road, which soon becomes narrow and winding. Drive to Rowardennan car park at the road end.

The upper reaches of Loch Lomond are dominated by Ben Lomond, a mountain rising steeply from the east shore. This is Scotland's most southerly Munro, standing on its own, miles from any other hill of similar height. More than 30,000 people a year climb the mountain and enjoy the unrivalled views over both Highlands and Lowlands. The main path up it has recently been rebuilt.

The Ben Lomond hill path begins from the car park, where it is signposted at the rear of a white building housing information and toilets. The path climbs steeply out of the oakwood into an area with felled trees. It crosses a forest trail and a little bridge, then goes up steps in a rock slab. As it levels off, look left for the view up Loch Lomond and to Ben Lomond and the lower, pointed peak of Ptarmigan.

❶ **Out of the Woods** Leave the forested area by a kissing gate and enter open moor with rough grassland stretching ahead. The path climbs steadily and then zigzags uphill and goes through a gate in a stock fence. After a brief respite, another steep haul takes you onto the south ridge of Ben Lomond.

❷ **Sron Aonaich** The gradient levels off as you gain the promontory, Sron Aonaich, at the near end of the ridge. Suddenly, you can see eastwards to the Trossachs.

Look backwards and the panorama is even more impressive—a bird's-eye view of the south end of Loch Lomond, studded with islands. The next 1.6km (1 mile) is relatively easy walking along the broad ridge with views to both sides.

❸ **Summit Ridge** When you reach the foot of the summit cone, the path again zigzags steeply uphill. Reaching the summit ridge gives you a new view, looking down on Loch Ard and larger Loch Katrine to the northeast. The path skirts the crest of the narrow ridge, and it is only when it dips to a notch that you can see the cliff on your right.

❹ **On Top of the World** A final short climb takes you to the trig point on the summit of Ben Lomond (974m/3,195 ft.). At last you have a 360-degree view, which stretches more than 80km (50 miles)—all the way to Ben Nevis—on a clear day.

To the south and east, look over the flat river plains and low ranges of hills that make up the central Lowlands, and Glasgow sprawling beyond Loch Lomond. Mountains dominate to the north and west, with the dividing line—the Highland Boundary Fault—running through the islands of Loch Lomond. In the southwest, the jagged mountains of the Isle of Arran stand above the peninsulas of southern Argyll and northwards, in the far distance, is Ben Nevis, Scotland's highest mountain.

You now have a choice of returning the way you came or completing a horseshoe over Ptarmigan—it's a similar distance, but the path is more challenging.

⑤ Northwest Ridge The circuit continues with a very steep descent of the northwest ridge, which drops away a few meters from the trig point. If the rock is wet or the visibility is poor, the route may appear too demanding. Once you get going, you realize that it is a well-trodden path, but you'll probably need to steady yourself with your hands as you descend.

In only 0.4km ($^1/_4$ mile), you descend 198m (650 ft.) to a point where the ridge levels off and the path turns left towards Ptarmigan.

⑥ Ptarmigan Drop down into a dip where stepping stones provide a sure footing across two small bogs; then climb a short slope. The path meanders pleasantly along the knobbly ridge to a lochan, after which you make the final short ascent onto Ptarmigan (731m/2,398 ft.).

This peak is named after the ptarmigan, a mountain grouse that turns pure white in winter. In summer, its plumage is a mixture of white and grayish brown, which helps it blend surprisingly well into the lichen-covered rocks.

Enjoy the elevated view; then continue straight on downhill. The path goes steeply down zigzags, following the ridge southwards.

⑦ Kissing Gate After crossing a small stream, the way runs diagonally down the right side of the ridge, passing under heather-covered crags, to a kissing gate in a fence. It continues on the same line across the hillside, which is now covered in

A Natural Memorial

The area where you will be walking was bought for the nation after World War II, with the support of the National Land Fund. Conserving beauty and wildlife, coupled with peaceful recreation for the living, was seen as the most appropriate way to commemorate those who died.

In 1996, the land was officially dedicated in perpetuity as the Ben Lomond National Memorial Park. It now lies at the heart of Scotland's first National Park— Loch Lomond and the Trossachs, which the Scottish government established in 2002, soon after devolution. Today, the National Trust for Scotland and Forestry Commission Scotland own and manage it for conservation and public enjoyment. Although ancient oakwoods fringe the shore of Loch Lomond, the slopes above them have been covered in dark spruce plantations. Now foresters are gradually restoring natural habitats by felling all trees and shrubs that are not native to Scotland. The hillsides that currently appear devastated will soon be covered in a softer mantle of trees that merge naturally with the open hillside above.

For the best panorama of wood and mountain, take the A82 up the west shore of Loch Lomond and stop at Firkin Point to look across the water.

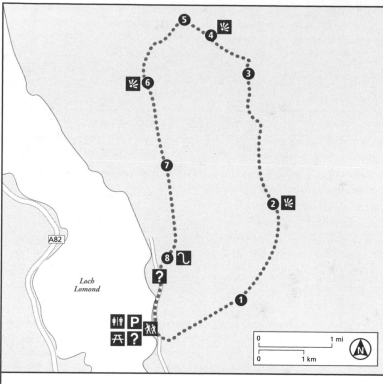

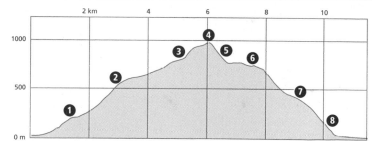

🏔 NS 35917 98679 (0 km): Trailhead

❶ NS 37172 99121 (1.6 km): Follow path out of forested area

❷ NN 37608 00452 (3.1 km): Path levels off near end of the ridge

❸ NN 37298 02455 (5.3 km): Zigzag up on to narrow summit ridge

❹ NN 36707 02856 (6 km): Summit of Ben Lomond

❺ NN 36374 03090 (6.5 km): Descend down northwest ridge

❻ NN 35838 02179 (7.7 km): Short ascent to Ptarmigan summit

❼ NN 36122 01002 (9 km): Pass through kissing gate in fence

❽ NS 35918 98674 (10.3 km): Left at T-junction on to West Highland Way

7

bracken and in places is rough and muddy underfoot. Another kissing gate takes you into a wooded area, and soon you are walking under the shade of oak trees.

❽ West Highland Way Shortly after passing through an open gateway beside a waterfall, you come to a T-junction. Turn left onto the track, which is part of the West Highland Way. The second house on the left is Ardess Lodge Ranger Centre and the start of the Hidden History Trail. A little farther on, pass the entrance to Rowardennan Youth Hostel. Now the track runs along the shore, passing two shingles beaches before you arrive back at the car park.

ARROCHAR ALPS ★★

Difficulty rating: Strenuous

Distance: 14.2km (8.9 miles) round-trip

Estimated time: 8 hours

Elevation gain: 1,006m (3,300 ft.)

Costs/permits: £1 car parking

Best time to go: Make an early start to get a space in the car park.

Website: www.forestry.gov.uk

Recommended map: Harvey Superwalker Arrochar Alps

Trailhead GPS: NN 29500 04930

Trailhead directions: Take the A82 up Loch Lomond and go west on the A83 at Tarbet. Go through Arrochar, around the head of Loch Long, and turn into the lochside car park opposite the turning for Succoth. Arrochar and Tarbet rail station is on the West Highland line. Scottish Citylink coach service 926 (Glasgow to Campbeltown) stops at Arrochar.

The Cobbler, with its three rocky peaks, has one of the most distinctive mountain profiles in Scotland. It is the most popular of the dramatic Arrochar Alps, which rise steeply from the sea in the northern part of Argyll Forest Park. This challenging route combines the Cobbler—a Corbett (a mountain 762–914m/2,500–3,000 ft. in height)—with two neighboring Munros, Beinn Narnain and Beinn Ime.

Cross the busy road from the car park and go around wooden railings that mark the start of a smooth new path. After only 50 paces, turn right onto a very rough path that leads straight uphill through young trees.

❶ Old Trackway Cross a horizontal track and keep straight on up on a very eroded "path." This was once a trackway supplying materials for construction of a hydroelectric scheme, but all but a few concrete footings have been washed away, leaving a deep gouge to scramble up.

❷ Foot of Crags Rise up onto open ground where a path goes left along the hillside (to the dam on Allt a' Bhalchain).

Here clamber up through a crack between the crags above.

Above the first crags, see if you can spot a small plaque on a rock. It remembers Charles Paterson, a founding member of the Arrochar Mountain Rescue Team.

The route continues straight up Beinn Narnain via the southeast ridge, which gradually becomes more defined. At a leveling in the ridge, you gain a fine view of the Cobbler, silhouetted against the skyline.

❸ Cruach Nam Miseag The ridge narrows to the little top of Cruach nam Miseag and then dips to a broad col. A high prow of rock now looms above. A slight path goes up the left side and crosses over to

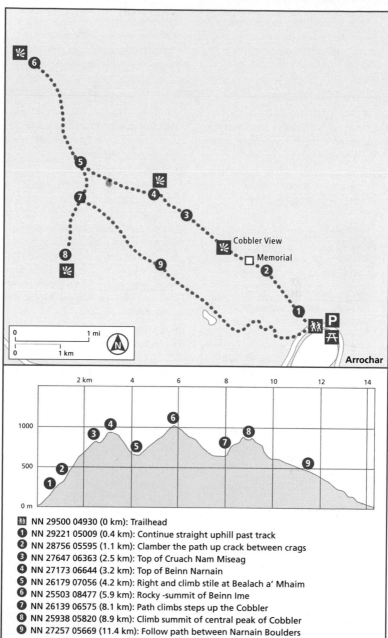

Arrochar

🏃 NN 29500 04930 (0 km): Trailhead
1 NN 29221 05009 (0.4 km): Continue straight uphill past track
2 NN 28756 05595 (1.1 km): Clamber the path up crack between crags
3 NN 27647 06363 (2.5 km): Top of Cruach Nam Miseag
4 NN 27173 06644 (3.2 km): Top of Beinn Narnain
5 NN 26179 07056 (4.2 km): Right and climb stile at Bealach a' Mhaim
6 NN 25503 08477 (5.9 km): Rocky -summit of Beinn Ime
7 NN 26139 06575 (8.1 km): Path climbs steps up the Cobbler
8 NN 25938 05820 (8.9 km): Climb summit of central peak of Cobbler
9 NN 27257 05669 (11.4 km): Follow path between Narnain Boulders

(Tips)   Feeling Nervous?

The day starts with a tough climb straight up Beinn Narnain, where some easy scrambling takes you through tiers of crags. It finishes with a gentle descent down a well-made path recently built up the Cobbler. If you prefer to avoid difficulties, you can use that path to climb all three mountains via the Bealach a' Mhaim.

the foot of the Spearhead, a prominent buttress. Scramble up the rock slabs in the gully on its right side.

❹ Beinn Narnain   From the top of the gully, stroll across Beinn Narnain's flat top to the trig pillar (926m/3,038 ft.).

Look east to see Ben Lomond, the conical peak on the far side of Loch Lomond, and south for a view down Loch Long. The nearest mountains are the Cobbler (southwest), Beinn Ime (northwest), Ben Vane (north), and the knobbly ridge of A' Chrois (northeast).

Continue northwest along the top to a small cairn. A path kinks slightly left to descend through a rocky area that ends with a boulder field. Beyond, walk down grassy slopes all the way to the Bealach a' Mhaim.

❺ Bealach a' Mhaim   Veer right over the flat wet area to a stile in a fence that runs over the bealach. Beyond, climb straight up the grassy shoulder of Beinn Ime. A worn path leads upwards, but it is drier underfoot a little to the right, nearer to the crags that bite into the east side of the mountain. As you approach the top, cross a stream and pass a jutting rock, then bend left along the summit ridge.

❻ Beinn Ime   The highest point of Beinn Ime (1,011m/3,316 ft.) is a rocky platform topped by a bit of concrete and metal—all that remains of a trig pillar. Enjoy a view into Glen Kinglas; then

return by the same route to the Bealach a' Mhaim. After crossing the stile, swing right towards the Cobbler.

❼ Cobbler Climb   From the foot of the Cobbler, follow the re-engineered path of rock steps that zigzags straight up the steep north ridge. Where the new path ends, the north peak rises on your left and the main central peak is straight ahead. If you wish to visit the North Peak, it involves scrambling up (and back down) sloping rock slabs. This promontory overhangs the cliffs—go very carefully as there are sheer drops on three sides.

❽ The Cobbler   Keep going up to the flat summit of the central peak of the Cobbler (881m/2,890 ft.). The very highest point is atop a rock outcrop, but I've never risked scaling it, as it involves squeezing through a "window" and then scrambling up the far side above the cliffs.

The Cobbler is so called because its profile looks like a cobbler, or shoemaker, bent over his last, with his wife watching him from the other side. The mountain's "real" name is Ben Arthur.

Return by the new path to the foot of the Cobbler. (You may see people using a precipitous path that descends through cliffs from the col between central and north peaks, but you are safer on the main route.) At the foot of the hill, the path bends right and runs gently downhill beside the Allt a' Bhalachain.

❾ Narnain Boulders   Halfway down the valley, the path weaves between the Narnain Boulders, two giant blocks of rock that climbers use for bouldering practice. Beyond a small dam, the path zigzags down into the forest. After contouring northeast along the hillside, the path zigzags some more, down to a level track by a mast. Go left a short way to a path marked by a post; then go right, downhill again. This takes you back down to the road opposite the car park.

GLEN NANT (Kids)

Difficulty rating: Easy

Distance: 4km (2.5 miles) round-trip

Estimated time: 2 hours

Elevation gain: 46m (150 ft.)

Costs/permits: None

Best time to go: March and April for spring wildflowers; October for autumn colors

Website: www.forestry.gov.uk

Recommended map: Glen Nant leaflet available from local Tourist Information Centres

Trailhead GPS: NN 01943 27268

Trailhead directions: At Taynuilt (on the A85 19km/12 miles east of Oban), turn south on the B845 (signed KILCHRENAN) for 4km (2.5 miles); then turn right at the forest sign for Glen Nant National Nature Reserve. Bus service 415 runs from Oban to Kilchrenan.

Glen Nant is a prime example of Atlantic Oakwood—the lush west coast woodland that is Scotland's "rainforest." Follow the Ant Trail to learn about the wildlife of the wood and to see how the trees were coppiced—cut back to promote regrowth—and turned into charcoal to fire the historic Bonawe Iron Furnace. Children will enjoy finding tidbits of information along the way.

The Ant Trail is waymarked by posts with a white ant and an arrow indicating the direction. Along the way, you will pass several information boards and fingerposts (guide posts), where a panel pulls out to reveal interesting facts. These show a few Gaelic words in red, so you can even start picking up the old Highland names for plants and animals.

❶ **Path from the Car Park** Take the track leading out of the top of the car park and go through a gate in a deer fence. Walk up the track to a bend by an information board, where trees in the adjacent enclosure have been coppiced, using traditional techniques.

By cutting trees down to stump level and encouraging new shoots to grow, coppicing produces a sustainable supply of wood that can be harvested every 20 years. In the past, the wood was turned into charcoal and the bark used for tanning cowhide to make it into leather.

❷ **Woodland Path** About 100m (328 ft.) beyond the board, leave the track by turning right at a post and going up steps to a woodland path. This gradually climbs up and around a wooded hill, passing information panels about pine marten and the sounds of the wood.

❸ **Oak Fingerpost** At a slight leveling in the path, a fingerpost explains that the oak trees are so large because they have not been coppiced for 150 years. Now the path goes downhill, coming to wetter ground that is open on the right. A board here describes the ecology of wood ants, whose nests you can see in the wood. They are mounds up to 0.6m (2 ft.) high, covered by a thatch of fine twigs.

❹ Routes Divide Cross a footbridge over a burn and pass a fingerpost about Gaelic names, just beyond which the path divides.

To cut 0.8km (¹/₂ mile) and quite a lot of climbing off the walk, turn left at the path junction (signed SHORTER ROUTE). This follows the burn upstream and rejoins the longer route at the next footbridge (point 6).

Turn right for the longer route on a path that climbs uphill through tall oak, ash, and elm. To the left of another post there is a particularly splendid coppiced oak.

❺ Bench View The path breaks out onto open ground at the top of the hill where a bench is positioned with a fine view over the trees to Ben Cruachan. Return downhill on another marked path (left as you arrive at the top). A stretch of boardwalk carries you over wetter ground. Many of the trees are full of character; look out for one on the left that fell over years ago; it is still growing and its branches are dripping with moss and ferns. Beyond,

the path goes down steps and winds down more steeply to the stream.

❻ Routes Meet The shorter and longer routes meet at a footbridge. Cross over and follow the path upstream to the right, walking through hazel coppice.

Where the path levels off by a post, walk a little off it to the right to see out of the wood. This is a similar view to the one from the hilltop, looking over the rolling canopy of trees to the soaring peak of Ben Cruachan.

The path now runs on the level above the stream.

❼ Charcoal History Come to another information board that explains how timber was stacked tightly to exclude air and burned slowly to produce charcoal, which was then used to smelt iron, since it creates more heat than wood.

Glen Nant was a busy place 200 years ago, as hundreds of people were employed to fuel the furnace, which produced up to 700 tons (711 tonnes) of iron per year. To make just one ton of iron, about 0.5 hectares (1.25 acres) of wood had to be cut

Bonawe Iron Furnace

The charcoal produced in Glen Nant was loaded into sacks and then transported by pony down to Bonawe Iron Furnace, beside Taynuilt on the shore of Loch Etive. The scenic, grassy site of the furnace is now a peaceful open-air museum. It is well worth a visit and makes a pleasant complement to the Glen Nant walk, helping to bring to life the rich history of these oakwoods.

The ironworks were founded in 1753 and closed in 1876, by which time coke had superseded charcoal as the preferred fuel. You can see how the furnace operated, and wander around the buildings, following the numbered plaques that explain the function of each. The ore shed contains displays that describe how the smelter worked and why it was built here, while the vast charcoal stores now provide nesting sites for swallows.

Bonawe is in the care of Historic Scotland and open to the public daily throughout the summer; from late March through September, it's open 9:30am to 5:30pm; and in October it's open 9:30am to 4:30pm. Entry costs £4.20 for adults and £2.10 for children; concessions are £3.20. ℂ **01866 822432;** www.historic-scotland.gov.uk.

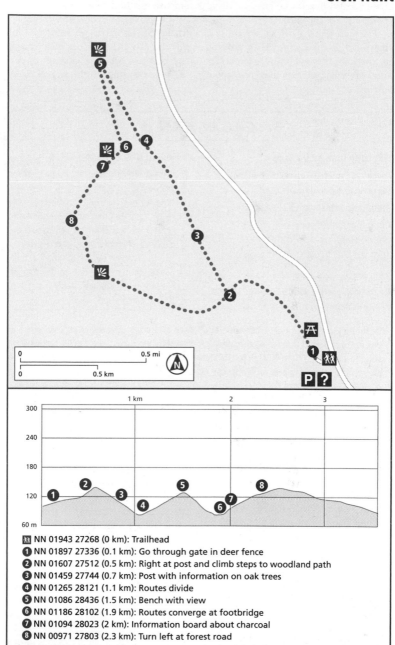

0.5 mi
0
0
0.5 km

N

300
240
180
120
60 m

1 km
2
3

🏃 NN 01943 27268 (0 km): Trailhead
❶ NN 01897 27336 (0.1 km): Go through gate in deer fence
❷ NN 01607 27512 (0.5 km): Right at post and climb steps to woodland path
❸ NN 01459 27744 (0.7 km): Post with information on oak trees
❹ NN 01265 28121 (1.1 km): Routes divide
❺ NN 01086 28436 (1.5 km): Bench with view
❻ NN 01186 28102 (1.9 km): Routes converge at footbridge
❼ NN 01094 28023 (2 km): Information board about charcoal
❽ NN 00971 27803 (2.3 km): Turn left at forest road

down. That provided 12 to 14 tons of timber, which in turn produced 2 tons of charcoal to fire the smelter.

The path winds above the stream to a fingerpost describing the lichen growing on the trees. Beyond, cross a footbridge and walk up to another fingerpost about woodpeckers.

❽ **Forest Road** Go up steps to the forest road and turn left to return to the car park. Soon there is a view west over an area where conifers have been felled to a hillside that is a patchwork of rough pasture and native woodland. Follow the track all the way back down to the car park.

CRUACHAN ★

Difficulty rating: Strenuous

Distance: 16km (10 miles) round-trip

Estimated time: 8 hours

Elevation gain: 1,074m (3,525 ft.)

Costs/permits: None

Pet friendly: No

Best time to go: May to July for long days

Website: www.visitcruachan.co.uk

Recommended map: OS Explorer 377 (OS Landranger 50)

Trailhead GPS: NN 08016 26728

Trailhead directions: Start from Cruachan railway station (a request stop) between Taynuilt and Dalmally. It is signed on the A85 opposite Cruachan Power Station Visitor Centre, 32km (20 miles) east of Oban. If arriving by car, park in one of the pull-in bays beside the road, not the visitor center car park. Scottish Citylink service 977 (Oban to Glasgow) stops at the power station.

The shapely mountain rising between Loch Awe and Loch Etive catches your eye from miles around. This is Ben Cruachan, which is linked by a narrow, rocky ridge to the neighboring Munro, Stob Diamh. A circuit of them—the Cruachan horseshoe—involves some easy scrambling and is one of Scotland's classic skyline traverses.

Keep this walk for a fine day when you can enjoy the views—it's no fun to be on the exposed ridge in wind and rain!

Steps link the busy trunk road to the railway platform. At the bend halfway up, go through a metal gate and a tunnel under the railway line. Walk up concrete steps to an electricity substation and go left on a rough woodland path that climbs steeply up the east side of Cruachan Burn. Cross a stile beside the Falls of Cruachan and continue less steeply, passing under power lines. Keep going to a tarmac road.

❶ **Bridge Below the Dam** Turn left, cross a bridge over the burn, and follow the road up to the foot of the dam. Go left to zigzag up steps; then climb a metal ladder

to a gate on top of the dam wall. Go left along the dam and through another gate. Turn left on a wide stony track running southwest.

❷ **Hill Climb** Leave the track near its crest and climb northwest up the hillside to a knoll. Turn slightly right to pass another knoll, and climb the pleasant grassy ridge to Meall Cuanail. Higher up you can follow a ruined wire fence that bends left near the top, where crags drop off on the right.

❸ **Meall Cuanail** From the summit of Meall Cuanail, the view stretches way down Loch Awe, while ahead you look up to the imposing peak of Ben Cruachan. Descend steeply down loose rocks to a col;

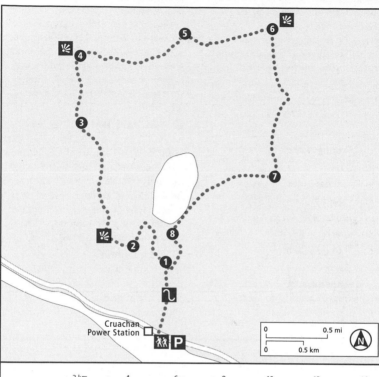

Cruachan
Power Station

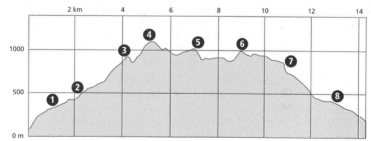

NN 08016 26728 (0 km): Trailhead
1 NN 08123 27717 (1 km): Turn left and cross bridge over burn
2 NN 07691 27934 (2.1 km): Leave track and climb up hill to knoll
3 NN 06979 29552 (4.2 km): Summit of Meall Cuanail
4 NN 06972 30457 (5.1 km): Summit of Ben Cruachan
5 NN 08491 31049 (7.2 km): Summit of Drochaid Ghlas
6 NN 09482 30840 (8.9 km): Summit of Stob Diamh
7 NN 09544 28846 (11.2 km): Turn right down slopes of col
8 NN 08164 28083 (12.8 km): Follow access road downhill from
   Cruachan Dam and turn right below it

then continue up Cruachan's south ridge. As you near the top, you reach the summit cone, which is composed of large pink granite boulders.

④ Ben Cruachan Scramble up the boulders to the cairn on top of Ben Cruachan (1,126m/3,694 ft.). The adjacent trig pillar (a 1m-high [3¹/₃-ft.] marker used by surveyors) is broken off at half height.

What makes the view from Ben Cruachan special is that as well as the usual mountainscape of peaks receding into the distance, you can see over the west coast to the Hebrides. The large Isle of Mull is spread out below, and on a clear day you will see many other, more distant, Hebridean islands, such as Coll and Tiree.

The airy ridge now stretches 2.8km (1³/₄ miles) eastwards to Stob Diamh. There are several kinks in direction, and

subsidiary ridges branch north in a couple of places, so careful navigation is needed in poor visibility.

Start by scrambling down Ben Cruachan's narrow east ridge. Where a chasm opens up on the left, you can scramble ahead over exposed slabs or drop right on a path that bypasses the difficulties and then returns to the crest for pleasant, high-level walking.

⑤ Drochaid Ghlas The ridge path bends left onto Drochaid Ghlas (1,009m/3,310 ft.), whose rocky summit is a conglomeration of boulders and slabs. You can scramble to the top, which is on a north-running ridge, but you need to return along it and descend southeast to continue along the main ridge. The ridge narrows and drops to a col.

⑥ Stob Diamh A steady climb now takes you onto Stob Diamh (980m/3,215 ft.). Turn south and cross a dip to the lower top of Stob Garbh. Continue along the broad south ridge for 300m (984 ft.)

The Hollow Mountain

A massive cavern, high enough to house the Tower of London, is hidden under your feet; it houses Cruachan Power Station, which lies 1km (²/₃ mile) within Ben Cruachan. Here, enormous turbines convert the power of water into electricity. Guided tours take visitors inside by bus to a viewing platform, overlooking the generating hall that houses four generators.

Opened by the Queen in 1965, Cruachan power station was the first reversible pump storage hydro system to be built in the world. During periods of peak demand, water flows down from Cruachan Reservoir, in the corrie above, to drive the turbines. However, when demand is low, surplus electricity is taken from the national grid and used to power the turbines in reverse, lifting water back up into the reservoir and effectively "storing" the energy.

The **Cruachan Visitor Centre** (✆ **01866 822618**) attracts over 60,000 people each season. It houses an exhibition, gift shop, and cafeteria with views over Loch Awe, and is open from February to mid-December. Open hours in summer (Easter to late Oct) are daily 9:30am to 5pm and in winter are Monday through Friday 10am to 4pm. Guided tours are normally every 30 minutes and can be booked; they cost £5.50 for adults, £4.50 for seniors and students, and £2 for children (6–16 yrs); kids under 6 are free.

to where it forks. Descend the ridge running southwest and then south towards Beinn a' Bhuiridh.

❼ Lairig Torran As you reach the wide col—the Lairig Torran—before Beinn a' Bhuiridh, turn right to go down broad slopes. Keep to the north of the steep-sided burn flowing down from the col. Near the bottom, a rough path crosses the burn and then contours along muddy ground above Cruachan Reservoir. Join a trail beyond a concrete water channel flowing out of the hillside.

❽ Cruachan Dam The trail leads to the east end of the dam and curves downhill. Follow it to a junction and go right below the dam. Just before the bridge over Cruachan Burn, turn left on the rough path that descends beside the stream to the road.

TOBERMORY Ⓚⁱᵈˢ

Difficulty rating: Easy

Distance: 4km (2.5 miles) one-way (return by bus)

Estimated time: 1.5 hours

Elevation gain: Downhill from start

Costs/permits: £13 in ferry and coach tickets

Pet friendly: Yes

Best time to go: May and June, before school holidays begin

Website: www.calmac.co.uk

Recommended map: Isle of Mull forest walks leaflet, available from local Tourist Information Centres

Trailhead GPS: NM 50868 54048

Trailhead directions: From Oban pier, take the Caledonian MacBrayne ferry to Craignure on the Isle of Mull; then catch the Bowman's Coaches bus that meets each ferry. Passengers must buy tickets (£7.25 round-trip) and be on board at least 10 minutes before the ferry sails. The ferry crossing takes 45 minutes, and the bus journey (£5.30 round-trip) is about 40 minutes.

If you can't spare longer, at least take a day trip to the Isle of Mull to enjoy its lovely scenery and visit the much-photographed capital, Tobermory. This walk explores the waterfalls and water-lilied lochan (small lake) in Aros Park before approaching the town along the shore path, which gives you the best views of the pretty harbor surrounded by buildings of many vivid colors.

Get off the bus at Aros Park gates, a mile before Tobermory. This is a request stop, so ask the driver to let you know when you are there.

❶ Aros Lodge A Forestry Commission sign marks the entrance to Aros Park. Go through the gates and past the flower-decked gate lodge. Walk down the tarmac drive, ignoring a couple of paths going left. Keep on to noisy Aros Burn, which you will hear before you see it.

❷ Waterfalls Path Cross the bridge over the burn and immediately beyond it turn left down the Waterfalls Path, signed LOWER FALLS. Keep left beside the rushing stream until you come to another post, and here go right on the link path to the car park. Enjoy a glimpse of Tobermory as you contour around to a grassy area with toilets, barbeques, and picnic tables.

❸ Lochan Trail Walk across the grass to an information board beside the car park; then follow the post marking the Lochan Trail. Cross a trail and drop down to the small loch, where you go right on the shore path to walk a circuit of the lochan. The white and yellow water lilies that fringe the lochan are at their best in late July and August.

4 Head of the Loch A small bridge crosses a stream at the head of the loch. Just beyond, go left at a path junction to return down the far shore.

Beside the path, you'll find some adventure play equipment. It's an opportunity for children of all ages to let off steam by jumping, climbing, and balancing.

Pass a bench on the shore where the loch narrows and ignore a right turn. Go left to cross a concrete bridge over the outflow from the loch and turn right down a track.

5 Aros Pier The path leads down to the pier, from where you can see across the bay to Tobermory. Cross a footbridge opposite the pier buildings and follow the Shore Path towards the town. Go right at a trail junction and cross a bridge below the lower waterfall. Soon the path zigzags uphill with benches on practically every bend.

Now that you've climbed above the wooded cliffs, your view stretches over Calve Island and far across the Sound of Mull. Ben Hiant, the highest hill on the Ardnamurchan Peninsula, is particularly noticeable.

6 Picnic Table Pleasant walking above the cliffs leads to a picnic table. Beyond, keep right at a path junction sign for Tobermory. Walk under mature pine trees with open pasture on your left. Soon steps lead down to a lower level where you pass another cascading stream, Sput Dubh.

7 Tobermory View After rounding a corner, you come to a bench overlooking Tobermory Bay.

> This is the delightful view that appears on so many postcards. A neat row of buildings, painted in an array of bright colors, curves around a bay full of moored yachts.

Continue along the path, passing above the marina and a white building with a round tower, Taigh Solais, which houses toilets and other visitor facilities. You arrive at the Ledaig car park, at the south end of Tobermory. The bus for Craignure leaves from the car park, but it's worth exploring the waterfront before returning.

Fun Facts   **Balamory**

Tobermory is the real life setting for *Balamory,* a series on children's television that attracted an enormous following. Various houses in the town featured as the homes of characters such as Miss Hoolie, the nursery school teacher; P. C. Plum, the policeman; and Spencer, the painter responsible for the houses' colorful appearance.

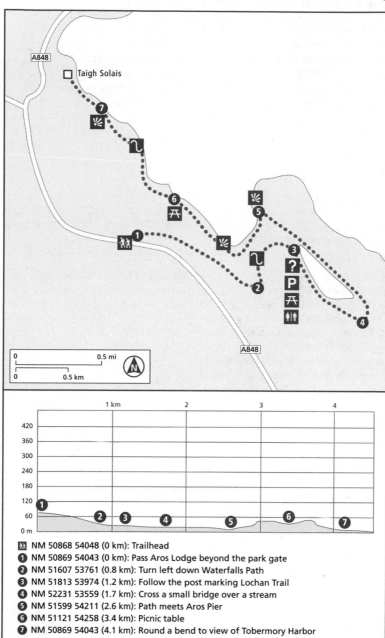

🚶 NM 50868 54048 (0 km): Trailhead
1 NM 50869 54043 (0 km): Pass Aros Lodge beyond the park gate
2 NM 51607 53761 (0.8 km): Turn left down Waterfalls Path
3 NM 51813 53974 (1.2 km): Follow the post marking Lochan Trail
4 NM 52231 53559 (1.7 km): Cross a small bridge over a stream
5 NM 51599 54211 (2.6 km): Path meets Aros Pier
6 NM 51121 54258 (3.4 km): Picnic table
7 NM 50869 54043 (4.1 km): Round a bend to view of Tobermory Harbor

KILMARTIN GLEN ★★

Difficulty rating: Easy

Distance: 6.4km (4 miles) round-trip

Estimated time: 2 hours

Elevation gain: None

Costs/permits: None

Pet friendly: Yes, but you may meet cattle and sheep.

Best time to go: September and October, when the glen is quieter

Website: www.kilmartin.org

Recommended map: OS Explorer 358 (OS Landranger 55)

Trailhead GPS: NR 83502 98831

Trailhead directions: Start from the public parking area opposite the Kilmartin Hotel in Kilmartin village, which is on the A816 13km (8 miles) north of Lochgilphead and 45km (28 miles) south of Oban, and accessible by bus from either town.

Over 5,000 years of human history are etched into the landscape of Kilmartin Glen, which has one of the greatest concentrations of archaeological sites in Scotland. This walk takes in many of the finest sites, including stone circles, burial cairns, and the carved grave slabs of medieval knights.

Begin by walking across the grass to a viewpoint that looks southwards over Kilmartin Glen; an interpretation board picks out several features you will visit on this walk. Then have a look around the adjacent churchyard—it's crowded with ancient gravestones, bearing testament to Kilmartin's past significance as a seat of royal power and a center of Christianity. Don't miss the amazing array of deeply carved slabs that are protected from the weather in a stone outbuilding. They date from around A.D. 1300 to 1700. Continue to the right past Kilmartin House and following the pavement downhill.

❶ **Old Coach Road** Turn left after Sona House onto a path that crosses a bridge and cattle grid. Keep straight ahead across a field; then go left on a trail and left again when you meet another track. This old coach road runs down the west side of the flat, fertile glen. To your left is Glebe Cairn, which may be visited by a footbridge, though there is little to see other than a heap of stones. This is the most northerly of five remaining burial cairns that form a linear cemetery through the glen.

❷ **Nether Largie North Cairn** Keep going until you see a stile leading to a cairn in the field on your left. This one is well worth a visit and has interesting interpretation.

This is exciting for children of all ages, be they 7 or 70. Clamber up the pile of rounded stones and slide open the trapdoor. If you dare, go down steps into a chamber with a stone burial cist in the center.

Nether Largie Mid Cairn, about 200m (656 ft.) farther on, again has interpretation and is a good viewpoint. Continue down the track to Kilmartin Primary School, where you go straight over a crossroads and soon turn left off the road to Nether Largie South Cairn. This was the first to be built—over 5,000 years ago—and predates the pyramids.

❸ **Lady Glassary Wood** Walk through the South Cairn enclosure and take a grassy path on the far side, signed

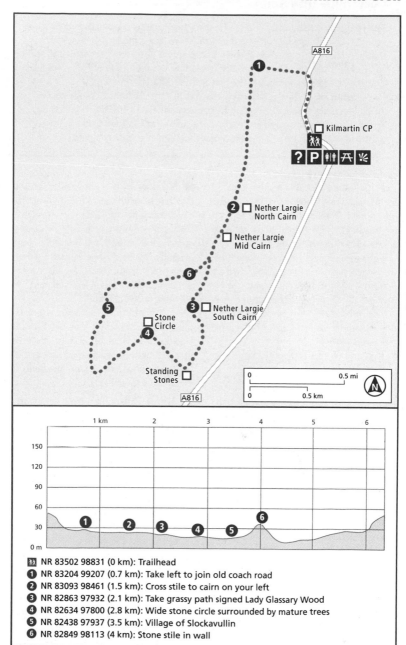

🚶 NR 83502 98831 (0 km): Trailhead
1 NR 83204 99207 (0.7 km): Take left to join old coach road
2 NR 83093 98461 (1.5 km): Cross stile to cairn on your left
3 NR 82863 97932 (2.1 km): Take grassy path signed Lady Glassary Wood
4 NR 82634 97800 (2.8 km): Wide stone circle surrounded by mature trees
5 NR 82438 97937 (3.5 km): Village of Slockavullin
6 NR 82849 98113 (4 km): Stone stile in wall

(Kids) Kilmartin House

The center for archaeology and landscape interpretation housed in Kilmartin House is an absolute gem. It's no dusty museum, but a modern complex with audiovisual show, interactive models, and plenty to fascinate children. Here you'll gain a wider picture of Kilmartin Glen, including the multitude of rock carvings and the 7th-century fortress of the first Scottish kings.

It is open all year, every day, from 10am to 5:30pm. Entry is £3.90 for adults, £1.20 for children, and £9 for a family; concessions are £3.10. Tickets last all day, so you can come and go as you explore the area. The Wildfood Café has Taste of Scotland accreditation and is a great place for a fresh and tasty lunch.

LADY GLASSARY WOOD. The path runs up to the wood and along its edge to a gate into a field. Walk across the field to a set of standing stones before going right to another path, signed TEMPLE WOOD.

I like to walk to the far end of these tall stones and position myself so that they are perfectly aligned with the center stone between the far pair, pointing up the glen. It helps me feel their power reaching across the millennia, as I wonder who erected them and why.

❹ **Temple Wood Stone Circles**   Follow the path back to the road; then go straight over to a wide stone circle surrounded by mature trees. A smaller, older circle stands under the trees on the right. Turn right out of the gate and walk south to a T-junction, where you go right.

❺ **Slockavullin**   The road takes you into Slockavullin, an old mill village that has a babbling burn running through it. Walk past cottages with flowery gardens, over a stone bridge, and around a couple of bends. Where the road ends at a gate, go right on a path that leads into trees. It runs along the top of a wooded bank and then goes diagonally downhill.

At the bottom of the slope, you pass a square stone structure—an old limekiln. During the era of agricultural improvements, limestone was burned here and the resulting lime spread on the fields to improve their fertility.

❻ **Stone Stile**   The path comes to a stone stile in a wall behind the primary school. Go left on a track that merges with the old coach road. Follow it back past the Mid and North Cairns to Kilmartin village.

CARRADALE ★

Difficulty rating: Moderate
Distance: 12km (7.5 miles) round-trip
Estimated time: 4 hours
Elevation gain: 239m (785 ft.)
Costs/permits: None
Pet friendly: Yes, with one stile crossing

Best time to go: July and August for lingering on the beaches
Website: www.carradale.org.uk
Recommended map: OS Explorer 356 (OS Landranger 68)
Trailhead GPS: NR 81381 37469

Trailhead directions: From Lochgilphead, take the A83 to Kennacraig, 8km (5 miles) south of Tarbert. Turn left onto the B8001 (signed SKIPNESS) and go right at Claonaig Bay along the coast on the B842 to Carradale. Turn into the village, go right at a sign for Port Righ, and then take the track to Carradale Bay car park (gates to open). Allow plenty of time, as the B-roads are single-track. The bus services to Carradale run via Campbeltown.

Carradale, on the east side of the Kintyre peninsula, is peaceful paradise remote from the busy world. The village and its surroundings are a microcosm of Scotland's west coast. In just one walk, you can visit beautiful beaches, an active fishing harbor, a heather-topped hill, and a rocky point inhabited by wild goats.

The car park is at the east end of Carradale Bay, where a mile of golden sand tempts you to spend the day swimming and sunbathing. Start off by walking to the west end of the beach—stroll along the sand or take the Waterfoot path, marked by one of many signposts you will see around Carradale Estate. The path leads over a footbridge and stile into fields, where you pick up a grassy track behind the beach.

❶ **Waterfoot** At the end of the beach, pass Carradale Bay Caravan Park—well screened by gorse bushes—and turn right up a wide track beside Carradale Water. Go left at a triangular junction and then left again in 100m (328 ft.) onto a path. This runs pleasantly under old pines before you turn right and return to the drive via Sally's Walk.

❷ **Network Centre** Continue left up the drive to an information board about the Kintyre Way by the main road. Cross over to the Network Centre (open Fri–Wed 10am–5:30pm, Easter to Sept; closed Thurs), where you can pop in for insight into Carradale's history, culture, and wildlife, or tuck into delicious home baking in the tearoom.

Walk between the tearoom and colorful Heritage Centre, passing a forest walks information board and going straight ahead up steps. Turn left on a path leading up to a forest trail, go left for 49m (160 ft.), then right up a path signed DEER HILL WALK. Climb steeply through trees, leaving the forest as the gradient eases. The grassy path meanders across the open hill until east of the summit.

❸ **Cnoc Nan Gabhar** At a junction, fork left up to a trig point (a concrete marker) on the hilltop. Arran appears to be only a stone's throw away across Kilbrannan Sound, its jagged mountains silhouetted against the sky. Looking inland, you see into the wild and rugged interior of Kintyre, while the sparsely inhabited coast runs away to north and south.

Continue along the main path, soon going downhill. At a junction, turn right onto a wider path—part of the Kintyre Way. Follow it all the way to the foot of the hill; then go right on a track past playing fields. Fork left to walk through the Port na Storm car park to the main road.

❹ **Carradale Harbor** Turn left and walk through the village, passing grocers, a bakery, a post office, and two hotels. The road runs downhill to the harbor, which is still used by several fishing boats. Take a path between the houses on the right, signed AIRDS CASTLE (a feature that time has almost completely obliterated).

❺ **Golf Course** A kissing gate leads onto the golf course, where you need to proceed with care. Follow a ruined stone wall to a hillock; then walk along its right side, keeping to the edge of the fairway. Turn right at the corner and continue along the sea edge of the course. Head for

ARGYLL & THE WEST HIGHLANDS WALKS

7

CARRADALE

Carrad
Harbour

☐ Fishing boats

Network
Centre

B879

Carradale
Bay

B842

0   0.5 mi
0   0.5 km

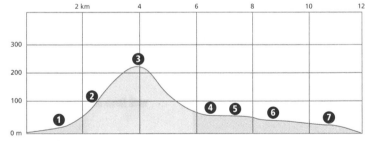

2 km   4   6   8   10   12

300
200
100
0 m

NR 81381 37469 (0 km): Trailhead
1 NR 80450 37319 (1.1 km): Pass campsite and turn right up wide track
2 NR 80044 38162 (2.3 km): Network Centre
3 NR 80372 39597 (4 km): Take left fork at junction to top of hill
4 NR 81127 38313 (6.4 km): Turn left down the road through the village
5 NR 81893 38582 (7.3 km): Take the path signed Airds Castle
6 NR 81745 37806 (8.6 km): Walk past Port Right beach
7 NR 81523 36485 (10.7 km): Tidal island at tip of the point

Kintyre Way

Scotland's newest long-distance path opened in summer 2006. It runs the length of Kintyre from Tarbert to Southend. The 140km (87-mile) route crisscrosses the peninsula from side to side, as it is designed to visit communities where accommodations and refreshments are available. Largest of these is Campbeltown, which in its heyday had 34 distilleries.

Away from the coast, the terrain is hilly and uninhabited—you may see no one all day. Several sections of road walking are faster going, but hard on tired feet. It is worth visiting various attractions along the way, such as Skipness Castle and Saddell Abbey; although impressive, they are off the beaten track and not widely known. You can even divert on a day trip to the Isle of Gigha, a short ferry hop from Tayinloan. See www.kintyreway.com.

a cottage and take a path down its left side to a road.

❻ Port Righ Turn left on the tarmac towards a row of cottages overlooking Port Righ, a perfect crescent of white sand enclosed within rocky headlands.

In the center of the bay, steps lead down to a bench with a lovely view over the water, which shades through turquoise to aquamarine. It's a great place to picnic while gazing across the sea to Arran. Alternatively, go a bit farther along and take the steps down to the beach.

Both bay and road end at the Dunvalanree Hotel. Drop left onto a little path through trees to a stile in a wall. Climb over and begin a rough walk along a terrace of rock and salt marsh between the sea and a line of crags. It is hard work

following the shore all the way to Carradale Point, but you may see wild goats, seals, dolphins, or even basking sharks.

If you tire of rock hopping, take a shortcut halfway down the east shore. At a break in the crags, go right up a marshy slope and then head northwest across the peninsula, back towards the car park.

❼ Carradale Point Persist in scrambling around the shore and you come to a tidal island at the tip of the point. Cross the gravel beach (don't worry, the water is only ankle-deep at high tide) and climb to the top, crowned by a vitrified fort. Look carefully at the encircling banks for exposed sections of wall to see glassy rocks, fused by fire.

Leave the island and scramble up between rocks to a path that runs high along the west side of the point. It returns to Carradale Bay, descending to a gate in a fence just before the beach.

KINLOCHLEVEN

Difficulty rating: Moderate

Distance: 10km (6.5 miles) round-trip

Estimated time: 4.5 hours

Elevation gain: 381m (1,250 ft.)

Costs/permits: None

Best time to go: April and May for spring colors and maybe views of snowy mountains

Website: www.kinlochleven.co.uk

Recommended map: OS Landranger 41 (OS Explorer 384)

Trailhead GPS: NN 18798 61943

Trailhead directions: Leave the A82 at Glencoe village and follow the B863 to Kinlochleven. Park by the public toilets just before the bridge over the River Leven; the Ice Factor is on the other side of the road. Local buses go to Kinlochleven; see www.travelinescotland.com.

The West Highlands are where Scotland's mountains meet the sea—never more so than in Kinlochleven. Lying between Glencoe and Fort William, the village at the head of Loch Leven grew up to serve an aluminum smelter, powered by the great volume of water running off high mountains. On this circuit to Loch Eilde Mor, one of the sources of that water, you see deep into majestic mountain terrain.

From the public toilets, cross the road bridge, with the tailrace from the hydroelectric power station thundering in your ears. Take the first road on the right for the Grey Mare's Tail waterfall.

❶ **Grey Mare's Tail** Walk up the left side of the waterfall car park (an alternative start point) and turn left behind a white church. The path rises to a viewpoint where you can see through the trees to the long plume of white water. Keep left down concrete steps and to a footbridge in the shady woodland. The route goes right beyond the bridge, but first walk left to a confluence of streams where you can look up at the high cascade. Return past the footbridge and go left at a post—you are going to follow the yellow arrows all the way uphill. Initially the path is deeply eroded and you step up bare rock in many places.

❷ **Open Views** At a post above the waterfall, go right. As you leave the trees, the gradient eases and the path surface improves. The large white Mamore Lodge Hotel is on the hillside to the left. Go through a gate in a deer fence; then cross a burn with large slabs as stepping stones. Beyond two smaller streams, come to another post and again go right. Climb up to a heavy metal gate at the top of the enclosure fenced against deer.

❸ **Hill Track** Just above the metal gate, join a wide stony track and turn right along it.

A very solid memorial bench overlooks the track junction. As you've now completed most of the climb, enjoy the reward of relaxing with a splendid view down Loch Leven. The prominent conical hill above the south shore is the Pap of Glencoe; behind it the hills rise to the narrow Aonach Eagach ridge, whose traverse is a famous mountaineering challenge.

The track continues to climb, but much more gently. Although you only rise up to 399m (1,310 ft.), you feel as if you are in wild mountain country, remote from civilization. On your left, the dramatic Mamores range soars upwards to peaks over 1,000m (3,280 ft.) high.

❹ **Loch Eilde Mor** As you crest the rise, Loch Eilde Mor comes into view ahead. The glistening 3.2km-long (2-mile) loch and its smaller twin, Loch Eilde Beag, fill the valley between the mountains. Soon turn right onto a path that immediately crosses a burn by stepping stones. The path crosses the foot of the loch, curving around a moraine to a small dam where a water intake feeds a large pipeline.

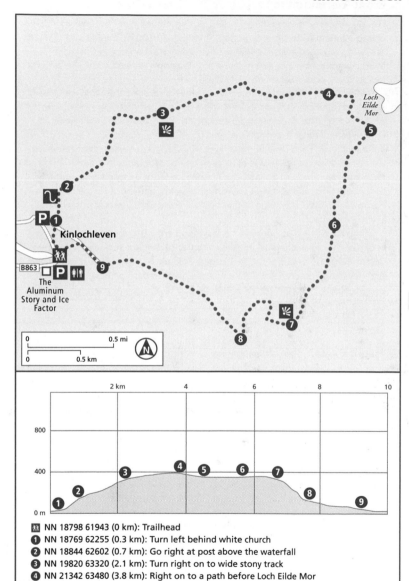

NN 18798 61943 (0 km): Trailhead
1. NN 18769 62255 (0.3 km): Turn left behind white church
2. NN 18844 62602 (0.7 km): Go right at post above the waterfall
3. NN 19820 63320 (2.1 km): Turn right on to wide stony track
4. NN 21342 63480 (3.8 km): Right on to a path before Loch Eilde Mor
5. NN 21761 63175 (4.5 km): Path crosses the dam and turns right
6. NN 21418 62263 (5.5 km): Cross metal bridge
7. NN 21001 61289 (6.6 km): Path turns right and downhill
8. NN 20504 61193 (7.5 km): Right at junction then through gap in wall
9. NN 19232 61854 (9.1 km): Walk through junction along stony trail

From Aluminum to Ice

The aluminum works were built in 1907, during the reign of King Edward VII, who visited Mamore Lodge to go shooting. Smelting aluminum requires vast amounts of energy, and it was worth shipping in ore to take advantage of the cheap hydroelectric power available here. Up to 800 people worked in the smelter, and Kinlochleven grew to accommodate them.

By the end of the century, other newer smelters around the world were out-producing Kinlochleven, and in 1994 Alcan announced that they would close the works in 2000. The electricity produced locally could be used in their works at Fort William or fed into the national grid.

Kinlochleven Land Development Trust was set up to oversee regeneration of the village and take advantage of its position as a stopping-off point on the West Highland Way. The Trust opened The Aluminium Story, a museum about the history of smelting, and obtained grants for a training scheme in footpath maintenance. Many local paths were upgraded as a result, although, sadly, they have since degenerated.

The greatest success story was the development of the Ice Factor, established in one of the old smelter buildings. It contains the biggest indoor ice-climbing wall in the world as well as the UK's largest articulated rock-climbing wall and a high-level rope course. With shop, sauna, cafe, bistro bar, and adjacent brewery, there is plenty to occupy the avid mountaineer in even the wettest west-coast weather (www.ice-factor.co.uk).

---

❺ Pipeline Path The path crosses the dam and turns right to follow the pipeline along the hillside. The pipe contours for some 8km (5 miles) to the Blackwater Reservoir, in order to add to the volume of water powering the hydroelectric plant in Kinlochleven. Drainage is poor on this path, and you have to cross several patches of peat bog.

❻ Metal Bridge After swinging around a stream valley and crossing a decrepit metal bridge—where care is needed—the surface becomes a bit firmer. The path may be inferior, but the views are exceptional, especially northwards to the Mamores and along the West Highland Way, which passes through a glen to the west of them.

❼ Downhill Path Before the pipeline and hillside bend away to the left—2km (1¼ miles) beyond the dam—the path turns right, straight downhill. You have wonderful aerial views of Kinlochleven from the steep but sound path as it zigzags down. Near the bottom, the path runs above the Allt na h-Eilde, the stream flowing out of the loch, then enters woodland and winds down past dripping crags to a stone wall.

❽ Rushing Rivers Go through a gap in the wall and turn right on the path just beyond. Look up to a waterfall on the Allt na h-Eilde before crossing a footbridge over the stream. Beyond the bridge, you have views of the larger River Leven, tumbling over tilted rocks.

Although this valley appears thoroughly wet, extraction for hydroelectricity has considerably diminished the flows in both watercourses. Turbines in the power station in Kinlochleven are driven by the water delivered through the steep pipelines you can see on the opposite hillside—these originate at the Blackwater Reservoir.

The path runs through the delightful birch woodland surrounding the River Leven and crosses several side streams, including four in close succession that have been carefully cobbled to create little fords.

❾ Track Junction As you near Kinlochleven, turn left onto a path going downhill, just before some overhead power lines. The path goes through a gap in a deer fence, passes under the power lines, and drops down to a wide track junction. Walk straight ahead along a stony trail that becomes Wades Road. Turn left onto a tarmac path running through trees beside the River Leven. At the main road, turn left back across the road bridge to the start point.

SLEEPING & EATING

ACCOMMODATIONS

★★★ **Ardanaiseig Hotel** This luxurious hideaway sits amid wooded gardens on the shores of Loch Awe. Once a private home, the hotel has formal sitting rooms with big upholstered chairs, fresh flowers, and polished tables. The guest rooms, named after local mountains and lochs, are furnished with antiques; some have four-poster beds.

Kilchrenan by Taynuilt PA35 1HE. ✆ **01866 833333.** www.ardanaiseig.com. 16 units. £124–£193. Rates include breakfast. AE, DC, MC, V. Closed Jan to mid-Feb. **Close to:** Cruachan, Glen Nant.

Arden House This stone-built Victorian B&B was the setting for the popular BBC series, *Dr. Finlay's Casebook.* It has a quiet setting below Callander Crags and close to Bracklinn Falls. The public areas boast antiques, while the high-ceilinged guest rooms are tasteful and comfortable.

Bracklinn Rd., Callander FK17 8EQ. ✆ **01877 330235.** www.ardenhouse.org.uk. 5 units. £35–£40. Rates include breakfast. MC, V. Free parking. Children under 14 not accepted. **Close to:** Callander Crags and Bracklinn Falls.

Argyll Hotel This waterfront inn, built in 1755, has a wood-and-gilt public bar, a guests-only cocktail lounge, and a dignified restaurant serving five-course dinners featuring the best of local produce. The comfortable guest rooms have decors ranging from flowered chintz to modern functional, and most open onto panoramic views of Loch Fyne.

Front St., Inveraray PA32 8XB. ✆ **01499 302466.** www.the-argyll-hotel.co.uk. 37 units. £52–£79, but advanced booking rate as low as £35. Rates include breakfast. AE, DC, MC, V. **Close to:** Arrochar Alps, Kilmartin Glen.

★ (Kids) **Carradale Bay Caravan Park** Ideal for a relaxing, family holiday, this peaceful caravan (motorhome) and camping park lies behind a mile-long sandy beach that offers safe swimming. It is part of Carradale Estate and surrounded by waymarked paths. Bring your own caravan or tent, or book a log cabin or luxury caravan.

Carradale, Kintyre PA28 6QG. ✆ **01583 431665.** www.carradalebay.com. For a family of 4 per night: tent pitch £22, serviced caravan pitch £25; luxury caravan, sleeps 5, £348 per week; log cabin, sleeps 4, £447 per week. MC, V. Closed Oct–Mar. **Close to:** Carradale.

★ (Finds) **Foxholes** Far from a foxhole, this is actually a spacious country house set in a tranquil glen to the south of Oban. The cozy, comfortable bedrooms are painted in soft pastels and furnished traditionally. All rooms have panoramic views of both the countryside and the hotel's well-maintained gardens.

Lerags, Oban PA34 4SE. ℂ **01631 564982.** www.foxholeshotel.co.uk. 7 units. £47–£51; with dinner £68–£79; single supplement £19. Rates include breakfast. MC, V. Free parking. Closed Dec–Mar. **Close to:** Cruachan, Glen Nant, Tobermory, Kilmartin Glen.

Ⓥalue **Ledard Bothies**   Aimed at people actively enjoying the outdoors, these budget-priced accommodations are set in the heart of the Trossachs. Ledard is a working hill sheep farm and the base of the Scottish Sheepdog School. It has a clay-pigeon range, fishing on the adjacent loch, and strong connections to Rob Roy MacGregor.

Ledard Farm, Kinlochard, by Aberfoyle FK8 3TL. ℂ **01877 387219.** www.highland-adventure.co.uk. 4 units, each sleeping 2 people. £15 with own sleeping bag; £20 with bed linens. Closed Nov–Mar. **Close to:** Callander Crags and Bracklinn Falls, Ben Lomond, Conic Hill.

RESTAURANTS

★ **Clachaig Inn** INTERNATIONAL/SCOTTISH   The Clachaig is a famous mountaineering destination, somewhere to savor hearty food, real ale, and malt whisky by a roaring fire after a day on the hills. Try haggis, neeps n' tatties, or a wild boar burger. Live folk music brings the place to life on Saturdays and other nights.

Glencoe. ℂ **01855 811252.** www.clachaig.com. Main courses £8.25–£16. MC, V. Daily 11am–11pm. Reservations not accepted. **Close to:** Kinlochleven.

★ Ⓕinds **Dunvalanree** SCOTTISH   Feel like a country houseguest at this small hotel overlooking the turquoise waters of Port Righ. Non-residents are welcome at the convivial dinner. The whole evening experience starts with drinks in the lounge while choosing from a menu that features locally caught seafood and other fresh local produce.

Port Righ Bay, Carradale, Kintyre. ℂ **01583 431226.** www.dunvalanree.com. Reservations recommended. 2 courses £21, 3 courses £25. AE, MC, V. Arrive 7pm for 8pm dinner. B&B including dinner £50–£70. Closed Christmas and Jan–Feb. **Close to:** Carradale.

Kilted Skirlie INTERNATIONAL/SCOTTISH   Set in a modern shopping and leisure complex at the main gateway to the National Park, this restaurant and cocktail bar has a magnificent view up Loch Lomond to Ben Lomond. Dishes such as Venison and Drambuie Stew give traditional Scottish ingredients a contemporary twist.

Loch Lomond Shores, Balloch. ℂ **01389 754759.** www.kiltedskirlie.co.uk. Reservations recommended. Main courses lunch £6.50–£9, dinner £12–£20. AE, MC, V. Lunch daily noon–5:30pm; dinner Sun–Thurs 6–9pm, Fri–Sat 6–10pm. **Close to:** Ben Lomond, Arrochar Alps, Conic Hill.

★★ **Knipoch Hotel Restaurant** SCOTTISH   Situated 10km (6 miles) south of Oban on the shores of Loch Feochan, Knipoch offers truly fine dining. The daily five-course menu relies heavily on Scottish produce and is supported by an excellent wine cellar. Typical choices would be cock-a-leekie soup and Sound of Luing scallops.

Knipoch, Kilninver, by Oban PA34 4QT. ℂ **01852 316251.** www.knipochhotel.co.uk. Reservations required. Main courses £15–£20; B&B £84–£110. AE, DC, MC, V. Daily 7:30–9pm. Closed mid-Dec to mid-Feb. **Close to:** Cruachan, Glen Nant, Tobermory.

Ⓜoments **Lade Inn** SCOTTISH   Inviting from the outside and welcoming inside, this family-run inn specializes in real ales and locally sourced produce, including shepherd's pie made with local lamb and baked Trossachs trout. The adjacent Scottish Real Ale shop stocks over 100 beers. Experience the atmosphere of a ceilidh in the cozy Bothy Bar.

Kilmahog, Callander. ℂ **01877 330152.** www.theladeinn.com. Reservations recommended in high season and on weekends. Main courses £8–£16. DC, MC, V. Food served noon–8:45pm, Sept–June kitchen closed 3–5pm. Live Scottish Folk Music Fri–Sat from 8:30pm. **Close to:** Callander Crags and Bracklinn Falls.

(Kids) **Melfort Mermaid** INTERNATIONAL   Housed in a new timber building, this restaurant has a glorious view over tranquil Loch Melfort. It offers well-priced, freshly cooked local food and serves mainly luxury self-catering holiday houses built around a private harbor. Non-residents are very welcome, especially families with children.

Melfort Pier and Harbour, Melfort Village, Kilmelford, by Oban. (C) **01852 200324.** www.mellowmelfort. com. Reservations recommended. Main courses £4–£22. MC, V. Daily 11am–10pm (last orders 9pm). Closed Mon Oct–Mar. **Close to:** Kilmartin Glen.

The Northeast Highlands Walks

by Felicity Martin

Rising from the North Sea to the Grampians Mountains, this region covers a vast land mass. Its northern edge is the south coast of the Moray Firth, the big wedge of sea at Scotland's top right corner. At Fraserburgh the coast bends south and runs down past Aberdeen, which faces east over the North Sea.

Fishing villages and towns—some still active—line the coast, while part of Scotland's most productive farmland stretches over the plains behind. Vast acreages of barley are grown for malting, to supply the numerous whisky distilleries in the area, and for winter feed for the herds of black, glossy-coated Aberdeen Angus cattle that dot the pastures. The climate here is much drier than in the west, and the Moray Firth is famed for often being sunny when the rest of Scotland is enveloped by clouds.

Farther inland, several small ranges of hills surround the Cairngorms, the high central mountains that are one of Scotland's most distinctive features. Glaciers have carved into the mountain plateau, gouging out corries (deep cliff-ringed hollows) and sheer-walled glens. A very special environment exists on the high tundra-like tops, which bear a fragile carpet of sub-arctic vegetation. Creation of the Cairngorms National Park in 2003 recognized the importance both of the mountains' natural heritage and their popularity as a place for recreation.

Two great rivers run through this region: the Dee, draining the eastern Cairngorms and flowing down to Aberdeen, and the Spey, draining the western and northern slopes and meeting the sea midway along the Moray Firth. Deeside is often known as Royal Deeside, because the royal family has had their summer home here since Queen Victoria bought Balmoral in 1848. It is a valley of castles, pinewoods, and well-to-do towns with attractively proportioned stone houses. Nearer Aberdeen, Scotland's oil capital, property prices rise and many places have become commuter villages.

On first acquaintance, Strathspey has a similar character, but it is subtly different (and has even more whisky distilleries!). The River Spey is wilder in nature, spilling over into the Insch marshes and fringed by birchwoods. Aviemore, developed to support the Cairngorms ski center, is a busy, brash resort with a high street of pizza parlors and outdoor gear shops. The quickly built tourist facilities of the 1960s have been partly redeveloped in recent years, but the only really charming building is the Victorian railway station. Aviemore's growth has drained some of the life out of older, neighboring towns, such as Kingussie and Newtonmore.

The geography of the northeast provides a lot of walking opportunities. Most famous are the Cairngorms routes, which typically involve a "long walk in" to high, remote places. Such walks require commitment—there is no quick, easy escape—and they become a much more serious

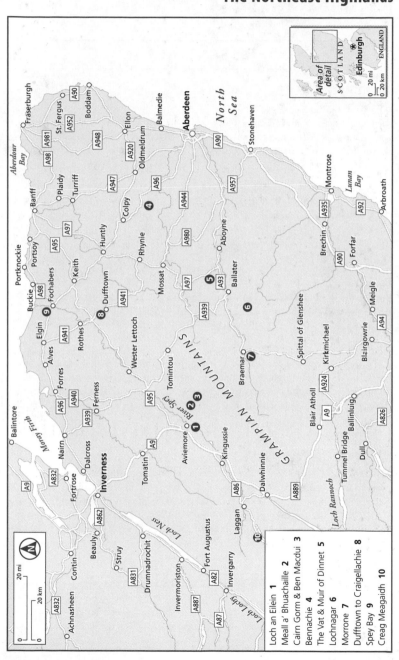

Loch an Eilein **1**
Meall a' Bhuachaille **2**
Cairn Gorm & Ben Macdui **3**
Bennachie **4**
The Vat & Muir of Dinnet **5**
Lochnagar **6**
Morrone **7**
Dufftown to Craigellachie **8**
Spey Bay **9**
Creag Meagaidh **10**

proposition in winter, when weather on the Cairngorms plateau can be as savage as in the Arctic. However, there are also many gentle coastal, river, and woodland walks, as well as routes up moderately high hills and the long-distance Spey Way.

ESSENTIALS

GETTING THERE
By Air
Air travelers can fly into **Aberdeen airport** ((℡ **08700 400006;** www.aberdeenairport.com) in the east or **Inverness airport** ((℡ **01667 464000;** www.invernessairport.com) in the north, and hire a car for onward travel.

By Car
If driving from the south to Aviemore and Strathspey, take the M80/A9 from Glasgow or the Forth Road Bridge/M90/A9 from Edinburgh (the two routes meet at Perth). To reach Aberdeen and Deeside, you can branch off the M90 at Kinross and head east on the A91/A914 to Dundee then take the slower A92 coast road or faster A929/A94. Alternatively, go through Perth and take the A93 via Blairgowrie and over the scenic Glenshee pass to Braemar.

By Bus
Scottish Citylink ((℡ **08705 505050;** www.citylink.co.uk), the national coach operator, has bus service to the major towns in the region; Edinburgh to Aberdeen takes about 3.5 hours, and a standard single costs £24; Edinburgh to Aviemore takes a similar time for £21.

By Train
Rail travelers have a choice of the east-coast line to Aberdeen or the Highland line, which has stations at Newtonmore, Kingussie, and Aviemore. **First Scotrail** ((℡ **08457 484950;** www.firstgroup.com/scotrail) runs the trains on both. Edinburgh to Aberdeen takes 2.5 hours, and an anytime single costs £33; Edinburgh to Aviemore takes nearer 3 hours for £37.

The exact coach or rail price depends on time of travel, and saver tickets are available.

VISITOR INFORMATION
VisitScotland ((℡ **08452 255121;** www.visitscotland.com), the Scottish tourist board, provides information on the area and a booking service. It has many Tourist Information Centres throughout the region; they include Aberdeen ((℡ **01224 288828**) at Exchange House, 26/28 Exchange St.; and Aviemore ((℡ **08452 255121**) at Unit 7, Grampian Rd. For in-depth information, see VisitScotland's websites www.visithighlands.com and www.aberdeen-grampian.com, and the National Park website www.cairngorms.co.uk.

ORIENTATION
You will need to decide on which side of the Cairngorms you wish to base yourself, because the mountain massif puts a lot of distance—and time—between east and west. The link road between the two sides—from Cockbridge to Tormintoul—resonates with everyone who listens to British weather forecasts, as it is always the first route to be closed by snowfalls.

south, both the A9 trunk road and adjacent railway line rise over the 457m (1,500-ft.) Drumochter Pass. The A93 through Deeside provides the main gateway to the eastern Cairngorms, while the A96 runs between Aberdeen and Inverness.

GETTING AROUND

Traveline Scotland ((*C* 08712 002233; www.travelinescotland.com), the national travel service, can help you plan your journey using public transport. The service has details of both small bus companies that provide local services and major transport operators.

The Cairngorms Explorer booklet published by the National Park Authority (and downloadable at www.cairngorms.co.uk) contains local bus timetables and much other useful information. The Heather Hopper provides a cross-Cairngorms Park bus service from May to September, with one route running twice daily between Strathspey and Deeside, and another more southerly once a day between Deeside and Perthshire.

LOCH AN EILEIN ★

Difficulty rating: Easy

Distance: 5km (3.1 miles) + optional 1.6km (1-mile) round-trip

Estimated time: 1.5 to 2 hours

Elevation gain: 20m (65 ft.)

Costs/permits: Parking £1.50 per person or £4.50 per car

Best time to go: Summer evening for quiet sunset walk (but remember the midge repellent!)

Website: www.rothiemurchus.net

Recommended map: Rothiemurchus Estate walks leaflet available from Rothiemurchus Centre

Trailhead GPS: NH 89706 08516

Trailhead directions: Take the Coylumbridge B970 road from the roundabout at the south end of Aviemore; then turn right at Inverdruie, opposite Rothiemurchus Centre. After 1.6km (1 mile), turn left at the brown tourist sign for Loch an Eilein and keep going to the car park at the end of the road.

Loch an Eilein is a sparkling sapphire set amid the ancient Caledonian pine forests of Rothiemurchus. Delightful views appear around every corner, including a ruined castle on the island that gives the loch its name, "Lake of the Island." If you don't mind some muddy walking, you can add in a circuit of the adjoining loch, which is smaller and wilder.

Take the path out of the back of the car park and walk past an information board to the visitor center, a small white cottage with adjacent toilet block. Turn towards the loch, where a bench overlooks the shore. Go straight across a wide junction for a clockwise circuit of the loch.

❶ **North End** The path soon crosses a footbridge over the stream flowing northwards out of the loch. Turn right when you meet a stony track, which rises slightly uphill with glimpses of the loch through

the tall, straight trees. Pass a cottage and go through an open gateway in a fence.

❷ **East Corner** Immediately after crossing a bridge over a stream flowing into the loch, a path branches left for the Lairig Ghru. Ignore it and keep straight on past a bench with a boulder backrest. The path bends right into a more natural area with mature pines, juniper, and heather.

❸ **South Shore** After entering denser, young woodland, the path bends right and passes a heap of boulders, which passers-by have piled up into little spires. Now there are attractive views over the loch as the path runs along the south shore. Pass a bench that looks across to Ord Ban, the wooded hill on the far side; then go over a small stream into a more open area with young, self-seeded pines.

❹ Loch Gamhna Come to a footbridge over a stream flowing out of another, smaller loch—Loch Gamhna. For the shorter circuit, cross the footbridge and keep straight on. To add in the extra mile round Loch Gamhna, walk left on a rough path and keep right when you join a better path. When the path forks, go right and enjoy scenic views over the loch.

Loch Gamhna is Gaelic for "Loch of the Stirks" (young cattle). Centuries ago, cattle raiders used the Thieves' Road past the loch to reach the fertile lands of Strathspey. To distract the raiders from their main herds, local folk used to leave a few cows tied to a tree beside Loch Gamhna.

After crossing a footbridge over the stream that feeds the loch, you'll find the peaty path is soft and muddy around the head of the loch. It improves as it runs along slightly higher ground along the west side of the loch.

❺ Between the Lochs If you have gone round Loch Gamhna, turn left when you meet the main path circuiting Loch an Eilein. If you didn't visit Gamhna, keep straight ahead at this junction. At the west corner of Loch an Eilein, a bench faces the water, looking up the length of the loch.

You are now over half-way around the loch, and this bench is a pleasant, sheltered place to rest. Many "granny pines," trees with thick trunks that can be a few centuries old, grow around it. While sitting quietly, you might see some of the wildlife characteristic of these old pinewoods: red squirrels, crested tits, or Scottish crossbills.

❻ Forest Walk Beyond the bench, turn right at a path junction to return along the north shore on a broad path through the attractive pine forest. After 1km (²/₃ mile), go around a gate to Loch Eilein Cottage, in an idyllic setting overlooking the shore.

Rothiemurchus Estate

Loch an Eilein is part of Rothiemurchus Estate, which stretches from Aviemore eastwards to Loch Morlich and Glenmore Forest Park, and southwards to Braeriach, one of the highest Cairngorm peaks. The estate lies at the heart of Cairngorms National Park and has a very special environment, containing both ancient Caledonian pinewood and wild mountain terrain.

The estate has been owned by the Grant family for 450 years and is now cared for by Johnnie and Philippa Grant, who have done much to develop the facilities for outdoor recreation. Visitors are offered a warm welcome, stunning scenery, and a wide range of outdoor activities. I've had fun quad biking, clay-pigeon shooting, and hand feeding their farmed red deer, but you could chose anything from canoeing, mountain biking, or fishing to a sled dog trip.

Drop into the **Rothiemurchus Centre** at Inverdruie (✆ **01479 812345;** www.rothiemurchus.net) to book an activity, buy produce (including home-grown venison and beef) from the farm shop, browse the gift shop, or take a break in the restaurant cafe. It is open February through October daily from 9:30am to 5:30pm.

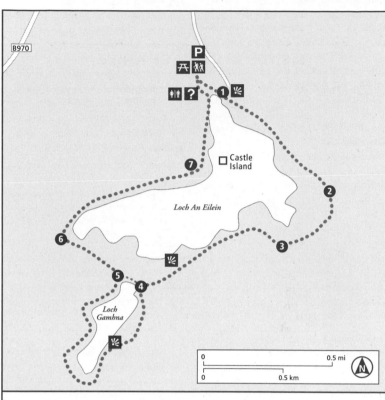

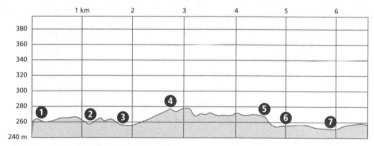

NH 89706 08516 (0 km): Trailhead

1 NH 89851 08353 (0.2 km): Footbridge over stream flowing from the loch

2 NH 90547 07713 (1.2 km): Keep ahead at junction with Lairig Ghru path

3 NH 90232 07365 (1.8 km): Path bends right and passes heap of boulders

4 NH 89337 07116 (2.7 km): Footbridge over stream from Loch Gamhna

5 NH 89233 07178 (4.5 km): Trail junction

6 NH 88834 07398 (5 km): Turn right at path junction beyond bench

7 NH 89691 07867 (5.9 km): Water's edge below Loch Eilein Cottage

⑦ Castle Island Walk down to the water's edge below the cottage for a view to the ruined castle on a wooded islet just off shore. Then return to the path and continue along it. Soon you are back by the bench at the north end of the loch. Go left at the wide junction and right before the visitor center to return to the car park.

MEALL A' BHUACHAILLE ★

Difficulty rating: Moderate

Distance: 8.4km (5.25 miles) round-trip

Estimated time: 4 hours

Elevation gain: 495m (1,625 ft.)

Costs/permits: £1 car parking

Best time to go: July and August for heather blooming

Website: www.forestry.gov.uk

Recommended map: Glenmore Forest walks leaflet available from Aviemore Tourist Information Centre and Forest Visitor Centre

Trailhead GPS: NH 89706 08516

Trailhead directions: Take the Coylumbridge B970 road from the roundabout at the south end of Aviemore and follow signs for Glenmore Forest to the Visitor Centre, opposite Glenmore campsite. Local buses run from Aviemore to Glenmore.

Walk through ancient Caledonian pine forest to a magical little green loch before climbing to the summit of Meall a' Bhuachaille, which is often clear when the higher mountains are shrouded in cloud. This Corbett is at the edge of the main Cairngorms massif and looks across to the ice-sculpted northern corries. The start point is near the Cairngorm Reindeer Centre and you may meet free-roaming reindeer on the hill.

Behind the visitor center and cafe, cross a paved track and take a path going slightly right uphill. It is marked by a post with a blue ring, indicating the Ryvoan Trek, which you follow as far as Lochan Uaine.

① Junction and Information Board Climb steadily uphill to a junction with an information board about the history of shepherding on Meall a' Bhuachaille.

Meall a' Bhuachaille is Gaelic for the rounded hill of the shepherd. It is so named because in summer herders from the many small farms nearby would bring their cattle and sheep here to grow fat on the lush grass. Since livestock grazing ceased, trees have re-colonized the slopes, though the harsh climate and strong winds prevent them growing all the way up the hill.

Turn right and then keep right on a track that goes slightly downhill. It brings you to a junction by a house, where you turn left. Follow this path for 1.6km (1 mile) through the forest. You'll see both tall, straight pines in plantations and older, naturally grown pines, which have broad, spreading crowns.

② Caledonian Pine Forest The trail emerges into an open area of ancient Caledonian pine forest shortly before it ends at a bench with a view across the Pass of Ryvoan to Cairn Gorm. Keep straight on along a rough path that weaves around gnarled pines and pushes between juniper bushes. The path winds around, then goes down rock steps to the bottom of the pass.

③ Lochan Uaine The path meets a stony track, where your route turns left. However, first go straight over and down steps to sheltered Lochan Uaine, whose deep blue-green waters contrast with a fringe of golden sand. Not far beyond the loch, the trail splits—take the left fork, signed NETHY BRIDGE, and pass a sign that you are entering Abernethy National Nature Reserve.

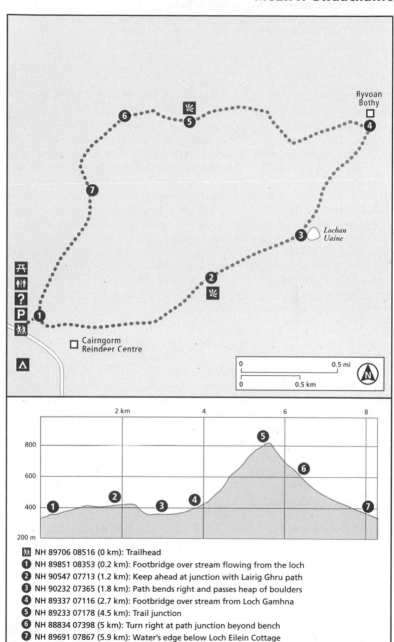

THE NORTHEAST HIGHLANDS WALKS

8

MEALL A' BHUACHAILLE

NH 89706 08516 (0 km): Trailhead
1 NH 89851 08353 (0.2 km): Footbridge over stream flowing from the loch
2 NH 90547 07713 (1.2 km): Keep ahead at junction with Lairig Ghru path
3 NH 90232 07365 (1.8 km): Path bends right and passes heap of boulders
4 NH 89337 07116 (2.7 km): Footbridge over stream from Loch Gamhna
5 NH 89233 07178 (4.5 km): Trail junction
6 NH 88834 07398 (5 km): Turn right at path junction beyond bench
7 NH 89691 07867 (5.9 km): Water's edge below Loch Eilein Cottage

(Kids) Cairngorm Reindeer Centre

Reindeer became extinct in Britain about 8,000 years ago, but were re-introduced into Scotland in 1952 by a Swedish Reindeer Herder, Mikel Utsi. In Scandinavia, reindeer, which are the same species as North American caribou, have long been semi-domesticated, living in large herds whose annual migrations are followed by the indigenous Sami people who own them.

The Cairngorm reindeer herd is Britain's only herd of free-ranging reindeer. There are currently around 130 reindeer, living in their natural environment on the Cairngorm Mountains and the Cromdale Hills. They mainly eat ground, rock, and tree lichens, which are plentiful here and of little use to other animals.

The **Cairngorm Reindeer Centre** ((C) **01479 861228;** www.reindeer-company. demon.co.uk) is next door to Glenmore Forest Visitor Centre. The Reindeer House has information and a shop, and from here you can visit the reindeer paddocks, where a few animals are kept on a rotational basis, or make a hill visit to the herd. The reindeer are tame and friendly, with soft, velvety noses, and very willingly feed from the hand. A new way to interact with them is to go trekking with them on the mountain trails—booking is essential for this.

Daily hill visits are made at 11am (weather permitting in winter) and also at 2:30pm in summer (May–Sept). Admission charges are as follows: adult £9, child (ages 6–16; under 6 free) £4.50, family £27; concessions are £6.50.

④ Ryvoan Bothy The track rises gently into an open heathery area with a small stone building—Ryvoan Bothy.

You can find respite in a bothy—a simple hut or small cottage—from the worst of weathers. Like others scattered through the mountains, Ryvoan Bothy is cared for by the Mountain Bothies Association, which preserves the tradition of maintaining basic shelters for people visiting remote places. You can find out more and read the rules inside—please shut the door behind you and leave no rubbish.

Turn left at the bothy onto a path that angles uphill through the heather. The path is well-made, with stone steps on the steeper sections.

⑤ Meall a' Bhuachaille After climbing about 396m (1,300 ft.) up from the bothy, you reach the summit cairn, which is built into a small shelter wall. Meall a' Bhuachaille (801m/2,657 ft.) catches a lot of wind, so you'll be glad of the windbreak as you survey the 360-degree view.

Below lies your start point in Glenmore Forest, near silvery Loch Morlich, while on the opposite side of the hill there is a similar scene—Loch Garten surrounded by the pinewoods of Abernethy National Nature Reserve. However, what really draws the eye is the great sweep of the northern corries and Cairn Gorm itself, rising above the paraphernalia of the ski slopes.

Follow a path down towards the broad col between Meall a' Bhuachaille and Creagan Gorm, the next, lower hill in the ridge that rolls away to the northwest.

⑥ Col Path Junction Shortly before reaching the lowest point of the col, come to a path junction and turn left.

If you are enjoying being up high and feel like going farther (an extra 8km/5 miles), you can keep going on the path over Creagan Gorm to Craiggowrie at the north end of the ridge. The path then drops west into the trees and you can follow orange waymarkers back through the forest.

If continuing on the recommended route, walk downhill—in the direction of Loch Morlich—quickly losing height as you descend into an area with scattered pines. Keep a lookout for reindeer; I saw a herd of 10 roaming free the last time I did this walk.

❼ Forest Path Re-enter the forest by a post with an orange ring—these waymarkers lead back to the car park. The path soon crosses a burn and runs downhill beside it. Recently, much of the plantation to either side has been felled. Continue down to the information board about shepherding and go right down the path back to the visitor center.

CAIRN GORM & BEN MACDUI ★★

Difficulty rating: Strenuous

Distance: 24km (15 miles) round-trip

Estimated time: 9 hours

Elevation gain: 762m (2,500 ft.)

Costs/permits: None

Best time to go: May to June for the longest hours of daylight

Website: www.cairngormmountain.org.uk

Recommended map: Harvey Superwalker Cairn Gorm

Trailhead GPS: NH 99785 07435

Trailhead directions: Take the Coylumbridge B970 road from the roundabout at the south end of Aviemore and follow signs for The Cairngorms through the forest and up the mountain. Near the top, fork left into the Coire na Ciste car park. Local buses run from Aviemore to Cairngorm Ski Centre.

Climb the mountain that gives the Cairngorms their name and cross the high plateau to Scotland's second highest mountain, Ben Macdui, at their very heart. Most of the route is above 1,000m (3,281 ft.) and at this altitude you are in an elemental world of sub-Arctic tundra, glacier-carved cliffs, and boulder fields. The route starts up Cairn Gorm's little-visited north ridge, avoiding most of the man-made structures that litter the mountain.

The Cairngorms plateau is not the place to be in bad weather; conditions can quickly become savage, and navigation is challenging with few landmarks. So save this walk for a day with a good forecast, when you can appreciate the feeling of striding across the roof of the world.

Before setting off, look northeast to your first target—forest plots that show up as a strange patchwork grid of lighter ground on the heathery hillside. Walk towards the ski building, and just before it go left on a path that passes behind a ski tow.

❶ Allt na Ciste A boardwalk takes you down and across the Allt na Ciste, which flows out of Coire na Ciste. Turn left on a peaty and indeterminate path that follows the burn downstream a little and then bends right along a ridge of moraine. Dip down and cross a burn, then climb the next moraine and pass to the right of hidden Lochan na Beinne.

❷ Forest Plots The small path continues up to the plots, which contain some clumps of trees, although most have been felled. Go right along the bottom of the plots; then turn uphill at their corner. Climb to the ridge, joining it near a cleft, and turn right up it. Initially, the ascent is fairly steep, but gradually the gradient eases and the walking is delightful, with views to both sides—Strath Nethy and

(Fun Facts **Mystery Presence**

Many people have experienced strange sensations while walking on Ben Macdui. If you hear footsteps behind you or feel a shiver up your spine, you may be being followed by the Big Grey Man, a giant ghost who is said to haunt the mountain.

Bynack More on the left, and down to Loch Morlich in Glenmore Forest on the right.

❸ **Sub-Arctic Tundra**   After passing a rocky knoll, you are walking on a fragile cushion of sub-Artic vegetation—ground-hugging mosses, lichens, and sedges. Cross this to the first top, with a height of 1,028m (3,372 ft.).

Now the ridge broadens and your direction swings slightly west of south. Climb to a small cairn, from where you can see a path ahead. Pass to the right of Cnap Coire na Spreidhe to the top station of a ski tow and just beyond join a well-made path. Walk uphill past a spring called the Marquis' Well (a good place to refill your water bottle).

❹ **Cairn Gorm**   At the summit of Cairn Gorm (1,245m/4,085 ft.), you'll find a weather station—a squat building connected to a communications mast—and a large cairn with a view down to Aviemore. Southwards, you see over Loch Etchachan, cradled between two rocky peaks, to Ben Macdui.

Continue over the top and down to the rim of the northern corries, whose spectacular curved cliffs bite into the rolling mountain plateau. From the next col, you see into wild Coire an t-Sneachda. Clamber up and over the following hill, Stob Coire an t-Sneachda (1,176m/3,858 ft.), enjoying dramatic views of the cliff edge.

❺ **Coire Domhain**   At the next col, between the head of Coire an t-Sneachda and Coire Domhain, you can chose whether to include Ben Macdui—the high, gray dome to the south—in your

walk. If you want to omit it (and cut 8km/5 miles off the walk), continue ahead over Cairn Lochan and join the descent path down the spur on the far side (see waypoint 9).

To include Ben Macdui, turn left on a pleasant path that climbs slightly up the side of Coire Domhain and then runs on a level with fine, open views over the Cairngorms.

❻ **Lochan Buidhe**   The path swings around Lochan Buidhe, on the watershed between east and west drainages of the plateau. It then climbs a boulder field, where its course is marked by occasional cairns. Walking becomes easier again as it levels off and runs to the foot of Ben Macdui's stony summit dome.

❼ **Ben Macdui**   Climb steadily uphill and curve slightly right to reach the trig point marker atop a high pile of rocks.

 You've now reached the second highest point in all of Britain (after Ben Nevis). The nearby viewpoint indicator helps identify the surrounding peaks, from Cairn Toul, the Angel's Peak, and Braeriach—just across the deep cleft of the Lairig Ghru—to more distant Lochnagar in the east. On a clear day Ben Nevis and the Moray Firth are visible.

Return down the summit dome by the same route towards Lochan Buidhe.

❽ **March Burn**   As soon as you have descended the boulder field, move about 100m (328 ft.) left to the other side of the watershed to get onto the path parallel to

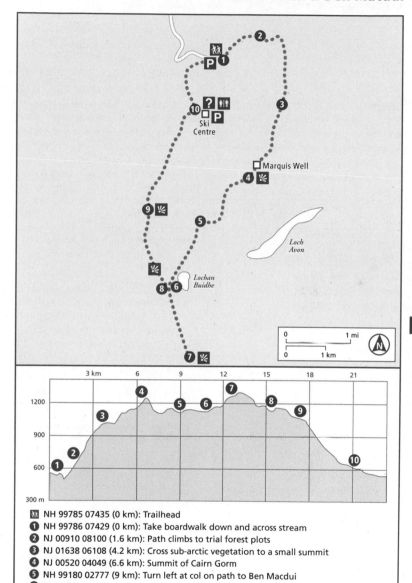

[🚶] NH 99785 07435 (0 km): Trailhead
1 NH 99786 07429 (0 km): Take boardwalk down and across stream
2 NJ 00910 08100 (1.6 km): Path climbs to trial forest plots
3 NJ 01638 06108 (4.2 km): Cross sub-arctic vegetation to a small summit
4 NJ 00520 04049 (6.6 km): Summit of Cairn Gorm
5 NH 99180 02777 (9 km): Turn left at col on path to Ben Macdui
6 NH 98326 01072 (10.8 km): Path passes Lochan Buidhe
7 NN 98902 98929 (13.1 km): Summit of Ben Macdui
8 NH 98253 00958 (15.4 km): Cross the head of March Burn
9 NH 97680 03122 (17.8 km): Top of spur on west side of Coire an Lochain
10 NH 98986 05944 (21 km): Coire Cas car park

the one beside Lochan Buidhe. This path crosses the head of March Burn, which flows in the opposite direction. As you rise up over the shoulder of Cairn Lochan, you see down the Lairig Ghru to Lurcher's Crag, a popular climbing cliff. Soon the path descends to the plateau west of Cairn Lochan, where it is vague for awhile.

❾ Spur   Head north to the top of the broad spur on the west side of Coire an Lochain, enjoying views down to two small lochs below encircling cliff walls. Follow the path down the crest of the spur, passing a post with a small sign asking you to avoid tramping the adjacent reseeded areas. Enjoy an easy descent down the well-made path, with Speyside laid out below. Once on the lower ground, stepping stones take you over the burns and across a stretch of hillside running with water.

❿ Coire Cas   Pass under a couple of ski tows and arrive at the Coire Cas car park, where the main Cairngorm Ski Centre is located. This is also the base station for the funicular railway that runs up to the Ptarmigan restaurant. Turn left along the road and fork right to walk around the hillside back to the Coire na Ciste car park.

BENNACHIE ★★ (Kids)

Difficulty rating: Moderate

Distance: 8.9km (5.5 miles) round-trip

Estimated time: 4 hours

Elevation gain: 375m (1,230 ft.)

Costs/permits: None

Best time to go: July and August for heather blooming (Bennachie Centre closed Mon)

Website: www.forestry.gov.uk

Recommended map: Bennachie walks leaflet available from the Bennachie Centre

Trailhead GPS: NJ 69851 21679

Trailhead directions: Leave the A96 just north of Inverurie (which is 26km/16 miles from Aberdeen) for Chapel of Garioch. From the village, follow brown tourist signs to the woodland car park at the Bennachie Centre.

Bennachie is the northeast's favorite hill. Mither Tap, the most prominent summit of the range, has been the first "mountain" climb for generations of children and provides an unsurpassed view over Aberdeenshire.

Allow time to look around the recently refurbished Bennachie Centre; you'll find the interpretive displays make the history and environment of the hill come alive. Start off along the track on the left of the building, waymarked ALL WALKS. Where routes divide, go right.

❶ Ancient Monument   Go right at the next junction; then look out for the ruins of a house, marked by the sign ANCIENT MONUMENT.

Keep right at the next junction and, higher up, go right and then immediately left onto a steeper, narrower path.

❷ Seat with a View   A steady climb through the forest takes you to a seat where you get the first view out over the patchwork of fields and woods below. The trees become more scattered and you leave the forest where a flight of stone steps begins. The steps zigzag up through the heather to the foot of the summit, where there are some marker posts.

❸ Mither Tap   Keep left and walk through a corridor in the stone rampart surrounding the top; then scramble up the final rough rocks to the trig point marker. In Scots, Mither is mother and Tap is head or top.

THE NORTHEAST HIGHLANDS WALKS

8

BENNACHIE

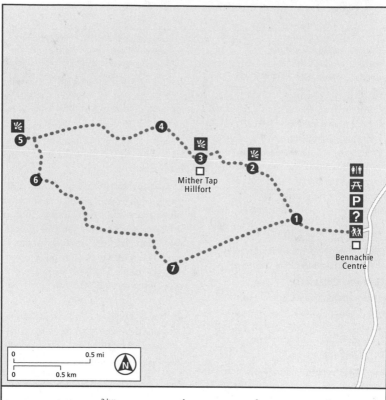

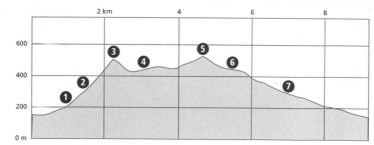

NJ 69851 21679 (0 km): Trailhead

1 NJ 69279 21749 (0.7 km): Ruins of old house past trail junction

2 NJ 68755 22276 (1.5 km): Seat with view

3 NJ 68227 22377 (2.2 km): Viewpoint indicator at top of Mither Tap

4 NJ 67801 22746 (2.9 km): Keep left at path junction

5 NJ 66283 22580 (4.6 km): Summit of Oxen Craig

6 NJ 66447 22161 (5.3 km): Turn left along Gordon Way at T-junction

7 NJ 67940 21190 (7.2 km): Take second left at meeting of paths

The top of Mither Tap (518m/1,700 ft.) is like a natural castle. During the Iron Age, the local tribe of Picts (ancient Celtic tribes who lived in Scotland until the 10th century) surrounded it with an enormous wall, which still stands about 3.3m (10 ft.) high. A viewpoint indicator shows the places you can see all around, from the Cairngorms to Aberdeen and Peterhead.

Return carefully down the rocks and through the wall to the posts. Now go left on a path around the summit to the far side. Just beyond a bend, go right at a junction. (For a quicker way back to the car park, go left at the junction and follow arrows marking the Mither Tap circuit.)

Ahead, high moorland stretches into the distance, punctuated by the rocky tops of Oxen Craig and Craigshannoch.

❹ Path Junction Descend to a path junction and keep left (unless you want to add Craigshannoch into your circuit). Ignore another turn when level with Craigshannoch and head straight on for the highest point.

❺ Oxen Craig The path gradually climbs up to Oxen Craig (528m/1,732 ft.), leveling out on reaching the broad summit. Here go left, past a shelter cairn to another viewpoint indicator.

Being the highest point for miles around, Bennachie is exposed to the full force of the wind. By now you have probably been thoroughly buffeted (and possibly chilled to the bone). The shelter cairn is one of the few places where you can hunker down and relax in relative peace.

Return to the path and retrace your steps back down the slope, turning right after about 100m (328 ft.) onto a well-made link path.

❻ Gordon Way The path runs southwards, taking you downhill to a T-junction where you join the Gordon Way and turn left along it. Pass above the spur of Bruntwood Tap, heading towards Garbit Tap until you have crossed Garbit Burn and veer downhill. The path runs along the edge of the forest before turning downhill again and crossing Ginshiel Burn.

❼ Heather Brig After more descent through the trees, you come to a felled area close to Heather Brig where there is a meeting of paths. Take the second left, signed BENACHIE CENTRE, and thereafter follow the Gordon Way (GW) markers back to the car park. The only place where you might go wrong is when you come to a path—go across it and continue on a track down the far side. For the final stretch, you rejoin your outward route, walking beside Clachie Burn.

THE VAT & MUIR OF DINNET ★ (Kids)

Difficulty rating: Easy

Distance: 1.1km (0.7 miles) and 2.9km (1.8 miles) round-trip

Estimated time: 45 minutes and 1 hour, respectively

Elevation gain: 35m (115 ft.)

Costs/permits: None

Best time to go: Early morning if you want the Vat to yourselves

Website: www.snh.org.uk

Recommended map: OS Explorer 405 (OS Landranger 37)

Trailhead GPS: NO 42931 99699 (Burn O' Vat) NJ 45044 00070 (New Kinnord)

Trailhead directions: From Ballater, go east 6.4km (4 miles) along the A93; then turn left onto the A97. The Burn O' Vat visitor center is on the left in 2.4km (1½) miles.

These two loops around a National Nature Reserve, which has a rare mix of open water, marsh, and heathland, can be combined into one walk. The shorter circuit visits a remarkable glacial feature—the Vat—a round chasm entered by a small crack. The second runs between two lochs, passing Iron Age hut circles and a Pictish carved stone. The Muir of Dinnet was designated as a National Nature Reserve in 1977 to celebrate the Queen's silver jubilee—25 years on the throne.

First explore the Vat on the circuit waymarked with purple arrows. Walk past the small visitor center and the toilet block. The path zigzags down to the burn and heads upstream. Go over one footbridge and keep straight on past the second.

❶ **The Vat** Suddenly rock walls seem to form a barrier ahead, with the burn trickling out of a crack beside a great chock stone. This is your route into the Vat! It looks intimidating, but it isn't very difficult—there are plenty of natural stepping stones in the burn.

Squeeze through and enter an astonishing space where the rock has been hollowed out by meltwater running under a glacier to create a great chamber. The floor is composed of rust-red gravel, and a waterfall tumbles down rocks at the back.

Return out of the Vat to the footbridge and turn left across it. Climb stone steps and then walk on the level above the burn to a junction where you go left on a path diagonally uphill.

❷ **Loch Kinnord Viewpoint** At a T-junction, turn right to a viewpoint overlooking the Muir of Dinnet.

The main feature you see is silvery Loch Kinnord, glinting among the trees. It and nearby Loch Davan fill kettle holes, depressions in the moraine created by large masses of ice that persisted as the last glaciers retreated, some 10,000 years ago. Until the 1940s, regular muirburn kept the surrounding area as open heather and bearberry moorland, but now birchwood has colonized much of it.

THE NORTHEAST HIGHLANDS WALKS

8

THE VAT & MUIR OF DINNET

Getting to Little Ord

It is easiest to drive round to the New Kinnord car park for the second walk: Return to the A93 and go along it to Dinnet; then turn left onto the B9119; the car park is on the left after 1.6km (1 mile).

However, you can also walk there on paths through the heather and birch (reversing the red-marked Loch Kinnord Circular). Cross the road from the visitor center and go left on a path. Walking parallel to the road, go right on a path through a small parking area, then left at a T-junction. After a barrier, veer right into another parking area, with a memorial to the opening of the reserve, and continue on a winding path. At a grassy track, go right 100m (328 ft.) to another track where you join the Little Ord circuit at point 4.

THE NORTHEAST HIGHLANDS WALKS

8

THE VAT & MUIR OF DINNET

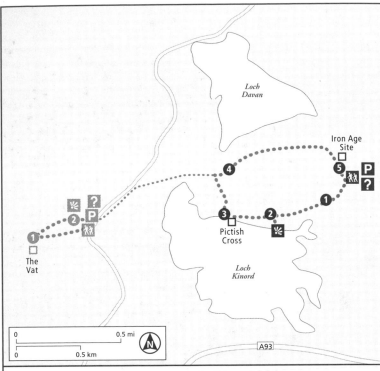

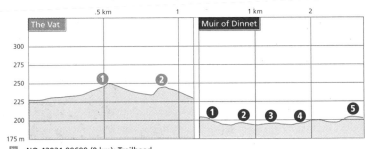

NO 42931 99699 (0 km): Trailhead
1 NO 42500 99577 (0.5 km): Walk through crack in rock wall into the Vat
2 NO 42872 99719 (0.8 km): Turn right at T-junction to viewpoint

NJ 45044 00070 (0 km): Trailhead
1 NO 44818 99880 (0.3 km): Keep right of farm buildings and go through gate
2 NO 44378 99687 (0.8 km): Left to loch shore after going through open gateway
3 NO 43998 99772 (1.3 km): Go left on unmarked grassy path to Pictish Stone
4 NJ 44054 00094 (1.8 km): Old Kinnord farmhouse
5 NJ 44923 00123 (2.7 km): Iron Age hut circles

On leaving the viewpoint, follow the path as it bends downhill back to the car park.

This second walk is a pleasant circular route marked with blue arrows. From the New Kinnord car park, go left along a paved lane, past a cottage, and along to a farm.

❶ New Kinnord The substantial farm buildings of New Kinnord replaced those at Old Kinnord, whose ruins you will see later. Keep right of the buildings and go through a gate. Follow the track that heads towards Loch Kinnord and then runs above it.

❷ Loch Kinnord After going through an open gateway in a wall, it is worth going left down to the loch shore to see the birdlife, which includes large flocks of greylag geese in winter. Just offshore, you will see a wooded island—a crannog.

Crannogs are common in Scottish lochs and are man-made islands, built as defensive homesteads. Most date from the Bronze and Iron ages, though they often remained in use through medieval times. Access was via causeways, either built on stilts or made of stones and hidden just below the surface of the water.

Return to the track and keep on until it makes a right-angle bend around pastures on the right.

❸ Pictish Stone Just beyond the corner, divert left on an unmarked grassy path for 100m (328 ft.) to an easily missed Pictish Stone. The carved cross slab is a fine example of elaborate Pictish artwork, and one of the few you will find in its original position, rather than removed to a museum. The Picts were the native Celtic people who inhabited Scotland from prehistoric times; they lost their identity after merging with the Scots in the 9th century, shortly after their conversion to Christianity.

Continue on the grassy track to a junction, where the link route joins from the Vat.

❹ Old Kinnord Keep right (left if you've come from the Vat) and soon pass the ruin of Old Kinnord farmhouse. There is a glimpse on the left of Loch Davan, before you go through a gate in a wall into trees. Farther on, the path runs through an open, heathery area with cross-country horse jumps. At a post by a jump, turn right, back into trees.

❺ Hut Circles After going up a slight incline, you reach an open area under power lines. The saucer-like hollows ringed with stones are Iron Age hut circles, most easily seen in winter and spring before the bracken grows. Beyond the next gate, drop down to the paved lane and return left to the car park (or go right if you are finishing at the Vat).

LOCHNAGAR ★★★

Difficulty rating: Strenuous

Distance: 20km (12.5 miles) round-trip

Estimated time: 7.5 hours

Elevation gain: 750m (2,460 ft.)

Costs/permits: £3 car parking

Best time to go: Arrive early to ensure a car-parking place

Website: None

Recommended map: Harvey Superwalker Lochnagar

Trailhead GPS: NO 30986 85129

Trailhead directions: In Ballater, cross the River Dee and go right on the B976, then left at a sign for Glen Muick. Some 12km (7.5 miles) of single-track driving takes you to the car park at the end of the road.

Lochnagar is the highest and most impressive mountain in the Eastern Cairngorms. Its north-facing cliffs hold the snow late into the year and are the haunt of climbers, while the White Mounth, a high Arctic-type plateau, rolls away to the south. This walk takes the shortest route to the summit and then returns via a thundering waterfall and the shores of Loch Muick. It is entirely on the Balmoral Estate, which is owned by the Queen.

THE NORTHEAST HIGHLANDS WALKS

8

LOCHNAGAR

From the public car park, take the path across a stream and through a grassy area with picnic tables. Draw level with a pinewood, where a toilet block is set back under the trees.

❶ **Visitor Center** The next building is the Balmoral Estate Visitor Centre, which houses displays about the local ecology and is a base for the ranger service. Just beyond it, turn right on a track down the edge of the wood and into the open. The trail takes you over the River Muick and across the flat-bottomed glen, with a view of the holiday lodge, Allt na-guibhsaich, among rhododendrons on the far side. Aim for the stone barn to the right of the lodge and take the marked path up its left side.

❷ **Allt Na-Guibhsaich Path** The track leads you through the surrounding pinewood to a trail running behind the lodge. Go right (straight on) along it, soon crossing a ford in the Allt na-guibhsaich, the "stream of the pines." Initially, the climb is fairly gentle, but it steepens as you climb around into the headwaters of the burn.

❸ **Watershed** Where the track levels off at the watershed, go left down a path marked by a small cairn. Cross a shallow opening, heading towards Meikle Pap, a conical hill that is a northern boundary of Lochnagar. The path climbs through grouse moor to the high, windswept col between Meikle Pap and Lochnagar. It goes close to the edge of a corrie (cirque), then bends back to climb "the Ladder," a steep boulder field.

To see into the great amphitheater of the corrie and get a view of Lochnagar, the lochan at the foot of the cliffs, walk towards the edge from the bend. This is a great spot for a photo, but take care as it's a sheer drop. Your route will run around the rim of the corrie to the highest point of the plateau, a pimple on the far side—Cac Carn Beag.

❹ **Cuidhe Crom** Above the Ladder, the route levels off at the first top, Cuidhe Crom. Skirt this rounded summit and continue around the corrie rim, avoiding the gullies dropping down through the cliffs. The path drifts away from the edge before climbing steeply up the most massive summit on the plateau, Cac Carn Mor (1,150m/3,773 ft.), which is marked by a large cairn.

At this altitude the vegetation is fragile, Arctic-like tundra that grows at ground level amid the stones. Paths can be hard to see and are just paler strips where the surface is disturbed by regular passage of boots. If cloud covers the tops, you will need to use careful navigation to find your way around to the highest point.

❺ **Cac Carn Beag** To reach Lochnagar's summit, continue north-northwest across a dip and scramble up the higher rocky outcrop of Cac Carn Beag (1,155m/ 3,789 ft.). A trig point marker and a viewpoint indicator top the weather-worn rocks.

Most of the Cairngorms are visible, from Mayar and Driesh only 13km (8 miles) away in the south to Cairn Gorm,

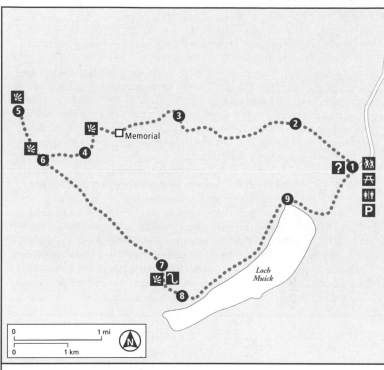

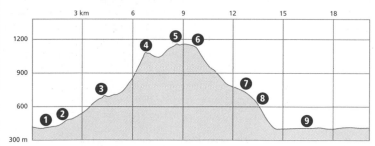

🏔 NO 30986 85129 (0 km): Trailhead

❶ NO 30807 85052 (0.7 km): Balmoral Estate Visitor Centre

❷ NO 29637 85862 (1.7 km): Cross the Allt Na-Guibhsaich stream

❸ NO 27398 86019 (4.3 km): Go left down path marked by small cairn

❹ NO 25634 85284 (6.7 km): Path levels and skirts summit of Cuidhe Crom

❺ NO 24371 86124 (8.6 km): Marker and viewpoint at top of Cac Carn Beag

❻ NO 24741 85297 (9.6 km): Down stone steps and enter valley of Glas Allt

❼ NO 27067 83097 (12.8 km): Path doubles back to foot of waterfall

❽ NO 27497 82563 (13.6 km): Cross footbridge above Glas-Allt Shiel lodge

❾ NO 29506 84402 (16.6 km): Turn right on path at stone boathouse

Balmoral Estate

Balmoral has been the Scottish home of the Royal Family since 1852, when it was purchased for Queen Victoria by her husband Prince Albert, who supervised the design and building of Balmoral Castle at Crathie (between Ballater and Braemar). The castle grounds, gardens, and exhibitions are open to the public, except during August, September, and October, when the Royal Family is in residence. Tours are hourly from 11am to 2pm and cost £8 for adults, £7 for seniors, and £3 for children. See www.balmoralcastle.com.

Lochnagar lies entirely within Balmoral Estate, a traditional Highland estate that extends to Glen Doll in the south. Deer stalking, grouse shooting, farming, and forestry are the main land uses, and the same access rights and responsibilities apply as to any other land in Scotland.

During the stalking season (mid-Aug to Oct 20), walkers are asked to phone Hillphones (© **01339 755532**) if they plan to venture off the recognized paths. This route stays on such paths, so a call is not necessary.

Lochnagar is named after the little, teardrop-shaped loch at the base of its north-facing cliffs—Lochan na Gaire, which is Gaelic for "the little loch of the noisy sound." In 1980, Prince Charles published *The Old Man of Lochnagar*, a children's story he dreamt up to entertain his younger brothers, Andrew and Edward, while they were on holiday at Balmoral Castle. The tale tells of an old man who drags a bathtub into a cave below the mountain's cliffs and makes a great commotion filling and heating it, upsetting the local pixies.

29km (18 miles) to the northwest. On a clear day, you can even see Ben Nevis (105km/65 miles) and the Bell Rock Lighthouse (77km/48 miles).

Return past Cac Carn Mor and continue southeast on the path.

❻ **Glas Allt** Walk down the stone steps, and this time keep going to the bottom, into the valley of the Glas Allt. The long glen stretches straight ahead for 3km (2 miles), and the path gradually angles down its left side. Eventually, the path crosses a footbridge to the other side. Not far beyond, you get a dramatic view, as the burn seems to drop into space and you have your first sight of Loch Muick.

❼ **Waterfall** The path makes a safe descent well away from the waterfall, then doubles back to its foot.

If you don't mind a bit of spray, this is a relatively sheltered place to stop and tuck into any food and drink you are carrying, or to take advantage of the free water supply (I [and others] drink vast quantities of mountain water and I haven't known it make anyone ill. Fast flowing water and springs are particularly safe.) Loch Muick seems far below, but you may make out white horses as the prevailing westerly whips along its surface.

Continue down the path, which runs beside rapids where rowan trees cling to the rocks, before zigzagging downhill.

❽ **Glass-Allt Shiel** The path enters the pinewood around the lodge, Glas-allt Shiel, going around the old stone wall that protected the trees when young from grazing red deer. Cross a footbridge over the burn and follow one of the paths through the trees to the lochside track. Turn left to leave the wood and walk along the loch with wide views over the water.

❾ Boathouse After 2.7km (1.7 miles), you reach a stone boathouse. Here, turn right on a path that runs across the foot of the loch, past a gravel beach. The path goes over a footbridge across the River Muick and angles up to a trail. Turn left and walk back 1km (²/₃ mile) to the visitor center and on to the car park.

MORRONE

Difficulty rating: Moderate

Distance: 12km (7.5 miles) round-trip

Estimated time: 4.5 hours

Elevation gain: 527m (1,730 ft.)

Costs/permits: None

Best time to go: September and October for autumn birch trees

Website: www.braemarscotland.co.uk

Recommended map: OS Landranger 43 (OS Explorer 387)

Trailhead GPS: NO 15149 91356

Trailhead directions: Braemar is in upper Deeside, where the A93 bends south to go over Glenshee into Perthshire. Turn into the village and go immediately left to the car park beside the public toilets. Buses run through Deeside from Aberdeen to Braemar.

Survey the eastern Cairngorms from Morrone, or Morven as it is sometimes called—the "Big Hill" rising to the south of Braemar. The path up this Corbett goes through the National Nature Reserve of Morrone Birkwood, the best British example of downy birch woodland with juniper. Returning by a trail and minor road provides an easy way to complete the circuit.

Go right, then left from the car park entrance, to cross the bridge over tumbling Clunie Water.

Walk between Braemar Mews, which contains shops and tourist information, and the Fife Arms Hotel as you head west on the Linn of Dee Road.

❶ Chapel Brae At a cobbled roundabout by the "green" cafe Taste, go diagonally left up Chapel Brae. Where the road ends at a car park, keep straight ahead on a path past a duck pond. At a fork, go left over a cattle grid and keep left at a triangular junction beyond.

You are now heading towards Morrone, and the track zigzags uphill through old birches with contorted shapes. Pass a cottage and at the next bend go straight uphill on a path (ignoring the arrow pointing right up the track).

❷ Birkwood Viewpoint The path leads directly to a viewpoint indicator and a bench that looks over the trees into the high Cairngorms. Braeriach, Cairn Toul, and Ben Macdui are among the summits visible.

Keep going, across a grassy trail, onto a path that climbs around the left side of a steep-sided knoll. Walk uphill through

Fun Facts Tall Tales

Look out for the butcher, R&D Gray, who sells delicious "locally caught" haggis. Scots regularly tell tourists that a haggis is a furry creature whose legs are shorter on one side so that it can more easily run around the hillsides.

heather to a gate in a deer fence; then pause to enjoy the view back over the village and the show ground used for the Braemar Gathering. The path now climbs southeast, diagonally uphill, following a low rocky outcrop.

❸ Stream Crossing By the time you cross a little stream, you are high enough to have a superb view over the River Dee. To the north across the valley, you can see up Glen Quoich, where large, old pines adorn the hillside. Eventually the path bends left, straight uphill. Before long, it broadens considerably and the gradient eases.

❹ Morrone Summit The top of the Morrone (859m/2,818 ft.) has been tamed in a rather messy fashion; the trig point marker is squeezed between an untidy cairn and a radio mast that is attached to an ugly building.

Stay long enough to identify some of the hills—massive Beinn Bhuird and Ben Avon to the north, the Glenshee hills to the south, and Lochnagar in the east, to the left of Loch Callater. Immediately west, the River Dee winds through green fields past red-roofed Mar Lodge.

Continue over the stony, weather-beaten summit on a track that runs southwest over the next lump in a wide, meandering ridge. As you go over it, the track swings left and drops to a col where it bends left again, heading downhill.

❺ Glen Clunie Cairn A long, straight stretch takes you downhill towards Clunie Water. As you descend, the vegetation gradually changes from windswept,

ground-hugging moorland plants to thick heather. Where the path bends again, to run closer to the stream on your left, a small cairn marks a good viewpoint into Glen Clunie.

All the hillsides around have a strange pattern of crisscross stripes. In August, when the heather is blooming, the landscape is a patchwork of green, brown, and purple. This is the result of muirburn—a traditional practice carried out by the keepers of grouse moors—that involves burning strips of heather to encourage the growth of new shoots.

❻ Clunie Water Follow the trail down to the minor road that runs along the west side of the glen and turn left to walk beside Clunie Water. The pastures on either side are fenced against deer, so that they don't eat the grass grown for cattle and sheep. Pass a pine plantation and cottage; then go over a cattle grid.

❼ Braemar Golf Club The road runs through Braemar golf course, the highest 18-hole course in Britain (at 351m/1,150 ft.). Walk by the clubhouse and go over another cattle grid. Beyond the 30 mph speed limit sign (48kmph), pass some fine stone houses and a church. The road takes you to the center of the village, with Braemar Mews on your left.

Just before you cross the bridge back over Clunie Water, look out for an aircraft engine sculpture the right. It is a memorial to the crew of a Vickers Wellington bomber that crashed near Braemar on a training flight in 1939. They were from Canada, Australia, New Zealand, and England.

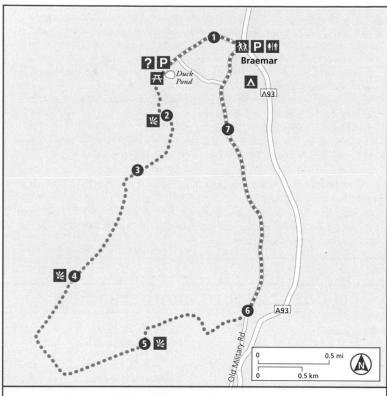

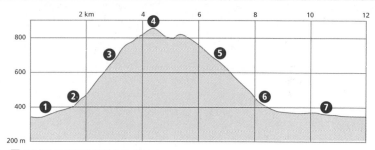

NO 15149 91356 (0 km): Trailhead
1 NO 14830 91456 (0.4 km): Left up Chapel Brae at cobbled roundabout
2 NO 14279 90511 (1.7 km): Viewpoint indicator and bench
3 NO 13921 89851 (2.7 km): Cross small stream
4 NO 13201 88628 (4.2 km): Summit of Morrone
5 NO 14019 87819 (6.6 km): Small cairn with view over Glen Clunie
6 NO 15234 88217 (8.2 km): Turn left at minor road
7 NO 14982 90350 (10.5 km): Walk by Braemar golf course clubhouse

The Braemar Gathering

The Queen is patron of the Braemar Gathering, a traditional Highland Games held on the first Saturday in September. Most Highland Games are earlier in the summer, but in 1848 this gathering was moved to September so Queen Victoria, who was coming to Balmoral for the first time, could experience a real flavor of the Highlands. Since then the reigning Monarch and members of the Royal Family have regularly attended.

The event has been running since 1816, when the Braemar Royal Highland Society was born, though the games can trace their roots back to the time of King Malcolm Canmore (1031–1093).

All the classic Highland Games elements are included, from the "heavy" events of throwing the hammer and tossing the caber to bagpipe and Highland dancing competitions. Hill runners race up and down Morrone in shockingly fast times, and teams from H. M. Forces compete with all their strength in the Inter Services tug-of-war championship.

Admission to the field on games day is as follows: adult £8, child £2; or tickets can be pre-booked for the seated areas (£14–£28). ✆ **01339 741098;** www. braemargathering.org.

DUFFTOWN TO CRAIGELLACHIE

Difficulty rating: Easy

Distance: 7.2km (4.5 miles) one-way (return by bus)

Estimated time: 2 hours

Elevation gain: Downhill from start

Costs/permits: None

Best time to go: April to June for fresh spring woodlands

Website: www.dufftown.co.uk and www. maltwhiskytrail.com

Recommended map: OS Explorer 424 (OS Landranger 28)

Trailhead GPS: NJ 32311 40892

Trailhead directions: From Aberdeen take the A96 to Huntly, then the A920 to Dufftown. From Aviemore, follow the A95 to Craigellachie, then the A941. Turn at signs for Glenfiddich and Balvenie Castle into the large car park beside Glenfiddich Distillery, on the north edge of town. Local buses serve the area.

This walk has no hills and is a good way to stretch your legs while following the Malt Whisky Trail through Speyside. It runs along a disused railway line beside the River Fiddich, going gently downhill from Dufftown to Craigellachie. Bountiful fresh water has been key to the development of so many distilleries in this area, but you'll also see its destructive power.

First pick up a bus timetable from the Tourist Information Centre in the Clocktower at the center of Dufftown. You'll complete the linear walk by returning from Craigellachie on the number 336 bus, which runs approximately hourly Monday to Saturday and every 2 hours on Sundays.

From the car park beside Glenfiddich Distillery, turn right onto the A941.

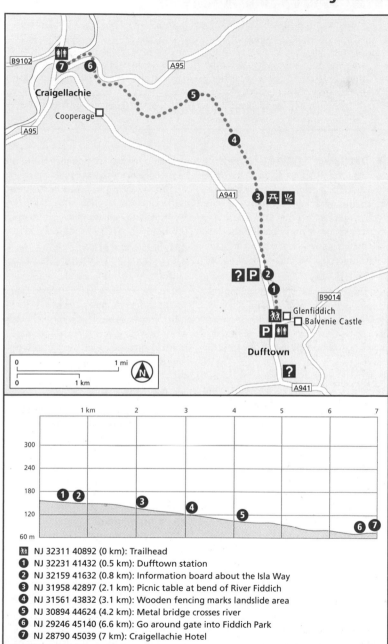

NJ 32311 40892 (0 km): Trailhead
1 NJ 32231 41432 (0.5 km): Dufftown station
2 NJ 32159 41632 (0.8 km): Information board about the Isla Way
3 NJ 31958 42897 (2.1 km): Picnic table at bend of River Fiddich
4 NJ 31561 43832 (3.1 km): Wooden fencing marks landslide area
5 NJ 30894 44624 (4.2 km): Metal bridge crosses river
6 NJ 29246 45140 (6.6 km): Go around gate into Fiddich Park
7 NJ 28790 45039 (7 km): Craigellachie Hotel

(Kids) Keith & Dufftown Railway

Enjoy the fun of a ride on this heritage railway, which was reopened by volunteers in 2001. The Spirit of Speyside, a diesel engine built around 1958, pulls the old-fashioned carriages through picturesque countryside, where you may spot roe deer, heron, or other wildlife. Dufftown Station has a quaint Victorian air and offers light refreshments at the Buffer Stop and occasional dining events in stylish 1930s Pullman cars. Open weekends March to September, and also Fridays June to August. Call ℂ **01340 821181** for fares and timetables.

❶ **Dufftown Station** Follow the pavement for 0.5km (¹/₃ mile) to Dufftown Station, passing the entrance to Balvenie and Kilvinie distilleries. Walk through the car park and around the side of the ticket office to the platform.

Turn left along the platform and continue ahead on a path beside the rail line.

❷ **The Isla Way** After going through a wooden gate, cross a driveway to picnic tables and an information board about the Isla Way, a new 20km (13-mile) route linking Dufftown to Keith. For the next stretch you follow the Isla Way along the disused railway line.

Beyond Convalmore Distillery—closed and with a rather derelict air—go around a gate with a yellow sign warning about landslides. By the time you reach the next footpath sign, you have left the busy road behind, and rural tranquillity has descended. Here the Isla Way goes right, but you continue straight ahead, with silver birch trees lining the embankment and three large whisky bond stores in the field below.

❸ **River Fiddich** Soon, come to a picnic table facing a bend in the fast-flowing River Fiddich that here rushes over shingle bars.

This is one of the few places along the route where a break in the riverside woodland lets you see the surrounding countryside of rolling farmland and wooded hills.

Hill of Newton rises on the left and steeper Scaut Hill on the right.

The wide path now runs fairly straight along the steep, wooded banks of the river. In spring and early summer, birdsong fills the air.

❹ **Landslide Notice** Wooden fencing marks the area of landslides that happened in 2002. Weave through the fences; then watch your footing for the short section where the path has narrowed to 0.9m (3ft.) wide in a couple of places. The damage is much less dramatic than the notices suggest, but it caused the authorities to remove the route's designation as a spur of the Speyside Way.

❺ **Gauldwell Bridge** Keep straight on until, beyond a bench, the old railway begins a slow curve to the left. This leads to a metal frame bridge that crosses the river by the Braes of Gauldwell. Note the old wooden walkways on either side of where the rails would have been. There are now more bends, as the old line follows the winding river.

❻ **Fiddich Park** Just after crossing another large bridge that takes you back over the river, go around a gate into Fiddich Park. Pass the car park and toilet block in this small country park and keep straight on, directing you towards Aberlour. Soon pass under the A95 and go around a gate. Beyond, the River Fiddich

The Malt Whisky Capital of Scotland

The local saying is:
"Rome was built on seven hills
Dufftown stands on seven stills."
 Nowhere in the world has such a concentration of distilleries. You can smell them as soon as you enter the town. The malty aroma from fermentation of the barley in large tubs mingles with heady vapors from the distillation process and the "Angel's Share," the 2% of spirit that evaporates from stored casks each year during the whisky's maturation.
 The Grant family built and still owns Dufftown's most famous distillery—Glenfiddich. It is a major visitor attraction and is open during the summer from 9:30am to 4:30pm Monday to Saturday, and noon to 4:30pm on Sunday (more limited opening in winter). Regular tours are free, while the connoisseur's tour costs £20 and requires pre-booking. See www.glenfiddich.com.
 Dufftown has a Whisky Museum, open most weekdays from mid-June to September, and a Whisky Shop, with an exceptional selection of single-malt Scotch whiskies. If visiting during the summer, try to be there for the whisky nosings on Tuesday evenings, or on Thursday night when you can let your hair down at the weekly ceilidh.

joins the River Spey, and the next view you have is of the wider river. Downstream, the modern road bridge partially obscures the splendid cast-iron Telford Bridge. Opened in 1814, it was revolutionary in the length of its single span.

❼ **Craigellachie Hotel**   After crossing a plank bridge over a tiny stream, turn right into Craigellachie's recreation ground. I couldn't resist a go on the zip wire before walking around the tennis courts to a path that slopes up to the main road. Cross the road to the public toilets; then go left a short distance to the bus stop in front of Craigellachie Hotel, which is renowned for its sumptuous Highland hospitality.

Balvenie Castle

This formidable ruin stands on a wooded hill behind Glenfiddich Distillery and is well worth a visit. The castle is surprisingly large inside and provides an insight into life centuries ago. It dates from the 1200s and was built by the Comyns, unsuccessful rivals to the Bruces for the crown of Scotland.
 Within the massive curtain wall is the Atholl Lodging, a fine example of Renaissance architecture built in 1550 when the then owner, the Earl of Atholl, required more comfortable accommodations.
 The castle became a ruin after being abandoned in 1720 in favor of a more "modern" house. Cared for by Historic Scotland, it is open daily Easter to the end of October, from 9:30am to 5:30pm (Oct closing 4:30pm). Entry is £3.70 for adults and £1.85 for children; concessions are £3 (✆ **01340 820121;** www.historic-scotland.gov.uk.)

SPEY BAY

Difficulty rating: Moderate

Distance: 16km (10 miles) round-trip

Estimated time: 4.5 hours

Elevation gain: 15m (50 ft.)

Costs/permits: None

Best time to go: July and August for osprey and other wildlife

Website: www.speysideway.org

Recommended map: Harvey Map of Speyside Way

Trailhead GPS: NJ 34110 59052

Trailhead directions: Travel by car or bus on the A96 to Fochabers, which is roughly midway between Aberdeen and Inverness. At the junction for Spey Bay on the west edge of the village, turn into the car park in Fochabers Community Woodland, marked by a brown tourist sign for the Spey Way.

The Spey is Britain's fastest-flowing river and it has a large natural floodplain, where the force of water is constantly carving new channels, creating islands, eroding banks, and dumping stones. See it in action as you follow the Spey Way to the ever-shifting river mouth at Spey Bay. It is a wonderful wildlife habitat, rich in food for ospreys, otters, seals, and dolphins.

Start by the information board under a spreading sweet chestnut tree and walk down the right side of a grassy area to the river. Turn right on the Spey Way, marked by a thistle symbol, along the wooded riverbank. Soon pass a picnic table, where there is a good view over the water, and keep left on an earth track running beside the river.

❶ Old Spey Bridge Frequent flooding means that the way can be rough and muddy as you go under the old stone bridge and modern road bridge that span the river. Keep straight ahead on a path along a raised embankment through dense deciduous woodland. Cross a track and ignore a fork to the left before the path narrows and runs beside the B9104. Beyond a bench, walk through a corridor cut between gorse bushes before good views over a bend in the river, where you may see anglers in waders, up to their waists in the water.

❷ Warren Wood On meeting a path, go right and take the first left past a barrier onto a track through the middle of Warren Wood. Shady mixed woodland soon gives way to open pine forest. Ignore side turnings, keeping on past an area of felled trees to a repaired section of riverbank. In March 2008, a flood swept away the riverside track, but it has been reinstated and is now protected by enormous stones.

❸ Shifting Shingle Continue on the trail, with your view of the river obscured by a high, vegetated bank, to a junction. Turn right to an information board, "Shifting Shingle," about the river and its amazing ability to wash stones and sediment down from the mountains. Then go right again and follow the track as it curves back to the north, running past barley-growing fields.

❹ Bogmoor Now the trail runs fairly straight all the way to Spey Bay, and you should ignore side turnings, including one

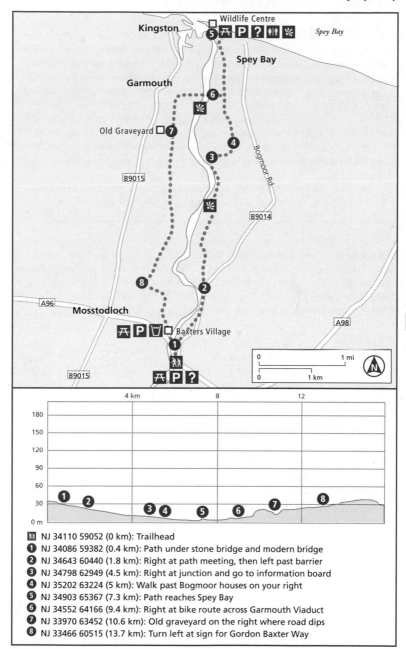

🏔 NJ 34110 59052 (0 km): Trailhead

❶ NJ 34086 59382 (0.4 km): Path under stone bridge and modern bridge

❷ NJ 34643 60440 (1.8 km): Right at path meeting, then left past barrier

❸ NJ 34798 62949 (4.5 km): Right at junction and go to information board

❹ NJ 35202 63224 (5 km): Walk past Bogmoor houses on your right

❺ NJ 34903 65367 (7.3 km): Path reaches Spey Bay

❻ NJ 34552 64166 (9.4 km): Right at bike route across Garmouth Viaduct

❼ NJ 33970 63452 (10.6 km): Old graveyard on the right where road dips

❽ NJ 33466 60515 (13.7 km): Turn left at sign for Gordon Baxter Way

Moray Firth Wildlife Centre

From 1768 to 1991, Spey Bay was a salmon-fishing station where fish were netted as they swam into the river. The buildings at Tugnet are now a wildlife center run by the Whale and Dolphin Conservation Society, who have a daily program of talks and tours. A resident population of around 130 bottlenose dolphins lives in the Moray Firth, and some of them are regularly seen from the center. You can learn more about dolphins in the lively exhibition, which is free, although donations to WDCS are welcome.

The most prominent building on site is Tugnet Ice House, a stone shed with three rounded roofs. Most of it is below ground, where it's cooler so the stored ice stayed frozen longer. Before refrigeration was invented, ice was used to keep the fish fresh. It was gathered in winter from the Spey and stored in the ice house.

The Centre (© **01343 820339;** www.wdcs.org) is open daily April to October from 10:30am to 5pm and on weekends during most of the winter.

to Bogmoor—the houses you see off to the right. Walk between fields and wet woodland, passing an information board, "Roots in the River," about the trees that manage to colonize the unstable riverside environment.

❺ **Spey Bay** About 1km (²⁄₃ mile) after crossing a raised paved path, part of the Aberdeen-to-Inverness cycling route, you reach Spey Bay. At cream-painted Tugnet House, which stands out amid the stone buildings, turn left to the Moray Firth Wildlife Centre.

Caféwild in the center has great-value light snacks, including hearty Scottish breakfasts and a selection of home-baked cakes. Allow time to explore the exhibition and see what wildlife is on the shingle bars and sheltered pools of the river mouth, where numerous swans, ducks, gulls, and waders rest and feed.

Walk to the far side of Tugnet Ice House for the best views and to see the results of the Tugnet Sculpture Project. At the edge of the car park take a small path that crosses a bridge over a stream, then runs beside the river before rejoining the path that brought you here.

❻ **Garmouth Viaduct** Walk back as far as the bicycle route, and this time turn right along it to cross the Garmouth Viaduct.

The old railway bridge is very long, as it was built to cross the Spey at one of its widest points, where it is braided into many streams between shingle islands. The elevated structure provides an osprey's-eye view of the Spey Bay Wildlife Reserve below.

On the far side, pass Kingston golf course; then go left up steps just before an archway. Turn left along a peaceful minor road, which runs along a bank overlooking the floodplain with a view to a cone-shaped hill, Bin of Cullen.

❼ **Old Graveyard** Where the road dips downhill, look for an old graveyard on the right. Some of the stones are more than 250 years old—one behind the obelisk in the middle has deeply carved symbols. It's a fascinating place to explore, but you may have to brave dive-bombing gulls during the nesting season (May–July). Continue on, passing Essil and Newton

Baxters Highland Village

In 1868, George Baxter opened a grocery shop in Fochabers. Since then, four generations of his family have grown the business into an international food group. Their premium brands of soups and preserves use the finest Scottish ingredients and include traditional recipes such as Royal Game soup and Cullen Skink (smoked haddock and potato soup).

The Highland Village is an old-world style collection of shops and restaurants where you can sample and stock up on their products. After a long walk, I recommend the famous Baxters pancakes to restore your energy levels.

Open daily 10am to 5pm. Call (C) **01343 820666; www.baxters.com.**

farms and their fields of beef cattle, to Speymouth Parish Church, known as the "Red Kirk" because of the color of its walls. Stynie farm is just beyond.

8 **Gordon Baxter Way** After Stynie Cottages, turn left at a sign for the Gordon Baxter Way and Mosstodloch. Follow a track across fields to Redhall cottages; then go right on a grassy path just before them.

Keep straight ahead past a pine wood (ignoring another path signposted up steps) to Mosstodloch, where you turn left into Baxters Highland Village. From the visitor center, cross the road with care; then go left on the pedestrian and bicycle route that goes over Old Spey Bridge. Keep straight on to the car park.

CREAG MEAGAIDH ★★

Difficulty rating: Strenuous

Distance: 21km (13 miles) round-trip

Estimated time: 8.5 hours

Elevation gain: 881m (2,890 ft.)

Costs/permits: None

Best time to go: September and October for autumn colors

Website: www.snh.org.uk

Recommended map: OS Landranger 34 (OS Explorer 401)

Trailhead GPS: NN 48291 87273

Trailhead directions: Take the A86 from Laggan (or Spean Bridge in the west), and halfway along Loch Laggan turn into the marked Creag Meagaidh car park.

The most impressive feature of Creag Meagaidh, a massive mountain with complex topography, is Coire Ardair, where a dark lochan lies below deep-gullied cliffs that are a prime winter climbing site. Walkers can gain the summit by climbing through The Window up to a high plateau. This route includes the two lower Munros that punctuate the long ridge bounding the north side of Coire Adair.

Follow the hill trail, a marked path that runs parallel to the path that leaves the car park by an information board about the National Nature Reserve.

1 **Aberarder** The path passes the white farm buildings at Aberarder, which are a base for the Scottish Natural Heritage staff who look after the reserve. A shelter on the corner contains more information and has a whiteboard where returning walkers are invited to record their wildlife sightings. Continue along the wooded path, which soon passes through a gap in a wall, then steadily rises through an open heathery area.

❷ **Birch Wood** Enter a birch forest, where many young saplings grow amid hoary older trees. The well-made path levels off, making walking easier. Initially, you are looking up to the ridge running west from Carn Liath, but as the glen curves left the view changes with every step. First you see Stob Poite Coire Ardair, then the V-shaped Window, and eventually the cliff face above the lochan.

❸ **Lochan a' Choire** The little oval loch below the cliffs (Lochan a' Choire) doesn't come into sight until the last minute. The path runs above the lochan and ends at the two streams that feed it.

I stopped at the last burn to drink deeply and refill my water bottle, as there is no running water on the summits. It's important to have enough liquid to keep you going until you come back down from Carn Liath.

A peaty path worn by many boots continues steeply uphill, following a ridge of moraine. The gradient eases across a grassy area, then steepens again up a boulder field, where a loose path winds up through rock and scree (an area prone to avalanches in winter).

❹ **The Window** As you reach The Window, the path runs along the right side of the rocky, narrow pass to a grassy col. Turn left and climb southeast—a slight path zigzags up to the right of some old metal fence posts—until you are above the cliffs of Coire Ardair. The plateau rises up to a broad, grassy dome, which has a large cairn on its north side, overlooking crags that drop to Lochan Uaine. Climb the dome and curve to the right above the crags. In poor visibility, you will need a series of bearings to reach the summit while keeping well away from the edges.

❺ **Creag Meagaidh** The top narrows to the west of the grassy dome and dips before rising to a higher cairn at Creag Meagaidh's main summit (1,130m/3,707 ft.).

From here, you have a beautiful view of the west Highlands. Due south, a river runs towards you from small Loch Ghuibinn. To the right (west) of this are the peaks of the Grey Corries. Around from them, you can see over Aonach Mor, to Britain's highest mountain, Ben Nevis.

Return back across the high plateau to The Window and climb the hill on the far side.

❻ **Stob Poite Coire Ardair** A path worn in the grassy slope bends right above cliffs, bringing you quite quickly to the cairn that marks the summit of the next Munro, Stob Poite Coire Ardair (1,053m/3,454 ft.). Now continue along the high, level ridge, passing another cairn. You start to see Loch Laggan below. After 1.2km (³/₄) miles (1.2km), bend left and follow the ridge around the lip of Coire a' Chriochairein.

As you walk along this ridge, you cross from the west side of Scotland to the east. The streams flowing north from Stob Poite Coire Ardair drain into the River Spean, which reaches the west coast near Fort William. However, by the time you are above Coire a' Chriochairein, the streams going north are flowing into the headwaters of the River Spey, which runs northeast to the Moray Firth on the east coast.

❼ **Sron Coire a' Chriochairein** The ridge narrows to a rocky point (991m/3,250 ft.) above the basin. Translated from Gaelic, this is Point of the Hollow of the Boundary Keeper. Drop steeply northeast into a col and climb up the far side. Now the ridge broadens and you pass over the

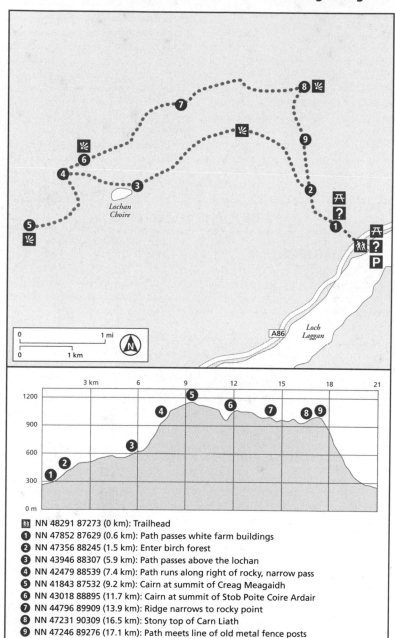

NN 48291 87273 (0 km): Trailhead

1. NN 47852 87629 (0.6 km): Path passes white farm buildings
2. NN 47356 88245 (1.5 km): Enter birch forest
3. NN 43946 88307 (5.9 km): Path passes above the lochan
4. NN 42479 88539 (7.4 km): Path runs along right of rocky, narrow pass
5. NN 41843 87532 (9.2 km): Cairn at summit of Creag Meagaidh
6. NN 43018 88895 (11.7 km): Cairn at summit of Stob Poite Coire Ardair
7. NN 44796 89909 (13.9 km): Ridge narrows to rocky point
8. NN 47231 90309 (16.5 km): Stony top of Carn Liath
9. NN 47246 89276 (17.1 km): Path meets line of old metal fence posts

rounded top of Meall an t-Snaim and go down to another col, which has two clefts in the bottom.

❽ Carn Liath Climb steadily up rounded slopes onto the stony top of Carn Liath (1,006m/3,300 ft.), the Grey Hill. Ardverikie House, which starred in the British television series *Monarch of the Glen,* lies below on the shore of Loch Laggan, with the Ben Alder mountains rising behind.

Return about 200m (656 ft.) along the stony ridge; then turn south down slopes of grass interspersed by boulder fields.

Soon your target, the white buildings of Aberarder, comes into sight below.

❾ Na Cnapanan Descend towards the rocky lump of Na Cnapanan, aiming for the west (right) side of the saddle before it. Here pick up a line of old metal fence posts. Follow them diagonally downhill, passing below rock outcrops and stepping through heather and dwarf trees. A slight path helps, but it is a rough descent. The fence line descends through the birch wood to the well-made path. Turn left and return down it to the car park.

SLEEPING & EATING

ACCOMMODATIONS

Deeside Hotel This well-managed guesthouse occupies an 1890 pink-granite house surrounded by late-Victorian gardens, and is a 3-minute walk from the center of Ballater. The guest rooms are simple, with white walls, wood furniture, and bathrooms with showers. Dinner menus change nightly, while breakfast ingredients come from suppliers to the Royal Family.

45 Braemar Rd., Ballater AB35 5RQ. ℂ 01339 755420. www.deesidehotel.co.uk. 9 units. £50 room, £75 including dinner. MC, V. Rates include breakfast. Closed Jan. Pets welcome. **Close to:** The Vat and Muir of Dinnet, Lochnagar.

(Finds) Froach Lodge Hill-walkers will immediately feel at home in this cozy house with hostel-style accommodations, which is the base for a small mountaineering business. Availability of beds depends on what courses and holidays are running. Andy has a great knowledge of the Cairngorms, while Rebecca's food is legendary.

Mountain Innovations, Deshar Rd., Boat of Garten PH24 3BN. ℂ 01479 831331. www.scotmountain. co.uk. 6 twin rooms. B&B £18, £31 including dinner. MC, V. **Close to:** Lochan an Eilein, Meall a Bhuachaille, Cairn Gorm and Ben Macdui.

(Kids) Glenmore Caravan and Camping Site Here you can stay in the middle of beautiful Glemore Forest, on a large, open touring site with its own sandy beach. Loch Morlich watersports center is next door, and there's plenty of space for children to play. The facilities are clean and modern.

Forest Holidays, Glenmore, PH2 1QU. ℂ 01479 861271. www.forestholidays.co.uk. 220 units. 2-person pitch £12–18, family of 4 17–£26. MC, V. **Close to:** Lochan an Eilein, Meall a Bhuachaille, Cairn Gorm and Ben Macdui.

★ (Kids) Hilton Coylumbridge This is Aviemore's best hotel for children because of its extensive sports and leisure facilities, set on 26 hectares (65 acres) of tree-studded grounds. Kids love the Fun House and Adventure Park, with dry ski slope and climbing wall. The guest rooms are spacious and well appointed.

Coylumbridge, by Aviemore PH22 1QN. © **01479 810661.** www.hiltonhotels.com. 88 units. £70–£100.
Rates include breakfast. AE, DC, MC, V. **Close to:** Lochan an Eilein, Meall a Bhuachaille, Cairn Gorm and
Ben Macdui.

★★ **Kildrummy Castle Hotel** This 19th-century mansion, on acres of landscaped
gardens, overlooks the ruined castle of Kildrummy. Its guest rooms, many furnished with
antiques, vary in size; some of the master rooms feature four-poster beds and fireplaces. The
public rooms have oak-paneled walls and ceilings, mullioned windows, and window seats.
Kildrummy, by Alford AB33 8RA. © **01975 571288.** www.kildrummycastlehotel.co.uk. 16 units. £85–
£100. Rates include breakfast. AE, MC, V. Closed Jan. **Close to:** Bennachie, The Vat and Muir of Dinnet.

Rucksacks Centrally placed in Braemar, this hostel is owned by a mountain-lover,
Kate, who knows just what walkers need. The Alpine-style hut, for those on a tight
budget, and the Cottage and Cabin, with a dormitory and twin room each, are arranged
around a quiet garden.
15 Mar Rd., Braemar AB35 5YL. © **01339 741517.** www.hostel-scotland.co.uk. 5 units. £7–£15. No credit
cards. **Close to:** Morrone, Lochnagar.

RESTAURANTS

★★ (Finds **Craigellachie Hotel** SCOTTISH Savor the style and elegance of a classic hotel while enjoying fine dining in the Ben Aigen Restaurant. Fillet of Aberdeen
Angus beef and poached Scottish salmon crowned by avruga caviar are typical fare. For
an after-dinner dram, choose from over 700 single-malt whiskies in the Quaich Bar.
Craigellachie, Speyside. © **01340 881204.** www.craigellachie.com. Reservations recommended. Dinner
menu £32 (desserts extra), or full Taste of Scotland menu £38; lunch mains £3.95–£11. AE, MC, V. Daily
noon–2pm, 6–9:30pm. **Close to:** Dufftown to Craigellachie, Spey Bay.

★★ **The Cross** SCOTTISH This chic restaurant serves superlative meals that have
put The Cross on Scotland's gastronomic map. The main building is an old tweed mill.
Specialties depend on the availability of produce in the local markets and might include
wild Scrabster seabass or breast of Gressingham duck.
Tweed Mill Brae, off the Ardbroilach Rd., Kingussie. © **01540 661166.** www.thecross.co.uk. Reservations
recommended. Fixed-price 3-course dinner £47–£50. MC, V. Tues–Sat 7–9pm. Closed Dec–Feb. **Close to:**
Lochan an Eilein, Meall a'Bhuachaille, Cairn Gorm and Ben Macdui.

(Kids **The Gathering Place** INTERNATIONAL This small, family-run bistro welcomes children and serves locally sourced food, fine wines, and draught real ale. Sip
aperitifs in the woodland garden before dining on dishes such as collops of Mar Lodge
venison or Scottish lamb steak with a red-currant and red wine jus.
9 Invercauld Rd., Braemar. © **01339 741234.** Main courses: lunch £6–£7, dinner £12–£17 (reduced-price
children's portions 6–7pm). MC, V. Mon–Sat noon–2pm; Wed–Sun 6–9pm. Reservations recommended.
Close to: Morrone.

★ **Ord Ban Restaurant Cafe** SCOTTISH/INTERNATIONAL Delicious, locally
sourced food is prepared simply and served in what was a Victorian schoolroom. Rustic
lunches include produce from the Rothiemurchus Estate deli, plus home baking and
great coffee. In the evening, the dishes range from local salmon, beef, and venison to fresh
pea, chanterelle, and parmesan risotto.
Rothiemurchus Centre, by Aviemore. © **01479 810005.** www.ordban.com. Reservations required for
dinner. Main courses: lunch £5–£7, dinner £13–£16. AE, MC, V. Daily 9:30am–5:30pm; Thurs–Sat 6:30–
9pm. **Close to:** Lochan an Eilein, Meall a' Bhuachaille, Cairn Gorm and Ben Macdui.

★ **Taste of Speyside** SCOTTISH   True to its name, this restaurant avidly promotes Speyside cuisine, as well as the product of Speyside's 46 distilleries. Try the platter of smoked salmon, smoked venison, smoked trout, pâté flavored with malt whisky, locally made cheese, salads, and homemade oat cakes, or a bowl of nourishing homemade soup.

10 Balvenie St., Dufftown. ⓒ **01340 820860.** Reservations recommended. Main courses £15–£17, Speyside platter £18. AE, MC, V. Tues–Sun noon–2pm, 6–9pm. Closed Mon, also closed Sun in winter. Closed Jan. **Close to:** Dufftown to Craigellachie, Spey Bay.

The Northern Highlands Walks

by Patrick Thorne

The romantic glens and rugged mountain landscapes of the north Highlands are timeless and pristine. Deer graze only yards from the highway (be wary if you see these and you're driving that they're not actually on the road ahead too!), and, at a secluded loch, you can enjoy a picnic or fish for trout and salmon. The shadow of Macbeth still stalks the land (locals will tell you that this 11th-c. king was much maligned by Shakespeare). The area's most famous resident, however, is said to live in mysterious Loch Ness: First sighted by St. Columba in the 6th century, "Nessie" has cleverly evaded searchers ever since.

Centuries of Highland invasions, rebellions, clan feuds, and land clearances of the local population by rich lairds may now be distant memories, but they remain part of the national psyche for many Highlanders. Although the region isn't as remote as it once was, the features on the landscape are still shaped by the results of those actions a century and more ago.

For hikers, therefore, you may feel you are walking through time as well as over the heather as you climb up through some of Scotland's wildest, highest, and least spoiled countryside, enjoying the superb views out over the sometimes rugged, sometimes desolate, but always spectacular scenery, usually ending with the sea in most directions.

There are hikes of all kinds here, and this chapter endeavors to give you a taste of all. You don't have to always head upwards in the Highlands: The region has hundreds of miles of coastline with some great walks to

some of Europe's best beaches, even if the water is a tad cold. Most hikes do head upwards, but it's up to you how far and how high you go as the whole range is here, from gentle hills to rocky scrambles on the country's highest peaks.

One thing never to underestimate here, perhaps more than anywhere else in Scotland, is the extremity of weather that can blow in unexpectedly, making it easy for even experienced hikers to lose their way and sadly leading to a number of casualties every year, despite the best efforts of the well-organized volunteer mountain rescue services. Always ensure you are fully prepared for all eventualities when you head out, however pleasant it seems as you set off.

Spring and autumn are often the best times to visit. Although unpredictable, the weather tends to be better than in the summer; you also avoid the worst of the tourist crowds and on the west coast the worst of the infamous midge clouds, which descend in the thousands on hot, still days, not giving a serious bite but causing huge irritation.

Fort William is a major center for the west Highlands, surrounded by wildly beautiful Lochaber, the "land of bens, glens, and heroes." Dominating the area is Ben Nevis, Britain's highest mountain. This district is the western end of what is known as the Great Glen, geologically a fissure dividing the northwest of Scotland from the southeast and containing Loch Lochy, Loch Oich, and Loch Ness. The Caledonian Canal, opened in 1847, linked these lochs, the River Ness, and the Moray Firth at Highland capital Inverness on the East, another good base, indeed a better one for most of the hikes listed.

This Great Glen is the southern border of our region, the western, eastern, and northern all made up of coastline. In between, the land becomes increasingly wild and sparsely populated as you move north and west through Inverness-shire, Ross-shire, Sutherland, and Caithness.

ESSENTIALS

GETTING THERE

By Air

The northern Highlands and Islands are best reached by air from Aberdeen (www.aberdeenairport.com), Inverness (www.invernessairport.com), Edinburgh (www.edinburgh airport.com), and Glasgow (www.glasgowairport.com) airports. Glasgow is the main international hub, but the other three smaller airports are well connected from London and other major British cities, and in the case of Aberdeen and Edinburgh, from other European capitals too.

Inverness Airport, located 13km (8 miles) east of the city, is the fastest gateway to the region. This receives services either daily or several times a week from a dozen U.K. airports, including London Gatwick, London Luton, Manchester, Birmingham, Southampton, Exeter, Bristol, Nottingham, Glasgow, Edinburgh, and Belfast. Flight operators include Easy Jet, Flybe, British Airways, and Ryanair. The airport's website provides a constantly updated online travel planner, which links through to the airlines involved on each route: www.hial.co.uk/inverness-airport.html, The two main operators from London are **Easy Jet** (✆ **08712 442366;** www.easyjet.com) and **Flybe** (✆ **08717 000535;** www.flybe.com).

By Bus

There are several buses running daily from Edinburgh, Glasgow, and other cities in the U.K. to Inverness, taking 3 hours from Edinburgh and Glasgow. As with rail services, schedules and prices vary according to the season and the bus operating company. For the latest information, visit www.travelinescotland.com, or call the 24-hour Travel Line Scotland at ✆ **08712 002233,** available 7 days a week. This is also the source for information on bus services in the local area.

There are several buses running daily from Glasgow and other cities to Fort William, taking 3 hours from Glasgow. For current schedules and prices, go to www.citylink.co.uk, or call ✆ **08705 505050.**

By Car

Arriving by road or rail, you must choose between the east- or west-coast routes, the East being the major artery to the north, with the modern A9 highway and rail line, which continues via Inverness right up to Britain's northwest tip at Wick and Thurso. The west-coast route, primarily to Fort William, follows the A82, and there is also a rail link.

The main road from the South to Inverness is the A9. The drive takes 3 to 4 hours from Glasgow or Edinburgh. The A82 to Fort William is a slower and more winding route, although it does pass through some spectacular scenery, particularly Gelcoe.

All of the hikes listed, with the exception of Ben Nevis, are most easily reached via the east-coast route to Inverness.

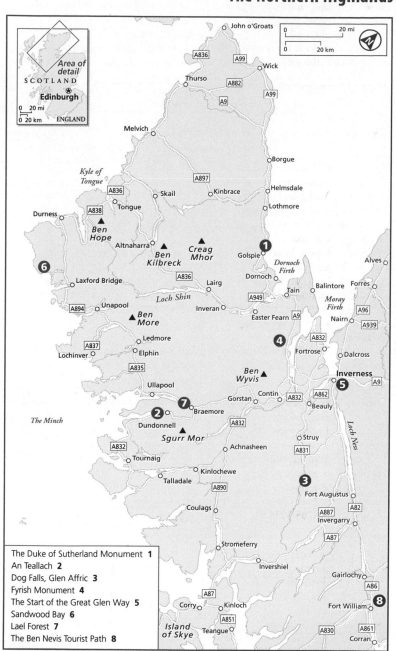

John o'Groats

A836

A99

Wick

Thurso

A882

A99

A9

Melvich

Borgue

Kyle of Tongue

A897

Helmsdale

Skail

Kinbrace

Lothmore

A836

Tongue

Durness

A838

Ben Hope

Altnaharra

Ben Kilbreck

Creag Mhor

Golspie

1

Dornoch Firth

Alves

6

Laxford Bridge

A836

Lairg

Dornoch

Tain

Balintore

Forres

Loch Shin

Inveran

A949

Moray Firth

Nairn

A96

A894

Unapool

Ben More

Easter Fearn

A9

A939

A837

Ledmore

A832

Lochinver

Elphin

Fortrose

Dalcross

A835

Ben Wyvis

Ullapool

Gorstan

Contin

A832

A862

Inverness

5

A9

The Minch

2

7

Braemore

Beauly

Dundonnell

A832

Sgurr Mor

Struy

Achnasheen

A832

Tournaig

A831

Kinlochewe

Loch Ness

Talladale

A890

3

Coulags

Fort Augustus

A887

A82

Invergarry

A87

Stromeferry

Invershiel

Gairlochy

A86

Corry

Kinloch

A87

Fort William

8

Island of Skye

Teangue

A851

A830

A861

Corran

The Duke of Sutherland Monument **1**
An Teallach **2**
Dog Falls, Glen Affric **3**
Fyrish Monument **4**
The Start of the Great Glen Way **5**
Sandwood Bay **6**
Lael Forest **7**
The Ben Nevis Tourist Path **8**

Area of detail

SCOTLAND

Edinburgh

0   20 mi

0   20 km

ENGLAND

0   20 mi

0   20 km

Inverness is connected to most of the UK's major cities by rail. Direct services from Glasgow and Edinburgh take about 3.5 hours each, or 8 hours from London Kings Cross station. There is also an overnight sleeper train service (first class single berth, standard class twin berth, or carriages with reclining seats) from London Euston, departing around 9pm and arriving in Inverness around 8am, but times may vary. For current schedules and price—as well as online booking for the lowest prices—go to www.thetrainline.com or call ✆ **08456 015929.** For overnight sleeper services, visit www.firstgroup.com/scotrail/caledoniansleeper/index.html or call ✆ **08457 550033.** Lowest prices are available by booking online.

To Fort William, the scenic West Highland rail line begins at the Queen Street Station in Glasgow and ends at Mallaig, on the west coast. Three trains a day run this route; for current schedules and prices go to www.firstgroup.com/scotrail or call ✆ **08456 015929.**

VISITOR INFORMATION

VisitScotland (✆ **08452 255121;** www.visitscotland.com), the Scottish tourist board, provides information on the area and a booking service. The Inverness branch of the **Highlands of Scotland Tourist Board** is at Castle Wynd, off Bridge Street (✆ **01463 234353;** www.visithighlands.com/inverness-loch-ness). The Fort William branch of the Highlands of Scotland Tourist Board is at the Cameron Centre in Cameron Square (✆ **01397 703781;** www.visithighlands.com/fort-william-lochaber). For in-depth information, see VisitScotland's website for this region: www.visithighlands.com/northern-scottish-highlands.

ORIENTATION

The northern Highlands encompass Scotland's highest mountains, most impressive beaches, and largest wilderness areas. The southern border of the region is the Great Glen, home to Loch Ness, which contains more water than the rest of the UK's rivers, lakes, and lochs combined, as well as its famous monster. The Glen runs southwest from Inverness on the east coast to Fort William on the western side of the country. The west, dominated by the Gaelic culture (the reason for the bilingual road signs that have now spread across the region), is an area of sparse population, rugged land, and nearly inaccessible fishing communities. The eastern part of the region, north of Inverness, has strong Viking influences and contains most of the agriculturally productive land, as well as most of the region's population of a quarter million. Here the coastal road has been modernized and taken on causeways and bridges over three sea inlets, or firths, to provide fast access along the coast. From this route, there are half a dozen roads crossing to the west, typically allowing you to reach west-coast communities such as Ullapool or Lochinver more quickly than by following the winding road up the west coast instead.

GETTING AROUND

The main road north of Inverness is the A9, running up the east coast to Scotland's northeast tip and which can be used to directly access several of the hikes (Fyrish, Duke of Sutherland Monument). For Sandwood Bay, Lael Forest, and An Teallach, leave the A9 at Tore and take the second turn on the left at the roundabout onto the A835, another good modern road, heading northwest.

Rail service from Inverness station can take you close to the start of several of the north Highland hikes. It is approximately 45 minutes from Inverness to Alness for the Fyrish walk (you will need to take a taxi the final few miles from the station) or 70 minutes to Golspie for the Duke of Sutherland walk, which you can join straight from the train station.

Bus services are also available, the times and prices for which unfortunately change frequently. There are local bus services to the bottom of the Ben Nevis walk from Fort William.

THE DUKE OF SUTHERLAND MONUMENT ★

Difficulty rating: Moderate

Distance: 9.7km (6 miles)

Estimated time: 4 hours round-trip

Elevation gain: 360m (1,181 ft.)

Costs/permits: None

Pet friendly: Yes

Best time to go: The waterfall is often most impressive in spring as the snow melts.

Website: None

Recommended map: OS Explorer - Active Map sheet 441 Lairg, Bonar Bridge & Golspie

Trailhead GPS: NC 84212 01222

Trailhead directions: Drive north through Golspie (about an hour's drive north of Inverness and also accessible by rail or bus), on the A9. As the road climbs out of the village, take the turn onto a single-track road to the left, about 0.4km (1/4 mile) farther on. The small car park is located about 0.8km (1/2 mile) up this road on the left side. The circular walk also passes through Golspie, so it is possible to park anywhere in the village and start it from there.

THE NORTHERN HIGHLANDS WALKS

9

THE DUKE OF SUTHERLAND MONUMENT

The walk up to the Duke of Sutherland's imposing monument, clearly visible from the village of Golspie below and for many miles as you approach, is a good mid-length hike through a wonderful variety of terrain—with lots of time to ponder the controversial legacy of the man depicted in the 32m-high (106 ft.) monument.

The hike up to the Duke of Sutherland's statue is a walk in two parts. A short lower section takes you into the Big Burn, a famous and long-established local beauty spot with some pleasant waterfalls at its head. You then climb up what is initially the route of the burn, through woodland, and into open country as you climb to the top of Ben Bhraggie (396m/1,300 ft.), where the Duke's statue is located.

❶ **The Big Burn** Go through the gateway in the dry stone wall at the back of the car park and turn down to the right. You are now descending into the Big Burn valley,

which is crisscrossed by multiple paths, although they are all following the stream on one side or the other; as long as you move uphill and against the flow of the small stream, you are on the right track. The path descends a steep escarpment through mature woodland containing ash, sycamore, oak, and beech trees and takes you to the stream itself. Turn right to follow it upwards, and after 200m (656 ft.) cross the metal foot bridge over it (if you come upon a wooden footbridge, you have emerged a little too far downstream; stay on the right bank and follow the stream up to the metal footbridge).

A short walk (49m/160 ft.) along the left bank of the burn takes you to the bottom of the waterfall that makes this such a popular local beauty spot. The waters cascade over a fault between the older sandstone that forms the mountains beyond and the softer Jurassic-era sandstone of the coastal plain. The result is a very pretty picture, with the lower section of the falls, approximately 5m (16 ft.) high, visible.

② Above the Falls Return to the metal bridge and turn right. The path climbs steeply out of the valley as you begin a 3.2km (2-mile) unremitting climb towards the summit of Beinn a Bhragaidh, where the Duke's statue is located. The solidly made steps and steep path first lead you to a small bridge over the top of the waterfall.

The path now follows the right bank of the stream again and has a gentle incline. The woodland gradually thins to small birch trees, broom, and rhododendron bushes. Now, 1.1km (²/₃ mile) from your start point, a fourth bridge crosses back over the stream to your left. Take that and begin to climb again, now passing into coniferous woodland. A 46m (150-ft.) ascent takes you to a single-track road above the wood. Turn left on this and follow it for 198m (650 ft.). You will see fields and woodland above, with moorland above that, and a vista of the east coast with Golspie comes into view below.

③ Benvraggie Wood At the crossroads, turn right, uphill just before you reach the cottage on the corner there, and follow the forest track which leads you up to Benvraggie Wood. This is an active forestry plantation and also marks the lower end of an exciting mountain-bike track that has recently been created. Most of this is separate from the walking route, but still be aware of the possibility that a high-speed biker may come hurtling past.

The track climbs through the wood, which varies between areas which have seen widespread tree felling and areas that still have thick Scots pine planted in the no-longer favored way—so close together than no other plant life can exist between them.

Continue straight on up the path and ignore other forestry trails it crosses en route. After 1.2km (²/₃ mile) you reach a large deer fence with a smaller walkers' gate you pass through.

④ Beinn a Bhragaidh (Ben Bhraggie) The path now climbs through open moorland, and the wind may well start to pick up. The heather-clad hillside brings an air of desolation to the landscape, or perhaps it is just your legs getting a little tired. The path continues to climb and then, after another 0.8km (¹/₂ mile), begins to plateau at 396m (1,300 ft.).

The route actually passes behind the hill's summit, and the increasingly ominous monument of the Duke is lost from view to your left, before you turn and find yourself walking in the opposite direction towards the coast, with the Duke beginning to appear on the horizon.

⑤ The Duke of Sutherland Monument The massive monument provides shelter from the wind and a place to stop, take in the view, and reflect on the statue itself.

There are superb views to the south towards Easter Ross and the Black Isle. To the north, the town of Brora may be seen, and nearby the splendid Dunrobin Castle, the Duke's seat, which should also be included in your itinerary if you have time.

⑥ The Descent The route down descends more steeply than the ascent, with a zigzagging path cutting down through the heather, before re-entering Benvraggie wood. You are in fact descending the hill about 0.8km (¹/₂ mile) to the

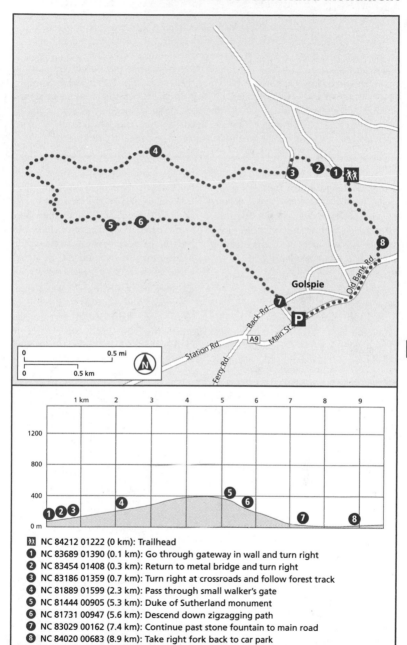

🚶 NC 84212 01222 (0 km): Trailhead
1 NC 83689 01390 (0.1 km): Go through gateway in wall and turn right
2 NC 83454 01408 (0.3 km): Return to metal bridge and turn right
3 NC 83186 01359 (0.7 km): Turn right at crossroads and follow forest track
4 NC 81889 01599 (2.3 km): Pass through small walker's gate
5 NC 81444 00905 (5.3 km): Duke of Sutherland monument
6 NC 81731 00947 (5.6 km): Descend down zigzagging path
7 NC 83029 00162 (7.4 km): Continue past stone fountain to main road
8 NC 84020 00683 (8.9 km): Take right fork back to car park

> (Fun Facts **A Stony Stare**
>
> The massive statue to the first Duke of Sutherland is a poignant symbol which generates strong passions to this day, and a controversy as to whether or not it should still be there. The statue was erected in memory of the Duke, who became the largest landowner in Britain when he married the wealthy Countess of Sutherland in 1785. However, he is remembered for the often brutal removal of more than 5,000 of his tenants from their simple homes and farms in the Highland Clearances, to make room for thousands of sheep. There is therefore some irony, to say the least, in part of the inscription on the statue which reads, ". . . of loved, revered and cherished memory, erected by his tenantry and friends."

south of the path you took going up. Again you cross the forestry track following the BBFP, or Ben Bhraggie Footpath, sign posts, which lead on to a farm trail. Pass to the left of Rhives Farm and you reach the outskirts of Golspie.

7 Golspie The first thing you will see is a pretty stone fountain in the center of a roundabout, dedicated to the first Duke of Sutherland's wife, the Duchess Elizabeth. Continue past this to the main road through the center of Golspie (this is the A9 you drove along to reach the trailhead).

Follow the pavement through the village. It bends to the left and then, after 0.8km (1/2 mile), at the Sutherland Arms Hotel, to the right. Leave the road here and follow the path signposted WATERFALL that heads into the wooded valley straight ahead when the road bends away.

8 Back at the Burn You now have a 15-minute walk back up to the trailhead. Keep to the right side of the valley, and when the path forks steeply up the embankment to the right take that and climb back up to the car park.

AN TEALLACH ★★

Difficulty rating: Strenuous

Distance: 18km (11 miles) round-trip

Estimated time: 12 hours

Elevation gain: 1,050m (3,445 ft.)

Costs/permits: None

Pet friendly: No

Best time to go: Between June and October, to enjoy the long daylight hours

Website: None

Recommended map: OS Explorer - Active Map sheet 435 An Teallach and Slioch

Trailhead GPS: NH 09251 87918

Trailhead directions: Follow the A832 towards Dundonnell. If you are coming from Inverness and Ullapool to the east, you will park in an area about 400m (1,312 ft.) before the Dundonnell Hotel (to the east). Many walkers stay in the hotel before and after tackling An Teallach.

The An Teallach hike is long, extremely strenuous, and involves rock scrambles, with the most experienced mountaineers opting to include small rock climbs and rappelling back down to reach the highest points en route. The compensation for all the effort is an exceptionally rewarding walk with spectacular views, on what is regarded by many as arguably the best mountain in Britain, but the hike should only ever be undertaken by very experienced hikers, ideally with mountaineering experience, as well as full mountain survival equipment and training and accompanied by a local guide. Indeed some of the higher sections on the ridge are best tackled roped together to your fellow walkers, so it's certainly not wise to tackle An Teallach alone. As the start of the hike is a good distance from major tourist centers, it is also worth staying close to the trailhead so that you do not have a long journey at the start or end of the day. Dundonnell is also home to a regional volunteer mountain rescue service, which has been called out to An Teallach many times.

After parking, continue to walk away from Dundonnell eastwards along the road. Look for a right turn onto a path before you reach some homesteads. The path heads generally south, leading you behind some houses. For the first kilometer it crosses open moorland, which can get boggy in or after wet conditions.

After the easy beginning, the path begins to climb more steeply, zigzagging up past Creag nan Soithichean to the ridge of Meall Garbh. The spectacular views, which are the great reward of this hike, begin to emerge quite soon, and, if you stop to look, views out over Scotland's beautiful west coast become increasingly impressive. Don't stop for too long too soon, however, as this is a long walk.

You now continue on past Meall Garbh up towards Sron a Choire. Initially the gradient eases once again, but the terrain becomes increasingly rocky as you climb a further 250 vertical meters (820 ft.) over the next 2km (1¼ miles) alongside the Coir' a' Mhuilinn with the peak of Glas Mheall Mor to the east (your right as you climb).

❶ The Bidein a' Ghlas Thuill Ridge
Once again the ascent eases off for a brief period as you cross over relatively smooth rocky terrain before the steepest and most challenging climb to date begins as you ascend to Bidein a' Ghlas, marginally the highest point of the route. As well as the gradient, you will need to cope with scree and larger rocks as you climb.

Once you reach the trig point marker at the peak of Bidein a' Ghlas Thuill, the views become still more impressive, with 360-degree views. The most stunning outlook is to the south, where you will see the peaks and pinnacles that lie ahead against a spectacular backdrop, which many experienced Scottish hikers regard as the best view in all of the Highlands.

❷ The Ridge The most demanding section of the trail now begins as the route follows a ridge heading south. There are dangerous drops on either side, and in several sections it may be wise to rope together with your fellow walkers.

The ridge initially descends a little before starting the extremely steep climb up to Sgurr Fiona, reached either with a rock scramble, for which climbing skills are a great advantage, or by taking a path up the northern side of the mountain. The summit is only 2.1m (7 ft.) lower than Bidein a' Ghlas Thuill, and the views are again superb, if marginally less dramatic than those from the previous peak.

From Sgurr Fiona onwards, there is a choice for experienced mountaineers of following the ridge walk, which can involve climbing a series of rock pinnacles, some so infamous they have been named. The best known, Lord Berkeley's Seat, actually overhangs the lochan far below. The Lord in question is reputed to have climbed the pinnacle then stopped for a smoke on top, probably not a wise thing to do.

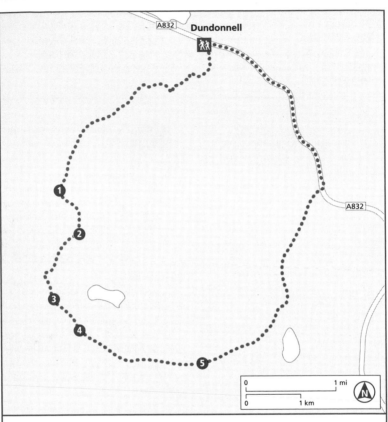

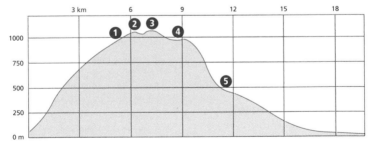

🏃 NH 09251 87918 (0 km): Trailhead
❶ NH 06535 85215 (5.1 km): Ascent eases briefly at Bidein a' Ghlas ridge
❷ NH 06839 84396 (6.1 km): Ridge descends before climbing up Sgurr Fiona
❸ NH 06341 83225 (7.7 km): The pinnacles of Corrag Bhuidhe
❹ NH 06788 82621 (8.4 km): Cadha Gobhlach
❺ NH 08984 81874 (11.5 km): Take path heading northeast

> **ⓕun Facts   A Deserved Reward**
>
> No hike to An Teallach is complete without a drink of the local An Teallach Ale, brewed by the local Teallach Brewery, opened in 2002 by David and Wilma Orr. Walkers are welcome to visit the microbrewery to sample the ale (most sensibly after, rather than before the hike!), which is located at Camusnagaul on the other side of Dundonnell on the A832.

❸ **Corrag Bhuidhe** More pinnacles follow over a distance of about 0.5km (¹/₃ mile) crossing by Corrag Bhuidhe. For these, climbing skills are required to reach the top of each and probably rappel up to 20m (65 ft.) back down. There are various routes to avoid some or all of these pinnacles by by-passing them on the southern side, but the route remains extremely exposed and treacherous. The safer route circles down below the pinnacles following a relatively easy path that follows a steep grass slope between gullies and around buttresses. It is quicker than the ridge scramble, which can also be a factor if it is later in the day. The final section down from Corrag Bhuidhe is treated as rock climbing rather than hiking, and people have died on this section of the route, so once again both extreme care and experience are essential.

❹ **Cadha Gobhlach** Once you reach Cadha Gobhlach, the more difficult sections of the hike are behind you. The route continues southeastwards over Sail Liath and begins to descend more gently over open ground. Look out for the small Lochan na Brathan and head east to the south of this until you reach a path heading northeast.

❺ **Gleann Chaorachain** You still have about 8km (5 miles) of your walk left, continuing the circular route heading north on a largely well-maintained track that eventually meets the A832 again at Corrie Hallie. Turn left (to the north) and follow the A832 back to the car park at Dundonnell.

DOG FALLS, GLEN AFFRIC ★

Difficulty rating: Moderate

Distance: 6km (3.8 miles)

Estimated time: 3 hours round-trip

Elevation gain: 110m (360 ft.)

Costs/permits: None

Pet friendly: Yes

Best time to go: The route is especially stunning in the autumn with fall foliage.

Website: www.glenaffric.org

Recommended map: OS Explorer - Active Map sheet 431 Glen Urquhart & Strathglass, Drumnadrochit & Muir of Ord

Trailhead GPS: NH 28366 27699

Trailhead directions: Take the A831 to Cannich and then the single-track road for approximately 3.2km (2 miles) towards Tomich, but turn right at the Fasnakyle Power Station and into Glen Affric. The Dog Falls walk car park appears on your left after about 3.2km (2 miles) more. This has a small toilet block, picnic benches frequented by the local chaffinch bird population, and a notice board with information on the walk.

Dog Falls is the start and end of a beautiful walk through Glen Affric, often acclaimed as the most beautiful glen in Scotland. The walk is located about 1 hour's drive from Inverness, making for a perfect day trip. The route encompasses a pretty waterfall in a rocky gorge and rare wildlife, including, if you're lucky, pine martens, capercaillie (wood grouse), and crossbills, as well as a small loch and great views up the glen. Glen Affric has inspired many poets and artists over the centuries, most notably the Victorian painter Landseer, who set his famous work "Monarch of the Glen" here. The Glen stretches for 50km (31 miles) from the west coast to Strathglass on the eastern side. It's also famous for its natural woodland, which includes some of the oldest surviving natural forest in Britain and Europe, known as the ancient Caledonian Forest. This great wood once covered Scotland almost entirely and is currently the subject of a major regeneration effort.

There are several walks in and around Glen Affric, of varied lengths, many of them waymarked with colored posts. Benches are provided for resting and taking in the magnificent scenery at crucial spots, and there are also several good-quality information panels. You can even hike along the side of Loch Affric and carry on to the west coast, perhaps spending a night en route in a hostel or bothy. However, Dog Falls brings together the best elements of this beautiful area into a shorter walk, which begins by crossing the bridge over the River Affric, running right next to the car park and beginning the climb uphill.

You will want to stop and look at the river as you cross. If it is a warm day, it's likely there'll be children playing in the shallows. You will see that the section back in the direction from which you've come is a series of small rapids. The main falls are some distance downstream and reached towards the end of your walk.

Once over the bridge, the path is moderately steep and you are making virtually all of the entire walk's ascent during this 1km (²/₃-mile) section through evergreen woodland.

❶ **Forest Path** As you near the top of the hill, at least as far as the makers of the path are concerned, it bends around to the left and levels out. You are now walking back in the direction of Cannich, parallel to the river and roads in the valley below.

Continuing on the forest track instead, you will see at regular intervals on your left that there are viewpoints, usually with a bench provided, where you can sit awhile and marvel over the idyllic views below. There are several interesting information panels en route covering the flora, fauna, and geology of the area.

Ignore the first turn you come to after the forest starts to thin, signposted down to the falls, and instead stay on the track which bends to the right, descending a little before climbing again. Look out for a post marked with yellow, which indicates that you should turn left and descend back into the valley. This path takes you on a scenic winding route down to the secluded Coire Loch. Look out for the old Granny Pine on your right as you descend towards the loch.

Coire Loch is a special place, hidden from most routes and of special interest to scientists, as 14 different types of breeding dragonfly have been identified here, including some very rare species. If you visit earlier in the year, during the first month of spring, you will find it heaving with toad life! The banks of the loch can be boggy, so it is best to rest a little above it and enjoy the view.

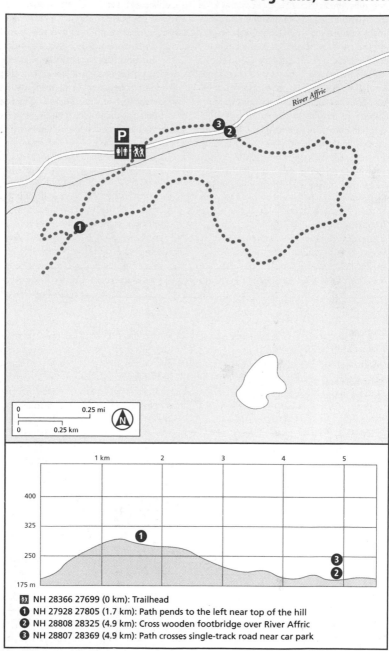

NH 28366 27699 (0 km): Trailhead
1 NH 27928 27805 (1.7 km): Path pends to the left near top of the hill
2 NH 28808 28325 (4.9 km): Cross wooden footbridge over River Affric
3 NH 28807 28369 (4.9 km): Path crosses single-track road near car park

❷ The Footbridge at the Falls The path now bends back to the left (west) and takes you on a still winding and undulating but clearly marked route through the lower hillside, where you'll find a great mixture of grassland, birch trees, and fallen dead trees, which have been left in place to encourage natural regeneration of the woodland as it would have been before mankind started to manage the local landscape.

A long wooden footbridge, only wide enough for one person to traverse at a time, crosses back over the River Affric, and you can see the small gorge that the water cascades through to form the main falls. You can walk up along side the falls to get a closer view, but be wary of the sudden drop, especially when the ground is wet and slippery.

❸ Over the Road The final stretch of the walk winds through the pine forest just across from the single-track road you arrived on (watch for traffic as you cross). The path continues for 0.8km ($^1/_2$ mile) before crossing back over the road opposite the car park at the trailhead.

There is the option to turn off to the right at the top of the initial climb from the river (the turning is marked with a white post) onto a path which will eventually take you above the southern banks of Loch Affric, but that is off our route. However, if you have time, it is worth following the path for around 0.5km ($^1/_3$ mile), as it provides wonderful views of the wider Glen.

FYRISH MONUMENT

Difficulty rating: Moderate

Distance: 5.6km (3.5 miles) round-trip

Estimated time: 3 hours

Elevation gain: 130m (425 ft.)

Costs/permits: None

Pet friendly: Yes

Best time to go: May to June, for the long, sunny spring days

Website: None

Recommended map: OS Explorer - Active Map sheet 438 Dornoch & Tain

Trailhead GPS: NH 62909 70956

Trailhead directions: From the coastal A9, turn left, inland, at the junction with the B9176. The road climbs uphill; after 3.2km (2 miles), take a left again onto a single-track road with a sign posted BOATH. After about 488m (1,600 ft.), you will see a small car park at the edge of woodland on your left, which marks the trailhead.

The Fyrish monument is an impressive 18th-century hilltop building constructed by the local laird (lord and landowner) of the time to provide work for impoverished locals, although not necessarily out of a generous spirit. Clearly visible from the coastal A9 road below, it is built in the style of an Indian bridge, and so is quite an unusual structure to see at the top of a Scottish hill. There are also superb views of the region from the top.

The walk up to Fyrish is best undertaken by way of the Millennium Path. The walk is a relatively constant uphill trek of moderate pitch, initially through thick woodland, but the trees clear a little over halfway up to reveal heather moorland to your right and the wonderful view of the firth below. The walk is well worth tackling at any time of the year, but between May and September the local midge population (mosquito-like

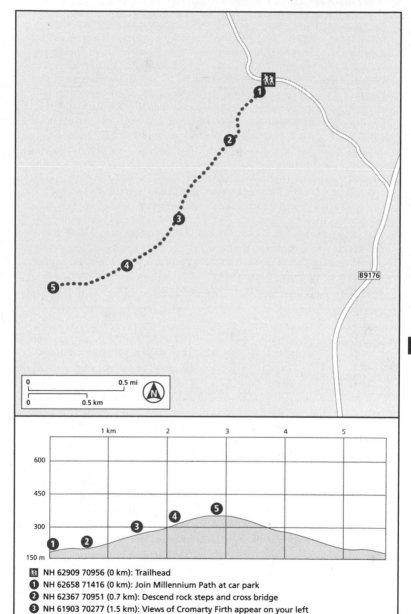

THE NORHTERN HIGHLANDS WALKS

9

FYRISH MONUMENT

🚶 NH 62909 70956 (0 km): Trailhead

❶ NH 62658 71416 (0 km): Join Millennium Path at car park

❷ NH 62367 70951 (0.7 km): Descend rock steps and cross bridge

❸ NH 61903 70277 (1.5 km): Views of Cromarty Firth appear on your left

❹ NH 61448 69853 (2.1 km): Clear the top of the forest and enter an area of heather moorland

❺ NH 60772 69702 (2.9 km): Fyrish Monument

Fun Facts   A Little Piece of India

The Fyrish monument is built of nine circular stone towers, the five central ones linked above to form three arches. The structure is a replica of the gates of Negapatam in India; it was built by impoverished locals who labored on the hilltop under the orders of the local lord and master, Sir Hector Munro, in 1783. Sir Hector was a commander of the colonial British Forces in India and had just finished a successful 21-year career in the country, including taking control of the coastal settlement of Negapatam in 1782, which had been under Dutch control for the previous 120 years. When Munro returned home, the forcible eviction of the local population from their small farms in the infamous Highland Clearances had begun, and many people were starving. Rather than just provide food and, as the thinking was at the time, risk encouraging laziness, Sir Hector set them to work building the architectural replica that broadcasts his military victory.

A number of legends surround the construction of the monument. One is that Sir Hector had, in fact, wanted to give the locals money to stop them from starving, but they were too proud to accept it, so for this reason Sir Hector commissioned the monument. Being so generous, the story goes, the noble lord had all the rocks that were carried up the hill to build the moment rolled down to the bottom again, so that the men could bring them back up and he could pay them twice. This story seems unlikely when you consider that it was Sir Henry who helped clear the land of local families to create more room for his sheep to graze.

flies) can make it a bit of an endurance feat on rare still days, particularly in the shelter of the trees.

❶ Trailhead Car Park The hike begins much as it remains for the full ascent, following a relatively direct route straight up the hill towards the monument. This lower section is cut through mature woodland and crosses several intersections with forest tracks used by workers for the local Novar Estate. At all these points, simply continue straight on uphill—there are wooden posts marking the route if you are ever uncertain, but it is very straightforward. The walk is popular with visitors and locals alike, the latter often walking their dogs, so there's usually someone passing to say "hello" to.

❷ The Burn After about a kilometer (²/₃ mile) the path descends a little way down some rock steps to cross a bridge over a fast-moving burn before climbing

up more stone steps on the other side and continuing on up through the forest.

❸ The View Southwest As the woodland begins to thin, you will begin to get increasingly impressive views to your left of the wide Cromarty Firth below you and the Black Isle across from it. On the other side of this lies Inverness, with the Monadhliath Mountains beyond (if it is a clear day). Looking out over the firth, the village of Evanton is down to your left and you will see the Cromarty Firth causeway beyond it, which you may have crossed driving up from Inverness. In the opposite direction, you will see the port town of Invergordon, likely alongside several oil-drilling platforms anchored in the Firth. These large structures are no longer built in the area, but there are invariably several in for repair.

❹ The View East Climbing higher, you will clear the top of the forest and enter an area of heather moorland, with the top of the folly itself beginning to appear on the horizon a few hundred meters farther on. If it's summertime, it's worth scouring the heather for blaeberries, a small, dark purple colored fruit that makes a fine jam, jelly, or pie. If you look back over your left shoulder, you will be able to see the Souters, two large hills on either side of the entrance to the Firth from the North Sea. They are named after an apparent resemblance to two giant shoemakers (known in the local Scots dialect as souters) bent over their work. Legend has it that they shared their giant tools and tossed them across the gap between them.

⑤ Fyrish Monument The monument itself offers the best views yet and shelter from the wind that is often blowing. It is impressive to see it towering above you when it seems so small from the road and to consider the work that went into its construction at a time when most people's homes were far less substantial. On a clear day, you should have an excellent view across the Cromarty Firth—famous for seals, oil-rig repairs, and cruise liners, as well as its natural beauty—to the Black Isle and beyond to the Moray coast.

The return walk is normally back down the same route. There is a signposted option to take an alternative route about halfway back down by turning left onto a forest track and following the signposts back around, but this adds little variety and is really just a slightly different route for the sake of it.

THE START OF THE GREAT GLEN WAY

Difficulty rating: Moderate

Distance: 6.4km (4 miles) round-trip

Estimated time: 3 hours

Elevation gain: 190m (625 ft.)

Costs/permits: None

Pet friendly: Yes

Best time to go: Late summer to pick raspberries and blackberries from the hedgerow en route

Website: www.greatglenway.com

Recommended map: Inverness, Loch Ness & Culloden Ordnance Survey OS Explorer - Active Map 416 covers first section of walk from Inverness to Fort Augustus.

Trailhead GPS: NH 66648 45173

Trailhead directions: Starting at the eastern end of the walk in Inverness city center, the Great Glen Way begins at the bottom of High Street, where the B862 (Bank Rd.) crosses the B861 (Young St.) at the bridge over the River Ness.

The 117km (73-mile) Great Glen Way is in one respect the youngest of the famous multi-day hiking routes across Scotland. In another respect, it is one of the oldest, with large sections based on ancient drovers' roads above Loch Ness and elsewhere on the route. The path was officially opened in 2002 by His Royal Highness Prince Andrew and links Fort William on the west coast to Inverness on the east, along the north side of the famous glen. This route covers the first section walking out of the town towards Loch Ness. Hikers can turn round, jump on a bus, or into a taxi at many points on the walk. On this first section of the walk you will walk from the heart of the city following the pleasant riverside area of Inverness before climbing out through the suburbs into increasingly rural and eventually wild terrain, now enjoying spectacular views back over the Highland capital and the Moray firth and Cairngorm Mountains beyond.

With the Highlands famous for their desolate moors, empty beaches, and abandoned glens, it feels odd to set off on a hike that, if you wished, could continue all week. But the best thing about the Great Glen Way is that you can follow it for as far or as little as you like, and the first few miles, as you walk out of Inverness, are very pleasant and full of variety. So even if you have only a few hours free in the Highland capital, it's worth just following the first mile or so of the route.

❶ Beneath Inverness Castle The start of the walk, marked by a metal signpost, begins on the eastern side of the River Ness, an attractive, wide river that drains from the famous loch. Depending on the time of your visit, the river can be a gentle flow, with fishermen wading in to the middle, or it can be a mighty torrent close to the tops of its banks. In recent spring thaws, it has broken its banks and even swept away railway bridges.

The route continues along the riverside, initially passing shops and hotels on Bank Street, with Inverness Cathedral visible on the opposite bank, before reaching the Infirmary pedestrian suspension bridge over the river, and a beautifully maintained war memorial, about 0.8km (¹/₂ mile) from your starting point. Here a pedestrian section begins and the surrounding buildings become gradually more residential.

❷ The Ness Islands After a further 0.8km (¹/₂ mile), you will pass the very attractive Bellfield Park on your right, with its formal gardens, putting green, tennis courts, and paddling pool, before the path reaches the historic Ness Islands, a series of small islands in a wide section of the river, linked together by a series of small foot bridges. The islands have long been a popular recreational area for Invernessians, and you are likely to pass dog walkers and joggers as well as those using the route to cross the river.

Once across the river, look out for blue wooden posts which mark the route of the Great Glen. These take you west now, passing the Floral Hall Botanical Centre—well worth a stop if you are in no hurry.

The municipally owned Floral Hall, with its gardens and coffee shop, was opened in 1993 by Prince Edward. The facility boasts a climatically controlled two-story glass house, with paths throughout and impressive sub-tropical plants fighting for space. Particularly popular on cold Highland days, the hall is also popular with children for the friendly Koi Carp in the pond. There is a linked cactus house, with another impressive display built up over many years by the local Inverness Cactus & Succulent Society. The outdoor garden is surrounded by a high stone wall and contains a good variety of gardening styles.

This is also a decision point if you are thinking of an easy stroll back to the city center. For a small change of route, it is easy to follow the west side of the river back, rather than crossing back to the east.

❸ The Caledonian Canal After walking 3.2km (2 miles) from your start point, you reach the Caledonian Canal as it flows beneath the A82 Glenurquhart Road, which is heading out of town towards Loch Ness (you can also catch any bus here for the 5-min. ride back to the city center). This is the point from which cruise boats depart on tours of the Loch. The Great Glen Way crosses the canal using the historic swing bridge, then crosses the A82 and follows the wide paved tow path on the west side of the canal, heading northwest for a further 0.4km (¹/₄ mile) before the little blue sign posts direct you down some steps into the undergrowth of the canal embankment.

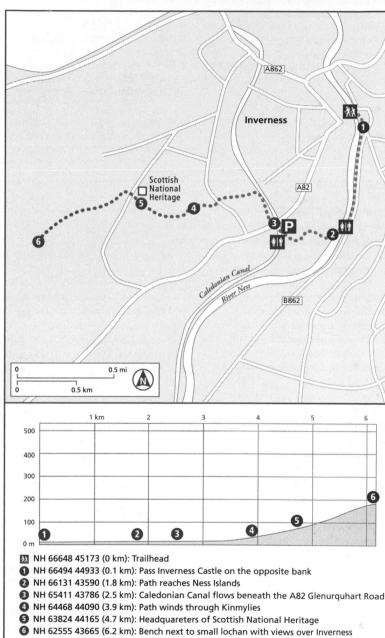

NH 66648 45173 (0 km): Trailhead
1 NH 66494 44933 (0.1 km): Pass Inverness Castle on the opposite bank
2 NH 66131 43590 (1.8 km): Path reaches Ness Islands
3 NH 65411 43786 (2.5 km): Caledonian Canal flows beneath the A82 Glenurquhart Road
4 NH 64468 44090 (3.9 km): Path winds through Kinmylies
5 NH 63824 44165 (4.7 km): Headquareters of Scottish National Heritage
6 NH 62555 43665 (6.2 km): Bench next to small lochan with views over Inverness

(Fun Facts **The Caledonian Canal**

Completed in 1803 after 20 years of construction, at a cost of £840,000, the canal was intended to provide a shortcut for ships that would otherwise need to sail around the northern coast of Scotland. Unfortunately, it never achieved its hoped-for commercial success, as it was initially dug too shallow; it was deepened in the mid–19th century, but by then ships had grown bigger again, so it was still inadequate for many, and soon afterwards the railway arrived. However, it remains a popular route for pleasure craft. Designed by the great engineer Thomas Telford, it includes some impressive sets of lochs (29 in total), particularly at the east-coast end by the Muirtown Basin and in Fort Augustus at the south end of Loch Ness. The 100km-long (62-mile) canal links Lochs Dochfour, Ness and Oich, and Loch Lochy.

❹ **Kinmylies** For the next 0.8km (¹/₂ mile), it is important to keep your wits about you as the path winds its way across the municipal golf course, under a road, and through the final housing development on the outskirts of Inverness at Kinmylies, before finally beginning to climb away from the city limits.

Despite its twists and turns, the route remains very well marked, with the blue posts giving directions, so just fix on the next one visible at each one you reach.

❺ **SNH** The path now ascends for 0.8km (¹/₂ mile) through farmland towards famous buildings in the past and present of Inverness. First visible is the modern wooden structure that is the headquarters of the Scottish National Heritage (known locally simply as SNH) organization, one of the major agencies responsible for managing Scotland's many natural attractions. This has a bus terminus outside, providing another option to return to the city center in about 15 minutes.

Passing the building, you enter a new housing development—evidence demonstrating that Inverness is one of Europe's fastest growing cities—and the large gothic building that was once the city's mental health hospital, Craig Dunain, to your left.

Finally you leave the last buildings of Inverness and continue a moderate climb through mature broadleaved woodland and open fields, with a lovely view of your entire walk beginning to appear behind you.

❻ **Craig Leach Forest** Now 6.4km (4 miles) from Inverness, you have reached the long ridge along which the old drovers' road leads through the Dochfour Estate towards open moorland above Loch Ness. There is a bench looking back out over Inverness next to a small lochan here that provides the best view of the entire city that you will find anywhere. The sea beyond is also clearly visible.

This is where I recommend turning back to get a bus or taxi from Scottish National Heritage. The next 4km (2.5 miles) ahead continue through rather monotonous forestry plantation, and there are now limited opportunities to find transport back to Inverness before you reach Drumnadrochit, another 16km (10 miles) away.

Difficulty rating: Moderate

Distance: 13km (8 miles) round-trip

Estimated time: 6 hours

Elevation loss: Minimal

Costs/permits: None

Pet friendly: Yes

Best time to go: In late summer the days are long, the insect pests are reduced, and the sea as warm as it gets.

Website: www.jmt.org/sandwood-estate.asp

Recommended map: OS Explorer Map sheet 446 Durness & Cape Wrath

Trailhead GPS: NC 20361 60927

Trailhead directions: Follow the A838 to Rhiconich, turning left onto the single-track B801 shortly afterwards. Follow this to Kinlochbervie (4.8km/3 miles), where you take a right turn uphill past the Kinlochbervie Hotel rather than driving to the harbor. Follow this winding road a further 4.8km (3 miles) to the small Blairmore car park on the left of the road, which has an information point and well-maintained toilets.

Sandwood Bay is a truly spectacular beach 16km (10 miles) south of mainland Scotland's northwestern tip at Cape Wrath. The drive to the trailhead at Blairmore takes you through some spectacular coastal scenery, while the walk itself covers a sweeping plain of peatland. However, it is the stunning sandy bay itself, framed by towering sandstone cliffs with an impressive sea stack at the south end of the bay, that makes this walk one you will remember for the rest of your life.

Sandwood Bay is a wonderful place to visit year-round, but if you are visiting between May and October, it is crucial to ensure you are wearing insect repellent before you leave your car at Blairmore trailhead. Attacks by swarms of the infamous Scottish midge will not be a problem on breezy days, but on hot, still days, they can be very annoying indeed, until you reach the midge-free beach.

❶ **Blairmore Car Park**   Cross over the road and through the gateway where the wide gravel path, suitable for vehicle access, cuts a way through the heather. For the first few hundred meters, you will skirt Loch Aisir to your right, with the coast to your left obscured all the way to the bay by a series of low hills, first Cnoc poll a Mhurain (152m/500 ft.) and then Druim na Buainn (153m/503 ft.). If you look beyond the loch, a huge expanse—including much of the 4,452-hectare (11,000-acre) Sandwood Estate that is owned by the wild land protection charity the John Muir Trust—is laid out before you in a vast heather-covered plain, rising in the distance to higher west-coast peaks.

The estate is made up of croft land, a traditional hereditary type of tenancy, operated by 10 working crofters (tenant farmers). This is the same John Muir who began life in East Lothian, Scotland, before his family emigrated to the USA in 1849 when he was aged 11. Arriving in California at age 30, he went on to achieve fame as a naturalist, leading the campaign to protect Yosemite, the world's first national park.

② Loch na Gainimh After 1.6km (1 mile), the path reaches the southern tip of the larger Loch na Gainimh, which has a small sandy beach, a taste of things to come. Resist the temptation to have a paddle (especially if the midges are nipping!) and carry on along the gently undulating track, which is very well-marked the rest of the way.

Look closely for sphagnum mosses, which hold huge volumes of water in their leaves, or the simple butterwort plant, which carries out the noble task of "eating" the midges in its purple flowers, which have in-turned petals and a sticky solution that traps the unfortunate insect before dissolving it. These are just 2 of the 200 different plants living in the area, including 8 varieties of wild orchid.

③ Loch a Mhuilin At our third loch, the wide track comes to an end and a short stroll on the sandy beach of its southern shores is required before cutting away northwest. The path crosses a few wee burns (small streams), each only a couple of feet wide, before gently climbing along the southern flank of Druim na Buainn. Watch for the outlines of simple old stone buildings beneath the heather. These were turf-roofed structures used by local people to protect cattle, which grazed the area largely in and before the 19th century.

Most of the original inhabitants were evicted by the local landowner (the laird) in the late 1840s to make way for sheep farming, and it was not until 50 years later that a British government Act of Parliament brought in protection and tenant land rights for those who had not left for southern cities like Glasgow or the New World. Any fragments of tree stumps you notice in the peat are likely to be the preserved remains of woodland that covered the area in a drier time some 2,000 years ago.

④ Above Sandwood Loch About 5.4km (3¹/₂ miles) from the trailhead, the gentle climb reaches its peak and Sandwood Loch, which feeds into the bay. It's an impressive sight down to your right past ruined old stone buildings, but is just a taste of what's ahead, as the path turns downhill to the left and you begin your descent towards the bay.

A spectacular vista opens up, with views of much of the vast 3.2km-wide (2-mile) beach, which extends over a huge area bordered by dunes—which themselves give way to an area known as "the machair," located between the peatland you have hiked across and the coast. This is a region of huge interest to botanists and geologists (the area is officially designated an SSSI or "Site of Special Scientific Interest") with a rich diversity of flora and rare bird species present, including skylarks and corncrake, the latter returning to the area in recent years after a long absence.

⑤ Above the Beach A couple of minutes before the beach, you will begin to see the cliffs rising above you, particularly to the south on your left, and the impressive sand stone sea stack, Am Buachaille ("the shepherd") will become visible, a useful landmark for generations of fishermen. You are likely to have the area either entirely to yourself, or at most only have a handful of fellow souls to share its magnificence with. As the calls of the sea birds echo around the cliffs, you'll feel as if you are entering a forgotten world.

⑥ Sandwood Bay Beach Sandwood Bay's beach is of the finest sand with crystal-clear waves breaking on the shore. It's the perfect place to wander, beach-comb, or just sit and read a book. Although you reach the sea after walking about 6.4km

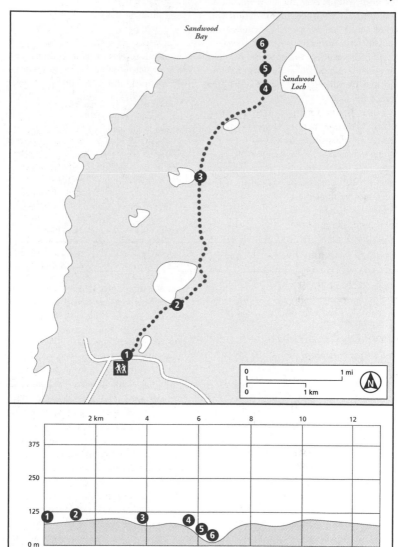

🚶 NC 20361 60927 (0 km): Trailhead
❶ NC 19388 60029 (0 km): Cross the road and through gateway to wide gravel path
❷ NC 20283 60889 (1.3 km): Southern tip of Loch na Gainimh
❸ NC 20695 62972 (3.9 km): Wide track comes to an end at Loch a Mhuilin
❹ NC 21891 64411 (5.7 km): Climb to Sandwood Loch
❺ NC 21919 64752 (6.1 km): Sandstone sea stack becomes visible
❻ NC 21882 65189 (6.5 km): Sandwood Bay beach

(4 miles) from the trailhead, you are likely to want to keep walking for several more miles around the huge expanse of sand and cliffs to explore the area. At low tide, it is possible to continue northwards along the beach into smaller adjacent bays, but it is important to be aware of the changing tide to be sure you are not caught out by its return.

There is little point stopping for long en route to the beach, but once here you are likely to want to stay for hours, so make sure you bring food and drink along. You'll need some fortitude to take a dip, tempting as it may be on a warm day, as the water temperature will be challenging for all but the most hardy. Small rocky outcrops punctuate the beach and can be scrambled up for a view down to the sea when the tide is out. In mid-summer, daylight lasts until about 11pm in the evening, so there is no reason to hurry back, just make sure someone at your accommodations knows where you are and that you might be late returning.

LAEL FOREST

Difficulty rating: Easy

Distance: 2.9km (1.8 miles) round-trip

Estimated time: 2 hours

Elevation gain: 122m (400 ft.)

Costs/permits: None

Pet friendly: Yes

Best time to go: The woodland is full of autumn color during October and November.

Website: None

Recommended Map: OS Explorer Map sheet 436 Beinn Dearg & Loch Fannich

Trailhead GPS: NH 18832 82379

Trailhead directions: Lael Forest is 14km (9 miles) before Ullapool on the north (right) side of the A835 road when driving from Inverness, an approximately 75-minute drive. There are two small car parks, free of charge, at each end of the forest garden section which lies along the roadside, with paths ascending into the wider forest surrounding it at each end, meeting above to form a circuit. The car parks are clearly marked by roadside signs and have picnic areas and information boards. The hike described begins in the farther car park, closer to Ullapool, but it is equally good to start at the other.

Lael Forest is centered on its "forest garden," a collection of several hundred varieties of trees and shrubs ranging from common specimens to some very rare varieties. The wider forest surrounding it is mostly made up of plantation woodland for commercial forestry, which climbs up the steep hillside of the valley. The area has great scenic beauty with famous peaks, including Beinn Dearg and An Teallach; the shorter forest trails described here can be extended to day-long hikes into the wider wilderness.

Before setting off over the small foot bridge on your right as you enter the car park, follow the banks of the wee burn (small stream) it crosses to the top corner of the car park, where you'll see a pleasant little waterfall that is worthy of a few moments' admiration.

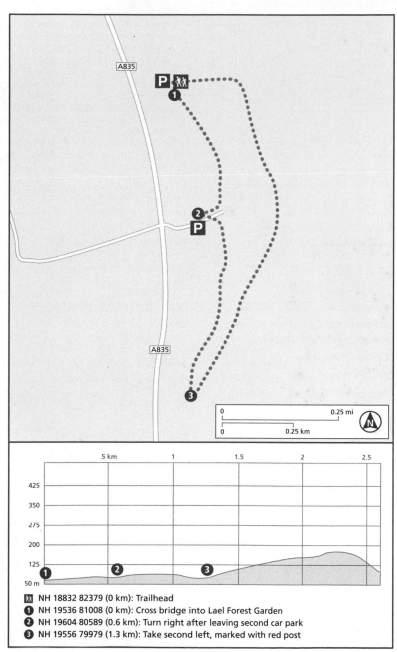

NH 18832 82379 (0 km): Trailhead
1 NH 19536 81008 (0 km): Cross bridge into Lael Forest Garden
2 NH 19604 80589 (0.6 km): Turn right after leaving second car park
3 NH 19556 79979 (1.3 km): Take second left, marked with red post

Lael Forest Garden

The Garden, which covers 6.9 hectares (17 acres), was created over many years by successive owners prior to it coming under public ownership in 1929. It contains more than 200 varieties of trees and shrubs collected from all over the world. Rare trees include specimens of Delavay's Silver Fir and Forrest's Fir, reputedly the best examples in the country, as well as Britain's most northerly specimen of Italian Cypress trees. New species are still added every year.

❶ The Forest Garden It's worth reading the display board, which gives some background to the route. You will see color-coded marker posts indicating different levels of walks available, with the two shorter options being red or green, both about 1.2km (³/₄ mile) long. Our route combines the two.

Now, cross the bridge and you are in Lael Forest Garden. This contains several hundred trees and shrubs ranging from common specimens to many rarities—a kind of tree zoo! Nearly all of the trees have small notices displaying their names. Look out for trees from all over the world, including cricket bat willows, Chilean yew, Corsican and Macedonian pine, Oregon maples, and Serbian spruce, as well as examples from other corners of the world, including New Zealand and the Himalayas.

The garden also contains more than 20 giant sequoia trees of great size, although they are not (yet) the tallest trees in Britain. They are, however, some of the widest, with up to 8m-circumference (27-ft.) trunks. Although not as massive as the famous sequoias of western America, they are nonetheless impressive examples, particularly on a British scale.

The path divides into three routes, going through the middle, top, and bottom of the forest garden as it continues for about 0.4km (¹/₄ mile) back along the edge of the road to the other car park. If you are in no hurry, it is well worth wandering back and forth around all three paths to see it all.

❷ The Forest Follow the marker posts out of the far side of the second car park and turn right almost straightaway to follow the edge of the woodland above the road. You are entering the surrounding forest of Lael, which was planted in the 1930s and '40s for commercial forestry. Indeed, sections of the original forest have now been felled and replaced with deciduous rowan, oak, and birch rather than the regimented firs of the original era. However, much of the woodland surrounding you as you climb is evergreen.

The path covers gently undulating ground as you head in a southerly direction through tall trees; the route is marked with green posts. Keep quiet for the chance of seeing the pine marten, which live in the area.

After about 0.8km (¹/₂ mile), as you pass a small car park, follow the path around to the left as it becomes a trail climbing upwards, running parallel to the valley road below, but this time heading back in the direction you came.

❸ The Forest Trail Now you are returning in the opposite direction above the forest garden. It is easy walking above the pines for about 1.2km (³/₄ mile). You will pass a junction on your left, which leads you back to the car park you crossed on your walk after the forest garden, but ignore this and continue on to a second left turn, marked with a red post this time. It leads you down through woodland, again with tall pine trees, next to the waterfall observed at the start. At the bottom there are well-made wooden steps leading you back to the car park where you started.

THE BEN NEVIS TOURIST PATH ★

Difficulty rating: Strenuous

Distance: 16km (10 miles) round-trip

Estimated time: 10 hours

Elevation gain: 1,326m (4,350 ft.)

Costs/permits: None

Pet friendly: No

Best time to go: June to October to make the best of daylight hours and hopefully good weather.

Website: None

Recommended map: Harvey Superwalker 1:25,000 scale map Ben Nevis

Trailhead GPS: NN 12597 72978

Trailhead directions: At the A82 roundabout, just east of Fort William center, take the clearly marked Glen Nevis Road. Drive for 0.8km (¹/₂ mile) to the visitor center on your left, which has a large car park. It is also possible to walk up from Fort William.

Ben Nevis, at 1,344m (4,408 ft.), is the highest mountain in the British Isles and for many Scots the most important hill for them to climb in their lifetime. Indeed, once conquered, they may no longer feel the need to climb any other. Although there are spectacular views if weather conditions are good, they rarely are, and the hike is largely an unremitting slog. However, the sense of achievement in reaching the summit is hard to match at any other point in the U.K. for the recreational hiker.

The two most misleading words in "The Ben Nevis Tourist Path" are "tourist" and "path." Although mountain rescue teams often complain that hikers they recover are ill-prepared in skimpy summer wear and with no basic survival equipment (hopefully still alive—there's an average of 13 deaths on the mountain per 5 years), those two words don't really help matters.

The "tourist path" begins gently enough, with a large tourist facility at the trailhead on the outskirts of Fort William. From the car park, a footbridge takes you over the river Nevis and then for a few hundred meters along the far side of the river, before you turn uphill and begin an initially gentle ascent.

From here on in, however you are on Britain's biggest vertical ascent, a largely unremitting 5-hour uphill slog over increasingly rough ground facing the likelihood of very challenging weather conditions. It is not reported how many of the 100,000 people who start the walk up Ben Nevis persevere to the top.

So it's worth stopping a moment just before you cross the bridge, as a large notice board on your left gives a list of the items you are advised to carry with you up the mountain, and a page is posted detailing the expected weather conditions. The things-to-bring list runs to 20 items, but suggests thin thermal fleece layers, water- and wind-proof jackets, hat and gloves (even in summer, for there is snow at the summit), survival bag, first aid kit, torch, whistle, compass, and a mobile phone. This being Scotland, the weather conditions listed should be considered a guide only and you should be prepared for the worst. If the weather is bad, abandon your trip here.

After presenting such a doom-laden vision of the ascent, I should now stress, the views can be spectacular!

❶ **Glen Nevis** The mountain path initially ascends along the side of Meall an Suidhe (708m/2,322 ft.), with beautiful Glen Nevis stretching out to your right below you. This scenic wonder has been

(Fun Facts)   **Not Your Average Climb**

Ben Nevis means "mountain of heaven" in Gaelic and was first reported to have been climbed in 1771. The path you are walking up was created in 1883, built to service a permanently manned year-round observatory, the ruins of which you will find at the top. It operated for 20 years, until funds ran out, and in 1 year it reported more than 260 gales; the annual rainfall recorded was 401cm (158 in.). In 1911, a Model-T Ford car successfully made the ascent, and in 1981 a group of students pushed a bed up. Every year there is a running race up the mountain and you may be annoyed by fit young racers sprinting past you as you struggle up. The record ascent and return time for the race is less than 2 hours. Many other stunts and records have been set on the mountain, and a piano was discovered at the summit in May 2006 during a tidying-up exercise.

used as a film location for many movies, including *Braveheart, Highlander,* and the *Harry Potter* series. The path is well-maintained and is often busy with coach parties of boy scouts or youth clubs, and your greatest challenge initially may be getting past these if they stop for a breather on a narrow stretch of the path.

❷ **Lochan Meall an Suidhe**   Often known as "halfway loch" (although it isn't yet quite halfway in terms of vertical ascent), the path is in its best condition and gentlest as it crosses a sheltered plateau, skirting to the right side of the loch. As you reach 610m (2,000 ft.), the only major division in the long ascent appears, with a left turn onto the CIC hut path, which skirts below the spectacular north wall of Ben Nevis before descending back down to the valley. However, the route up lies in clear view ahead of you as you reach the steep sides of Ben Nevis proper and the scree fields, which you cross for the last 686m (2,250 ft.) of your ascent.

❸ **Red Burn**   The path now climbs steeply through the scree field, close to the descent of the Red Burn steam. It is hard going for the inexperienced mountain hiker, with parts of the path strewn with sizable boulders, and other parts running with water except in the driest weather.

❹ **Five Finger Gully**   As the climb passes the 914m (3,000-ft.) point, the top of the path comes into view and you will be tempted to ask descending hikers if you're nearing the summit. Resist the temptation, as their answer may be depressing—you still have a few hours to go! Be wary at this point, especially in bad weather, as the path is at its least discernable among the scree slides and the notorious cliffs of Five Finger Gully that lie just to your right.

❺ **The Summit**   As you near the summit, the mist and fog are likely to increase, as will the strength of the wind. It is important to keep your wits about you and keep a close eye on the path, marked by cairns, as there are steep drops nearby. Whatever time of year you make your ascent, it is very likely you will need to cross one or two small snow fields, and despite the warmth your ascent may have generated, you will feel the air temperature dropping.

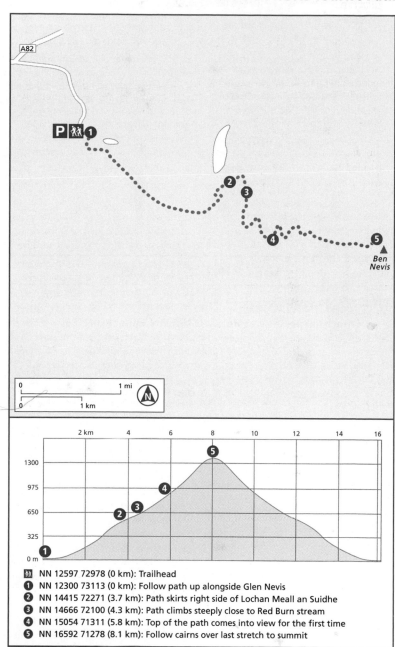

A82

Ben
Nevis

0   1 mi
0   1 km

2 km   4   6   8   10   12   14   16

1300

975

650

325

0 m

🚶 NN 12597 72978 (0 km): Trailhead
① NN 12300 73113 (0 km): Follow path up alongside Glen Nevis
② NN 14415 72271 (3.7 km): Path skirts right side of Lochan Meall an Suidhe
③ NN 14666 72100 (4.3 km): Path climbs steeply close to Red Burn stream
④ NN 15054 71311 (5.8 km): Top of the path comes into view for the first time
⑤ NN 16592 71278 (8.1 km): Follow cairns over last stretch to summit

Hopefully you will be one of the lucky few who arrive at the summit during the one-fifth of the time it is not shrouded in cloud, and can thus enjoy the full 360-degree views of spectacular scenery of the west coast and the Great Glen.

If it's fog-bound when you summit, there are still lots of interesting things to see at the top, including a peace cairn containing stones from all over the world, the ruins of an observatory, and a (very) small hotel that existed in the late 19th and early 20th centuries. The ruins of these can be used for shelter. Whatever the weather, you can bask in the feeling of satisfaction of having conquered Britain's highest peak and take a photograph on top of the highest cairn to prove it.

It is important to return by the same path you came up; taking a different route back down may look straightforward on the map, but can be fatal if you become lost in the fog, which can roll in at any time. The numerous cairns around the summit of the mountain are reputed to have been built in memory of various hikers who have died on the mountain.

SLEEPING & EATING

ACCOMMODATIONS

★★ **Dornoch Castle Hotel**   For a taste of Highland history, you can opt to stay in this castle (which was once the residence of the bishops of Caithness), built of stone in the center of town in the late 15th or early 16th century. Today, its winding stairs, labyrinthine corridors, and cellars have been converted into a well-directed hotel and restaurant.

Castle St., Dornoch IV25 3SD. ℂ **01862 810216.** www.dornochcastlehotel.com. 18 units. £82–£165 double. Rates include Scottish breakfast. AE, MC, V. **Close to:** The Duke of Sutherland Monument and Fyrish.

★★ **Dunain Park Hotel**   The Dunain Park stands in 2.4 hectares (6 acres) of garden and woods between Loch Ness and Inverness. This 18th-century Georgian house is furnished with fine antiques, allowing it to retain the atmosphere of a private country house.

Dunain Park, Inverness IV3 8JN. ℂ **01463 230512.** www.dunainparkhotel.co.uk. 11 units. £128–£198 double; from £200 suite. Rates include Scottish breakfast. AE, MC, V. Drive 1.6km (1 mile) southwest of Inverness on A82. **Close to:** Great Glen Way.

★ **Glen Mhor Hotel**   Located 300m (984 ft.) from the start of the Great Glen Way route, the Glen Mhor Hotel on the River Ness is a hospitable family-run hotel. From many of the individually styled guest rooms you have views of the river and cathedral; some are suitable for families.

9–12 Ness Bank, Inverness IV2 4SG. ℂ **01463 234308.** www.glen-mhor.com. 43 units. £80–£110 double; £110–£150 junior suite. Rates include Scottish breakfast. AE, DC, MC. **Close to:** Great Glen Way, Dog Falls, Fyrish.

★★★ **Ivybank Guest House**   This is one of the best B&Bs in Inverness. Located off Castle Road about a 10-minute walk north of the town center, Ivybank was built in

1836 and retains its original fireplaces and an oak-paneled and beamed hall with a rosewood staircase. It features a walled garden and comfortably furnished guest rooms.

28 Old Edinburgh Rd., Inverness IV2 3HJ. ℭ **01463 232796.** www.ivybankguesthouse.com. 6 units, 3 with private bathroom. £56 double without bathroom; £64 double with bathroom. Rates include Scottish breakfast. AE, MC, V. **Close to:** Great Glen Way, Dog Falls, Fyrish.

★ **Kingsmills Hotel**   Once a private mansion, this hotel is a charming 18th-century country house set amid a woodland garden that's adjacent to an 18-hole golf course. Over the years it has attracted royals, high-ranking government officials, film stars, and even Robert Burns himself.

Culcabock Rd., Inverness IV2 3LP. ℭ **01463 237166.** www.kingsmillshotel.com. 82 units. £150–£174 double; £180–£210 suite. Rates include Scottish breakfast. AE, DC, MC, V. **Close to:** Great Glen Way, Dog Falls, Fyrish.

★★ **The Lime Tree**   This well-kept B&B in the center of town is housed in what is reputed to be the oldest fully surviving building in Fort William. It was built in the early 1800s as the manse for the nearby Church of Scotland. Today, it offers pastel guest rooms (with small, shower-only bathrooms) and exhibition space for local painters.

The Old Manse, Achintore Rd., Fort William. ℭ **01397 701806.** www.limetreefortwilliam.co.uk. 5 units, 3 with private bathroom. £54–£74 double without bathroom; £90–£110 double with bathroom. DC, MC, V. **Close to:** Ben Nevis.

RESTAURANTS

★★ **Café 1** INTERNATIONAL/SCOTTISH FUSION   One of the most pleasant restaurants in town—just across the street from the castle and 250m (820 ft.) uphill from the start of the Great Glen Way—is in a century-old stone-fronted building on a street dotted with shops. Dine on generous portions of Angus rump steak with rocket and parmesan salad, as well as penne pasta with fresh tomatoes, spinach, garlic, and chilli Buffalo mozzarella.

75 Castle St., Inverness. ℭ **01463 226200.** Reservations recommended. Main courses lunch £7.50–£12; dinner £8.50–£18. MC, V. Mon–Sat noon–2pm and 6–9:30pm. **Close to:** Great Glen Way, Dog Falls, Fyrish.

★ **Ceilidh Place** INTERNATIONAL/SCOTTISH FUSION   When Robert Urquhart started the Ceilidh Place in Broomview Cottage in 1970, the building where he had been born nearly 50 years earlier, a sign outside invited passing musicians to come in and perform in exchange for their supper. Although its success has led to expansion with a hotel, larger restaurant, and book shop, it remains a wonderful place for eating, meeting, talking, and singing.

14 West Argyll St., Ullapool. ℭ **01854 612103.** www.ceilidhplace.com. Main courses lunch £5–£10; dinner £10–£20. MC, V. Daily 11am–11pm. Reservations usually essential. **Close to:** Lael Fortest, An Teallach, Sandwood Bay.

★★ **Crannog Seafood Restaurant** SEAFOOD   Occupying a converted ticket office and bait store in a quayside setting overlooking Loch Linnhe, this restaurant serves seafood so fresh that locals claim "it fairly leaps at you." Much of the fish comes from the owners' own fishing vessels or from their smokehouse. Bouillabaisse is a specialty, as are king prawns and langoustines. A vegetarian dish of the day is invariably featured.

Town Pier, Fort William. ℭ **01397 705589.** Reservations recommended. Main courses £10–£20. MC, V. Daily noon–2:30pm and 6–9pm. Closed Jan 1–2 and Dec 25–26. **Close to:** Ben Nevis.

★ **Golf Links Hotel** INTERNATIONAL/SCOTTISH FUSION   This hotel restaurant dates from the early 1900s, when it was built as the stone rectory for the local minister. Many of the guests are golfers drawn to the nearby Golspie, Royal Dornoch, and Brora courses. Scottish and continental cuisine is served in a dining room with a view of Ben Bhraggie.

Church St., Golspie. (*C*) **01408 633408.** www.golflinkshotel.co.uk. Main courses lunch £7.50–£12, dinner £8.50–£18. MC, V. Daily noon–2:30pm and 6–9pm. Reservations recommended. **Close to:** The Duke of Sutherland Monument and Fyrish.

★★★ **Inverlochy Castle** BRITISH   This is one of the grandest restaurants in Britain. The cuisine here has been celebrated ever since Queen Victoria got a sudden attack of the munchies and stopped in "for a good tuckin." The kitchen uses carefully selected local ingredients, including salmon from Spean, crabs from Isle of Skye, crayfish from Loch Linnhe, and produce from the hotel's own gardens. Dinner is served in rooms decorated with period and elaborate furniture, presented as gifts to Inverlochy Castle from the king of Norway.

Torlundy, Fort William. (*C*) **01397 702177.** Reservations required. Fixed-price lunch £30; set-price dinner £55. AE, MC, V. Daily 12:30–1:30pm and 7–9pm. Closed Jan–Feb. **Close to:** Ben Nevis.

★ **Storehouse of Foulis** SCOTTISH   The Storehouse of Foulis combines a modern restaurant and shop building in a wonderful location on the shore of the Cromarty Firth next to the fully restored 18th-century storehouse building, which houses a Clan Munro Museum. The restaurant serves good-value, high-quality, wholesome, homemade Scottish food, including breakfast and lunch, and has won awards for its cakes. The staff is friendly and efficient. A great warm-up stop en route to your hike or on the way back.

Foulis Ferry, Evanton. (*C*) **01349 830038.** www.clanland.com. Main courses lunch £4–£8. MC, V. Mon–Sat 9am–6pm; Sun 10am–5pm. Reservations not required. **Close to:** Fyrish and The Duke of Sutherland Monument.

Appendix A:
Fast Facts, Toll-Free
Numbers & Websites

1 FAST FACTS: SCOTLAND

AREA CODES The country code for Britain is 44. The area code for Edinburgh is 0131, for Glasgow 0141. When dialing from outside the U.K., add the country code and omit the leading zero in the area code.

ATM NETWORKS/CASHPOINTS Most people in Scotland get their cash from an automated teller machine (ATM) rather than bothering to go to a bank counter. You'll find ATMs ("cash machines") at most banks, high streets, and larger supermarkets. They take international credit cards, debit cards, and bank cards, providing they have a 4-digit pin encoded. The Cirrus (www.mastercard.com) and Plus (www.visa.com) networks span the globe. As a general rule, any cash machine that displays the Visa logo can be used by Plus cardholders, and those displaying the MasterCard logo can be used by Cirrus cardholders.

Britain has converted to the "chip and pin" system, and without a 4-digit pin you will be hard put to use your card anywhere—in an ATM, shop, restaurant, or hotel (these days few places accept signatures to verify purchases). Make sure you know your number before you travel!

CAR RENTALS If you want to rent a car in Scotland, you will get a better deal by planning ahead and booking at least 2 business days in advance. Think clearly about what you want, and make sure you understand what charges are being applied, particularly for insurance.

You'll find the cheapest day rate if you hire a car for a week or more. Hiring one for less than 3 days can cost almost as much. Longer hires normally offer unlimited mileage, but for 3 days or less, you'll probably be given a specified free mileage per day with a "per mile" charge on usage over this.

For listings of the major car-rental agencies, please see "Toll-Free Numbers & Websites," later in this appendix.

CELL (MOBILE) PHONES In Britain cellphones are called mobile phones. GSM (Global System for Mobile Communications) is the big, seamless network that makes for easy cross-border mobile-phone use throughout Europe and dozens of countries worldwide. In the U.S., T-Mobile and AT&T use this quasi-universal system; in Canada, Rogers customers are GSM; and all Europeans and most Australians use GSM.

GSM phones function with a removable SIM card, encoded with your phone number and account information. If your mobile is on a GSM system and you have a world-capable multi-band phone, such as many Sony Ericsson, Motorola, Samsung, and Nokia models, you can make and receive calls around much of the western world. Check with your mobile-phone provider before you leave that the "international roaming" function is activated on your phone. Unfortunately, charges can be high—again check with your provider.

You can buy a British prepay mobile phone including phone number and SIM card for as little as £30 in many high-street shops. You do not need to provide identification to purchase a prepay phone, but you will need to provide identification and proof of address in Britain to set up a mobile phone contract. Do ask about the network's coverage if you are going to be traveling around the Highlands—some networks, such as O2, Orange, and Vodafone, have much wider signal coverage than others. You can expect to get good coverage in cities, towns, and near major roads, but your signal will fall off—and may disappear completely—in more remote places. Often the only time you can get a signal on a walk is from the top of the hill, and even that's not guaranteed.

CREDIT CARDS   All credit cards that bear the Visa or MasterCard logo are accepted throughout Scotland, and American Express cards are also widely accepted. However, few places take Diners Club. If in doubt, ask the retailer in advance if you can use your card, or check if your card's logo is displayed in the payment area.

Note that many banks now add a 1% to 3% "transaction fee" to all charges you incur abroad.

CURRENCY   Britain's unit of currency is the Great British Pound (sterling)—GBP. The currency is based on the decimal system with 100 pence to each pound. Scotland shares this system, the only difference being that north of the border you will find Scottish bank notes in circulation as well as Bank of England ones. Three Scottish banks print notes: Bank of Scotland, Royal Bank of Scotland, and Clydesdale Bank. The notes are interchangeable, though many retailers in England are reluctant to accept Scottish notes as they are less confident of being able to check for counterfeits.

Bank notes have the values of £5, £10, £20, and £50. There are also still some Scottish £1 notes in circulation, though they are a rarity nowadays. Coins have the values of £2, £1, 50p, 20p, 10p, 5p, and 1p. British slang for pounds is "quid."

Foreign currency can be changed at banks, post offices, larger hotels, and at independent Bureaus de Change, which are found at international airports and most city centers. Exchange rates have been fluctuating wildly over the past year. The Financial Times website (www.ft.com) has a currency converter, or you can visit the VisitScotland one at www.visitscotland. com/guide/travel/currency.

DRINKING LAWS   The legal age for buying alcohol is 18. Children under 16 aren't allowed in pubs, except in certain rooms—generally where meals are being served, and then only when accompanied by a parent or guardian. Don't drink and drive; the penalties are stiff. Basically, you can get a drink from 11am to 11pm, but this can vary widely, depending on the discretion of the local tavern owner. The law allows 15 minutes for "drinking-up time." Certain licensed premises can have hours extended in some areas up to 4am, on a "local need" basis. Except in strongly Presbyterian places, such as the Isle of Lewis, pubs open on Sunday; but often they don't open until noon. Restaurants are allowed to serve liquor during licensed hours, but only to people who are dining on the premises. A meal, incidentally, is defined as "substantial refreshment." And you have to eat and drink sitting down. In hotels, liquor may be served from 11am to 11pm to both guests and nonguests; after 11pm, only guests may be served.

DRIVING RULES   Driving in Scotland, as elsewhere in the U.K., is always on the left-hand side of the road. Unless otherwise signposted, the maximum speed limits on U.K. roads are as follows:

- Motorways and dual carriageways: 113kmph (70 mph) and 97kmph (60 mph) for cars towing caravans or trailers.
- Built-up areas: 48kmph (30 mph)
- Outside built-up areas: 97kmph (60 mph) and 80kmph (50 mph) for cars towing caravans or trailers.

ELECTRICITY British electricity is 240 volts AC (50 cycles), roughly twice the voltage in North America, which is 115 to 120 volts AC (60 cycles). American plugs don't fit British wall outlets. Always bring suitable transformers and/or adapters—if you plug an American appliance directly into a European electrical outlet without a transformer, you'll destroy your appliance and possibly start a fire. Tape recorders, VCRs, and other devices with motors intended to revolve at a fixed number of revolutions per minute probably won't work properly even with transformers.

EMBASSIES & CONSULATES All embassies are in London, but several countries have consulates in Edinburgh. There's a U.S. Consulate at 3 Regent Terrace (© **01315 568315**), open Monday through Friday from 1 to 5:30pm.

The **Canadian High Commission** is at 50 Lothian Rd. (© **01314 736320**), open Monday through Friday from 8am to 4pm.

The Australian High Commission is at 69 George St. (© **01316 243333**), open Monday through Friday from 9:30am to 3:30pm.

The New Zealand Consulate is at 5 Rutland Sq. (© **01312 228109**), open Monday to Friday 9am to 5pm.

The Irish Consulate is at 16 Randolph Crescent (© **01312 267711**), open Monday through Friday from 9:30am to 1pm and 2:15 to 5pm.

EMERGENCIES In an emergency, call © 999. An operator will connect you to the emergency service you need: fire, police, ambulance, coastguard, or mountain rescue.

GASOLINE (PETROL) Fuel is taxed heavily in the U.K., making it among the most expensive in the world. It is sold in liters and the price fluctuates considerably. During 2008, it rose to well over £1 per liter, though it fell back to around 90p per liter by the end of the year. Taxes are already included in the printed price. One U.S. gallon equals 3.8 liters or .85 imperial gallons. In urban areas, some petrol (gasoline) stations stay open 24 hours a day, but in rural areas opening hours tend to be shorter, often with Sunday closings. Distances between stations can be considerable in rural areas (and prices much higher), so fill up when you get the chance. Motorway service stations usually have a markup on their fuel; the lowest prices are available from stations attached to major supermarkets.

HOLIDAYS The following holidays are celebrated in Scotland: New Year's Day (Jan 1–2), Good Friday and Easter Monday, May Day (May 1), spring bank holiday (last Mon in May), summer bank holiday (last Mon in Aug), Christmas Day (Dec 25), and Boxing Day (Dec 26).

HOSPITALS Citizens of E.U. countries are entitled to free medical treatment at National Health Service (NHS) hospitals on production of an E111 form. Several non-E.U. countries, including Australia and New Zealand, have reciprocal healthcare arrangements with the U.K. Citizens of other countries get free emergency treatment at Accident and Emergency (A&E) units at NHS hospitals, but are charged for all other medical services.

INSURANCE Medical Insurance Although it's not required of travelers, health insurance is highly recommended. Most health insurance policies cover you if you get sick away from home—but check your coverage before you leave.

For travel overseas, most U.S. health plans (including Medicare and Medicaid) do not provide coverage, and the ones that do often require you to pay for services upfront and reimburse you only after you return home.

As a safety net, U.S. travelers may want to buy travel medical insurance. If you require additional medical insurance, try MEDEX Assistance (© 800/732-5309; www.medexassist.com) or Travel Assistance International (© 800/821-2828; www.travelassistance.com; for general information on services, call the company's Worldwide Assistance Services, Inc., at (© 800/777-8710).

Canadians should check with their provincial health plan offices or call **Health Canada** (© **866/225-0709;** www.hc-sc. gc.ca) to find out the extent of their coverage and what documentation and receipts they must take home in case they are treated in the United Kingdom.

Travel Insurance The cost of travel insurance varies widely, depending on the destination, the cost and length of your trip, your age and health, and the type of trip you're taking, but expect to pay between 5% and 8% of the vacation itself. You can get estimates from various providers through **InsureMyTrip.com.** Enter your trip cost and dates, your age, and other information, for prices from more than a dozen companies.

U.K. citizens and their families who make more than one trip abroad per year may find an annual travel insurance policy works out cheaper. Check **www.money supermarket.com,** which compares prices across a wide range of providers for single- and multi-trip policies. The **Post Office** (© **0800 294 2292** www.postoffice.co.uk) offers both annual and single trip insurance coverage, which can be arranged online or at any post office counter.

Most big travel agents offer their own insurance and will probably try to sell you their package when you book a holiday. Think before you sign. **Britain's Consumers' Association** recommends that you insist on seeing the policy and reading the fine print before buying travel insurance. **The Association of British Insurers** (© **02076 003333;** www.abi.org.uk) gives advice by phone and publishes Holiday Insurance, a free guide to policy provisions and prices. You might also shop around for better deals: Try **Columbus Direct** (© 08700 33 9988; www.columbusdirect.net).

Trip Cancellation Insurance Trip-cancellation insurance will help retrieve your money if you have to back out of a trip or depart early, or if your travel supplier goes bankrupt. In the U.K., trip cancellation is normally included in travel insurance policies. Trip cancellation traditionally covers such events as sickness, natural disasters, and State Department advisories. The latest news in trip-cancellation insurance is the availability of **"any-reason"** cancellation coverage—which costs more but covers cancellations made for any reason. You won't get back 100% of your prepaid trip cost, but you'll be refunded a substantial portion. **TravelSafe** (© **888/885-7233;** www.travelsafe.com) offers both types of coverage. Expedia also offers any-reason cancellation coverage for its air-hotel packages. For details, contact one of the following recommended insurers: **Access America** (© 866/807-3982; www.accessamerica. com); **Travel Guard International** (© 800/ 826-4919; www.travelguard.com); **Travel Insured International** (© 800/243-3174; www.travelinsured.com); and **Travelex Insurance Services** (© 888/457-4602; www.travelex-insurance.com).

INTERNET ACCESS To find public Wi-Fi hotspots in Scotland, go to www. jiwire.com; its Hotspot Finder holds the world's largest directory of public wireless hotspots. You will find plenty of coverage in major cities, large hotels and at airports, but Wi-Fi access is more sporadic in other areas. However, an increasing number of accommodations providers, even small B&Bs, are supplying it.

LEGAL AID Your consulate, embassy, or high commission (see above) will give you advice if you run into trouble. They can advise you of your rights and even provide a list of attorneys (for which you'll have to pay if services are used), but they can't interfere on your behalf in the legal processes of Great Britain. For questions about American citizens arrested abroad, including ways of getting money to them, call the **Citizens Emergency Center of the Office of Special Consulate Services,**

in Washington, D.C. (© 202/647-5225). Other nationals can go to their nearest consulate or embassy.

LOST & FOUND Be sure to tell all of your credit card companies the minute you discover your wallet has been lost or stolen and file a report at the nearest police precinct. Your credit card company or insurer may require a police report number or record of the loss. Most credit card companies have an emergency toll-free number to call if your card is lost or stolen; they may be able to wire you a cash advance immediately or deliver an emergency credit card in a day or two.

For cards lost in the U.K., you can phone the following toll-free numbers: **Visa** © 0800 89 1725; **MasterCard** © 0800 96 4767; **American Express** © 0800 521 313.

If you need emergency cash over the weekend when all banks and American Express offices are closed, you can have money wired to you via **Western Union** (© **800/325-6000;** www.westernunion.com).

MAIL Post offices and subpost offices are open Monday through Friday from 9am to 5:30pm and Saturday from 9:30am to noon.

Sending an airmail letter to North America costs 56p for .35 oz. (10 grams,), and postcards require a 56p stamp. British mailboxes are painted red and carry a royal coat of arms. All post offices accept parcels for mailing, provided they are properly and securely wrapped.

MEDICINE Many medicines are available at pharmacies (chemists), but stronger drugs require a doctor's prescription.

If you want to bring medicine with you, first check that it is licensed for use in the U.K. Always carry medicines in the labeled container supplied by the pharmacist. If you are likely to require additional supplies, bring a letter from your doctor or a personal health record card giving details of the drug prescribed. For further information, contact HM Customs and Excise Advice Centre © **020 8929 0152.**

PASSPORTS On arrival in the United Kingdom, you must show a valid national passport or other equivalent official document that satisfactorily establishes your identity and nationality. Visitors to the U.K. who require a visa may normally stay in the U.K. up to a maximum of 6 months.

The websites listed in this section provide downloadable passport applications as well as the current fees for processing applications. For an up-to-date, country-by-country listing of passport requirements around the world, go to the "International Travel" tab of the U.S. State Department at **http://travel.state.gov.**

For Residents of the United States: Allow plenty of time before your trip to apply for a U.S. passport; processing normally takes 4–6 weeks (3 weeks for expedited service) but can take longer during busy periods (especially spring). And keep in mind that if you need a passport in a hurry, you'll pay a higher processing fee. Whether you're applying in person or by mail, you can download passport applications from the U.S. State Department website at http://travel.state.gov. To find your regional passport office, check the U.S. State Department website.

For Residents of Canada: Passport applications are available at travel agencies throughout Canada or from the central **Passport Office,** Department of Foreign Affairs and International Trade, Ottawa, ON K1A 0G3 (© **800/567-6868;** www.ppt.gc.ca). *Note:* Canadian children who travel must have their own passport. However, if you hold a valid Canadian passport issued before December 11, 2001, that bears the name of your child, the passport remains valid for you and your child until it expires.

For Residents of Australia: You can pick up an application from your local post office or any branch of Passports Australia, but you must schedule an interview at the passport office to present your application materials. Call the **Australian Passport Information Service** at ℂ **131-232,** or visit the government website at www.passports.gov.au.

For Residents of Ireland: You can apply for a 10-year passport at the **Passport Office,** Setanta Centre, Molesworth St., Dublin 2 (ℂ **01/671-1633;** www.irlgov.ie/iveagh). Those under age 18 and over 65 must apply for a 3-year passport. You can also apply at 1A South Mall, Cork (ℂ **21/494-4700**), or at most main post offices.

For Residents of New Zealand: You can pick up a passport application at any New Zealand Passports Office or download it from their website. Contact the **Passports Office** at ℂ **0800/225-050** in New Zealand or 04/474-8100, or log on to www.passports.govt.nz.

POLICE The best source of help and advice in emergencies is the police. For non-life-threatening situations, dial "0" (zero) and ask for the police, or ℂ 999 for emergencies. If the local police can't assist, they'll have the address of a person who can. Losses, thefts, and crimes should be reported immediately.

SMOKING It is against the law to smoke in all business premises in Scotland. "Business premises" includes all hotels, pubs, restaurants, indoor places of entertainment, public transport, and taxis. Basically, it is only legal to smoke out of doors or in private homes. However, hotels and B&Bs are allowed to designate one or more bedrooms for smoking guests. If you want one of these, ask at the time of booking.

TAXES There's no local sales tax. However, Great Britain imposes a standard value-added tax (VAT) on most goods and services. Normally, the rate is 17.5%, but

from 1 December 2008 to 31 December 2009 it has been reduced to 15% to encourage expenditure. Hotel rates and meals in restaurants include VAT; the extra charge is included in the price quoted and on the final bill. This can be refunded if you shop at stores that participate in the Retail Export Scheme (signs are posted in the window).

Britain imposes an air passenger duty (departure tax) on air travel. The standard rates are £20 for most European destinations and £80 for all other destinations, including flights to the United States.

Reduced rates, payable by economy-class passengers, are £10 for short-haul flights within Europe or £40 for most international flights. This tax is accounted for in your ticket.

TELEPHONES Public payphones are found in most places. Some of the traditional old red phone boxes have been retained, especially in conservation areas. In larger places, you'll find a choice of payphones taking coins, phone cards (which you can purchase from news-agents), or credit cards.

If calling from a coin-operated phone box, you'll need to pay a minimum of 40p, which will give you 20 minutes to a standard U.K. number.

Standard-rate numbers, where the call costs less if it is local, begin 01—or in London and a few other places 02. Numbers beginning 0800 are free to call, and 0845 numbers are normally charged at 5p per minute and 0870 numbers at 10p per minute. Charges may be higher from mobile phones.

If you need help making a call, phone the operator on ℂ 100 for U.K. calls or ℂ 155 for international calls.

To call overseas from the U.K., dial the international access code—00—followed by the country code for the place you are calling, then the local number. Common country codes are U.S. and Canada 1; Australia 61; New Zealand 64; and South Africa 27. Or call through one of the following long-distance access codes: **AT&T USA Direct** (✆ 1800/CALL-ATT [225-5288]), **Canada Direct** (✆ 0800/890-016), **Australia** (✆ 0800/ 890-061), and **New Zealand** (✆ 0800/890-064).

For calling collect or if you need an international operator, dial ✆ **155.**

For directory inquiries, phone the British Telecom service on ✆ **118 500** or one of the many private services advertised.

TIME The U.K. follows Greenwich Mean Time (GMT), with the clocks moved forward 1 hour to British Summer Time (BST) from the end of March to the end of October. For most of the year, including summer, Britain is 5 hours ahead of the time observed in the eastern United States. Because of different daylight-saving-time practices in the two nations, there's a brief period (about a week) in autumn when Britain is only 4 hours ahead of New York, and a brief period in spring when it's 6 hours ahead.

TIPPING Tipping is a matter of personal choice in Scotland and is not practiced as rigorously as in North America. If you want to show your appreciation of service, the following guidelines provide an idea of how much is appropriate. For cab drivers, add about 10% to 15% to the fare shown on the meter. If the driver personally unloads or loads your luggage, add 50p per bag. For hotel porters, give 75p per bag, even if you have only one small suitcase. For maids, give £1 per day. In hotels, you may also want to tip the concierge if he or she has been particularly helpful.

Hotels sometimes add a service charge of 10% to 15% to bills, but it is normally left to the customer to decide what tips to give. In B&Bs, the tip isn't likely to be included.

In restaurants and nightclubs, a 10% or 15% service charge may be added to the bill, so check before you leave a tip. Tipping in pubs is not common, although in cocktail bars the waiter or barmaid usually gets about £1 per round of drinks.

Barbers and hairdressers expect 10% to 15%. Tour guides expect £2, but it's not mandatory. Petrol station attendants are rarely tipped. Theater ushers also don't expect tips.

TOILETS Public toilets are clean and often have an attendant. Hotels toilets can be used, but they discourage non-guests. In cities and large towns, department stores have toilets for the use of customers. Likewise, all but the smallest cafes and restaurants have toilets. Garages (filling stations) often, but not always, have facilities for the use of customers. There's no need to tip, except to a hotel attendant.

WATER Tap water is considered safe to drink throughout Scotland. It tastes good and is free! If you ask for tap water with a meal, restaurants and cafes must provide it without charge.

In more remote rural areas, hotels, restaurants, and homes may be on a private water supply because they are too far away to receive a piped mains supply. Private supplies are registered with local authorities, which check that they comply with safety standards. The water may be slightly discolored (brownish) if it comes from a peaty area; however, it will be perfectly safe and the taste should not be affected.

Don't drink untreated water from streams, rivers, or lakes, unless you are walking in the hills above grazing animals and habitation that could pollute the water. When you are in the outdoors, help keep Scotland's water pure by going to the toilet well away from open water, rivers, and streams.

2 TOLL-FREE NUMBERS & WEBSITES

MAJOR U.S. AIRLINES
(*flies internationally as well)

American Airlines*
☎ 800/433-7300 (in U.S. or Canada)
☎ 020/7365-0777 (in U.K.)
www.aa.com

Cape Air
☎ 800/352-0714
www.flycapeair.com

Continental Airlines*
☎ 800/523-3273 (in U.S. or Canada)
☎ 084/5607-6760 (in U.K.)
www.continental.com

Delta Air Lines*
☎ 800/221-1212 (in U.S. or Canada)
☎ 084/5600-0950 (in U.K.)
www.delta.com

JetBlue Airways
☎ 800/538-2583 (in U.S.)
☎ 080/1365-2525 (in U.K. or Canada)
www.jetblue.com

Midwest Airlines
☎ 800/452-2022
www.midwestairlines.com

North American Airlines*
☎ 800/371-6297
www.flynaa.com

Northwest Airlines
☎ 800/225-2525 (in U.S.)
☎ 870/0507-4074 (in U.K.)
www.nwa.com

United Airlines*
☎ 800/864-8331 (in U.S. and Canada)
☎ 084/5844-4777 (in U.K.)
www.united.com

US Airways*
☎ 800/428-4322 (in U.S. and Canada)
☎ 084/5600-3300 (in U.K.)
www.usairways.com

Virgin America*
☎ 877/359-8474
www.virginamerica.com

MAJOR INTERNATIONAL AIRLINES

Air France
☎ 800/237-2747 (in U.S.)
☎ 800/375-8723 (in U.S. and Canada)
☎ 087/0142-4343 (in U.K.)
www.airfrance.com

Air India
☎ 212/407-1371 (in U.S.)
☎ 91 22 2279 6666 (in India)
☎ 020/8745-1000 (in U.K.)
www.airindia.com

Air New Zealand
☎ 800/262-1234 (in U.S.)
☎ 800/663-5494 (in Canada)
☎ 0800/028-4149 (in U.K.)
www.airnewzealand.com

Alitalia
☎ 800/223-5730 (in U.S.)
☎ 800/361-8336 (in Canada)
☎ 087/0608-6003 (in U.K.)
www.alitalia.com

American Airlines
☎ 800/433-7300 (in U.S. and Canada)
☎ 020/7365-0777 (in U.K.)
www.aa.com

bmi
☎ 0870 6070 555 (in U.K.)
☎ 1332 64 6181 (outside U.K.)
www.flybmi.com

British Airways
☎ 800/247-9297 (in U.S. and Canada)
☎ 087/0850-9850 (in U.K.)
www.british-airways.com

China Airlines
☎ 800/227-5118 (in U.S.)
☎ 022/715-1212 (in Taiwan)
www.china-airlines.com

Continental Airlines
☎ 800/523-3273 (in U.S. or Canada)
☎ 084/5607-6760 (in U.K.)
www.continental.com

Delta Air Lines
☎ 800/221-1212 (in U.S. and Canada)
☎ 084/5600-0950 (in U.K.)
www.delta.com

EgyptAir
☎ 212/581-5600 (in U.S.)
☎ 020/7734-2343 (in U.K.)
☎ 09/007-0000 (in Egypt)
www.egyptair.com

El Al Airlines
☎ 972/3977-1111 (outside Israel)
☎ *2250 (from any phone in Israel)
www.elal.co.il

Emirates Airlines
☎ 800/777-3999 (in U.S.)
☎ 087/0243-2222 (in U.K.)
www.emirates.com

Finnair
☎ 800/950-5000 (in U.S. and Canada)
☎ 087/0241-4411 (in U.K.)
www.finnair.com

Iberia Airlines
☎ 800/722-4642 (in U.S. and Canada)
☎ 087/0609-0500 (in U.K.)
www.iberia.com

Icelandair
☎ 800/223-5500 ext. 2, prompt 1 (in U.S. and Canada)
☎ 084/5758-1111 (in U.K.)
www.icelandair.com
www.icelandair.co.uk (in U.K.)

Japan Airlines
☎ 012/025-5931 (international)
www.jal.co.jp

KLM Royal Dutch Airlines
☎ 800/225-2525 (in U.S. and Canada)
☎ 0871 222 7474 (in U.K.)
www.klm.com

Korean Air
☎ 800/438-5000 (in U.S. and Canada)
☎ 0800/413-000 (in U.K.)
www.koreanair.com

Lufthansa
☎ 800/399-5838 (in U.S.)
☎ 800/563-5954 (in Canada)
☎ 087/0837-7747 (in U.K.)
www.lufthansa.com

Olympic Airlines
☎ 800/223-1226 (in U.S.)
☎ 514/878-9691 (in Canada)
☎ 087/0606-0460 (in U.K.)
www.olympicairlines.com

Quantas Airways
☎ 800/227-4500 (in U.S.)
☎ 084/5774-7767 (in U.K. and Canada)
☎ 13 13 13 (in Australia)
www.quantas.com

SAS Scandinavian Airlines
☎ 1 800 221 2350 (in U.S. or Canada)
☎ 0871 521 2772 (in U.K.)
www.flysas.com

Swiss Air
☎ 877/359-7947 (in U.S. and Canada)
☎ 084/5601-0956 (in U.K.)
www.swiss.com

United Airlines*
☎ 800/864-8331 (in U.S. and Canada)
☎ 084/5844-4777 (in U.K.)
www.united.com

US Airways*
☎ 800/428-4322 (in U.S. and Canada)
☎ 084/5600-3300 (in U.K.)
www.usairways.com

Virgin Atlantic Airways
☎ 800/821-5438 (in U.S. and Canada)
☎ 087/0574-7747 (in U.K.)
www.virgin-atlantic.com

Aegean Airlines
ⓒ 210/626-1000 (in U.S., Canada, and U.K.)
www.aegeanair.com

Aer Arann
ⓒ 0870 876 7676 (in U.K.)
ⓒ 08 18 210 210 (in Ireland)
ⓒ 353 818 210210 (all others)
www.aerarran.com

Aer Lingus
ⓒ 800/474-7424 (in U.S. & Canada)
ⓒ 087/0876-5000 (in U.K.)
www.aerlingus.com

Air Berlin
ⓒ 087/1500-0737 (in U.K.)
ⓒ 018/0573-7800 (in Germany)
ⓒ 180/573-7800 (all others)
www.airberlin.com

Air Transat
ⓒ 020 7616 9187 (in U.K.)
www.airtransat.com

bmi baby
ⓒ 870/126-6726 (in U.S.)
ⓒ 087/1224-0224 (in U.K.)
www.bmibaby.com

easyJet
ⓒ 870/600-0000 (in U.S.)
ⓒ 090/5560-7777 (in U.K.)
www.easyjet.com

Flybe
ⓒ 0871 700 2000 (in U.K.)
ⓒ 00 44 1392 268500 (outside U.K.)
www.flybe.com

flyglobespan
ⓒ 0871 971 1440 (in U.K.)
www.flyglobespan.com

JetBlue Airways
ⓒ 800/538-2583 (in U.S.)
ⓒ 801/365-2525 (in U.K. or Canada)
www.jetblue.com

Ryanair
ⓒ 1 353 1 249 7700 (in U.S.)
ⓒ 081/830-3030 (in Ireland)
ⓒ 087/1246-0000 (in U.K.)
www.ryanair.com

Southwest Airlines
ⓒ 800/435-9792 (in U.S., U.K., and Canada)
www.southwest.com

Thomson Airways
ⓒ 0871 231 4691 (in U.K.)
http://flights.thomson.co.uk

Wideroe
ⓒ 47 75 11 11 11 (outside Norway)
www.wideroe.no

CAR RENTAL AGENCIES

Advantage
ⓒ 800/777-5500 (in U.S.)
ⓒ 021/0344-4712 (outside of U.S.)
www.advantage.com

Alamo
ⓒ 800/462-5266 (in U.S.)
ⓒ 0870 400 4562 (in U.K.)
www.alamo.co.uk

Arnold Clark
ⓒ 0844 576 5425 (in U.K.)
www.arnoldclarkrental.com

Auto Europe
ⓒ 888/223-5555 (in U.S. and Canada)
ⓒ 0800/2235-5555 (in U.K.)
www.autoeurope.com

Avis
ⓒ 800/331-1212 (in U.S. and Canada)
ⓒ 084/4581-8181 (in U.K.)
www.avis.com

Budget
ⓒ 800/527-0700 (in U.S.)
ⓒ 800/268-8900 (in Canada)
ⓒ 087/0156-5656 (in U.K.)
www.budget.com

Dollar
© 800/800-4000 (in U.S.)
© 800/848-8268 (in Canada)
© 080/8234-7524 (in U.K.)
www.dollar.com

Easycar.com
© 08710 500 444 (in U.K.)
www.easycar.com

Enterprise
© 800/261-7331 (in U.S.)
© 514/355-4028 (in Canada)
© 012/9360-9090 (in U.K.)
www.enterprise.com

Hertz
© 800/645-3131 (in U.S.)
© 800/654-3001 (for international reservations)
www.hertz.com

National
© 800/227-7368 (in U.S.)
© 0870 400 4581 (in U.K.)
www.nationalcar.co.uk

Practical
© 0121 772 8599 (in U.K.)
www.practical.co.uk

Thrifty
© 800/367-2277 (in U.S.)
© 918/669-2168 (international)
www.thrifty.com

MAJOR HOTEL & MOTEL CHAINS

Apex
© 0845 365 0000 (in U.K.)
© 44 (0) 131 666 5124 (outside U.K.)
www.apexhotels.co.uk

Best Western International
© 800/780-7234 (in U.S. and Canada)
© 0800/393-130 (in U.K.)
www.bestwestern.com

Crowne Plaza Hotels
© 888/303-1746
www.ichotelsgroup.com/crowneplaza

Days Inn
© 800/329-7466 (in U.S.)
© 0800/280-400 (in U.K.)
www.daysinn.com

Dreamhouse
© 0845 226 0232 (in U.K.)
www.dreamhouseapartments.com

Express by Holiday Inn
© 0871 423 4896 (in U.K.)
www.hiexpress.co.uk

Hilton Hotels
© 800/HILTONS (445-8667) (in U.S. and Canada)
© 087/0590-9090 (in U.K.)
www.hilton.com

Holiday Inn
© 800/315-2621 (in U.S. and Canada)
© 0800/405-060 (in U.K.)
www.holidayinn.com

InterContinental Hotels & Resorts
© 800/424-6835 (in U.S. and Canada)
© 0800/1800-1800 (in U.K.)
www.ichotelsgroup.com

Macdonald Hotels & Resorts
© 0844 879 9000 (in U.K.)
© 44 (00 1506 815 142 (outside U.K.)
www.macdonaldhotels.co.uk

Marriott
© 877/236-2427 (in U.S. and Canada)
© 0800/221-222 (in U.K.)
www.marriott.com

Novotel
© 800 NOVOTEL (668-6835) (in U.S. and Canada)
© 0870 609 0962 (in U.K.)
www.novotel.com

Quality
© 877/424-6423 (in U.S. and Canada)
© 0800/444-444 (in U.K.)
www.qualityinn.choicehotels.com

Radisson Hotels & Resorts
ⓒ 888/201-1718 (in U.S. and Canada)
ⓒ 0800/374-411 (in U.K.)
www.radisson.com

Ramada Worldwide
ⓒ 888/2-RAMADA [72-6232] (in U.S. and Canada)
ⓒ 080/8100-0783 (in U.K.)
www.ramada.com

Sheraton Hotels & Resorts
ⓒ 800/325-3535 (in U.S.)
ⓒ 800/543-4300 (in Canada)
ⓒ 0800/3253-5353 (in U.K.)
www.starwoodhotels.com/sheraton

Swallow Hotels
ⓒ 0870 050 20 20 (in U.K.)
www.swallow-hotels.com

Thistle
ⓒ 0871 376 9016 (in U.K.)
ⓒ 44 (0) 870 333 9132 (outside U.K.)
www.thistle.com

Travelodge
ⓒ 800-578-7878
www.travelodge.com

Westin Hotels & Resorts
ⓒ 800-937-8461 (in U.S. and Canada)
ⓒ 0800/3259-5959 (in U.K.)
www.starwoodhotels.com/westin

Appendix B:
Language & Place Names

Scotland has been inhabited for thousands of years and has seen many waves of invaders and immigrants who spoke various tongues. The oldest languages, which were never written down, have been lost in the mists of time. When the Romans invaded, 2,000 years ago, the native Celtic people—the Picts—were speaking a language related to Welsh. The only traces of Pictish remain in places names, such as "Aber-", meaning river mouth as in Aberdeen, and "Pit-", meaning portion or share as in Pittenweem.

Gaelic was the language of the Scots, a people who came from Ireland and colonized the western parts of Scotland after the Romans had left. When the kingdoms of the Scots and the Picts were unified in the 9th century, the Gaelic language supplanted Pictish and by 1000 A.D. was spoken throughout Scotland.

By then another language had also come on the scene—Scots, which developed from northern Old English with a strong touch of Norse, the language that Viking occupiers brought from Scandinavia. By about 1500 A.D., Scots had replaced Gaelic in most of lowland and eastern Scotland. These days Gaelic is only commonly spoken in the far northwest, particularly in the Western Isles, although it is found in place names all over the country. These names have often been "Anglicized" in their spelling, as shown in parentheses below. With the advent of greater mobility and modern communications, Scots has become somewhat diluted by English. However, there are still many distinctly different words in common use.

Most place names are descriptive, so knowing what they mean can add an extra dimension to a walk. For instance "Meall Buidhe" is a rounded yellow hill (colored by mountain grasses and sedges) and is likely to be an easier walk than climbing "Sgurr Dubh," the rocky black peak.

Here are some words you will often see on maps and in the walk descriptions, including a few English ones that may confuse North American visitors.

GAELIC WORDS
HILL NAMES

Beag	Little	Meall	Round hill
Beinn (Ben)	Mountain	Mor	Big
Carn (Cairn)	Heap of stones	Sgurr (Sgor)	Rocky peak
Creag (Craig)	Crag, rock, cliff	Stob	Point
Cnoc (Knock)	Hillock		

COLORS

Ban	White, pale	Glas	Green, grey
Buidhe	Yellow	Gorm	Blue, green
Dearg	Red	Ruadh	Red-brown
Dubh	Black	Uaine	Green
Fionn	White, fair		

Abhainn	River	Dun	Fort
Allt	Stream	Gleann (Glen)	Narrow valley
Caol (Kyle)	Narrows	Eas	Waterfall
Ceann (Kin-)	Head (as in Kinloch)	Eilean	Island
Cille (Kil-)	Church	Loch	Lake or arm of the sea
Clach	Stone	Lochan	Small lake, pond
Coille	Wood	Srath (Strath)	Broad valley
Coire	Hollow in mountainside	Taigh (Tigh)	House
Bealach	Pass through mountains		

SCOTS WORDS

Auld	Old	Linn	Waterfall, narrow gorge
Birk	Birch tree	Muckle	Big
Brae	Slope of a hillside	Stane	Stone
Brig	Bridge	Steading	Farm buildings
Burn	Stream	Tap	Head, hill, heap
Den	Deep wooded valley	Wee	Small
Firth	Estuary, inlet of the sea		

ENGLISH WORDS

Col	Pass or dip in a mountain chain.
Folly	A decorative building constructed to enhance the landscape.
Kissing-gate	A pedestrian gate designed to stop livestock passing through, with an enclosure at one end only large enough for one person at a time (who, while trapped, may receive a kiss from another person on the other side of the gate!)
Lay-by	Pull-in for parking at the side of a road
Track	A path wide enough for a wheeled vehicle
Trig point/pillar	Trigonometrical station used by surveyors to create accurate maps in the pre-GPS era (a pillar about 1m high, often found on the summit of hills)

INDEX

See also Accommodations and Restaurant indexes, below.

GENERAL INDEX

Abbey Street (Melrose), 100
Abbotsford House, 96–98
Abbotsmoss House, 98
Aberarder, 211–212
Abernethy National Nature
   Reserve, 186
Access America, 252
Accommodations. *See also*
   Accommodations Index
   Argyll and the West
      Highlands, 177–178
   best, 8–9
   Edinburgh and
      Glasgow, 69
   green-friendly, 20
   northeast highlands,
      214–215
   northern highlands,
      246–247
   southern Scotland, 107
   Tayside and Fife, 144–145
   toll-free numbers &
      websites, 259
Ailsa Craig, 81, 82, 93
Airports, 14
Air travel, 13–14
   Argyll and the West
      Highlands, 148
   Edinburgh and
      Glasgow, 34
   green-friendly, 20
   northeast highlands, 182
   northern highlands, 218
   southern Scotland, 72
   Tayside and Fife, 110
   toll-free numbers &
      websites, 256–258
Allt a' Chobhair, 130
Allt Eigheach, 142
Allt Mhairc, 132
Allt na Ciste, 189
Allt Na-Guibhsaich Path, 198
Allt na h-Eilde, 176

The Aluminium Story
   (Kinlochleven), 176
Aluminum works,
   Kinlochleven, 176
Am Buachaille, 238
Ancrum Moor, 103
Angus, 109
Anstruther Harbor, 120
An Teallach, 224–227
An Teallach Ale, 227
Ant Trail, 159
Aonach Eagach ridge, 174
Aonach Mor, 212
Arbroath, 138
Arbroath Smokie, 138
Area codes, 249
Argus butterflies, 104
Argyll and West Highlands
   walks, 147–179
   Arrochar Alps, 156–159
   Ben Lomond, 153–156
   Callander Crags and Brack-
      linn Falls, 150–152
   Carradale, 170–173
   Cruachan, 162–165
   getting around, 148, 150
   getting there, 148
   Glen Nant, 159–162
   Kilmartin Glen, 168–170
   Kinlochleven, 173–177
   orientation, 148
   sleeping and eating,
      177–179
   Tobermory, 165–167
   visitor information, 148
Argyll Forest Park, 156
Aros Burn, 165
Aros Lodge, 165
Aros Park, 165
Aros Pier, 166
Arrochar Alps, 3–4, 62–64,
   69, 156–159
Arthur's Seat, 5, 43–46
A719, 80
AT&T USA Direct, 255
Atholl Estates, 132, 134

Atholl Lodging (Balvenie
   Castle), 208
ATM networks/cashpoints,
   249
Auchenlaich, 152
Auld Kirk
   Ayr, 81
   St. Monans, 118
Australia
   customs regulations,
      11–12
   High Commission, 251
   passports, 253–254
Aviemore, 180
Ayr, 74, 80
Ayrshire, 75, 78–81

Balamory (television
   series), 166
Balmaha, 66, 68, 69
Balmoral Castle (Crathie),
   200
Balmoral Estate, 200
Balmoral Estate Visitor
   Centre, 198
Balvenie Castle, 208
Bass Rock, 38, 46, 120
Battle of Glen Trool, 92
Battle of Loch Trool, 88
Baxters Highland Village, 211
Bealach a' Mhaim, 158
Bealach Ard, 68
Beatrix Potter Garden, 126
Beinn a Bhragaidh (Ben
   Bhraggie), 222
Beinn a' Ghlo, 126, 134
Beinn Ghlas, 128, 130
Beinn Ime, 158
Beinn Narnain, 156, 158
Ben Chonzie, 122
Ben Cruachan, 162–165
Ben Lawers, 4, 128–131
Ben Lomond, 4, 64, 68,
   153–156, 158
Ben Lomond National
   Memorial Park, 154

Ben Macdui, 189–192
Ben More, 130
Bennachie, 4, 192–194
Bennanbrack, 87, 92
Ben Nevis, 3, 212
    Tourist Path, 243–246
Ben Vorlich, 68, 122
Benvraggie Wood, 222
Benyellary, 93
Bidein a' Ghlas Thuill, 225
The Big Burn, 221–222
Bird-watching
    Coldingham Bay to
        Eyemouth, 106
    Falls of Clyde, 52
    The Hermitage, 125
    Kinross, 116
    Loch Leven, 116
    Peebles, 94
    Portpatrick, 81–82
    St. Abb's, 104
    Seaton Cliffs, 135, 136
    Southern Upland Way, 81
    Wood of Cree walk, 86
    Yellowcraigs Beach, 38
Birnam Institute, 126
Birnam Oak, 109, 126
Birnam Wood, 126
Bishop Hill, 116
Blackwater Reservoir,
    142, 176, 177
Blair Castle, 134
Blairmore Car Park, 237
The Blowhole, 135, 136
Boathouse bird hide
    (Kinross), 116
Boat trips and cruises
    Castle Island, 116
    Craigleith Island, 38
    Falkirk Wheel, 48
Bogmoor, 208, 210
Bonawe Iron Furnace, 160
Bonnington iron bridge, 52
Bonnington Linn Power
    Station, 50
Bonnington Weir, 52
Borders Abbeys Way, 97, 98
Borders Gunroom (Melrose),
    102
Bowden, 102
Braan Walk, 125
Bracklinn Falls, 150–152
Braehead Road, 102
Braemar, 141
The Braemar Gathering, 204
Braemar Golf Club, 202
Braemar Mews, 201
Braes of Doon, 152
Braes of Gauldwell, 206

Braes of Mulgarvie, 92
Braigh Clais Daimh, 132
Branklyn Garden (Perth),
    112, 114
Brig o' Doon (Bridge of
    Doon), 78
Broad Wood, 102
Brora, 222
Bruce's Stone, 87, 92
Bruce's Stone Car Park, 87, 92
Buchanan Street Bus Station
    (Glasgow), 36
Buchan Burn, 92
Buchan Hilland, 93
Buchan waterfall, 92
Bugs (ticks and insect
    bites), 22
Burleigh Sands (Kinross), 116
Burn of Edramucky, 128, 130
Burn of Kilbo, 140
Burn O' Vat visitor center,
    195
Burns, Robert, 75, 78
    cottage and birthplace,
        80–81
Bus travel (coach travel)
    Argyll and the West
        Highlands, 148
    Edinburgh and
        Glasgow, 34
    northeast highlands, 182
    northern highlands, 218
    Tayside and Fife, 110
Buxton House (Selkirk), 97
Bynack More, 190

Cac Carn Beag, 198
Cadha Gobhlach, 227
Caiplie Caves, 120–121
Caiplie Farm, 120
Cairn Gorm, 3, 189–192
Cairngorm Reindeer Centre,
    188
The Cairngorms, 180, 182,
    183, 189, 190, 198, 214
Cairngorm Ski Centre, 192
Cairngorms National Park,
    138, 180, 184
Cairn Lochan, 190, 192
The Caledonian Canal,
    217, 234, 236
Caledonian MacBrayne
    (CalMac), 16, 150
Caledonian pine forest, 186
Callander, 150
Callander Crags, 5, 150–152
Campsie Fells, 59, 64

Canada
    customs regulations, 11
    health insurance, 252
    High Commission, 251
    passports, 253
Capel Mounth, 141
Cape Wrath, 237
Carbeth, 58, 59
Carbon offsetting, 20
Carlingheugh Bay, 136
Carnethy Hill, 42
Carn Liath, 212, 214
Carradale (Kintyre
    peninsula), 6, 170–173
Carradale Bay, 171, 173
Carradale Harbor, 171
Carradale Point, 173
Car rentals, 15, 249
    Glasgow and
        Edinburgh, 36
    green-friendly, 20
    for southern Scotland
        walks, 75
    toll-free numbers &
        websites, 258–259
Car travel, 14–15
    driving rules, 250
    Edinburgh and
        Glasgow, 34
    northeast highlands, 182
    northern highlands, 218
    southern Scotland
        walks, 74
    Tayside and Fife, 110
Carved bench, Falls of
    Clyde, 50
Castle Gate (the Three
    Sisters), 136
Castle Island, 115, 116, 186
Cellphones, 249–250
Chalybeate, 152
Chapel Brae, 201
Charcoal, 160
Clairinch, 69
Clan MacGregor, 69
Climate, 12, 19
Clunie Water, 202
C-N-Do, 23
Cnoc Nan Gabhar, 171
Cnoc poll a Mhurain, 237
Coastal Interpretative Centre
    (near Portpatrick), 82
The Cobbler, 156, 158
Coire a' Chriochairein, 212
Coire an Lochain, 192
Coire Ardair, 211, 212
Coire Cas, 192
Coire Domhain, 190

Coire Loch, 228
Coldingham, 103, 104
Coldingham Bay, 106
Collennan Quarry, 75
Common Riding Event
    (Selkirk), 97
Conic Hill (Loch Lomond),
    5, 66–69
Convalmore Distillery, 206
Coronation Road (Perth), 114
Corrag Bhuidhe, 227
Corra Linn Waterfall, 52
Corrie Fee, 138, 140
Corrie Hallie, 227
Corrour, 141–144
Costs and permits, 18
Cove Haven, 136
Cowal Walking and Arts
    Festival, 147
Craigallian Loch, 59
Craiganlet (wreck), 84
Craigellachie, 204
Craigellachie Hotel, 207
Craigend Castle, 58
Craigend Visitor Centre
    (Mugdock Country
    Park), 56, 59
Craiggowrie, 188
Craig Leach Forest, 236
Craigleith Island, 38
Craigvinean Cottage, 126
Craigvinean Forest, 126
Crail, 118, 121
Crannogs, 197
Creagan Gorm, 188
Creag Meagaidh (between
    Fort William and
    Aviemore), 4, 211–214
Credit cards, 250, 253
Creel Path, 104
Crieff, 121
Crieff Hydro Hotel, 122
Croftmore, 135
Cromarty Firth, 232, 233, 248
Cruachan, 162–165
Cruachan Burn, 162
Cruachan Dam, 165
Cruachan Horseshoe
    (Oban), 4
Cruachan Power Station, 164
Cruachan Reservoir, 164
Cruachan Visitor Centre, 164
Cruach nam Miseag, 156
Cuidhe Crom, 198
Culcrieff, 121
Culcrieff Wood, 124
Culsharg, 92

Currency and currency
    exchange, 250
Customs regulations, 11–12

David, King, 94
Deer Hill Walk, 171
Deer hunting (stalking), 42
Degree of difficulty rating,
    17–18
Deil's Heid, 135, 136
Dere Street (Melrose), 102,
    103
Diana's Grove, 134
Dickmont's Den, 136
Difficulty rating, 17–18
Dining. See also Restaurants
    Index
    Argyll and the West
        Highlands, 178
    best, 7–8
    Edinburgh and
        Glasgow, 70
    green-friendly, 20
    northeast highlands,
        215–216
    northern highlands,
        247–248
    southern Scotland,
        107–108
    Tayside and Fife, 145–146
Distance, 18
Dog Falls, Glen Affric,
    3, 227–230
Dolphins, Moray Firth, 210
Driesh, 138–140
Drinking laws, 250
Driving rules, 250
Drochaid Ghlas, 164
Druim na Buainn, 237
Drymen, 63, 64, 66
Dry-stane walls, 98
Dufftown, 204–207
Dufftown Station, 206
Duke of Sutherland monu-
    ment, 221–224
Dumgoyne, 5
    summit of, 62
Dumgoyne Hill by Killearn,
    59–63, 68
Duncryne Hill, 68
Dundee, 109
Dundonald (village), 76
Dundonald Castle, 76, 78
Dundonald Castle Visitor
    Centre, 76
Dundonald Glen, 75, 76
Dundonnell, 225, 227

Dunkeld Cathedral, 126
Dunrobin Castle, 222
Dunsky Golf Club, 82

Easyways, 24
Edinburgh
    getting around, 36
    getting there, 34, 36
    orientation, 36
    sleeping and eating, 69–71
    traveling to, 34
    visitor information, 36
Edinburgh and Glasgow
    walks, 33–71
    Arthur's Seat and Holyrood
        Park, 43–46
    Conic Hill, 66–69
    Dumgoyne Hill by Killearn,
        59–63
    Falkirk Wheel, 47–50
    Falls of Clyde, 50–52
    Kelvin Walkway, 53–56
    Mugdock Country Park to
        Carbeth, 56–59
    Queen's View and The
        Whangie, 63–66
    Scald Law—The Pentland
        Hills, 40
    Yellowcraigs Beach to
        North Berwick, 37–40
Edinburgh Castle, 46
Eildon Hill North, 100, 102
Eildon Hills, 98, 100, 102
Electricity, 251
Elevation gain, 18
Embassies and consulates,
    251
Emergencies, 251
Estimated time, 18
Ettrick Forest, 97
Evanton, 232
Eyemouth, 106

Faldonside Loch, 98
Falkirk Wheel (between
    Edinburgh and Glasgow),
    6, 47–50
Falkirk Wheel Visitor Centre,
    47, 48
Falls of Clyde, 2–3, 50–52
Falls of Clyde Wildlife
    Reserve, 50
Falls of Cruachan, 162
Falls of Fender, 132
Families with children, best
    walks for, 1–2

Famous Grouse Experience (Crieff), 121
Famous Grouse Experience tours, 124
Farragon Hill, 135
Ferguson, J. D., 112
Ferguson, Malcolm, 152
Ferguson Gallery (Perth), 112
Ferries, 15–16
 Tayside and Fife, 110
Fiddich Park, 206–207
Fidra Island, 37, 38
Fife and Tayside walks, 109–146
 Ben Lawers, 128–131
 Fife Coastal Path, 118–121
 getting there, 110
 Glen Tilt, 131–135
 The Hermitage, 124–128
 Knock of Crieff, 121–124
 Loch Leven Heritage Trail, 115–118
 Mayar and Driesh, 138–141
 Perth and Kinnoull Hill, 112
 Rannoch to Corrour, 141–144
 Seaton Cliffs, 135–138
Fife Coastal Path, 6, 118–121
Firkin Point, 154
First ScotRail, 34, 110, 148, 182
Firth of Clyde, 64, 75, 80, 82, 93, 148
Firth of Forth, 40, 42, 44, 46, 109, 121
Firth of Lorn, 148
Firth of Tay, 109
Five Finger Gully, 244
Fochabers, 207, 211
Forestry Road, 92
Forth and Clyde Canal, 56
Forth Rail Bridge, 43, 46
Fort William, 66, 147, 148, 217, 218, 220, 233, 243
 accommodations, 247
 restaurants, 247, 248
Friarton Bridge (Perth), 114
Frommers.com, 11, 23
Fyrish Monument, 6, 230–233

Galloway Forest Park, 87, 88, 90, 93
Gannochy, 115
Garmouth Viaduct, 210
Gasoline, 251
Gauldwell Bridge, 206
Gibson Street (Glasgow), 54

Gilbert's Bridge, 131, 132
Glas Allt, 200
Glasgow
 getting around, 36
 getting there, 34, 36
 orientation, 36
 sleeping and eating, 69–71
 traveling to, 34
 visitor information, 36
Glasgow and Edinburgh walks, 33–71
 Arthur's Seat and Holyrood Park, 43–46
 Conic Hill, 66–69
 Dumgoyne Hill by Killearn, 59–63
 Falkirk Wheel, 47–50
 Falls of Clyde, 50–52
 Kelvin Walkway, 53–56
 Mugdock Country Park to Carbeth, 56–59
 Queen's View and The Whangie, 63–66
 Scald Law—The Pentland Hills, 40
 Yellowcraigs Beach to North Berwick, 37–40
Glasgow and South Western Railway, 78
Glass-Allt Shiel, 200–201
Gleann Chaorachain, 227
Glen Affric, 227–230
Glen Clova, 138
Glen Clunie Cairn, 202
Glencorse Reservoir, 42
Glen Doll, 138, 200
Glendoll, 138, 140
Glen Fender, 135
Glenfiddich Distillery, 204, 208
Glengoyne Distillery, 62
Glen Lyon, 128, 130
Glen Nant, 3, 159–162
Glen Nevis, 144, 243–244
Glen Prosen, 140
Glen Quoich, 202
Glen Tilt, 131–135
Glentress Forest, 94
Glentrool, 84, 87, 90
Glen Trool Road, 90
Glen Turret, 122
Glenturret Distillery, 124
Golf
 Braemar Golf Club, 202
 Carradale, 171
Golspie, 224
Google Maps, 19
Gordon Baxter Way, 211
Gordon Way, 194

Gow's Bridge, 134
GPS
 coordinates, 21
 trailhead, 19
Great Glen, 220
Great Glen Way, 2
 start of, 233–236
Greenan Castle, 80
Greenan Road, 80
Green-friendly tips, 20
Grey Mare's Tail, 174
GSM (Global System for Mobile Communications), 249
Guided walking tours, 23–24

Ha'penny House (Kelvin Walkway), 56
Harestanes, 103
Harestanes Visitor Centre, 103
Harvey maps, 19
Health and safety concerns, 21–23
Health insurance, 251–252
Heather Brig, 194
Heathery Rig Plantation, 98
Hercules' Garden, 134
Heritage Centre (Carradale), 171
The Hermitage, 7, 124–128
Hermitage Bridge, 128
Hermit's Cave, 125
Hermit's Well, 121
High Greenan House, 80
Highland Boundary Fault, 66, 122, 154
Highland Clearances, 232
Highland Light Infantry Statue (Glasgow), 54
Hill of Newton, 206
Hill walks, best, 4–5
Holidays, 251
Holyrood Abbey, 44
Holyrood Park, 44
Hosh Path, 121, 124
Hospitals, 251
Hotels. See also Accommodations Index
 Argyll and the West Highlands, 177–178
 best, 8–9
 Edinburgh and Glasgow, 69
 green-friendly, 20
 northeast highlands, 214–215

northern highlands, 246–247
southern Scotland, 107
Tayside and Fife, 144–145
toll-free numbers & websites, 259
Hut circles, Iron Age, 197

Ice Factor, The, (Kinlochleven), 176
Insect bites, 22
Insurance, 251–252
car-rental, 15
InsureMyTrip.com, 252
Internet access, 252
Inverness
accommodations, 246–247
restaurants, 247
Inverness Castle, 234
Ireland
consulate, 251
passports, 254
The Isla Way, 206
Isle of Arran, 68
Isle of Gigha, 173
Isle of May, 120
Isle of Mull, 147, 148, 164
Itineraries, suggested, 25–32

Jedburgh, 103
Jesus Well, 121
Jim Aitken Arboretum (Perth), 114
Jock's Road, 141
Jubilee Cairn, 150
Jubilee Car Park, 114
Jubilee rifle range, 132

Kate McNieven's Craig, 122, 124
Keith & Dufftown Railway, 206
Keltie Glen Road, 152
Kelvin, Lord (William Thomson), 54
Kelvingrove Museum and Art Gallery (Glasgow), 53
Kelvin Walkway (Glasgow), 2, 53–56
Kelvin Way Bridge, 53–55
Kilbo Path, 140, 141
Killantringan Bay, 84
Killantringan Lighthouse, 6, 81, 82
Killearn, 62, 69
Kilmartin Glen, 168–170

Kilmartin House, 170
Kilrenny Mill, 120
Kinlochleven, 173–177
Kinlochleven Land Development Trust, 176
Kinmylies, 236
Kinnoull Hill, 112–114
Kinnoull Hill Woodland Park, 114
Kinnoull Tower (Perth), 114
Kinross Fisheries, 115
Kinross House, 116
Kinross Pier, 115
Kintyre Way, 147, 173
Kirkgate Park (Kinross), 116
Kirk Hill (St. Abb's), 104
Kirk Road Junction, 42
Kissing Gate, 154
Knock of Crieff, 5, 121–124

Ladybank Forest, 126, 128
Lady Glassary Wood, 168, 170
Lael Forest, 2, 240–242
Lael Forest Garden, 242
Lairig Ghru, 183
Lairig Torran, 165
Leachd a' Chaorainn, 142
Legal aid, 252
Lighthouses
Killantringan Lighthouse, 6, 81, 82
St. Abb's Lighthouse, 104
Lilliard's Stone, 102–103
Little Ord, 195
Loch Affric, 230
Loch a Mhuilin, 238
Lochan a' Chladheimh, 142
Lochan a' Choire, 212
Lochan Buidhe, 192
Loch an Eilein, 5, 183–186
Lochan Meall an Suidhe, 244
Lochan na Beinne, 189
Lochan na Gaire, 200
Lochan nan Cat, 130
Lochan Trail, 165–166
Lochan Uaine, 186, 212
Loch Ard, 153
Loch Eilde Beag, 174
Loch Eilde Mor, 174
Loch Eilein Cottage, 184
Loch Etchachan, 190
Loch Etive, 148
Loch Gamhna, 184
Loch Ghuibinn, 212
Lochie Brae, 115
Loch Katrine, 148, 153
Loch Kinnord, 195, 197

Loch Leven, 116, 174
Lochleven Castle, 115
Loch Leven Heritage Trail, 3, 115–118
Loch Linhe, 148
Loch Lomond, 62, 64, 147, 154
Loch Morlich, 184, 188, 190, 214
Loch Muick, 200
Loch na Gainimh, 238
Lochnagar, 4, 197–201
Loch Ness, 220, 233, 236
suggested itinerary, 30–32
Loch Ossian, 144
Loch Tay, 128, 130
Loch Trool, 87–90
Loch Venachar, 152
Loganlea Reservoir, 40, 43
Lord Berkeley's Seat, 225
Lost and found, 253
Lothian Buses, 36
Lovers' Walk, 121

Macpherson, Duncan, 141
Maidens and Dunure Light Railway, 78
Mail, 253
Malt Whisky Trail, 204
MapQuest, 20
Maps, recommended, 19
March Burn, 190, 192
Mary's Gate (Kinross), 116
Mary's Ponds, 116
Maxton Kirk (Melrose), 102
Mayar, 138–140
McNieven, Kate, 122
Meall a' Bhuachaille (Aviemore), 4, 186–189
Meall Cuanail, 162, 164
Meall Garbh, 225
Meall na Mucarach, 142
MEDEX Assistance, 251
Medical insurance, 251–252
Medicines, 253
Meikle Pap, 198
Melrose, 100–103
Melrose Abbey, ruins of, 100
Mermaids Kirk, 135
The Merrick (Galloway Forest Park), 4, 87, 90–93
Milkboys Path, 115
Millennium Path, 230
Mither Tap, 192, 194
Mobile phones, 249–250
Moncreiffe Island, 112
Monzie Castle, 124

The Moor, 141, 144
Moot Hill, 58
Moray Firth Wildlife Centre, 210
Morrone, 201–203
Morrone Birkwood, 201
Mosstodloch, 211
Mountain Innovations, 23–24
Mountain walks, best, 3–4
Mugdock Castle, 58
Mugdock Country Park, 2, 56, 57, 64
Mugdock Loch, 58
Mugdock Wood, 56, 58
Muir, John, 237
Muir of Dinnet, 195–197
Mulldonoch, 87, 92
Mull of Kintyre, 82
Mull Wildlife Week, 147
Munro, Sir Hector, 232
Myre Loch, 104

Na Cnapanan, 214
Narnain Boulders, 158–159
Nature Walk (Perth), 114
Navigation assistance, 19–20
Needle E'e, 135
Neidpath Castle, 94, 96
The Ness Islands, 234
Nether Largie North Cairn, 168
Nethy Bridge, 186
Network Centre (Carradale), 171
New Kinnord, 197
New Lanark Visitor Centre, 52
Newtown St. Boswell, 102
New Zealand
  consulate, 251
  customs regulations, 12
  passports, 254
North Berwick Pier, 38
Northeast highlands walks, 180–216
  Bennachie, 192–194
  Cairn Gorm and Ben Macdui, 189–192
  Creag Meagaidh, 211–214
  Dufftown to Craigellachie, 204–207
  getting around, 183
  getting there, 182
  Loch an Eilein, 183–186
  Lochnagar, 197–201
  Meall a' Bhuachaille, 186–189
  Morrone, 201–203

orientation, 182–183
  sleeping and eating, 214–216
  Spey Bay, 207–211
  The Vat and Muir of Dinnet, 194–197
  visitor information, 182
Northern highlands walks, 217–248
  An Teallach, 224–227
  Ben Nevis Tourist Path, 243–246
  Dog Falls, Glen Affric, 227–230
  Duke of Sutherland monument, 221–224
  Fyrish Monument, 230–233
  getting around, 220–221
  getting there, 218, 220
  Lael Forest, 240–242
  orientation, 220
  Sandwood Bay, 237–240
  sleeping and eating, 246–248
  the start of the Great Glen Way, 233–236
  visitor information, 220
North Woodside Flint Mill, 54
Novar Estate, 232

Oban, 147, 148
Old Corrour Lodge, 142
Old Kinnord, 197
The Old Man of Lochnagar (Prince Charles), 200
Old Spey Bridge, 208
Operation Peregrine Bird Hide, 52
Ordnance Survey, 19
Orion (wreck), 84
Orwell Churchyard, 118
Ossian's Hall, 125, 128
Owen, Robert, 52
Oxen Craig, 194

Packing tips, 13
Pap of Glencoe, 174
Passports, 11, 253–254
Peebles, 5, 93–96
The Pentland Hills, 40
The Pentlands, 33, 36, 40–43
Perth, 109, 112–115
  orientation, 112
Perth and Kinnoull Hill, 5
Perth Farmers' Market, 132
Perthshire, 25, 109
Peter's Rock, 142, 144

Pet-friendly walks, 18
Petrol, 251
Pictish Fort, 152
Pictish Stone, 197
Pittenweem, 120
Planning your trip to Scotland, 10–24
Police, 254
Portpatrick, 81, 82, 84
Port Righ, 173
Post offices, 252, 253
Potter, Beatrix, 125, 126
Pow Burn, 118
Prestwick International Airport, 72
Ptarmigan, 154

Queen's Ford, 134
Queen's View, 63, 64

Rail travel
Rannoch, 141–144
Rannoch Moor, 141
Rannoch Station, 142, 144
Red Burn, 244
Red Squirrel Trail, 134
Red Well, 152
Respiratory illnesses, 22
Restaurants. *See also* Restaurants Index
  Argyll and the West Highlands, 178
  best, 7–8
  Edinburgh and Glasgow, 70
  green-friendly, 20
  northeast highlands, 215–216
  northern highlands, 247–248
  southern Scotland, 107–108
  Tayside and Fife, 145–146
Rifle range, Jubilee, 132
River Affric, 228, 230
River Braan, 125, 126
River Dee, 180, 202
River Doon, 78, 80
River Fiddich, 206–207
River Kelvin, 53
River Leven, 174, 176
River Muick, 198, 201
River Ness, 234
River Spean, 212
River Spey, 180, 208
River Tay, 114, 126, 145
River Tilt, 131, 132

River Tweed, 94
RNLI lifeboat station
  (Portpatrick), 84
Robert Burns Heritage
  Museum (Alloway),
  78, 80–81
Robert II, King, 76
Robert the Bruce, King,
  87, 88, 100
Rob Roy, 98
Rothiemurchus Centre
  (Inverdruie), 184
Rothiemurchus Estate, 184
Rough Castle Tunnel, 48
Rumbling Bridge, 126
Ryvoan Bothy, 188

Saddell Abbey, 173
Safety and health
  concerns, 21
Sail Liath, 227
St. Abb's, 104
St. Abb's Head, 6, 103,
  104, 106
St. Abb's Head Cliff Walk, 104
St. Abb's Lighthouse, 104
St. Abb's National Nature
  Reserve, 104
St. Abb's Visitor Centre, 106
St. Andrews, 109
St. Andrew's Old Kirk (North
  Berwick), 38
St. Anthony's Chapel
  (Holyrood Park), 44
St. Cuthbert's Way, 100, 102
St. Fillan's Cave, 120
St. Monans, 118, 120
St. Vedas Hotel (St. Abb's),
  103, 104
Salisbury Crags, 33, 42,
  44, 46
Sandwood Bay, 6, 237–240
Sandwood Bay Beach, 238,
  240
Sandwood Estate, 237
Sandwood Loch, 238
Scald Law, 4–5, 40
  summit of, 43
Scars of Benyellary, 93
Scaut Hill, 206
Scenic walks, best, 5–6
Schiehallion, 135
Scott, Sir Walter, 98
  monument to (Selkirk), 97
Scottish Citylink, 36
  Argyll and the West
    Highlands, 148
  Tayside and Fife, 110

Scottish Fisheries Museum,
  120
Scottish Parliament
  (Edinburgh), 46
Scottish Seabird Center
  (North Berwick), 38
Scottish Witchcraft Act
  (1563), 122
Seamen's Grave, 136
Seasons, 12, 19
Seaton Cliffs, 2, 135–138
Seaton Den, 136
Second Beach, 82
Selkirk, 96, 97
Selkirk Hill, 97
Sgurr Fiona, 225
Shifting Shingle, 208
Shillinglaw Plantation, 98
Shipwrecks, 84
Skipness Castle, 173
Slockavullin, 170
Smoking, 254
Smugglers Trail, 75
Smuggling, 76
SNH (Scottish National
  Heritage; Inverness), 236
Southern Scotland walks,
  72–108
  Alloway, Ayrshire, 78–81
  Coldingham-St. Abb's
    Head-Eyemouth,
    103–106
  Dundonald Glen & The
    Smugglers Trail, 75–78
  getting around, 74–75
  getting there, 72, 74
  Loch Trool, 87–90
  Melrose to Harestanes,
    100–103
  The Merrick, 90–93
  Peebles, 93–96
  Portpatrick to Killantringan
    Lighthouse, 81–84
  Selkirk to Abbotsford
    House, 96–100
  Wood of Cree, 84–86
Southern Upland Way,
  72, 81, 82, 87, 88
Spey Bay (Moray Firth), 2,
  207–211
Sron a Choire, 225
Sron Aonaich, 153
Sron Coire a' Chriochairein,
  212, 214
Stalking (deer hunting), 42
Star ratings and icons, 17
Stevenson, Robert Louis,
  37, 38

Stirling, 152
Stob Binnein, 130
Stob Diamh, 162, 164
Stob Poite Coire Ardair, 212
Strathblane, 59, 60, 62, 63
Strath Garry, 135
Strath Nethy, 189
Strathspey, 180
  suggested itinerary, 28–30
Sub-arctic tundra, 190
Suggested itineraries, 25–32
The Superfast, 110

Taigh Solais, 166
Taxes, 254
Tayside and Fife walks,
  109–146
  Ben Lawers, 128–131
  Fife Coastal Path, 118–121
  getting there, 110
  Glen Tilt, 131–135
  The Hermitage, 124–128
  Knock of Crieff, 121–124
  Loch Leven Heritage Trail,
    115–118
  Mayar and Driesh, 138–141
  Perth and Kinnoull Hill,
    112–115
  Rannoch to Corrour,
    141–144
  Seaton Cliffs, 135–138
Teallach Brewery (An
  Teallach), 227
Telephones, 254–255
Temple Wood, 170
Ticks, 22
Time zones, 255
Tipping, 255
Tobermory (Isle of Mull), 2,
  165–167
Toilets, 255
Tomgarrow, 126
"To Old Friends" bench, 100
Torlum Hill, 122
Tourist information, 10–11
  Argyll and the West
    Highlands, 148
  Edinburgh and Glasgow
    walks, 36
  northeast highlands, 182
  northern highlands, 220
  southern Scotland
    walks, 74
  Tayside and Fife, 110
Towser, statue of, 124
Trailhead directions, 19
Trailhead GPS, 19

Trailhead safety and parking precautions, 23
Train travel
    Argyll and the West Highlands, 148
    Edinburgh and Glasgow, 34
    northeast highlands, 182
    northern highlands, 220
    southern Scotland walks, 74
    Tayside and Fife, 110
Transportation, green-friendly, 20
Travel Assistance International, 251
Travelex Insurance Services, 252
Travel Guard International, 252
Traveline Scotland, 112, 148
Traveling to Scotland, 13–17
Travel insurance, 252
Travel Insured International, 252
TravelSafe, 252
Trip-cancellation insurance, 252
The Trossachs National Park, 66, 68, 147, 148
Trossachs Trundler, 150
Tugnet Ice House, 210
Turnhouse Hill, 42
Turret Burn, 121, 124

Union Canal, 6, 47, 48
United States
    consulate, 251
    customs regulations, 11
    passports, 253
Upper Knock, 122, 124

Vat and Muir of Dinnet, The, 7, 194–197
Viaduct (near Peebles), 96
Victoria, Queen, 63, 204
Visitor information, 10–11
    Argyll and the West Highlands, 148
    Edinburgh and Glasgow walks, 36
    northeast highlands, 182
    northern highlands, 220
    southern Scotland walks, 74
    Tayside and Fife, 110

VisitScotland, 10, 110
VisitScotland Tourist Information Centre (Glasgow), 36

Wades Road, 177
Warren Wood, 208
Water, drinking, 255
Waterfalls Path, 165
Waterfoot path, 171
Waterloo Monument (Melrose), 103
Weather, 12
Websites, 19
Western Union, 253
West Highlands and Argyll walks, 147–179
    Arrochar Alps, 156–159
    Ben Lomond, 153–156
    Callander Crags and Bracklinn Falls, 150–152
    Carradale, 170–173
    Cruachan, 162–165
    getting around, 148, 150
    getting there, 148
    Glen Nant, 159–162
    Kilmartin Glen, 168–170
    Kinlochleven, 173–177
    orientation, 148
    sleeping and eating, 177–179
    Tobermory, 165–167
    visitor information, 148
West Highland Way, 56, 58, 59, 62, 64, 66, 68, 147, 156, 176
West Lomond, 116
Whale and Dolphin Conservation Society, 210
The Whangie, 64, 66
Whisky Museum (Dufftown), 207
Whitelee Farm Cottages, 102
White Mounth, 140, 198
Whiting Ness, 135
Whitlaw Kips, 98
Wilderness Scotland, 23
Wildflowers, 37, 56, 60, 80, 82, 87, 90, 102, 103, 106, 125, 126, 135, 136, 152, 159
Wildlife. See also Bird-watching
    best walks for seeing, 2–3
    Dundonald Glen, 76
    Moray Firth Wildlife Centre, 210
    Portpatrick, 81–82

Windmill, St. Monans, 118
The Window, 212
Woodlands (farm), 97
Woodland Trail, 86
Wood of Cree (Galloway), 3, 84–86
Worldwide Assistance Services, 252

Yellowcraigs Beach, 1–2, 37

ACCOMMODATIONS

Abode Hotel (Glasgow), 69
Ardanaiseig Hotel (Kilchrenan by Taynuilt), 177
Arden House (Callander), 177
Argyll Hotel (Inveraray), 177
Black Bull Hotel (Killearn), 69
Blair Castle Caravan Park, 144
Brig o' Doon House Hotel (Alloway), 107
Burts Hotel (Melrose), 107
Carradale Bay Caravan Park, 177
The County Hotel (Selkirk), 107
Craigtay Hotel (near Dundee), 145
Crieff Hydro Hotel, 145
Deeside Hotel (Ballater), 214
Dornoch Castle Hotel, 246
Dunain Park Hotel (Inverness), 246
Finds (Glasgow), 69
Foxholes (Oban), 177–178
Froach Lodge (Boat of Garten), 214
Glen Mhor Hotel (Inverness), 246
Glenmore Caravan and Camping Site, 214
Glenotter Guest House (Stranraer), 107
Hilton Coylumbridge, 214–215
Hilton Dunkeld House Hotel, 145
Ivybank Guest House (Inverness), 246–247
Kildrummy Castle Hotel, 215
Kingsmills Hotel (Inverness), 247
Ledard Bothies (Kinlochard by Aberfoyle), 178
The Lime Tree (Fort William), 247

Macdonald Holyrood Hotel (Edinburgh), 69
Malmaison (Glasgow), 69
New Lanark Mill Hotel and Waterhouses, 52
Parklands Hotel (Perth), 145
Rucksacks (Braemar), 215
Sauchope Links Holiday Park (Crail), 145
Scottish Youth Hostel Association (SYHA; Melrose), 107
SYHA Leith Walk (Edinburgh), 69
SYHA Park Circus (Glasgow), 70
Whitie's Guest House (Peebles), 107

RESTAURANTS
Abbotsford House (Melrose), 107
Balaka (St. Andrews), 145
Ben Lawers Hotel (Loch Tay), 145–146
Blair Atholl Watermill tearoom, 132
Café 1 (Inverness), 247
Caféwild (Moray Firth Wildlife Centre), 210
Ceilidh Place (Ullapool), 247

Clachaig Inn (Glencoe), 178
Corrour Station House, 144
Craigellachie Hotel, 215
Crannog Seafood Restaurant (Fort William), 247
The Cross (Tweed Mill Brae), 215
Duncan's (Perth), 146
Dunvalanree (Carradale), 178
East Haugh House (Pitlochry), 146
Falko Konditormeister (Gullane), 70
The Gathering Place (Braemar), 215
Glentrool Visitor Centre, 108
Golf Links Hotel (Golspie), 248
Inverlochy Castle (Fort William), 248
Kilted Skirlie (Balloch), 178
Knipoch Hotel Restaurant (Kilninver), 178
Loch Leven's Larder (Kinross), 146
McCallum's Oyster Bar (Troon), 108
Main Street Trading Company (St. Boswells), 108
The Mayview Hotel (St. Monans), 146

Melfort Mermaid, 179
Moments (Kilmahog), 178–179
Moor of Rannoch Hotel, 144
The Old Loans Inn (Loan), 108
Ord Ban Restaurant Cafe (Rothiemurchus Centre), 215
Papilio (Edinburgh), 70
Russell's Restaurant (Melrose), 108
Schottische (Glasgow), 70
Scottish Seabird Centre (North Berwick), 70
The Secret Garden (Alloway), 108
Stac Polly (Edinburgh), 70
Storehouse of Foulis (Evanton), 248
Sunflower (Peebles), 96, 108
Taste of Speyside (Dufftown), 216
Urban Angel (Edinburgh), 70
Wagamama (Glasgow), 70–71
The Waterfront Bistro and Bar (Portpatrick), 108
Wee Curry Shop (Glasgow), 71
The Wildfood Café (Kilmartin), 170

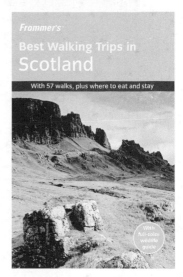

Explore over 3,500 destinations.

Frommers.com makes it easy.

Find a destination. ✓ Book a trip. ✓ Get hot travel deals.
Buy a guidebook. ✓ Enter to win vacations. ✓ Listen to podcasts. ✓ Check ou
the latest travel news. ✓ Share trip photos and memories. ✓ And much more

Frommers.com